Children and Childhood
in World Religions

The Rutgers Series in Childhood Studies

The Rutgers Series in Childhood Studies is dedicated to increasing our understanding of children and childhoods, past and present, throughout the world. Children's voices and experiences are central. Authors come from a variety of fields, including anthropology, criminal justice, history, literature, psychology, religion, and sociology. The books in this series are intended for students, scholars, practitioners, and those who formulate policies that affect children's everyday lives and futures.

Edited by Myra Bluebond-Langner, Distinguished Professor of Anthropology, Rutgers University, Camden, and founding director of the Rutgers University Center for Children and Childhood Studies

Advisory Board
Joan Jacobs Brumberg, Cornell University
Perri Klass, New York University
Jill Korbin, Case Western Reserve University
Bambi Schiefflin, New York University
Enid Schildkraut, American Museum of Natural History
    and Museum for African Art

Children and Childhood in World Religions

Primary Sources and Texts

EDITED BY DON S. BROWNING
AND MARCIA J. BUNGE

RUTGERS UNIVERSITY PRESS

NEW BRUNSWICK, NEW JERSEY, AND LONDON

LIBRARY OF CONGRESS CATALOGING-IN-PUBLICATION DATA

Don S. Browning and Marcia J. Bunge.
  Children and childhood in world religions : primary sources and texts /
  edited by Don S. Browning and Marcia J. Bunge.
      p.   cm. — (Rutgers series in childhood studies)
  Includes bibliographical references and index
  ISBN 978-0-8135-4517-2 (hardcover : alk. paper)
  1. Religions. 2. Children—Religious aspects. I. Browning, Don S. II. Bunge,
  Marcia J. (Marcia JoAnn), 1954–
  BL85.C45 2009
  200.83—dc22

                                              2008043378

A British Cataloging-in-Publication record for this book
is available from the British Library.

This collection copyright © 2009 by Rutgers, The State University

All rights reserved

No part of this book may be reproduced or utilized in any form or by any
means, electronic or mechanical, or by any information storage and retrieval system,
without written permission from the publisher. Please contact Rutgers University Press,
100 Joyce Kilmer Avenue, Piscataway, NJ 08854–8099. The only exception to this
prohibition is "fair use" as defined by U.S. copyright law.

Visit our Web site: http://rutgerspress.rutgers.edu

Manufactured in the United States of America

CONTENTS

PREFACE AND ACKNOWLEDGMENTS

This volume evolved out of a series of research programs sponsored by the Center for the Study of Law and Religion in the School of Law of Emory University. More specifically, it was part of the project called The Child in Law, Religion, and Society. This project began in 2003 and was the second phase of two research projects supported by generous grants from the Pew Charitable Trust. The first phase was called Sex, Marriage, and Family in the Religions of the Book and began in 2001. These two projects have produced over two dozen published books involving scores of authors. Both efforts were interdisciplinary, international, and interfaith in scope. They involved scholars from law, religion, the humanities, and the social sciences from several different countries representing many of the major religions of the world.

We wish to express our appreciation to the Pew Charitable Trusts for its support of the Center for the Study of Law and Religion and this specific book. We also want to express our gratitude for the vision and inspiration of John Witte, Jonas Robitscher Professor of Law and Ethics and director of the Center for the Study of Law and Religion and the Law and Religion Program at Emory. He encouraged us to take on this endeavor and provided the financial and logistical resources to make it possible.

Children and Childhood in World Religions is a companion volume to *Children and Childhood in American Religions*, also published by Rutgers University Press. We want to thank Christian Green of Emory School of Law, who did the original research required to determine whether these two volumes were possible and needed by the various disciplines concerned with children as well as pertinent to debates about children in the wider society. And we wish to give strong appreciation to Adi Hovav, our patient and insightful Rutgers editor, for her encouragement and guidance throughout.

The editorial work supporting this book was done at the Divinity School of the University of Chicago, where Browning is an emeritus professor. We want to thank Kevin Jung, Sarah Schuurman, and Antonia Daymond—all of whom were at one time graduate students of the Divinity School—for their various managerial and editorial talents that went into organizing, nurturing, and assembling this volume. All of them functioned as managing editors of this book. We also want to thank Richard Rosengarten, dean of the Divinity School, for supporting the project and providing office space and computers for the managing editors.

Valparaiso University, where Bunge is a professor, also contributed to the project in a variety of ways. President Alan Harre and Mel Piehl, Dean of Christ College, have enthusiastically supported Bunge's research on children and childhood for this project and for The Child in Religion and Ethics Project (funded by the Lilly Endowment). We would also like to thank Vicki Brody, administrative assistant at Christ College, and Daniel Jarratt and Libbi Bartelt, Christ College honors students. They heartily embraced the aims of the project and offered Bunge outstanding editorial and research assistance in her work for the Christianity chapter and the volume as a whole.

Behind the efforts taking place at our own institutions and the various institutions of all of the chapter editors for this volume was the support of Emory's Center for the Study of Law and Religion. More than financial help came from the Center. Witte and other administrators at the Center, including April Bogle, Eliza Ellison, Anita Mann, and Amy Wheeler, all shared their wisdom and experience with us, supporting this project in countless ways both large and small.

Don S. Browning
Marcia J. Bunge

Children and Childhood
in World Religions

Introduction

MARCIA J. BUNGE AND DON S. BROWNING

Since every person on earth once was or is a child, children and childhood are bound to be central themes in the world's religions. Indeed, references to children are often found in the authoritative texts, symbols, doctrines, and moral teachings of various religious traditions. Many religious rituals revolve around the birth, naming, coming of age, and education of children. Children often play a role in other rituals and celebrations of religious communities. These communities also have protected and disciplined children in distinctive ways, often affecting not only the family but also the religious and nonreligious institutions beyond the domestic realm.

Although religious traditions have addressed children and childhood, scholars of the world's religions have generally neglected these themes. What adults have done and said within a religious tradition has received far more attention within the academy. Certainly, scholars have studied issues related to children, such as abortion, sexuality, or the family, but they have not directly focused their attention on attitudes, practices, and teachings concerning childhood in various world religions. This has been a peculiar and regrettable oversight by scholars presenting the world religions to the reading public. To overlook how religions shape and are shaped by children and youth is to misunderstand both children and religion.

Recently, scholars of religion are realizing the importance and value of reflecting on children and childhood. Since the 1990s, a new and rich field of childhood studies is emerging not only in religious studies but also in a range of academic disciplines, challenging many assumptions about children and opening new lines of intellectual inquiry. Important studies on children and childhood are now undertaken not only in those fields typically devoted to children, such as education and child psychology, but also in history, law, literature, philosophy, sociology, and anthropology.[1] Furthermore, scholars in a number of areas in religious studies outside religious education (the field most commonly focused on children) are beginning to publish more work on children and childhood.[2] These publications include several major historical monographs that have already added important chapters to the history of Judaism, Christianity, Islam, Hinduism, Buddhism, and Confucianism, as well as to the history of childhood in general. Indeed, some of them have been authored by the editors of this volume.[3] Other interdisciplinary initiatives are examining the spiritual development and experiences of children and adolescents in various religions.[4] Studies in the areas of theology, ethics, and biblical studies have also appeared.[5] In all areas of theology and religious studies, scholars are also finding many more opportunities to present work on childhood at professional meetings or through specially funded national and international symposia or research projects.[6] Research in the area of childhood studies as a whole is inspiring conversation and collaboration among scholars from diverse disciplines and providing new intersections between scholarship and public policy.

In spite of this burgeoning interdisciplinary research, studies of specific religions on the subject of childhood are still rare, and most of them do not offer possibilities for comparison. Many of the historical studies focus on a particular period of time within one tradition alone. Literature on contemporary issues has been concerned primarily with particular problems of children—their lack of faith, their absorption into popular culture, or their lack of sexual boundaries. Such literature, as useful as it is, falls short of providing a comprehensive overview of children and childhood; and it fails to analyze the basic understandings of children within and across religious traditions.

The Contemporary Significance of This Book

This volume presents selected classic and formative texts on children and childhood from six major world religions—Judaism, Christianity, Islam, Hinduism, Buddhism, and Confucianism. As far as we can tell, no volume like this one currently exits. There has never before been an effort to bring together basic scriptures and documents that shaped the attitudes, practices, and teachings on childhood of these religions. The selections in this volume, although clearly not exhaustive, provide an introduction to central themes of children and childhood in these six world religions. By introducing and presenting classic texts on children from various traditions, the volume discloses a range of critical issues on relationships between children and religion and how these childhood traditions relate to their surrounding social contexts. Although this volume concentrates on texts that influenced a religious tradition's constructions of childhood and is not a social history, many of the chapters also provide valuable insights and bibliographical references to what is known about actual practices with children and their behaviors. In short, this book serves as a topography of the study of religion, children, and society; it fills a void in the current scholarship and functions as an indispensable guide to future research in the areas of religious studies and childhood studies.

The current volume is not only foundational for deepening our understanding of both children and religion and for strengthening research in a variety of academic disciplines; such a collection is also relevant to readers and audiences outside the academy, especially given our contemporary national and international situation. The texts assembled in this book are not just nice collections of interesting, perhaps curious, material; they are selections of readings vital to understanding aspects of contemporary social and political life in the United States and around the world. This is the case for several reasons.

First, because of the magnitude of impact that the major religions have had on culture and the life cycle of children and youth, it is important to understand them better. Religion shapes children through their socialization by parents and formal religious instruction, religious rituals in family and corporate settings, and religiously inspired views of marriage and gender. Even if children or their parents are not members of a specific religious community, religion nevertheless shapes them both directly and indirectly through its influence in many areas of cultural, social, and political life. Religious images and understandings of children are not confined to the inner life of a specific tradition; they spill over into the wider society, no matter how allegedly secular that society is thought to be.

Second, we must become more informed about relationships between religion and childhood because they are often a source of deep tension and heated debate here and abroad. Tensions surrounding the subject of children and religion can be found in the United States as well as in most countries where the forces of modernization and democracy have directly or indirectly challenged traditional religious beliefs and practices, raising questions about which authorities, institutions, and polities will shape the lives of children and families. On the one hand, some people are suspicious of what religions teach about childhood and whether or not religions benefit children in modern societies. Practices found within some strands of a tradition, such as the corporal punishment of children or child marriages, are often directly criticized. On the other hand, others perceive elements of modernization and contemporary culture as threats to children and their positive religious formation. Persons from a variety of religious traditions frequently express criticism of American culture, schools, media, and other institutions that influence their children. Such debates raise the important question of why some religious traditions feel that many aspects of modernization and democracy are threats to their children and others do not. There is no easy answer to this question, and responding to it is not the purpose of this book. Rather, our point is that even to begin to answer it, we must all know a great deal more about the childhood traditions of world religions.

Third, this volume is important because at the same time we are recognizing that the religion-childhood link may be a source of tension in the world, new social science research indicates that these religions may be sources of strength for children. Parents have historically tended to believe that passing on their particular religious tradition to their children positively influences them, and today there is a body of social-science studies suggesting that this intuition may be true, at least according to some measures of child well-being. Most of the research is still limited to the major religions in Western societies. For instance, Christian Smith and Melinda Denton in their exhaustive survey titled *Soul Searching: The Religious and Spiritual Lives of American Teenagers* (2005) showed that although most teens do not understand their religions deeply, those who are involved in religious life fare better in school, health, and job placement than the religiously unattached.[7] In 2003, a distinguished interdisciplinary panel of scholars released a report titled *Hardwired to Connect: The New Scientific Case for Authoritative Communities*. It argued that children, in order to attain psychological and physical well-being, need not only strong attachments to parents and families but also "deep connection to moral and spiritual meaning" of the kind generally provided by religious traditions.[8] The Search Institute has also found that involvement in a religious community is one of forty important "developmental assets" that strengthens child well-being.[9]

Fourth, since religious diversity is now the experience of every society and since all societies have children, many people want and need to know more about how the various religions relate to childhood. The great world religions are not just foreign realities in strange and distant countries. They are present everywhere—in the schools, marketplaces, neighborhoods, and voting booths of the United States as well as other countries around the globe. Thus, health experts, social workers, psychologists, and child advocates encounter this diversity when they meet in their practices individuals and families from different religious faiths. Teachers and professors at schools, colleges, and universities confront young people who were taught different faiths when children. Lawyers, doctors, and business people work with an increasingly diverse religious constituency and are often embarrassed by their lack of knowledge about religious traditions outside their own. Parents, too, desire to know more about what the world religions teach about childhood as their own children experience religious diversity in their schools and neighborhoods.

There have been efforts in recent years to compensate for this lack of knowledge and understanding. To remedy deficient knowledge in the medical and nursing professions, the Park Ridge Center published a book series titled *Health, Medicine, and the Faith Traditions*. These volumes examined several of the world religions from the perspective of what they taught about health, illness, aging, birth, and family. Childhood itself, however, was not a major theme.[10] There have been countless textbooks and sourcebooks assembled on the world religions, but children as such are generally neglected. A survey of introductory texts and sourcebooks over the last several decades found in their indexes only one reference to children, and this was to children as sources of "pollution" in Confucianism.[11] We can assure you that Confucianism has much more to say about children than this, as do all the major religions. Even one of the co-editors of this volume recently helped edit a major sourcebook titled *Sex, Marriage, and Family in the World Religions*, but it only addressed children as a category under marriage and family.[12]

Finally, this volume is also important within the context of mounting public concern about children and child well-being and the efforts of child advocates to address challenges facing children locally and globally. Across conservative and progressive lines, and both nationally and internationally, there is heightened awareness of the many challenges children face today. Many children here and abroad live in poverty and often are malnourished, receive inadequate educations, and lack proper health care.[13] These problems, in turn, often feed others, such as drug abuse, child labor, child soldiers, AIDS orphans, child-headed households, and sexually exploited children. Even children in affluent families often suffer neglect and abuse or struggle with addictions to drugs or alcohol. Scholars and child advocates also wonder about the effects of technology, the media, and global market pressures on rich and poor children alike. Child advocates around the world who represent both secular and faith-based nongovernmental organizations are taking increasing interest in religious traditions and beliefs because they shape a large part of the diverse social and cultural contexts in which child advocacy must be discussed and carried out, often determining the success or failure of child-focused programs. Furthermore, child advocates are seeking to learn more about varied religious responses to children's rights, particularly as these advocates participate in international debates surrounding the Millennium Development Goals and the ratification and implementation of the United Nations Convention on the Rights of the Child.[14]

For these reasons and others, *Children and Childhood in World Religions* is a valuable sourcebook for a variety of audiences and contexts in the academy and the public sphere both nationally and internationally.

Guiding Themes and Questions

As this volume shows, religions say a great deal about children, and each chapter explores some of the following central questions and themes. They are derived both from what these religions actually address and from our sense of the major concerns of the contemporary cultural conversation and debate about childhood and religion.

1. *The nature and status of children.* What are a religion's core beliefs about a child's nature and status? What are its metaphysical or theological beliefs

about children and their relation to what the religion holds as ultimate? What is a religion's understanding of birth, the moral status and agency of children, and a child's relation to good and evil?

2. *Gender and sexuality of children.* How does a religion speak about differences between boys and girls? How does it interpret the sexuality of children and youth? Are there any normative views of children in the world religions that prescribe or proscribe certain actions by children? What do these proscribed behaviors mean for issues of gender, sexuality, and impulse control?

3. *The role of children in central religious practices.* How do children participate in a religion's adult rituals? Are there special rituals for children? Does a religious community allow its children to participate in the secular rituals of the surrounding society?

4. *Obligations of parents and children.* How do religious traditions understand parental obligations to children and children's obligations to parents? How deep, long lasting, mutual, or asymmetrical are these obligations?

5. *Communal obligations to children.* How do religions speak about communal obligations to children and children's obligations to the community? Do particular religions have special institutions for children and youth, and how does the religion relate to external institutions dealing with children?

6. *Moral and spiritual formation of children.* How do the different traditions speak about the moral and spiritual formation of children? What practices and teachings are especially important in the process of spiritual formation? Who has responsibility for it? Is spiritual development forced or allowed to come freely?

The Structure of the Book

The selections have been chosen by leading scholars of six world religions. These scholars also have provided insightful introductions to the material they have assembled. The various editors have made no attempt to make parallel the periods from which the key texts have been chosen; the traditions develop in different ways and demand their own unique periodizations. Nor does every chapter give equal attention to the questions listed above; the religious traditions have different emphases and the editors were not always able to collect texts addressing in depth each of these issues. Editors have chosen selections representative of the history of the tradition, including some that reflect modern struggles to interpret—and perhaps reinterpret—a tradition. They have included selections that represent a variety of genres—legal, theological, poetic, and liturgical. However, not all traditions employ these genres to the same degree, and chapter editors have balanced their choices of texts on the basis of how each particular religion has communicated itself. Selections also have been chosen with an eye to their usefulness for comparison with texts from other religions.

Child, Children, and Childhood

A few sentences are needed about our use of the words child, children, and childhood. There is an important scholarly discussion as to whether it is possible to speak at all about "the child." Those on one side of this debate hold what has been called a "constructivist" view of childhood. They claim that there is no normative child or single cluster of characteristics pertaining to children. Hence, the best we can do is to speak of childhood—our cultural, historical, linguistic, and religious construal and constructions of children, and we should avoid references to "the child." Others hold what has been called an "essentialist" view of children. They believe there are characteristics common to all children, across history and cultures, and they sometimes use the term "child" to refer to these universal similarities.

In this book we use all three terms—childhood, children, and the child. On the one hand, bringing into conversation the traditions of six highly diverse religions is almost by definition acknowledging that there is some validity to the so-called constructivist view. On the other hand, to use the term "child" is not in itself to essentialize the term; its meaning is qualified by the sentences, paragraphs, and entire text in which the term is used. Hence, we should not be too fearful of trying to discover some common characteristics about children that may be cross-cultural and interreligious. Such documents as the United Nations Convention on the Rights of the Child—and in fact the entire human rights project—suggest that seeing children through different religious and cultural eyes yields overlapping insights that will aid us in raising and protecting children with some common guarantees and supports regardless of the religion, society, and culture within which they reside.

The Importance of Form and Context

Religious teachings and practices regarding children are shaped partially by the form and context of the religion. Judaism, Christianity, and Islam are religions with a sacred book: the Hebrew scriptures in the case of Judaism, both the Old and New Testaments in the case of Christianity, and the Qur'an in the case of Islam. The focus of these religions on their sacred book gives them a cohesion and compactness, even in the socialization of children, that arguably has not characterized Confucianism, Hinduism, and Buddhism. These latter three traditions each have multiple sacred texts that are variously honored in different strands and places but that do not constitute a single center of authority in quite the same way as the sacred books of Judaism, Christianity, and Islam.

In addition, although all of these traditions articulate norms and moral codes about children and childhood, they have distinctive ways of expressing them. For example, Judaism specifically represents itself as a religion based on law with identifiable legal teachings about children, education, and the duties of mothers and fathers. However, even though this law is seen as revealed by God, Judaism has not perceived it as static and unchanging. The interpretation of the law as it applies to children is a dynamically developing tradition. Islam is also a religion of the law—a body of law revealed in the Qur'an. Islamic law is also interpreted and codified in an evolving tradition, in this case the various traditions of law known as shari'a. Christianity, Confucianism, Hinduism, and Buddhism are not religions of the law in quite the same sense, even though they also evolved legal and moral codes. Their core is thought to lie elsewhere, for example the gospel (as in the case of Christianity), or meditative renunciation (as in the case of Hinduism and Buddhism), or family rituals (as in the case of Confucianism). Each one of these four religions, however, also has influenced the socialization of children and evolved rules, formal or informal, to guide this process. For example, Confucianism has developed powerful family traditions where children are taught to honor, if not worship, elders and ancestors in home-based rituals focused on the death and the remembrance of a parent or grandparent.

The social and geographical context of a religion makes a difference in its representations of children. No religion remains uninfluenced by its neighbors. For example, Christianity began as a movement within Judaism, and its attitudes to children were shaped by Jewish as well as Greek and Roman ideas and practices. In his chapter on Buddhism, Allen Cole shows how Buddhism unfolded differently in India and in China. In the Chinese context, Buddhism began to exhibit features of its Confucian host society. It gradually urged children to exhibit filial piety for elders, honor for the emperor, and interest in the fertility and the generational continuity of their extended families much the way these ideas were emphasized by the wider Confucian society. Such childhood emphases were less visible in the early days of the more world-renouncing teachings of Buddhism in India.

There often is tension within a religious tradition between what subeditors Marcia Bunge and John Wall have said could be called "low" versus "high" perspectives on childhood. By this distinction, they are pointing to whether a religion sees children as a source of wisdom and spirituality in their own right or whether their religious growth is viewed mainly as a matter of socialization from above or outside themselves by the authoritative teachings of an adult-transmitted truth or revelation. This tension can vary across and even within religions. For example, Yiqun Zhou in her chapter on Confucianism shows the tensions between Mencius (ca. 372–289 BCE) and Xunci (ca. 310–230 BCE). Although Mencius certainly believed that children needed to be socialized into Confucian teachings and ritual, he also saw them as potential symbols of moral perfection in themselves. Xunci, on the other hand, saw children as profoundly unruly and evil, and he believed that their spiritual perfection had to be cultivated entirely from above, that is, from the teachings and rituals adumbrated by the authoritative Confucius, his followers, and the extended Confucian family. This tension has continued in Confucianism throughout the centuries and exists even today as this tradition copes with the more child-centered cultures of Western societies.

Readers of the texts that follow should recall that all of these religions, in their ancient forms, saw children mainly through the eyes of adult men—fathers, grandfathers, and male religious leaders. This does not mean that we learn nothing of importance about children, mothers, or the relation of offspring to parents. It is rather that we do not gain these insights from the voice and perspective of children and women. However, in more modern times, all of these religions are beginning to acknowledge the independent angles of vision of children and their mothers. Furthermore, we are learning how to interpret ancient texts in ways that help us to see more deeply into the experience and agency of children.

Readers also should remember that, for the most part, we have very little direct knowledge of how children were actually raised in the formative periods of these traditions. It is difficult to construct on the basis of the texts alone the kind of social history that we value today which places religious teachings within the context of historical records about actual behaviors of children and their elders. Despite these difficulties, we welcome the work scholars are pursuing in this area.

Some General Themes

Despite the varied forms and contexts of these religions and the limitations of our sources, the texts assembled here tell us much about the ideals and normative models of childhood that shaped their respective religious traditions. They also engage several common themes. We present a few of them below. There are more. But what follows will give the reader a taste of the possible conversations that can emerge in comparing these traditions.

Within the history of these religions, most of them have ways of speaking of children as a blessing. For example, Elisheva Baumgarten tells us that the Hebrew Scriptures represent children as a central blessing and that, as a sign of this blessing, the ancestors of the Jewish people were promised by God that their offspring would be plentiful. Christianity continued to see children as a blessing, although it put less emphasis on procreation as such. Children as blessings and the importance of procreation were both emphasized in Islam. Avner Giladi points out that although progeny and lineage are perceived as blessings in Islam, this was often stated more in terms of sons than daughters. Yiqun Zhou tells us that Confucian parents certainly loved their children and actively showed them affection, especially in their early years, but their sacred value was seen more as something achieved as they came to occupy their roles in household rituals honoring elders and ancestors. One might argue that Buddhism's doctrine of *samsara*, that is, stopping the cycle of birth and suffering, implied negative attitudes toward the birth of the child. However, Alan Cole believes that its view of the perfection of the Buddha's childhood and its gradual identification over time of all children with the Buddha had the long-term effect of elevating the status of children in Buddhist territories. In ancient Hindu texts, as Laurie Patton claims, the birth of a son is understood to be a critical part of a prosperous life.

These views of the sacred importance of children were often associated with an element of realism, if not utility. Judaism valued children as gifts from God, but it also believed that males were religiously obligated to have children for what they contributed to the survival and continuity of the covenant community. This is an accent also found in Islam. As Laurie Patton claims, ancient Hindu texts also view the birth of a son as a form of social security and continuation of the lineage. Alan Cole points out that although Buddhism in its early years had little to say directly about children, it gradually over the centuries became quite interested in their birth and growth. This was not so much to value procreation itself; rather procreation was valued as a requirement for the replenishment of the Buddhist tradition and its teachings.

Religious traditions also show interesting similarities and differences in the extent to which children in themselves are deemed as sources of religious inspiration. Bunge and Wall refer to the well-known words attributed to Jesus indicating that children are in some ways models for adults, "for it is to such as these that the kingdom of heaven belongs" (Matt. 19:14). Baumgarten cites Jewish sources that claim the fetus studies the Torah in the mother's womb, and learning its teachings in later life is actually a matter of recollecting what was earlier known in utero. Within Hinduism, Patton finds the idea of the child as closer to the divine, especially in classic myths of Krishna, which juxtapose childhood vulnerability with divine strength.

Some modern people are disturbed by what they believe the religions of the world teach about the evil or sinful nature of the child. Actually, the religions vary significantly on this issue within and across traditions. Furthermore, views of a child's sin and evil are often coupled with notions of their accountability and responsibility. Even those religions that hold strong doctrines of original sin, such as the parts of Christianity influenced by St. Augustine (354–430 CE), often balance this teaching by equally strong images of children born in the image of God. Baumgarten points out that Judaism has no understanding of the original sin of children and in fact sees the purity of the newborn child as a source for perfecting the wider society. Although Hinduism and Buddhism believe children at birth are contaminated through *samsara* by the evil deeds of their ancestors, this state of affairs is more a matter of the human condition in general than any special commentary on the special sinfulness of children. Confucianism, as Zhou mentions, is divided on the question of children's natural inclinations toward evil, with different points of view on this matter emerging repeatedly throughout its long history.

All of these religions have articulate understandings of parental and communal obligations to children. These traditions generally expect adults to address a child's basic needs of food, shelter, and affection; to provide spiritual, moral, and cognitive guidance; and to protect a child's property or inheritance. Religious traditions offer explicit guidelines for treatment and care of orphans or abandoned children. Initiating children into a faith tradition generally takes place through various ritual practices and study both in the home and the religious community. Particular religious ceremonies mark transitions from one stage of life to the next. Within Hinduism, for example, children are "ritually formed," as Patton suggests, through a variety of rituals that include cutting the umbilical cord to the accompaniment of Vedic mantras; naming and first feeding ceremonies; rites for the first time a child's hair is cut; and initiations into studying the Veda. In many religious traditions, schools external to the home also play a role in children's formation and education, such as in the Jewish rabbinic schools, the public and parochial schools of the Christian Protestant Reformation, or the *pesantren*, *kuttab*, and *madrasa* of Islam. Confucianism progressively institutionalized rigorous examination systems through state-run civil service systems for boys as one of the few ways to increase prestige and master the social space between filial duties to the family and service to the emperor.

Religious traditions also address children's obligations to their parents. Within Christianity and Judaism, the command to "honor your father and mother" extends to adulthood. Confucianism, and to some degree both Hinduism and Buddhism, have strong expectations that children will care for their elders, with obligations thought to last beyond the grave and even across eons of time. In his introduction to Buddhism, Alan Cole shows how a religion that appears to renounce the world, and hence the importance of children and families, also evolved complex patterns of reciprocity between celibate monks and their own mothers, fathers, brothers, and sisters. Teachings in Buddhism that at first glance appear to be world-denying and even neglectful of children in fact accompany very complicated ways of directly and indirectly supporting parents and their offspring as they struggle with the realities of finite life on earth.

Conclusion

The reader, however, would be wise not to press too far any of the above generalizations about children and childhood in world religions. Her or his immersion in the expert introductions and collections of texts that follow will bring clarification and nuance to everything we have suggested. Furthermore, religious traditions inevitably have different strands, tributaries, and divisions that also change over time. This means that almost every dominant characteristic of a religious tradition that scholarly observers might advance will be humbled by some exceptions lingering somewhere in its various nooks and crannies.

Each chapter and the volume as a whole provide the reader with an amazing array of possible attitudes toward and ideas about children and childhood both within and across traditions. The chapters also shed light on central religious beliefs and practices and the role children play in them. And they invite us to explore further the complex place of children in these and other religious traditions. Finally, the selections that follow prompt all readers—regardless of our religious and philosophical commitments—to reexamine our own preconceptions and beliefs about children and to reevaluate our responsibilities and obligations toward children themselves.

NOTES

1. For a review of some of the recent studies in many fields, see Scott Heller, "The Meaning of Children Becomes a Focal Point for Scholars," *Chronicle of Higher Education,* August 7, 1998, 14–15; Mary Jane Kehily, *Childhood Studies* (New Brunswick: Rutgers University Press, 2004). For a comprehensive literature review that omits the perspective of religion, see Dominic Wyse, ed., *Childhood Studies* (Oxford: Blackwell, 2004).

2. For an overview of developments in these areas, see "The Child, Religion, and the Academy: Developing Robust Theological and Religious Understandings of Childhood," in the *Journal of Religion* 86.4 (October 2006), 549–579.

3. Elisheva Baumgarten, *Mother and Children: Jewish Family Life in Medieval Europe* (Princeton: Princeton University Press, 2004); Marcia J. Bunge, ed., *The Child in Christian Thought* (Grand Rapids: Wm. B. Eerdmans, 2001); Alan Cole, *Mothers and Sons in Chinese Buddhism* (Stanford: Stanford University Press, 1998); Avner Gil'adi, *Children of Islam: Concepts of Childhood in Medieval Muslim Society* (New York: St. Martin's Press, 1992) and *Infants, Parents, and Wet Nurses* (Leiden: Brill, 1999). Other examples of recent historical studies include, Ivan G. Marcus, *Rituals of Childhood: Jewish Acculturation in Medieval Europe* (New Haven: Yale University Press, 1998); and Anne Behnke Kinney, *Representations of Childhood and Youth in Early China* (Stanford: Stanford University Press, 2003).

4. For example, the Search Institute has opened a new Center for Spiritual Development in Childhood and Adolescence and recently published two books on child spirituality: one focusing on social scientific research and the other on religious perspectives, primarily within Buddhism, Christianity, Hinduism, Islam, and Judaism. See E. C. Roehlkepartain, P. E. King, L. M. Wagener, and P. L. Benson, eds., *The Handbook of Spiritual Development in Childhood and Adolescence* (Thousand Oaks, Cal.: Sage, 2006); and K.-M. Yust, A. N. Johnson, S. E. Sasso, and E. C. Roehlkepartain, eds., *Nurturing Child and Adolescent Spirituality: Perspectives from the World's Religious Traditions* (Lanham, Md.: Rowman & Littlefield, 2006). For more information on the project and the Search Institute, see Search-Institute.org.

5. Within the last eleven years alone, several theological and biblical journals here and abroad have devoted entire issues to the subject of children. See, for example, *Dialog* 37 (Summer 1998); *Interpretation* 55.2 (2001); *Conservative Judaism* 53.4 (Summer 2001); the *Jahrbuch für biblische Theologie* 17 (2002); *Christian Reflection* (July 2003); *The Living*

Pulpit 12.4 (2003); *Sewanee Theological Review* 48.1 (2004); *Theology Today* 56.4 (2000); and *African Ecclesial Review* 46.2 (2004). In biblical studies, see for example, *The Child in the Bible*, edited by Marcia J. Bunge (general editor), Beverly Roberts Gaventa, and Terence Fretheim (Grand Rapids: Wm. B. Eerdmans, 2008).

6. The American Academy of Religion (AAR), the American Historical Association, the Society of Church History, and the Society of Christian Ethics, for example, have devoted a few sessions at their national meetings to the themes of religion and childhood. Furthermore, in 2002 the Program Committee of the AAR approved a new program unit, the "Childhood Studies and Religion Consultation," which is now providing a forum for a more focused and sustained interdisciplinary and interreligious dialogue about children and religion. A program unit on "Children in the Biblical World" was also established at the Society of Biblical Literature (SBL) in 2008. For information on both the "Childhood Studies and Religion Consultation" and "Children in the Biblical World Section," see the Web sites of the AAR (aarweb.org) and SBL (sbl-site.org). Several academic projects and initiatives in the United States, such as "The Child in Law, Religion, and Society" (Emory University; Web site is law.emory.edu/cslr) and "The Child in Religion and Ethics" (Valparaiso University; Web site is childreligionethics.org), are also focusing on children and religion, generating new discussions and research opportunities for scholars in many areas of theology and religious studies.

7. Christian Smith, *Soul Searching: The Religious and Spiritual Lives of American Teenagers* (Oxford: Oxford University Press, 2005).

8. *Hardwired to Connect: The New Scientific Case for Authoritative Communities*, a report released by the YMCA of the USA, Dartmouth Medical School, and the Institute for American Values (New York: Institute for American Values, 2003), 5.

9. For more information, see Search-Institute.org.

10. *Health, Medicine, and the Faith Traditions* included books such as David Feldman, *Health and Medicine in the Jewish Tradition* (New York: Crossroad, 1986), Fazlur Rahman, *Health and Medicine in the Islamic Tradition* (New York: Crossroad, 1987), and Kenneth Vaux, *Health and Medicine in the Reformed Tradition* (New York: Crossroad, 1984).

11. The children as pollution index entry is in Willard G. Oxtoby, ed., *World Religions: Eastern Traditions* (Oxford: Oxford University Press, 1996). Other texts that we consulted that did not reference children at all are listed below. It must be admitted that omission of the words child, children, or childhood in the index does not mean these books do not mention them, but it does suggest that the subject was not seen as important enough to merit inclusion in the index. See also Mircea Eliade, *From Primitives to Zen* (New York: Harper and Row, 1967); S. Vernon McCausland, Grace Cairns, and David Yu, *Religions of the World* (New York: Random House, 1969); Ward J. Fellows, *Religions East and West* (New York: Religions East and West, 1979); Niels Nielsen, Norvin Hein, Frank Reynolds, Alan Miller, Samuel Karff, Alice Cochran, and Paul McLean, eds., *Religions of the World* (New York: St. Martins Press, 1983); Ninian Smart, *The Religious Experience of Mankind* (New York: Charles Scribner's Sons, 1964, 1976, 1984); Stewart Sutherland, Leslie Houlden, Peter Clarke, and Friedhelm Handy, eds., *The World's Religions* (Boston: G. K. Hall, 1988); Houston Smith, *The World's Religions* (San Francisco: Harper SanFrancisco, 1991); William Young, *The World's Religions: Worldviews and Contemporary Issues* (Englewood Cliffs, N.J.: Prentice Hall, 1995); John R. Hinnells, ed., *A New Handbook of Living Religions* (Oxford: Blackwell, 1997).

12. Don Browning, Christian Green, and John Witte, eds., *Sex, Marriage, and Family in the World Religions* (New York: Columbia University Press, 2006).

13. For more information about the situation of children, see the following Web sites: United States Census Bureau (census.gov); the Children's Defense Fund (childrens defense.org); the United Nations Children's Fund (unicef.org); and the National Center for Children in Poverty (nccp.org).

14. The UNCRC was passed in 1989 by the UN General Assembly. Since then, it has been ratified by all but two nations: the United States and Somalia.

1

Judaism

ELISHEVA BAUMGARTEN

Procreation, the commandment to bear offspring, is frequently noted as one of the central obligations in Judaism. Both because of the centrality of the commandment to procreate in the book of Genesis and because of the contrast between Jewish culture in antiquity and its sister religion, Christianity, the obligation to marry and have children is identified with one of the core obligations of the Jewish people. As such, children and childhood, which follow from the duty of procreation, can be expected to be central to the social organization of the Jewish people. Yet, while in practice Jews throughout history lived their lives as part of a family framework, and these families all aspired to raise children and educate them, there is little literature until the early modern period that discusses how these goals are to be attained.

The Jewish religion is organized around a body of Jewish teaching often called the Torah but which in fact consists of the Bible (Old Testament), the Oral Law (Mishnah and Talmud), and expansions on these literatures that vary in shape and form expanding and reinterpreting the basic texts. Historically considered, one can say that Judaism is a combination of three central ideas—belief in God, God's revelation of the Torah to Israel, and Israel as the people who obey the Torah as part of their obedience of God. Although the interpretation of these ideas has changed over time, the ideas themselves have remained constant.[1]

Judaism as a religion is organized around precepts that dictate the way every man and woman should conduct their everyday lives and contains many directives regarding all areas of life, including procreation, childrearing, education, and financial support of children. As such, traditional Jewish sources abound with discussions of various aspects of childhood and childrearing, and when examining sources on these issues over a long period of time, one can see both the change and the continuity that characterizes discussions of this topic.

Since Jews have lived under the rule of other nations and religions from antiquity until modern times, one can also discern the divergences in Jewish tradition and examine these changes in light of the cultures within which the Jews lived. Throughout history, whether in antiquity when Jews were sovereign over themselves, or after the destruction of the Second Temple (70 CE) when Jews lived among other nations, Jewish culture always existed alongside other cultures. Whether among Egyptians, Persians, Greeks, Romans, Christians, or Muslims, Jews were part of their surrounding cultures, absorbing and transforming ideas they learned from their neighbors and reinterpreting and explaining their traditions in light of the values they discerned around them. The Jewish tradition in its turn also helped shape neighboring religions and cultures, and constant dialogue between Jews and their surrounding cultures existed.

Jewish communities were scattered throughout the Mediterranean basin and all over Europe, Asia, and parts of Africa until the late Middle Ages. With the discovery of the Americas, Jews migrated to the new world as well, bringing their traditions and methods of education with them. The texts in this chapter will provide a look at many of these different areas. Although some texts refer to Near Eastern biblical and Hellenic cultures, the two religions with which the Jewish tradition is in dialogue for the longest time are Christianity and Islam. Since Christians and Muslims recognized the Hebrew Bible as part of their traditions as well, and reinterpreted these texts for their own purposes, these are the religions with whom Jews argued and agreed over scripture and its practical implications.

This chapter will focus on childhood in premodern Judaism from biblical times until the early modern era. After the onset of the Enlightenment in early modern Europe and with the secularization of Jewish culture first in Western Europe then in Eastern Europe and in the Ottoman Empire, Jewish conceptions of childhood and especially Jewish education underwent additional changes. The emancipation of Jews in European countries in the nineteenth century further challenged traditional frameworks. Modern Jewish education has differed from country to country on the basis of educational trends and fads in each country. Moreover, the branching out of different religious movements within Judaism, and especially the growth of the Reform and Conservative movements since the nineteenth century, make it difficult to discuss the tremendous variety of ideas and practices. The wide variety of scholarship in these directions is sufficient to demonstrate the different trajectories in which attitudes toward children, childhood, and education have blossomed. As a result, these developments deserve separate treatment and the challenges the modern period present are only hinted at in this chapter.[2]

Since Judaism is a religion of precepts, many discussions of children and childhood can be found in connection with religious obligations. Thus, for example, procreation, childhood rituals, religious education, and observance of Jewish ritual precepts are all discussed and debated at length in traditional sources, with explanations of what should and should not be done. These sources are evidence of both practice and belief concerning children and childhood.

In this chapter, the sources presented seek to display the richness of the different genres in which these topics were discussed–Bible, Mishnah, Talmud, biblical and Talmudic commentaries, Midrash, legal rulings, moral advice, tractates on education, poetry, and stories. Although not all these genres discuss childhood during all of the periods covered here, I have sought to bring together a representation of the various kinds of texts.

As noted, textual discussions are organized around precepts. Two examples will serve as a means of illustrating the methods employed in the sources. A first example is that mentioned above, reproduction, or the importance of reproducing a community of believers. When examining the commandment to "be fruitful and multiply" (*pru urvu*) one must begin with the book of Genesis, where it is outlined twice. God commands Adam and Eve to "Be fertile and increase, fill the earth and master it; and rule the fish of the sea, the birds of the sky and all the living things that creep on earth" (Doc. 1-4).[3] This command is reiterated after the flood, when God commands Noah and his sons: "Be fertile and increase and fill the earth" (Doc. 1-5). This directive continues and outlines a new relationship with nature that is not part of our subject at hand, ordering that the fear of man will be upon all beasts of the earth. Jewish authorities in later generations not only understood this command as an order to procreate and to abstain from celibacy but also saw procreation as a fundamental component of the Jewish religion.[4]

This obligation raises many questions both practical and theoretical. How many children must a person have to fulfill this requirement, and whose obligation is it to procreate–men, women, or both? If one's children die, can one still claim he or she has fulfilled this obligation? As we shall see, religious authorities argued over whether men and women had the same obligation to procreate, since men were commanded twice while woman was instructed to do so only once, and women were then excluded from the directive to Noah and his sons (Doc. 1-13). If a couple cannot have children and procreation is the central purpose of marriage, must a childless couple divorce (Doc. 1-10)? And when a child is born what must parents do for him or her and what must the Jewish community do if a parent is not present?[5]

All these obligations are interpreted in Jewish sources from the Bible through the codification of the oral law in the Mishnah and Talmud and then expanded in commentaries on these classic texts.[6] Midrashic texts, organized around biblical verses but incorporating pieces of the Oral Law, developed at the same time as the Oral Law itself and then continued to be written and recompiled throughout medieval times. Exegesis on the Bible, the Talmud, legal (halakhic response), and other literature led Jewish authorities to discuss conceptions of sex, the nature of childhood, education and rearing (both religious and commercial), and legal obligations of children toward their parents as well as those of parents toward their children. Rituals of childhood, such as circumcision or the beginning of education, also help outline understandings of children's place in society and expectations for children and their families. Since Jewish communities were often under the rule of a different religious majority, the question of how to promote children's identification with their religion and initiate them into it gained tremendous importance. Questions of gender are also of import when discussing childhood. Are boys and girls viewed and treated in the same way?

Another example of a central commandment regarding children, originating in the Bible and reinterpreted over time, is the commandment to honor one's father and mother. Over time, this obligation was expanded to include a variety of behaviors as well as obligation to one's grandparents and in-laws. Examining this directive allows a mirror image investigation—an understanding of what children must do in order to honor their parents and, at the same time, an exposition of what parents should do as part of their commitment to their children.

Both these examples and the commentary on them over time are key to understanding how to locate discussions of children and childhood within Jewish textual sources. Up until the Middle Ages, and even thereafter, few treatises or texts were written in which the focus was children: their care, education, or conception. Rather, through a variety of legal and philosophical issues, these topics were implicitly addressed.

Another way to uncover evidence about children in past Jewish societies is by studying central communal institutions. Since Jewish communities were built around a number of central social institutions throughout history and especially since the destruction of the temples, by looking for mention of children in sources regarding these institutions, childhood can be found. These institutions include the synagogue, the school, courts, cemeteries, and sites of rituals such as circumcisions, weddings, and funerals.

Research on Childhood in Jewish Culture

Like most researchers on childhood, scholars of Judaism began examining this topic during the last two decades of the twentieth century. In wake of the debate around Philippe Ariès's controversial thesis regarding childhood in the past, scholars became interested in the question of attitudes toward childhood in Jewish culture.[7] However, it is important to note that these discussions of family and childhood that originated in the 1980s were not by any means the first treatment of the topic. A number of scholars discussed it at the end of the nineteenth and the beginning of the twentieth centuries.[8]

In light of the Ariès thesis, which argued that in the Middle Ages Christian parents did not love their children as they do today and argued that children were defined and conceived of as young adults once they passed the stage of infancy, scholars set out to reexamine the Jewish sources.[9] Whereas the first scholars were eager to present the Jews as different from the Christians around them and sought to argue that this difference was inherent, more recent scholarship has recognized both similarities and differences between Jews and their surroundings.[10] Scholarship on childhood in Judaism began, much as in other fields, with the Middle Ages, and then expanded to other periods in history.[11] Other more specific issues—especially matters concerning education, procreation, and rituals—have also been examined in depth over the past twenty-five years and as part of a more general growing interest in social history and everyday life. Gender studies, which have been integrated into mainstream Jewish history and thought over the past decades, have also drawn attention to gender understandings and divisions concerning children.[12] However, the nature of the premodern Jewish sources have made it difficult to pull away from legal history and to attempt to reconstruct what daily life in the various communities might have been like for children.

Selection of Texts

At the outset, it is important to remember that the vast majority of the sources represent the norms and thoughts of an elite male group writing primarily for members of their own class. All of these texts, with the exception of a few very late ones, were written in Hebrew, a language many people who were not part of the elite did not have access to. Certainly most women did not know how to read Hebrew, and although many communities throughout Jewish history strove to provide their sons with the ability to read, those who did not continue their studies often knew only how to read and follow basic prayers. As such, the writings we now possess represent the social milieu of the elite writers and constrict our understandings of childhood to that which they tell us, excluding the thoughts and practices of men outside their class or those of women who were not privy to the same education. As we shall see, the first woman whose voice we can hear lived in the seventeenth century. In addition, since many of the texts discuss religious obligations, they are often prescriptive rather than descriptive. We will try to distinguish between these features of the texts in the selections that follow.

Throughout the chapter, I have brought a more thorough representation of ancient sources than modern ones (though they are far from comprehensive), trying to provide a glimpse at the development within Jewish society over time. The logic behind this is based on the fact that most of the later texts rely on ancient formulations, and as such it is important to be familiar with the earlier texts in order to understand the later ones. In addition, the later sources are divided almost equally between the Jewish communities living under Islam and those living under Christianity.[13]

Organization of Selections

After a brief introduction concerning the terms "childhood" and "child," the selections in this chapter are divided into four sections. The first section addresses procreation and conceptions of the life cycle, providing texts that illustrate the way the commandment was understood and theorized as well as some of the practical implications of these understandings. Among the topics addressed are the meaning of conception and birth, the definition of the relationship between children and evil, sin and purity, and the understanding of childhood as part of the life cycle.

The second section of the chapter is devoted to birth and child care. This section emphasizes texts that describe daily life, in order to provide a window not only to the world of those who wrote but also a picture of those who could not write and had no voice in the texts.[14] In Jewish texts, childbirth and child care are often discussed as part of the life-cycle rituals and in the context of daily life. Few texts contain childrearing instructions, especially in regard to young children. The main directives that appear deal with two issues: feeding them and initiating them into Judaism and religious education; both these issues will be taken up again in the section dealing with parental obligations. Early texts discuss changes to standard religious practice that stem from birth and child care, whereas texts from the medieval period and onward provide guidance and instruction for how to care for children. Sources that describe infancy and childhood focus mainly on feeding infants and on infant mortality and protection from death.

Because procreation was considered such an important obligation for men, Jewish law allowed divorce (and in some cases even enforced it) if a couple had no offspring after ten years. However, this issue underwent many changes over time, as I demonstrate below.[15]

The third section of the chapter addresses a variety of childhood rituals–rituals around birth, rituals that took place later on in a child's life before school began, and the bar mitzvah ritual, which in modern times is considered a central rite of passage. The first rituals Jewish children underwent were circumcision and naming. Whereas circumcision is a well-known precept from the time of the Bible and was performed on the eighth day, there is little information about naming ceremonies until much later on in the Jewish tradition. Moreover, even in the case of circumcision, it is only in the first centuries CE that instructions on how to perform the ritual survive in writing. The Mishnah is the first text in which the details of the ceremony appear comprehensively. As for girls, who were never circumcised in Judaism, we only hear of naming rituals from the early modern period and later.

Additional rites are initiation to schooling and, in early modern times, the bar mitzvah, as well as other less formal rituals for girls and other occasions. This section illustrates the organizing principles of these rituals and the way these rites changed throughout history alongside the preservation of key elements. In addition, since many of the ceremonies took place in public in front of the community at large, some of the sources in this section point to the ways children were included in communal events. As many of the sources reveal, initiating Jewish children into the community was simultaneously an attempt to negate external influences and ideas as well as an adaptation of values and ideals acculturated into Jewish culture from the surrounding society.

The fourth section of this chapter is the largest one, with the most expansive source material. It addresses legal and religious obligations toward children and the obligations that children had to others. The main topics discussed in the chapter are the legal obligations of parents toward their children: feeding and clothing the children along with educating them. The section on education encompasses both theories of education as well as descriptions of everyday events within schools and at home. These texts expose attitudes toward the induction of children into religion and religious practice and understandings of morality in the context of obligations toward children and their education. These sources expose both how children were expected to behave as well as the ways society dealt with misbehavior. Finally, the sources at the end of this section discuss an important obligation children had toward their parents, the fifth commandment (which required a child to honor his parents), address understandings of children's obligations to parents, and define the relationship between parents and children in terms of authority, obligation, and emotional ties.

All of the sections emphasize the variety of social institutions in which children took part. Attention is paid to gender divisions and conceptions throughout the chapter. The importance placed on actual descriptions of everyday life serves this purpose as well, providing a glimpse into the lives of those who did not write the texts, but feature in them prominently.

Each section opens with a brief introduction concerning the topics addressed within. Subsequently each specific source is introduced by providing historical and bibliographic information concerning the author or book from which the text was taken. Despite the division into sections, a number of the sources in the different sections shed light on sources in other parts of the chapter, and I have attempted to point to the recurring themes that emerge.

Introduction: Defining Childhood

The word "childhood" appears in the Hebrew scriptures only a few times, most significantly in the books Psalms and Ecclesiastes. Otherwise, the scriptures rarely discuss children or childhood as an abstraction. The following verses are presented in conjunction with commentary on them in order to illustrate understandings of childhood. As we shall see in the texts throughout the chapter, this idea of childhood as a happy and enjoyable period comes across in other sources as well. However, few texts discuss this topic as an issue in and of itself. Although there were few commentators on Psalms 110:3 (Doc. 1-1), some exegetes did remark on this verse, and I have included one by the medieval scholar Rashi (R. Isaac b. Solomon, northern France, d. 1203).

Document 1–1

Psalms 110:3

In majestic holiness from the womb from the dawn, yours was the dew of childhood.[16]

Document 1–2

Rashi's Commentary

This will be a nice chapter [of your life] and it will be like dew which is pleasant and will help create for you the fruits that will make you succeed.

Source: Rashi, ad locum, in standard editions of his commentary.

Document 1–3

Ecclesiastes 11:9–10

O youth enjoy yourself while you are in your childhood![17] Let your heart lead you to enjoyment in these days of your youth. Follow the desires of your heart and the glances of your eyes—but know well that God will call you to account for all such things—and banish care from your mind and pluck sorrow out of your flesh! For youth [lit., childhood] and black hair are fleeting.

Procreation and Birth

Biblical Origins

The book of Genesis provides the basic framework for ideas about procreation and birth within Jewish tradition. As noted above, procreation is commanded twice in the first ten chapters of Genesis. One can see that this commandment is closely linked both to dominion over the animal world and to the moral authority people have over their deeds, especially those regarding bloodshed. The book of Genesis presents bearing children as woman's lot in the world and as part of her punishment for eating from the tree of life.[18] Although, as we will see, procreation was considered a male obligation, at least in the earliest sources women are also tied to this function, and procreation is presented as part of their realm.

Children are considered one of the greatest blessings in the Bible. God promises the fathers of the Jewish people—Abraham, Isaac, and Jacob—that their offspring will be plentiful. The ability to bear children was in the case of all the patriarchs a challenge they and their wives had to meet. Through these stories, the Bible conveys the tremendous sorrow men and especially women felt when they were not able to conceive. We will also see how later Jewish sources follow up on the words and actions of the biblical figures, using them as examples and role models. An important biblical role model in the context of procreation is Hannah, the mother of Samuel (Sam. 1:1). The Babylonian Talmud (Doc. 1-10), compiled in Babylon during the fifth century, portrays her in this light.

Document 1–4
Genesis 1:28
God blessed them and God said to them: "Be fertile and increase, fill the earth and master it; and rule the fish of the sea, the birds of the sky and all the living things that creep on earth."

Document 1–5
Genesis 9:1–7
God blessed Noah and his sons and said to them, "Be fertile and increase and fill the earth. The fear and the dread of you shall be upon all the beasts of the earth and upon all the birds of the sky—everything with which the earth is astir—and upon all the fish of the sea; they are given in your hand. Every creature that lives shall be yours to eat; as with the green grasses, I give you all these. You must not, however, eat flesh with its life-blood in it. But for your own life-blood, I will require a reckoning: I will require it of every beast, of man too, will I require a reckoning for human life, of every man for that of his fellow man. Whoever sheds the blood of man, by man shall his blood be shed; for in his image did God make man. Be fertile, then, and increase; abound on the earth and increase on it."

Document 1–6

Genesis 3:16

And to the woman he said: "I will make most severe your pangs in childbearing; in pain you shall bear children. Yet your urge shall be for your husband and he shall rule over you."

Document 1–7

Genesis 22:16–18

[God to Abraham after the binding of Isaac:]

"Because you have done this and have not withheld your son, your favored one, I will bestow My blessing upon you and make your descendants as numerous as the stars of heaven and the sands on the seashore; and your descendants shall seize the gates of their foes. All the nations of the earth shall bless themselves by your descendants, because you have obeyed my command."

Document 1–8

Genesis 25:21

[Rebekah's barrenness:]

Isaac pleaded with the Lord on behalf of his wife, because she was barren; and the Lord responded to his plea and his wife Rebekah conceived.

Document 1–9

Genesis 30:1–2

[Rachel's barrenness:]

When Rachel saw that she had borne Jacob no children, she became envious of her sister; and Rachel said to Jacob: "Give me children or I shall die." Jacob was incensed at Rachel and said: "Can I take the place of God, who has denied you fruit of the womb?"

Document 1–10

Babylonian Talmud, Tractate Berakhot

Sovereign of the Universe, among all the things that Thou hast created in a woman, Thou hast not created one without a purpose: eyes to see, ears to hear, a nose to smell, a mouth to speak, hands to do work, legs to walk with, breasts to give suck. These breasts that Thou hast put on my heart, are they not to give suck? Give me a son so that I may suckle with them.

Source: BT Berakhot 31b.[19]

Children as Perpetuating Their Parents

Children were not only a blessing, they were also considered essential for their parents' and especially their fathers' perpetuation after death. If a man died without offspring, the Bible instructed his wife to marry one of his brothers in a process known as levirate marriage in order to perpetuate the dead brother's name. These texts emphasize the patrilineal orientation of the Jewish texts and the ways Jewish thought conceived of children as belonging to their fathers.

Levirate marriage (*yibbum*) was the primary obligation for the brother of a man who died without offspring. An alternative was *haliza* (lit., removal of a shoe).[20] Levirate marriage is exemplified in the story of Judah and Tamar (Gen. 38) and *haliza* can be seen in the marriage of Ruth and Boaz (Ruth 4). Until the Middle Ages, levirate marriage was still commonly practiced, and only after this period did *haliza* become the preferred course of action.[21]

Document 1–11

Deuteronomy 25:5–10

When brothers dwell together and one of them dies and leaves no son, the wife of the deceased shall not be married to a stranger outside the family. Her husband's brother shall unite with her: take her as his wife and perform the levir's duty. The first son she bears shall be accounted to the dead brother, that his name shall not be blotted out of Israel. But if the man does not wish to marry his brother's widow, his brother's widow shall appear before the elder's in the gate and declare: "My husband's brother refuses to establish a name in Israel for his brother; he will not perform the duty of a levir." The elders of the town should then summon him and talk to him. If he insists, saying: I do not want to marry her, his brother's widow shall go up to him in the presence of the elders, pull the sandal off his foot, spit in his face and make this declaration: "Thus shall be done to the man who will not build up his brother's house! And he shall go in Israel by the name of 'the family of the unsandaled one.'"

The Duty of Procreation

Rabbinic texts from the early centuries of the first millennium sought to define the obligation of procreation in a more exact manner. Hillel and Shammai are considered two of the greatest scholars in this period (1st century CE), and two distinct legal schools are named for them.[22] One of the issues they debated was what constitutes the duty of procreation and who is obligated to perform this duty.

Later sources accept the first opinion stated in this Mishnah, namely, that it is man's duty to procreate and not woman's duty. R. Johanan ben Baroka's opinion, which was the minority opinion, is not accepted on the grounds that it is not woman's nature to conquer and as such it is not within her realm to "fill the earth and master it" (Doc. 1–12).

One was supposed to have offspring to perpetuate one's place in the world to come. Some sources regard a man without a child as dead, while others explain that a sinner is punished by having his children die in his lifetime, leaving him without continuation. As part of the Jewish-Christian debate in the Middle Ages, Jews often argued that their Christian neighbors who were celibate were actually ensuring that they would have no place in heaven. As one medieval Jewish author concluded, "thus we see that having children is a characteristic of a God-fearing man," and this opinion seems to have prevailed.[23] Document 1–13 is an excerpt from a Midrash (exegesis) on Genesis 16 compiled in the fifth century CE that was frequently quoted in later centuries. It discusses a conversation between Sarah and Abraham before Sarah gives her maid Hagar to him (Gen. 16:2). The sentence "anyone who does not have a son is regarded as dead, as a ruined person" is quoted time and again when discussing the importance of procreation.

Traditional commentators echo this idea and focus mainly on men who have no children. Since women are not commanded with the obligation of procreation, they cannot file for divorce if they do not have children on grounds of not being able to fulfill the commandment like the men. Traditionally, a man could demand a divorce writ if he had no children on the grounds of not fulfilling his obligation to procreate, but a woman, whose duties did not include procreation, could not. Women could only claim they wanted a divorce and children so that they would have someone on whom to depend in their old age (BT Ketubbot 64a, BT Yevamot 65a).[24]

Until the early modern period, when a body of literature known as the *tekhine* literature flourished, we do not hear what women who were childless had to say or thought about the matter. *Tkhines* were supplicatory prayers said by women and men in Yiddish. Some of them were written by men while others were written by women. They became highly popular and were printed in many copies.[25] Document 1–14 is a prayer written for and said by a childless woman. One can see her anguish and desire for a child as well as her explanation for the misfortune that has befallen her.

Document 1–12

Who Should Procreate

No man may abstain from keeping the law "be fruitful and multiply," unless he already has children. According to the school of Shammai, two sons, according to the school of Hillel, a son and a daughter, for it is written "male and female he created them" (Gen. 1:27). If he married a woman and lived with her ten years and she bare no child, it is not permitted him to abstain. If he divorced her she may be married to another and the second husband may live with her for ten years. If she had a miscarriage the space [of ten years] is reckoned from the time of the miscarriage. The duty to be fruitful and multiply falls on the man but not on the woman. R. Johanan ben Baroka says: Of both of them it is written "And God blessed them and God said unto them be fruitful and multiply."

Source: Mishnah Yevamot 6:6.[26]

Document 1–13

Children as Perpetuating Their Parents

And Sarai said to Abram: "Look, the Lord has kept me from bearing. Consort with my maid, perhaps I shall have a son through her" (Gen. 16:2). They [the sages] said: Anyone who does not have a son[27] is regarded as dead, as a ruined person. Is regarded as dead [we learn from Rachel]: "Give me children or I shall die," as ruined for she [Sarah] says perhaps I shall have a son through her [lit., I will be built through her] and only something that is ruined is built.

Source: Genesis Rabbah, edited by Theodore Albeck (Jerusalem: Wahrmann Books, 1965), vol. 1, 45:2.

Document 1–14

Tkhine for Having Children (Tkhine for a Woman Who Has No Children)

Yehi rotsn [May it be]—God, my God and God of my ancestors, who has created me from clay and has given me a soul and everything in my life with his abundant grace and mercy. Since I have done but little good in this world, You have not granted me the merit of bearing children. Woe, how bitter is my life. I am like a tree which is fully grown but bears no fruit. A great sadness is upon me. I beseech heaven and earth to lament for me since my years are passing by like smoke. If I cannot correct my sins in this world, may my sorrow compensate for my sins, that I may merit to enter the world-to-come. O, woe is my life! My eyes overflow with tears, and my heart is sad within me; I cannot be happy. I must lament and cry because of the years that have passed since I was born. Woe is me! What can I say? I cry because of my bitter sins. Dear God! Who can heal my misfortune? Only

You, *hashem yisborekh* [blessed God], can repair it. If I cannot enjoy this world, let me merit to enter the other world, and may my soul not be humiliated in the world-to-come.

Source: Tracy Guren Klirs, *The Merit of Our Mothers: A Bilingual Anthology of Jewish Women's Prayers* (Cincinnati: Hebrew Union College, 1992), 114.

Creation of the Fetus

The classic Jewish account of how the fetus is created and what his or her life will look like appears in the Talmud. One can see the affinity between these ideas and concepts of embryology that were common in the Greco-Roman world.[28] These concepts and frames of references continued to accompany Jewish thinkers in the centuries to come (Doc. 1–15).

Traditional Jewish sources, like ancient Greek medicine, believe that the gender of the baby was determined forty or eighty days after conception, depending on the sex. Boys' souls were created forty days after conception, while girls' souls were created only after eighty days. Some sources expressed the idea that at the time of the formation of the soul it was declared who the baby would marry (Doc. 1–16).

The most famous discussion of this topic is attributed to R. Judah Nassi, who edited and compiled the Mishnah. R. Judah was well known not only as a legal authority but also as the head of the Jewish community in all political and local matters. The Jewish sources contain many tales of the close relations between R. Judah and the Roman governor, Antoninus (late second century CE). The discussion of the creation of the soul is attributed to them (Doc. 1–17).

These explanations of the creation of the fetus and the determination of children's future marriages were very popular throughout the ages, and many elements of this story were expanded to explain man's approach to the world and the stages of life. According to Jewish tradition, the fetus sits in the mother's womb and studies Torah and has to be forced to leave the womb when the time to be born arrives (Doc. 1–18). This source, which originated in late antiquity, was quoted throughout the Middle Ages and found its way into modern compilations of Aggadah.[29]

Another central issue researchers have discussed concerning conceptions of childhood has been the way children's souls are perceived. Are they pure in their youth or do they start life with evil inclinations that must be curbed? While on the whole it is accepted as commonplace knowledge that Jewish tradition certainly does not see conception as originating in sin and as such does not view infants or children as needing to purify themselves, there are some hints to such a notion in a variety of texts, beginning with the Bible. At the same time, many texts express the idea that children are pure and that their purity has the potential of purifying society. This is said especially in relation to young boys who study scripture and Jewish law.

Different sources debate at what age children begin to distinguish between good and bad, and at the same time they discuss at what age they begin to have an evil inclination. The texts seem to point to ages eight, nine, and ten as the central ages.

Document 1–15

Babylonian Talmud, Tractate Niddah

Our Rabbis taught: During the first three months, the embryo occupies the lowest chamber, during the middle ones it occupies the middle chamber, and during the last months it occupies the upper most chamber. . . . Our Rabbis taught: There are three partners in man, the Holy One blessed be He, his father, and his mother. His father supplies the semen out of which are formed the child's bones, sinews, nails, the brain in his head, and the white in his eye; his mother supplies the semen of the red substance out of which is formed his skin, flesh, hair, blood, and the black of his eye; and the Holy One blessed be He gives him the spirit and the breath, beauty of features, eyesight, the power of hearing, the ability to speak and to walk, understanding and discernment. When his time to depart from the world approaches, the Holy One blessed be He takes away his share and leaves the share of his father and his mother with them.

Source: BT Niddah 30b–31a.

Document 1–16

The Creation of Gender

Rab Judah has said in the name of Rab: "Forty days before the creation of a child, a Bath Kol [a voice from heaven] issues forth and proclaims The daughter of A is for B, the house of C is for D, the field of E is for F! There is no contradiction here, the latter dictum referring to a first marriage and the former to a second marriage."

Source: BT Sotah 2a.

Document 1–17

Babylonian Talmud, Tractate Sanhedrin

Antoninus also said to Rabbi: "When is the soul placed in man; as soon as it is decreed [that the sperm shall be male or female, etc.] or when [the embryo] is actually formed? He replied: "From the moment of formation." He objected: "Can a piece of meat be unsalted for three days without becoming putrid? But it must be from the moment that [God] decrees [its destiny]." Rabbi said: "This thing Antoninus taught me and Scripture supports him, for it is written 'And thy decree hath preserved my spirit'" (Job 10:12).

Antoninus also inquired of Rabbi: "From what time does the Evil Tempter sway over man; from the formation [of the embryo] or from [its] issuing forth [into the light of the world]?"—From the formation, he replied; "if so," he objected, "it would rebel in its mother's womb and go forth. But from when it issues."

Source: BT Sanhedrin 91b.

Document 1–18

Midrash Tanhuma-Yelamdenu

When at last the time arrives for his entrance into the world, the angel comes to him and says: "At a certain hour your time will come to enter the light of the world." He pleads with him saying: "Why do you wish me to go out into the light of the world?" The angel replies: "you know my son, you were formed against your will, against your will you will be born, against your will you will die, and against your will you are destined to give an accounting before the King of Kings, the Holy One blessed be He. . . . Then the seven stages of the life of man begin for him. In the first stage he is like a king, for everyone inquires about his health and is eager to look at him. They hug him and kiss him, since he is only one year old. In the second stage he is like a swine that grovels in dunghills, for a child waddles in dirt when he is two years old. In the third stage he is like a kid who skips about the pasture. He is a delight in the eyes of his mother and a joy to his father. He skips about here and there while laughing and everyone takes delight in him. In the fourth stage he acts like a horse about to run in a race. When is that? At the time of maturity when he is eighteen years old. Just as the horse prances about and preens himself, so the youth presents himself before his companions. In the fifth stage he is like an ass upon which a saddle has been placed. Men place a saddle upon him by giving him a wife who bears him sons and daughters. He roams hither and yon to obtain food and sustenance for his children. They pile additional burdens on him and he is overwhelmed with problems because of his sons and daughters. When is that? When he is forty years old. In the sixth stage he is like a dog who intrudes here and there and takes from one and gives to another and is not embarrassed. In the seventh stage he resembles a monkey, who is different from all other creatures. He asks about everything, he eats and drinks like a youngster and laughs like a child. He returns to his childish ways in discernment but not in other things. Even his children and the men of his household hate him. When he offers an opinion they say: "Ignore him, for he is an old fool." He behaves like an ape in all situations and in whatever he says. Even the children mock him and the wild birds can awaken him from his sleep.

Source: *Midrash Tanhuma-Yelamdenu*, translated by Samuel A. Berman (Hoboken, N.J.: Ktav, 1996), 656–657.

Document 1–19

Genesis 8:23

... and the Lord said to Himself: "never again will I doom the earth because of man, since the devisings of man's mind are evil from his youth."

Document 1–20

Psalms 51:7

"Indeed I was born with iniquity; with sin my mother conceived me."

Document 1–21

Midrash Tanhuma

And the Lord God said, "Now that the man" (Gen. 3:22) as it is written 'But see, this I did find: God made men plain [*yashar*]' (Eccles. 7:29), God who is righteous and plain created man to be righteous and plain in his image. And if you say, why did [God] create the evil inclination, for it says 'since the devisings of man's mind are evil from his youth' (Gen. 8:21), you are saying he is bad and who can make him good? He who is Blessed said: "You [people] make him bad for children of five, six, seven, eight, and nine years of age do not sin, only from age ten and older does he develop an evil inclination."

Source: *Midrash Tanhuma*, edited by Hanokh Zundel (Jerusalem: Levine-Epstein, 1969), Gen. 7. Further reference to these issues can be found in the section discussing education.

Birth and Child Care

Childbirth and the life of the newborn are perceived as special and important events in all societies. In Jewish texts, these events are treated as part of life-cycle rituals and in the context of daily life. Early texts discuss changes to standard religious practice that stem from birth and child care, whereas texts from the medieval period and onward provide guidance and instruction for how to care for children.

The primary caregivers for infants and young children were female—mothers, their servants, and wet nurses. The number of caretakers depended on the financial abilities of any given family, but the sources indicate that many families had servants and wet nurses that helped with the child care. They are frequently mentioned in discussions of feeding infants, infant mortality, and protection from death.

Boys were the ideal offspring in traditional Jewish society, as in many premodern societies. This preference emerges clearly from a discussion about what one is allowed to pray for. Since one is not allowed to pray in vain, one cannot pray for a boy after the fetus's sex has been determined (Docs. 1–22, 1–23). In addition, when discussing the births of the tribes of Israel in the Bible, reference is made to this preference. This preference is also often expressed in blessings recited after birth (Docs. 1–24, 1–25).[30]

Because procreation was considered such an important obligation for men, Jewish law allowed divorce (and in some cases even enforced it) if a couple had no offspring after ten years. However, this issue underwent many changes over time.[31] Moreover, some sources emphasize the importance of giving birth to sons in order to fulfill their obligation to procreate. This emphasis is especially heightened in texts written by Jews under Muslim rule; under Muslim rule statutes allow a man to marry an additional wife (since in these countries bigamy was practiced) if they did not produce male offspring with their first wife (Docs. 1–26, 1–27).[32]

Document 1–22

Praying for a Son

If a man cries out [to God] over what is past, his prayer is in vain. Thus if his wife was with child and he said "May it be thy will that my wife shall bear a male" this prayer is in vain."

Source: Mishnah Berakhot 9:3.

Document 1–23

Sefer Hasidim

The students were sitting in front of their rabbi. One said: May it be [God's will] that my wife will conceive, if the infant is born alive; if not, may she not conceive. His friend said: "may my wife conceive." His friend [the first speaker] said: "And if it [the baby] dies, it would be better if it were never born, for it says: 'Do not delude your maidservant' (2 Kings 4:16) and 'Don't mislead me' (ibid. 28). And when the baby is born I will pray that it will live."

Source: *Sefer Hasidim*, 2nd edition, edited by Judah Wistentski (Frankfurt am Main: Mekizei Nirdamim, 1924), #1526.

Document 1–24

Blessing of a Brother

[The blessing recited by a brother over his brother upon the birth of a son:]

"I ask you, O God, that He grace me with your life and his, and make him the brother of seven or eight (Eccles. 11:2), and that he strengthen your hand and fortify your position, and may it be said of him: 'your sons will succeed your ancestors: you will appoint them princes throughout the land' (Ps. 45:17). And may God grant me that the evil eye not fall upon you or upon him, and may He not show me any undesirable thing, neither in you nor in him, for all the days of our lives."

Source: Ms. Taylor-Schechter 16.179, published by Shlomo D. Goitein, *Sidrei Hinukh beYemei haGeonim uBeit haRambam,* translated by Jackie Feldman (Jerusalem: Ben Zvi Institute and Hebrew University, 1962), 24.

Document 1–25

Blessings upon the Birth of a Daughter

To my father Elpatael [the brother of the writer and sender]—may God preserve him—a daughter was born, and she called her Srura ["happiness"], in honor of my mother. May she merit coming into a happy and blessed home. May your two daughters [who were described by the writer with much enthusiasm] be happy and blessed. May God grant you what will raise your hearts [that is, a son. At that time, the two brothers had only daughters. As we learn from other letters, the wishes of the daughter came true].

Source: Ms. Taylor-Schechter 12.262; published by Shlomo D. Goitein, *Sidrei Hinukh beYemei haGeonim uBeit haRambam,* translated by Jackie Feldman (Jerusalem: Ben Zvi Institute and Hebrew University, 1962), 25.

Document 1–26

Male Offspring

If one marries a woman and lives with her for ten years and she has not borne male offspring, and even if she bore [sons] and they died at the end of ten years or more, since he has spent ten years with his wife and does not have male offspring, he can marry an additional woman over his wife.

Source: Raphael Berdugo, *Torot Emet* (Meknas: Brothers Tzaig Press, 1947), 82b (1593, Morocco).

Document 1–27

Having Only Girls

Most people who have only had girls born to them, trouble and despair find them day and night and they have worry constantly in their hearts concerning the future, from the day they [the girls] are born until they reach maturity and at all times.

Source: Avraham Ankawa, *Kerem Hemer* (Livorno: Elijah b. Amozag and Friends Press, 1871), part 2, #139 (1698, Fas).

Birth

Birth comes up in the sources both in exegetical contexts and when discussing the Laws of the Sabbath. During childbirth, as in all cases of severe sickness, one is allowed to help the woman giving birth in all ways, even if it involves desecrating the Sabbath or other holy laws.[33] In addition, the mother's life takes precedence over that of her unborn baby. The Mishnah and the Talmud both approve performing a caesarian section only when it is obvious the mother will not survive the birth.

There are few descriptions of birth in Jewish communities before early modern times. One such description exists in a seventeenth-century source that describes rituals for mothers after childbirth. The author of this description, R. Juspa of Worms, Germany, compiled a custom book in which he outlined the customs of his community in great detail.

Document 1–28

The Description of the Parturient's Ritual

The Custom of Parturients Who Give Birth to Males or Females

Immediately after birth they make a circle with a *neter* [chalk?] in the room of the parturients and write on it "barring Lilith"[34] and underneath this: "Adam and Eve." In this way, they write all around that circle, as is the custom everywhere. And some write on the entrance of the room: "Adam, Eve, barring Lilith, Sanoi, and Sansoi, and Samengloff,"[35] and this is a fitting custom. . . .

From the *jüdische Windel* [cloth diaper], after the third day preceding circumcision [*shlish hamilah*], they make the *wimpel*,[36] and they write on it the signatures of the child: when he will be called to the Torah, and also the day of his birth, the month of birth, as well as the year of his birth, and they draw in it the horoscope of that month. And the parturient does not go out of her house of birth until the fourth Sabbath after the birth and sometimes the fifth Sabbath until *der Kreis aus ist*.[37] . . . And the Sabbath afterwards, that is the same Sabbath on which she leaves her house of birth to go to the synagogue, on that Friday night, as the Sabbath arrives, she beautifies her bed with white sheets and pillows and the women come and visit her, and this they call *die weisse Pfühle*. It is also customary for neighbors and relatives to send food to the parturient. And most of them send cookies that are called *Brezel* and some send *Zucker Konfekt* [sugar candies] and some send whatever they wish and they honor the parturient with them. And she wears a pretty scarf and a *Sturz* on the *Schleier*[38] and she wears a *Röckli* [skirt or dress], a garment of shrouds underneath her outfit, when she goes from her house of birth to the synagogue on Sabbath morning. And after she goes out of the synagogue she wears a beautiful *Schleier* and she takes off the *Sturz* and the *Röckli*.[39]

During the morning prayers on that Sabbath, it is obligatory to call the husband of the parturient to the Torah and they make two blessings for him, [including] one for his promise to donate one liter of wax. And while he is still standing in front of the Torah scroll, his wife sends him the *Wimpel*, because here they put the *Wimpel* in the synagogue immediately on the Sabbath on which the parturient leaves her house for the synagogue. . . .

On that Sabbath, each parturient, whether she had a boy or a girl, sends small bowls filled with fruit and sugar to her relatives and neighbors and especially to those who honored her with the portions that are regularly sent to a parturient, as described above. For the three meals [of the Sabbath], the parturients invite female neighbors and relatives, whomever they want, and they eat, drink and rejoice with the parturients."

Source: R. Juspa of Worms, *Minhagim deKehilat Kodesh Wormeisa (Wormser Minhagbuch)*, edited by Benjamin S. Hamburger and Erich Zimmer (Jerusalem: Machon Yerushalyim, 1992), part 2, #288 (seventeenth century, Germany).

Document 1–29

Tkhine for a Woman Who Is about to Have a Child

Merciful and gracious God! Mighty Creator, have compassion on the woman *ploynes bas ploynes* [her name] that she may have this child safely. May the merit of our holy matriarchs—*Sore, Rivke , Rokhl*, and *Leye*[40]—and the merit of our prophetesses—*Miryem, Dvoyre, Khane*, and *Khulde*[41]—and the merit of *Yo'el*[42] sustain her in this time of danger so that she may have this child easily and without suffering.

For You, God, can perform such a miracle, through the merits of the righteous women from among our ancestors, that the child should be born a pure soul for Your service, a righteous person who will devote himself to the study of *toyre* and perform *mitsves* [commandments]. And if it is a female, may she be a modest woman, a God-fearing woman, and may she have good fortune.

Source: Tracy Guren Klirs, *The Merit of Our Mothers: A Bilingual Anthology of Jewish Women's Prayers* (Cincinnati: Hebrew Union College, 1992), 128.

Instructions for Care of Newborns

The texts below are examples of child rearing instructions found in texts from late medieval and early modern times.

R. Menahem Ibn Zerah, a Spanish rabbi who lived during the fourteenth century, wrote a compendium in which he tried to outline the essentials of Jewish life. His book *Zedah la-Derekh* [lit., baggage for the journey] is the first to provide an encyclopedia-like description of how different aspects of Jewish life are supposed to function. Among the chapter in his book are long chapters on everyday life and deportment that it is fitting in his eyes for Jews (Doc. 1–30).

More detailed instructions on rearing and education began to appear in manuals and books during the early modern period. Below is an excerpt from the *Brantspiegel*, written in Yiddish, primarily for female audiences during the seventeenth century. This book, written by an important member of the Prague Jewish community in the sixteenth century, was one of the most widely read books in its time (Doc. 1–31).[43]

Document 1–30

Zedah la-Derekh

Chapter 14–which speaks of the behavior of the child
from the day of his birth until old age

When the babe is born, it should be anointed with contracting substances, and its flesh should be salted, since it is tender and its flesh must be made harder so that it not be too easily injured by contact with external objects. It should be swaddled in a diaper, but its limbs should not be twisted while swaddling. And its body should be washed each day in lukewarm water and in temperate air, at times when there is no milk in its belly. And of this, the prophet said, in his rebuke of Israel, "for indeed you were not rubbed with salt, nor swaddled, nor were you bathed in water to smooth you" (Ezek. 16:4).

The food prepared by the Blessed Name for the newborn boy is milk, and whoever wishes to guard him from illness should give him no nourishment other than milk, which is natural food.

A man should always choose a wet nurse from twenty to thirty years of age, of good appearance without blemish, of even temper, neither thin nor fat. And she should avoid intercourse, which stimulates menstrual blood, so that her milk be white, sweet and odorless, neither too thin nor too thick but medium. The wet nurse should be of good character, neither irascible nor quick-tempered, since such traits reduce the quality of the milk. The food items which stimulate production of milk are sweet and fatty things and the flesh of lambs and goat kids, and moist fish, almond paste, and the like.

If the mother of the child can nurse her son, this is most effective, since it is the food the babe received in the womb, for it is menstrual blood which turns into milk. She should not nurse him overmuch, so that milk is not lost in the stomach, nor too little, lest his body heat up. Rather, she should nurse him moderately, according to the child's strength. And when first born, she should not nurse him until eight days pass, so that her milk stabilize.

The wet nurse should cheer up the child, singing to him so that he be happy and fall asleep, for sleep is beneficial to him; and he should sleep in a dark place. While he is awake, she should make him accustomed to see light and stars and hear music, for the organ stimulated to function will be strengthened. And she should teach him to speak, for babies imitate those who speak with them. One should always feed him with sweet things like honey, which cleanse the brain and aid in the development of his teeth.

And he should not be bled until he is fourteen or fifteen years of age, except from the ears or the calves. When the boy is weaned, he should be given light foods—pancakes with sugar and young chickens; his food should always be warm and moist, as he is like his food. When the time comes for him to move upon his own legs, he should be led step by step until his legs strengthen, so that he not become overly tired. Efforts should be made to impart character traits at an early age—that he be neither angry nor fearful, nor become cowardly nor hard-hearted or worrisome. This is the rule: warn him against becoming emotionally overexcited and take the middle path until he become of age. And so said Solomon in his wisdom: "train a lad in the way he ought to go," etc. (Prov. 22:6). For all this will aid him to be healthy. When he is five or six years of age, lead him to the house of study to train him in the commandments and in morals. Let him exert himself somewhat before eating. Let him abstain from wine while still a lad, until the age of twenty, especially if he is hot-tempered. From the age of twenty on, he should eat foods that tend towards heat and dryness, and be guided in the ways of health, as we specified above, until old age. And if he do so, fortunate be his lot. He shall be saved from evil afflictions and untimely death. And inherit many good days. From the beginning of the year until its end.

Source: R. Menahem Ibn Zerah, *Sefer Zedah la-Derekh,* translated by Jackie Feldman (Warsaw: H. Kalter, 1880), Chapter One, Rule Three, Chapter 14, 32a.

Document 1–31

Brantspiegel

Chapter 46. How to Educate Children in Proper Ways
One should not carry the infant naked, nor let him lie naked before people. Rather, he should be dressed or at least wrapped in his diaper so that the evil eye not behold him nor an evil spirit come over him, and also so that he not be bitten by flies or worms. And it is better that he should be clothed even in a short garment than that he lie naked. Moreover, already in their childhood, they may come to think that there is nothing wrong with going around naked and not be embarrassed to expose their flesh even when they grow older. It may also be that the sun will burn them during the day and the moon shine upon them at night, and this may harm them, for at times the moon may cause injury. . . . He should also not be permitted to urinate through a hole or through the window at night, for an evil spirit may harm him. He should not be dressed or undressed elsewhere than in his bed, so that he not grow accustomed to go around naked and know that it is fitting that he be ashamed before God, blessed be His Name, and before mankind. And if they sometimes go about naked, he should say to them: "a disgrace and a shame! Cover your nakedness!" He should train them not to perform their bodily functions before people, and tell them at all times that this is a disgrace. And he should threaten them with the rod so that they fear, and occasionally strike them lightly with it so that they know what the rod serves for. . . . If they sit at the dining table, and the infants dirty or soil themselves while eating, they should not be seated at the table, and certainly not brought to the synagogue. . . .[44]

They should be trained in infancy to extend their hand to their father and mother and to all their elders, and thus become accustomed to respect them when he grows up. . . .

Whole [?] clothes should be sewn for the infants and they should be taught to treat them with propriety and caution. And they should not wear new clothes, but old ones, for, as infants grow all the time, there's no need for new ones. Moreover, they cost much money, especially if a man has many children. Furthermore, if they grow accustomed to attractive clothes in their childhood, they shall desire them when they grow up as well and attempt to obtain them by all means, both permitted and prohibited, and many evils may result from this. For if a man whose house is abundantly blessed, adorn his sons with gold and silver jewelry—who knows how long the good days may last? For he may need to sell them later. And if he remain wealthy, they will enjoy the benefits soon enough, when they grow up—but his daughter should grow accustomed to this, so that she know how to adorn herself for her husband. Furthermore, he plants haughtiness in the hearts of his small children, and many troubles arise from haughtiness. . . . And in exile it is especially advised not to adorn children, in order not to arouse jealousy in the hearts of our despisers, who day and night plan and decree evil decrees upon us, whose revocation costs much money. Beautification and adornment also remove the fear of God from children's hearts. For if they go around in new clothes in their childhood, we worry that they may have to wear old ones in old age.

He should train them to go around with their heads covered. I have seen kerchiefs tied under the chins of infants so that they cannot remove them. . . . He should train them to have a belt sewn on to their clothes from behind, for when they become somewhat older, they will recite blessings which may not be recited without a belt. He should tie their shoes so that they cannot be removed from their feet. Thus, they may grow accustomed not to walk barefoot when they grow up. This is a shameful thing, and furthermore, they may stub their feet. One must take special attention that they not walk around barefoot in the months of Tevet and Shevat,[45] since this is a danger, as at those times the cats mate and defecate, and if a person touch the feces with his feet, they may become infected, and it takes much time to be healed from this.

When the infant begins to speak clearly, he should teach him "Moses charged us with the Teaching" (Deut. 33:4) and several other verses. As he grows older, he should continue to teach him verses, so that the fear of God become fixed in his heart already in childhood. When he is put to bed, his clothes should be properly folded, and he should be shown the folded clothes. And they should be trained to say "peaceful night" at night, "good morning" in the morning, "gut Shabbes" on the Sabbath, and "gut Yontef" on holidays. When people sit down to eat, he should be trained to say "blessed be those who are seated!" And when he takes leave of people, "with your permission." And when meeting people, "May the Name [of God] be with you!" When he grows somewhat older, he is taught to add the name of God to the blessings: "May God bless you with a good morning!" "May God bless you with a restful night!" If he is first greeted with the morning or evening blessing, he should reply with thanks and grace, and not pretend he has not heard what they have said, for people become angry when their blessings are not replied to.

It is good that he teach his children the Hebrew names for articles of clothing and household utensils, so that they may become accustomed to our holy language. And when they extend their hands towards someone, they should try to stand properly and their faces be welcoming. Before they learn how to walk, they should be carried to their father and mother on Sabbath and holidays to be blessed. Once they begin walking, they go to their parents themselves and stand before them with inclined body, and bend their heads to receive their blessing. In this way, they become acquainted with the commandment of respecting their elders and accept their authority. They should also go to their aunts and uncles to receive their blessing, for we are also commanded to respect them as well. And they should take care to honor elderly people, and request their blessings.

He should train them to eat every day at the same time, so that they not be constantly chewing their cuds like beasts, and not be gluttons. He should not give them sweets and dainties at all times, but give them what is of use for their bodies, and not more than is necessary. They should not desire to eat with strangers and be satisfied with what they receive in their parents' homes. And at mealtimes, they should be seated with culture and propriety and not gorge themselves on food and drink. Nor should they always desire to eat meat like wild animals. And when they eat, they should give of their bread to others so that they become accustomed to perform the commandment of welcoming guests. And they should eat gladly what they are given and not say: "this, I don't want to eat, and this I like!" This is a great sin, and people will hate them if they behave this way, and what people hate, The Holy One blessed be He hates as well. As R. Hanina ben Dosa said in the Ethics of the Fathers (3:6), "He in whom the spirit of mankind finds pleasure, in him the spirit of God finds pleasure." . . .

He must train the little children not to ask people for what they see in their homes, and not to be overly desirous to obtain such things—this matter is called "stretching out one's hand." And those people whose heart desires everything they see among others and prefer what others have to what they themselves possess—all their days will be evil. They shall know no tranquility in their bellies and their soul shall never be satisfied. . . . He should not let them eat quickly or ravenously. This is very shameful and may even cause damage, as the food will not be properly digested. It is imperative that his parents prevent him from being spoiled. For whoever is spoiled in his infancy desires to be spoiled all his life and cannot take leave of such things even in old age.

Source: R. Moses b. Henoch Altschul Yerushalmi, *Brantspiegel*, translated by Jackie Feldman (Basel: Konrad Waldkirche, 1602), 169b–179a (seventeenth century, Prague)

Children's Death and Illness

Death was commonplace in premodern times, and death of children comes up frequently in the sources. Because of the tremendous difficulty connected to dealing with death, many sources contain moral advice. A famous story in this context is that of a wise woman named Bruriah. If there was a historical woman of this name, she probably lived during the second century CE. The story tells of the death of her two sons and of the way she informed her husband of this death (Doc. 1-32).

Death was often understood as a punishment of sins. The classic explanation was that children died to atone for their parents sins (Doc. 1-33). As a result, a central issue discussed and objected to in the sources is excessive grief (Doc. 1-34), which was also seen as a refusal to accept God's will. At the same time, it is obvious from the sources that parents mourned their dead children and were far from indifferent about their deaths.

Document 1–32

Midrash Proverbs

It happened that while the rabbi was lecturing in the house of study on the afternoon of the Sabbath, his two sons died at home. What did their mother do? She lay them on a bed and spread a sheet on them. At the end of the Sabbath, Rabbi Meir returned home from the house of study to his own house. He said to her: "Where are my two sons?" . . . She said to him: "I want to ask you a question. . . . Some time ago a person came and entrusted an object to my care and now he came to collect it. Shall I restore it to him or not?" He answered: "My daughter, whoever has someone's pledge must return to its owner!" She then said, "Without asking for your consent I wouldn't gave it back to him." She thereupon clutched his hand and took him up into that room . . . and removed the sheet from the bodies. When he saw them both lying dead on the bed, he wept . . . and at that time she said to him, to R. Meir: "Did you not tell me that that which has been entrusted to one's keeping must be restored on demand? The Lord gave and the Lord hath taken away, blessed be the name of the Lord" (Job 1:21).

Source: *Midrash Proverbs*, edited by S. Buber (Vilna: Re'em Widow and Brothers Press, 1893), 31:1, 54b–55a.

Document 1–33

A Child's Death as Atonement

There are people of whom it is decreed that their children will die without successors, and they [the children] die at ten years of age and older. And why did they not die young, at age one, so that he [the parent] would not be so sad? Because it is known to the Creator of the world at what hour a person will experience great sorrow and be condemned to die, and the son dies so that the father or the mother will live. This is why the child lived until age ten, so that the father will be deeply sorrowful, and he will be atoned for [by the sorrow] and live.

Source: R. Judah the Pious, *Sefer ha-gematriyot le-Rabbi Judah heHasid* (Los Angeles: Cherubim Press, 1998), fol. 22b (thirteenth century, Germany).

Document 1–34

Extensive Grief over Child's Death

R. Judah said as citing Rav, Whoever indulges in grief to excess over his dead will weep for another. There was a certain woman that lived in the neighborhood of R. Huna; she had seven sons, one of whom died, and she wept for him rather excessively. R. Huna sent [word] to her. "Act not thus." She heeded him not [and] he sent to her: If you heed my word it is well; but if not, are you anxious to make provision [shrouds] for yet another? He [the next son] died and they all died. In the end he said to her, "Are you fumbling with provision for yourself?" And she died.

Source: BT Mo'ed Katan 27b.[46]

Rituals of Childhood

Circumcision and Naming Ceremonies

The first rituals Jewish children underwent were circumcision and naming. Circumcision is known from the time of the Bible (Doc. 1–35) but instructions on how to perform the ritual survive in writing only from the Mishnah. The sources concerning circumcision suggest that naming was part of the ritual from the start. As for girls, who were never circumcised in Judaism, we only hear of naming rituals from the early modern period and later.

Customs that were part of the circumcision ritual developed over time. Thus, for example, the custom of having the infant circumcised while being held by someone who sat in a chair called "Elijah the prophet chair" and the belief that the ritual was overseen by Elijah (2 Kings 17–21) is first mentioned in an eighth-century compendium of sources from Babylon (Doc. 1-36). In medieval Europe, the circumcision ceremony was moved from the home to the synagogue, turning it into an important communal affair. Moreover, additional roles were added in the ritual, such as the role of the *ba'al brit*–the co-parent or godparent who carried the infant to the synagogue and held him during the actual circumcision (Doc. 1-37).

Circumcision was a rite in which the father played a central role. Not only was this one of his obligations toward his son but this was a formal recognition of his paternity (Doc. 1-38). The mother was sometimes present and sometimes absent and had no fixed role in the rite. If the father was absent, then the local court was supposed to assume responsibility for the circumcision.

While the ritual of circumcision was practiced throughout all Jewish communities, and the blessings and the act of circumcision stayed constant, other parts of the ritual varied from place to place. In both Ashkenazic and Sephardic communities, there were additional rituals the night before the circumcision, extra figures were added to the ritual besides the father and the circumciser (*mohel*), and changes occurred over time.

Although women did not have any official role in the circumcision ceremony, over the generations they took on different tasks in the ritual. Ancient sources point to the fact that some women were circumcisers. The first woman mentioned in this role is Zipporah, the wife of Moses (Doc. 1-39). Sources from late antiquity point to women as circumcisers, at least in certain cases. By the Middle Ages, very few women were circumcisers, but a new role developed for women in the European communities–especially in Germany, Italy, and northern France. Women were those who prepared the infants for circumcision, brought them to the synagogue, and in some cases even held them on their laps during the ritual. During the Middle Ages, in northern Europe, the practice of having a female *ba'alat brit* (godmother) developed. While we know little of the custom during the periods when it was widespread, we have some evidence of it from the period after it was no longer seen positively and legal authorities tried (and succeeded) in banishing it. After this period, a woman's role was usually reduced to bringing the boy to the synagogue and handing him to her husband (Doc. 1-40), and playing a role in the preparations for the ritual.

Girls were not circumcised. Besides two short passages in the Mishnah regarding celebrations after the birth of a girl,[47] there is no discussion in the

Jewish sources of rites for girls until the fourteenth century in Germany. From this point and onward there is mention of a rite called the *Hollekreisch*. This rite was performed approximately a month after birth for boys and girls. On this occasion the children were given a non-Jewish name (Doc. 1–41).[48] In addition to the Hollekreisch, there were a number of other rituals that were symbolic and which were observed for boys (Doc. 1–42). Early modern texts from Jewish communities living under Moslem rule reveal a naming ceremony for girls that was customary among Middle Eastern Jews (Doc. 1–43).

Document 1–35

Genesis 17:1–5, 10–13

When Abram was ninety-nine years old the Lord appeared to Abram and said to him, "I am El Shaddai. Walk in my ways and be blameless. I will establish my covenant between me and you and I will make you exceedingly numerous." Abram threw himself on his face and God spoke to him further, "As for me, this is my covenant with you: You shall be the father of a multitude of nations. And you shall no longer be called Abram but your name shall be Abraham, for I will make you the father of a multitude of nations. . . . Such shall be the covenant between me and you which you shall keep: You shall circumcise the flesh of your foreskin and that shall be the sign of the covenant between me and you. And throughout the generations, every male among you shall be circumcised at the age of eight days. . . . Thus shall my covenant be marked in your flesh as an everlasting pact."

Document 1–36

Circumcision and Elijah's Chair

The elders of the generation told me that on the day that [my] father, our teacher, Abba Aluf,[49] brought me into the covenant, when he came to the synagogue with me on his arm, he sat for one moment on the prepared chair and then he stood up and placed me on the other chair of circumcision. And after he went out, they asked him what the reason for this was, for [they said that] they had never seen anyone doing this. And he said, I have learned from the elders that this prepared chair is for Elijah[50] and he is the angel of circumcision and I sat on it with the child so that perhaps he would bless the child for me, that he find wisdom in his blessing.

Source: Otzar HaGaonim, edited by Benjamin M. Lewin, *Thesaurus of the Gaonic Responsa and Commentaries, Shabbat* (Jerusalem: Mossad haRav Kook, 1930), 139, #425.

Document 1–37

Circumcision in the Synagogue

On the eighth day of circumcision they rise early to the synagogue to pray . . . and they light the candle . . . and they set up two chairs and they spread a mantle [probably a Torah mantle], or some thing of beauty to adorn it. One [chair] is for Elijah who comes and sits there and sees the commandment being performed . . . and one chair is for the *ba'al brit*[51] who sits in it with the child on his knees. And cloths are brought there for the circumciser to clean his hands with them . . . and they wash the child in warm water. And they dress him in fine clothes. A cloth gown and an overgarment and a beautiful hat for his head, as if he were a groom. And they carry him with pomp to the synagogue after the prayers. And the congregation rises to their feet for him when the child enters. And they say: " 'Blessed is he who comes' and the bearer says 'In the name of God.' And the father of the boy takes him and blesses 'to enter him into the covenant of Abraham' . . . and those standing there say 'As he has entered the covenant, so shall he enter Torah and the wedding canopy and good deeds. . . .' And the father gives him (the infant) to the ba'al brit. And he [the ba'al brit] sits on a chair and takes him in his hands. And the circumciser recites: 'Blessed art thou who has commanded us to circumcise' and he circumcises. . . ."

Source: *Mahzor Vitry*, edited by S. Horowitz (Nürnberg: Mekizei Nirdamim, 1892), #506, (twelfth century, northern France).

Document 1–38

Father's Role in Circumcision

An unmarried woman gave birth to a son and she gave him to someone [*ploni*] and said that he was his father. And he said "this is not my son." And they wanted to call him the son of ploni, to say ploni b. ploni. And R. Jacob [Mahar'i Segal] warned them not to embarrass him with this, as he would not admit [his paternity].

Source: R. Jacob Mulin, *Sefer Maharil. Minhagim,* edited by Shlomoh J. Spitzer (Jerusalem: Machon Yerushalayim, 1989), Hilkhot Milah, #19 (fifteenth century, Germany).

Document 1–39

Exodus 4:20–26

So Moses took his wife and sons, mounted them on an ass, and went back to the land of Egypt . . . At a night encampment on the way, the Lord encountered him and sought to kill him. So Zipporah took a flint and cut off her son's foreskin, and touched his legs with it, saying: "You are truly a bridegroom of blood to me!" And when he let him alone, she added, "A bridegroom of blood because of the circumcision."

Document 1–40

Women's Restricted Role

The custom which is practiced in most places does not seem to me permissible: A woman sits in the synagogue with the men and they circumcise the baby in her lap. And even if her husband is the mohel [circumciser] or her father or her son, it is not the way [of the world] that such an honored woman should enter among men and in the presence of the Shekhinah . . . especially since she is not commanded to circumcise, not even her own son, as it says "which God commanded him" (Gen. 17:23); "him" and not "her."[52] And if this is the case, why should they circumcise in her lap? Thus, they [the women] snatch this commandment from the men. And whoever can object should object, and whoever acts stringently in this case may he be blessed. Meir son of Barukh. . . .

Source: R. Samson b. Zadok,[53] *Sefer Tashbez* (Warsaw: Lewin-Epstein Brothers, 1901), #397 (thirteenth century, Germany).

Document 1–41

A Naming Ceremony for Girls

For after the parturient who gave birth to a girl leaves her house, it is a custom to name the baby, and that naming is called Hallekreisch. I heard a reason from my father, may his memory be blessed, who heard from his mentors, that the meaning of Hallekreisch is that they cry out at that time to the [female] baby a not holy name and the same for a baby boy. For example, if the "holy" name is Samuel and the *hol* [everyday, not holy] name is Zanvil, they call him Zanvil at that time, etc. . . . And Hallekreisch is made up of two words, Halle from *hol* and *kreisch* meaning to cry out. In other words the *shem hol* [not holy name] that is cried out and announced, for in the language of Lower Ashkenaz, they call a cry "kreisch."

Source: R. Moses Mintz, *She'elot uTeshuvot,* edited by Jonathan S. Domb (Jerusalem: Machon Yerushalyim, 1991), part 1, #19.

Document 1–42

A Naming Ceremony

It is a custom that at a convenient time, shortly after the circumcision ceremony, ten [men] gather. And they take a Pentateuch. And the little one is in the cradle dressed like on the day of his circumcision ceremony in grandeur. And they place a book on him and say "let this one [the boy] keep what is written in this [the Pentateuch]." And he says: "May God give you of the dew of heaven" (Gen. 27:28–29) and all the verses of blessings until "and only then you will be successful" (Josh. 1:8).[54] And they put a quill and ink in his hand so that he will be a scribe, adept in the paths of God.

Source: *Mahzor Vitry,* edited by S. Horowitz (Nurenberg: Mekizei Nirdamim, 1892), #507 (twelfth century, northern France).

Document 1–43

Blessing for Naming a Daughter

He who blessed our mothers Sarah, Rebecca, Rachel, and Leah and Miriam the prophetess and Abigail and Esther the queen, the daughter of Avihail, he will bless this pleasant girl and her name in Israel will be: [name] in this hour of blessing and good luck [*mazal tov*]. And he will raise her in health, peace, happiness and tranquility and may her father and mother merit to see her happiness and her wedding, male sons and wealth and honor, "they are full of sap and freshness in old age they still produce fruits [based on Ps. 32:15] and so may it be and we shall say AMEN."

Source: *Nahalat Avot veTikkun Yizhak* 19, excerpted from Eliezer Bashan, *Parents and Children as Reflected in the Literature of North African Rabbis* (Tel Aviv: Hakibbutz haMeuhad, 2005), 215.

Later Childhood Rituals

The premodern sources do not contain much information on rituals other than circumcision. However, a unique ritual of childhood existed during in Europe during the Middle Ages (Doc. 1–44), which had parallels in nineteenth-century Morocco, and only recently has been reconstructed throughout the orthodox world. This is a ritual that took place when the (male) child began his formal schooling. This ritual included going to the synagogue and being taken under the melammed (teacher's) wing. Then the children recited and read certain prayers and blessings.

Document 1–44

School Initiation Ritual

It is the custom of our ancestors to sit the children down to study [Torah for the first time] on Shavuot because that is when the Torah was given. The boys are brought [on Shavuot morning] to the synagogue to the teacher [according to the verse, "And it came to pass on the third day,] as morning dawned, there was thunder, and lightning" (Exod. 19:16). They bring over the tablet on which is written [the alphabet forward, beginning] *alef, bet, gimel, dalet;* and [the alphabet written backward, beginning] *tav, shin, resh, qof;* [and the verse, "When Moses] charged us with the Torah [as a heritage of the congregation of Jacob]" (Deut. 33:4); [the phrase] "May the Torah be my occupation"; and the first verse of Leviticus.

And the teacher recites aloud each letter, and the child recites [them] after him.

And he puts a little honey on the tablet, and with his tongue, the child licks the honey that is on the letters. These verses are written on a cake kneaded with honey: "as He said to me, 'Mortal, feed your stomach and fill your belly with this scroll that I give you.' I ate it, and it tasted as sweet as honey to me" (Ezek. 3:3); "The Lord God gave me a skilled tongue, to know how to speak timely words to the weary. Morning by morning, He rouses, He rouses my ear to give heed like disciples. The Lord God opened my ears, and I did not disobey, I did not run away (Isa. 50:4–5); "How can a young man keep his way pure?—by holding to Your word" (Ps. 119:9); "In my hurt I treasure Your promise; therefore I do not sin against You" (v. 11); "Blessed are You, O Lord; train me in Your laws" (v. 12); "Open my eyes, that I may perceive the wonders of Your teaching" (v. 18); "Give me understanding, that I may observe Your teaching and keep it wholeheartedly" (v. 34); "O how I love your teaching! It is my study all day long" (v. 97); "The words You inscribed give light, and grant understanding to the simple" (v. 130); "Your word is exceedingly pure, and Your servant loves it" (v. 140).

And he should write on an egg: "I have gained more insight than all my teachers, for Your decrees are my study" (v. 99); "I have gained more understanding than my elders, for I observe Your precepts" (v. 100); "How sweet is Your word to my palate, sweeter than honey to my mouth" (v. 103); "Your word is a lamp to my feet, and a light for my path" (v. 105). . . . And the teacher recites aloud with the boy everything [written] on the tablet, and on the cake, and on the egg. And the egg will be peeled and cooked. After the boys have completed their study, they feed the boy the cake and the egg because it is good for the opening of the heart.

The boys are covered under a cloak when they are taken from their house to the teacher's house or to the synagogue. And the reason is according to [the verse], "and they took their places at the foot of the mountain" (Exod. 19:17). And he is placed on the arm of the teacher, who sits him down to study, according to [the verse, "carry them in your bosom] as a nurse carries an infant" (Num. 11:12); and according to "I have pampered Ephraim, taking them into my arms" (Hosea 11:3).

After the study session, the boy is brought to the riverside, according to the Torah's being compared to water and [the verse] "Your springs will gush forth [in streams in the public squares]" (Prov. 5:16), so that the boy should have an expanded heart.

And the cake is prepared from three measures of fine flour corresponding to the manna, the well, and the quail [in the desert]. And one mixes into it honey, oil, and milk, symbolic of [the verse], "He fed him honey, etc. [from the crag, and oil from the flinty rock]" (Deut. 32:13), and it is written, "honey and milk are under your tongue" (Song of Songs 4:11).

Source: *Sefer haAsufot*, a thirteenth-century German manuscript that has never been fully printed. Excerpted from Ivan Marcus, "Honey Cakes and Torah: A Jewish Boy Learns His Letters," in *Judaism in Practice: From the Early Middle Ages through the Early Modern Period*, edited by Lawrence Fine (Princeton: Princeton University Press, 2001), 123–124.[55]

Document 1–45

Moroccan Torah Initiation Ritual

When the time comes that it is fitting that the child go to school, to study with the *melammed*, the father should rise early in the morning and wake the child and take him himself to the home of the teacher. And even if the father is older and important or a community provider [*parnas*] and a rabbi, it will not be embarrassing to him to lead his son once to the teacher's home. And he should thank the Holy blessed be He who allowed him to merit his son and bring him under the wings of *shekhina*. And the father or mother must cover the child under clothes when he is walking so that the child will not see any impure object in the world. And after he brings the child to the teacher's home, the father should put him in the teacher's lap as it says "as a nurse carries an infant" (Num. 11:12)."

Source: R. Shmuel Elbaz, *Rova HaKav* (Jerusalem: Elbaz Press, 1986), 6, #25 (late eighteenth, early nineteenth century, Safru).

Bar Mitzvah

Another childhood ritual is that of bar or bat mitzvah (bar mitzvah the male ritual; bat mitzvah the female ritual). As we will see below, age thirteen for boys and age twelve for girls have been noted as the age of maturity and of legal and ritual obligation since antiquity. However, no formal ritual for signifying this rite of passage exists before the Middle Ages. During the Middle Ages we find the first hints to a bar mitzvah ritual. This included reading a portion of the weekly Torah reading in synagogue and often a festive meal or a talk. Over the years, the bar mitzvah celebration also became the time at which males started to observe other rituals, primarily the use of phylacteries.[56]

Sources from North African Jewish communities note the significance of age thirteen,[57] but they do not describe a ritual such as that outlined above. Bat mitzvah celebrations became popular only over the last decades.[58] In the early modern period, when boys' bar mitzvahs were first celebrated, there was no parallel ritual for girls. In fact, many young girls were already betrothed and married when they reached age twelve.

Document 1–46

An Early Bar Mitzvah

A boy of thirteen years and one day is called bar mitzvah [son of commandments]. And for a month or more he dons phylacteries before he becomes bar mitzvah, so that he will learn how to train his hands and don them properly. And it is customary to teach him the laws of *tefillin* [phylacteries]. And they teach him to perform the commandments. And they tell him: You should know that until now all punishments for your sins were on your father, and now, as of age thirteen, the sins belong to the thirteen-year-old. And warn him not to commit any minor or major sins and he should be scrupulous to do the will of his creator.

On the Sabbath after he turns thirteen years and a day, most boys who are bar mitzvah lead the prayers during the public reading of the Torah portion,[59] and they start the prayer "Va'yazor Va'yagen"[60] in a nice tune that is special for boys who are bar mitzvah.[61] And it is obligatory to call the youth who is bar mitzvah to the scroll of the Torah. And while the cantor or his helper is blessing the youth, the youth's father goes and climbs onto the platform [lit., tower][62] and puts his hands on the head of the youth, his son, the bar mitzvah, and says: "Blessed art thou God that redeems me from this one's punishment." And he says this blessing quietly to himself and then the father returns to his seat. And some bar mitzvah boys have pleasant voices and they know how to pray in public and they pray . . . whatever prayers they can. And some don't even know how to read, and they don't read in public, but in any case they are called up to the Torah. . . .

And the father dresses his son in fine, new clothing that he wears for the first time at the beginning of that Sabbath. And in the afternoon,[63] he makes a meal for him, and the beadle does not call [people] to that meal. Just one hour before the afternoon prayers, the bar mitzvah boy himself calls the invited guests to his meal. . . . And they come and eat and drink and make merry with the boy and his father and mother and their friends. And the youth expounds [gives a speech] during this meal, a speech that is based on topics connected to bar mitzvah. And the custom is that the bar mitzvah youth blesses the Grace after Meals as the leader of the quorum for this meal.

Source: Juspa of Worms, *Minhagim deKehilat Kodesh Wormeisa (Wormser Minhagbuch)*, edited by Benjamin S. Hamburger and Erich Zimmer (Jerusalem: Machon Yerushalyim, 1992), part 2, #289 (seventeenth century, Germany).

Legal Obligations

There are a number of legal obligations that parents, and especially fathers, had toward their children. Central among them were maintenance (food and clothing) and education. Each of these will be a separate subsection within this part of the chapter. In addition, the sources at the end of this section discuss an important obligation children had toward their parents: the fifth commandment, which required a child to honor his parents.

Maintenance

A first legal obligation toward the child was that of *mezonot*, providing food for the child. While some saw this as an obligation from the Torah, it is only clearly discussed in later sources from the period of the redaction of the Mishnah and Talmud.[64]

During the first two years of a child's life the expectation was that his mother would nurse him or that a wet nurse would be hired. The legal obligation was constructed so that it was a woman's obligation toward her husband to nurse her infant and the father's obligation toward the infant (Doc. 1–47). If the couple were divorced, the father would pay the mother to nurse her own son.[65] In order to ensure that the baby's welfare would be preserved, a woman who was nursing her child was forbidden to remarry during the first twenty-four months of the child's life if she were divorced or widowed.[66] While the earlier sources do not indicate any differentiation between the time boys and girls were nursed, some later sources point to such a difference (Doc. 1–48). Another fear regarding the feeding of the infant was that the mother would become pregnant again and her impending birth would prevent her from being able to feed the infant. Jewish law did not forbid intercourse, rather it encouraged contraception.

The following sources lay out the conceptions that governed infant feeding and the relationship between parents and children vis-à-vis their nourishment in infancy. Once children were weaned, their fathers were obligated to provide their maintenance. The Bible does not discuss this issue, not even in the framework of the commandment of charity. The first possibility of imposing such an obligation on the father is developed in the period after the destruction of the second temple. During later years, the decree that a man must maintain both his sons and daughters was attributed to an ordinance given in Usha.[67] This ordinance is recounted both in the Palestinian and the Babylonian Talmud. The important distinction seems to be whether the child depends on his or her father for food or, in the words of the legal sources, *samukh al shulhan avihem* (Docs. 1–49, 1–50, 1–52).[68] The age until which a man had to support his children was debated in the sources. Some said age six, while others suggested age twelve. The sources also suggest that there were some who ignored this obligation (Doc. 1–51). In return for this provision, children's earnings were their fathers' (Doc. 1–53).

Mothers as opposed to fathers have no legal obligation to support their children. However, over the years it was suggested that women provide for their children out of charity.[69] Despite the central importance of these issues for sustaining a family and children, there is relatively little discussion of these topics in subsequent generations, with the exception of divorce cases. It seems that as a norm, Jewish society expected parents to care for, nourish, and support their children.[70]

Document 1–47

Duties of a Wife toward Her Husband

These are the works which the wife must perform for her husband: grinding flour and baking bread and washing clothes and cooking food and giving suck to her child and making ready beds and working in wool. If she brought him in one bondwoman she need not grind or bake or wash; if two she need not cook or give her child suck; if three she need not make ready his bed or work in wool; if four she may sit [all the day] in a chair.

Source: Mishnah Ketubbot 5:5.

Document 1–48

Length of Nursing

And if the woman died, the husband must hire a wet nurse for his son for twenty-four months and for his daughter for eighteen months. It seems this is specifically if she died, but if the husband died, she has to nurse her son for twenty-four months and the daughter for eighteen months.

Source: Raphael Berdugo, *Torot Emet* (Meknas: Brothers Tzaig Press, 1947), 83a (sixteenth century, Morocco).

Document 1–49

The Father's Obligation

The father is not liable for his daughters' maintenance. R. Eleazar b. Azaryah thus expounded it before the Sages in the vineyard at Jabneh:[71] "The sons inherit and the daughters receive maintenance; but just as the sons inherit only after their father's death, so the daughters receive maintenance only after the death of their father."

Source: Mishnah Ketubbot 4:6.

Document 1–50

Maintaining Small Children

R. Ulla Rabba expounded at the doorway of the patriarchs' house that even though they said: A man is not required to maintain his small sons and daughters, he must nevertheless maintain them whilst they are very small.

Source: BT Ketubbot 65b.

Document 1–51

Parents Who Refuse Support

When parents who refused to support their children were brought before R. Hisda, he would say: Make a public announcement: "The raven cares for its young but this man does not care for his young."

Source: Ketubbot 49b.

Document 1–52

Length of Father's Support

R. Isaac stated: It was ordained at Usha that a man must bear with his son until [he is] twelve years [of age]. From that age onward he may threaten his life. But could this be correct? Did not Rab, in fact, say to R. Samuel b. Shilath, "Do not accept [a pupil] under the age of six; a pupil of the age of six you shall accept and stuff him like an ox"?—Yes, "stuff him like an ox," but he may not "threaten him" until after [he has reached the age of] twelve years. And if you prefer I may say: This is no difficulty, since one may have referred to Scripture and the other to Mishnah; for Abaye stated: Nurse told me that a child of six [is ripe] for Scripture; one of ten, for Mishnah; one of thirteen, for a full twenty-four hours' fast, and in the case of a girl, [one who is of] the age of twelve.

Source: BT Ketubbot 50a.

Document 1–53

The Father Owns Children's Earnings

What is found by a man's son or daughter that are minors, what is found by his Canaanitish bondman or bondwoman, and what is found by his wife, belong to him; but what is found by his son or daughter that are of age, what is found by his Hebrew bondman or bondwomen, and what is found by his wife whom he has divorced (even though he has not yet paid her the *Ketubbah*), belong to them.

Source: Mishnah Baba Mezi'a 1:5.

Marriage and Sexual Maturity

One of the obligations fathers have toward children is finding them spouses. However, while the sources do not distinguish between the responsibility of the father toward boys and girls as far as alimony is concerned, when discussing obligations toward daughters, that of marrying off the girls is much more prominent.[72] This practice of arranged marriage can be found up to modern times. However, women were given the right to object to the marriages their fathers arranged once they reached the age of majority (age 12). Despite this, many sources point to this way of arranging marriages as the prevalent one.[73]

Central to the discussion of when children were to be married was the development of a theory concerning the beginning of adulthood and sexual maturity. An outline of the basics of such theory as well as a difference in attitudes toward male and female sexuality can be found in the sources. Earlier sources debate between physical maturity and biological age; later sources shift the importance they put on both, as can be seen in R. Moses Maimonides's summary of this issue (Doc. 1-56).

Document 1–54
Finding a Spouse

A father has authority over his daughter in respect of her betrothal [whether it was effected] by money, deed, or intercourse; he is entitled to anything she finds and to her handiwork; [he has the right] of annulling her vows and he receives her bill of divorce; but he has no usufruct during her lifetime. When she marries, the husband surpasses him [in his right] in that he has usufruct during her lifetime, but he is also under the obligation of maintaining and ransoming her and to provide for her burial. R. Judah ruled: even the poorest man in Israel must provide no less than two flutes and one lamenting woman.

Source: Mishnah Ketubbot 4:4.

Document 1–55
The Beginning of Adulthood

A girl who has produced two pubic hairs is liable to observe all of the commandments which are stated in the Torah. She either carries out the rite of *halizah*[74] or enters into levirate marriage. And so a boy who produced two pubic hairs is liable to observe all of the commandments which are stated in the Torah. He is able to enter into the status of a willful and rebellious son (Deut. 31:18). Once his [pubic] beard has filled out, he is able to be appointed the messenger of the community to pass before the ark and to raise his hands [in the priestly benediction]. And he does not take a share in the Holy Things of the sanctuary[75] until he produces two pubic hairs. Rabbi says, "I say, 'Until he is twenty years old,' since it says, *They appointed the Levites from twenty years old and upward, to have the oversight of the work of the house of the Lord* (Ezra 3:8)."

Source: Tosefta Hagigah 1:3.[76]

Document 1–56

Maimonides on Beginning of Maturity

A male child is called a minor or a little boy from his birth until he becomes thirteen years old. Even if he grows many hairs within this period of time, they do not constitute a token, but are considered the same as a mole. If after he becomes thirteen years and one day old, he grows two hairs in the nether part of the body, in the places known for growth of hair, he is considered an adult and is called a man.

Source: R. Moses Maimonides, *Mishneh Torah* (standard editions), Hilkhot Ishut, chapter 2, #10.

Custody

As a result of these obligations fathers had toward their children, many of these issues come up when discussing custody in cases of divorce. As a rule, below age six, children were always with their mothers. After this age, the law stated girls should remain with their mothers while boys should be with their fathers. Another occasion on which issues of custody arose was when one of the parents died and relatives demanded custody. Below are a number of sources that demonstrate some of these issues and variations on how different communities dealt with them.

Document 1–57

Custody of Daughters

Consequently, it must be inferred that [the place of] a daughter, whether she be of age or a minor, is with her mother.

Source: BT Ketubbot 103a.

Document 1–58

Sons and Custody

If a man's wife died leaving a son, and the mother-in-law says, "let him be raised by me," and his father says "let him be raised by me," and the son is over six years of age, and the man took another wife, what is the law? The father is right. Not only in the case when the mother died and his mother's mother wishes to raise him, should the father do so, but even if his mother was alive, and she [the mother-in-law] says "I will raise him," once he reaches the age of six, he is given to his father to raise, for the son is only legally attached to his mother until the age of six. . . . Thus, in the case where his mother dies, certainly one should not give him to his mother's mother, but to his father who teaches him Torah and a trade—as our rabbis taught, "the father is bound in respect of his son to circumcise, redeem him, teach him Torah, teach him a craft, and take a wife for him" (BT Kiddushin 29a). These are commandments which the father performs for his son, not the mother—and certainly not the mother's mother. For what should women know of the study of the Torah and of trades that they can teach to the sons of their daughters? For it is the father who is responsible for all these things. Thus, the son who reaches six years of age, it is fitting that he grow up in his father's house, so that these commandments may be performed. And we should not be concerned about his father's wife—for the substance of the household is that of the man and not the woman, and he should not be raised in his mother's mother's home as long as his father is alive. And this is the law and should not be deviated from in the slightest.

Source: *Responsa of the Geonim*, edited by Y. Harkabi (New York: Menorah, 1959), #553 (tenth century, Babylon).

Document 1–59

Granting Custody to Relatives

I am very ill and I don't know what will be my fate, death and life are in the hands of the Creator, may He be blessed, and I have children. For this reason I want to prepare a will; you will remember and preserve it in my name, so that all will be done according to it after my death and no one will veer away from it and my heart will be quieted when I leave this world. The first thing I instruct is that my mother-in-law who is called Mubaraka bat [daughter of] Hafat, may God keep him [he is dead], will be in charge of all my children. She will receive all that I leave and will extract from those who owe me money all that I deserve and everything will be in her hands for the good of the children, because I know that she loves them and has mercy on them and she will conduct herself carefully and she is a God-fearing woman.

Source: MS Hebrew 22, Archbishop Reiner collection, Vienna, published by Shlomo D. Goitein, *Sidrei Hinukh beYemei haGeonim uBeit haRambam* (Jerusalem: Ben Zvi Institute and Hebrew University, 1962), 32–33 (1137, Egypt).

Document 1–60

When Divorced Parents Move

QUESTION: Reuven[77] divorced his wife and he had two daughters and they remained with her, according to the law that daughters are with their mothers, and she [the mother] married and was at odds with her husband and for the sake of reconciliation [with the new husband] returned the girls to their father after he also married another woman. And then her husband traveled far away and did not want to return and he also sent her an instantaneous writ of divorce.[78] And the girls are miserable in their father's house with his [new] wife and they wish to return to their mother now that her husband is not with her, and also their mother has pity on them and wants to bring them home. And Reuven says, if you already gave them to me, I do not want to return them. Instruct us, our Rabbi if he can be forced to return them to her [the mother].

RESPONSE: . . . We learn from here that a daughter should grow up with her mother and learn women's crafts from her and modesty and the way of women. And if so, even if she agreed to give them to the father, he has to return them when she wants to her house, since what they said[79] the daughter is always with her mother, is not on account of intimacy or the greater love of the mother for her daughter that exceeds that of the father. Rather it is so that the daughter can be educated and learn proper behavior from her mother."[80]

Source: R. Moses b. Joseph Trani, *Shut haMabit* (Venice: Joani Callioni, 1639–1640), Part 2, #62 (sixteenth century, Safed, Israel).

Document 1–61

Custody of Orphans

On the 26th of Shevat 5533 [1773], a few days after I became bar mitzvah and my joy turned to sorrow, and my mother, as a result of her despair, took me to the holy city of Tiberias in order to see if she could find any relative who she could compel to support me and she befell a disappointment because all of them had wandered on account of the famine. And as a result of her great sorrow, she fell into her sickbed and died on the sixth day of Nissan that year, may her memory be blessed. And after these events, I went to Belgrade and I found favor in the eyes of one of the rich men and he promised to support me so that I would sit and study Torah [lit., on the Torah] until his virgin daughter grew older and that he would marry me to her with a dowry according to his honor. . . .

Source: R. Haim Isaac Musafia, *Sefer Haim vaHesed* (Livorno: Eliezer Otolingi Press, 1814), 3a–b (eighteenth century, Croatia).

Education and Religious Obligations

Education was another responsibility parents had toward their children, and more specifically fathers toward their sons. Education was primarily religious education as well as that for a trade. Religious education included knowledge of scripture as well of Jewish Law and, in the case of the males, a basic knowledge of Hebrew. The basis for all study was Torah study, which all boys received (Doc. 1-62). The texts throughout the ages expand on this responsibility, some commentaries including the educational content of this education, others enumerating all the different aspects of the education fathers must provide for their sons. Central to this discussion is the emphasis on the father, as opposed to the mother's obligation (Doc. 1-63). Although women do not have the obligation men have to educate and initiate their sons, and if a child is an orphan the community is obligated to fill in for the father, a variety of sources show that women took an active part in this education, although it was not their legal responsibility.

In addition, children were taught to fulfill a variety of religious precepts. Although both boys and girls were educated, there are many differences between the content and form of this education. Some sources below discuss the content that children should learn together with pedagogic instructions and emphases (Docs. 1-67 to 1-72). The boys often studied at a school situated in the local synagogue with teachers chosen by their parents or the community, or alternatively learned from private tutors in the home. Their studies were also supported by donations made by community members who obtained books and paper for them. Every Jewish boy learned how to read Hebrew and follow the prayers and the Bible. The most talented students continued to study for many years, whereas the others joined their families' trades or learned a new trade after two or three years of schooling.

Girls were educated in the home, often by male tutors. The most central dictum in this context is attributed to Ben Azzai (2nd century CE). The context of this pronouncement indicates the issue at hand. When discussing the bitter waters women who were suspected of adultery were forced to drink when the Temple was still standing, a discussion develops concerning women's education (Doc. 1-73).

Although there is little evidence of Jewish women's ability to read Hebrew, we know they were taught the basic laws pertaining to keeping a kosher household, observing the holidays, and ritual purity. Medieval sources also attest to women praying in Hebrew in the vernacular and being regular participants in synagogue life, which they were familiar with. In addition to religious education, girls were taught sewing, embroidering, and housework by their mothers and other women in their surroundings (Doc. 1–74). In general, the daughter, wives, and mothers of well-known scholars often displayed more extensive knowledge (Docs. 1–75, 1–76).

The age of religious obligation was the traditional age of thirteen for the boys and twelve for the girls, an age that was also associated with sexual maturity. However, as noted above, until early modern times, there is no evidence of a rite of passage connected with this transition. Sources from the medieval period also reveal that many obligations that are later considered to be those of adults were observed by children during the High Middle Ages, as soon as their parents and teachers thought they could accept these obligations (Docs. 1–64, 1–71). Despite the guidelines that exist in ancient literature it seems that throughout the centuries different categories served to define the age of obligation. Although ages twelve and thirteen remained essential for defining maturity, many religious obligations were undertaken before this age.[81] During the Middle Ages we can see a tightening of these categories and at the end of this period, certainly with the institution of the bar mitzvah, new emphases can be found.

A central term in this context is *gil hinukh*—the age of education—having to do with what the authors of the sources see children as being able to perceive and understand. Interesting parallels between this concept and the question of when children begin to have an evil inclination, as discussed above, can be noted.

Document 1–62

Father's Obligation

He used to say: At five years old [one is fit] for the Scripture, at ten years for the Mishnah, at thirteen for [the fulfilling of] the commandments, at fifteen for the Talmud, at eighteen for the bride-chamber, at twenty for pursuing [a calling], at thirty for authority, at forty for discernment, at fifty for counsel, at sixty for to be an elder, at seventy for grey hairs, at eighty for special strength, at ninety for bowed back, and at a hundred a man is as one that has [already] died and passed away and ceased from the world.

Source: Mishnah *Ethics of the Fathers* 5:21.[82]

Document 1–63

Respective Obligations of Parents

MISHNAH: All obligations of the son upon the father men are bound, but women are exempt. But all obligations of the father upon the son, both men and women are bound. All affirmative precepts limited to time, men are liable and women are exempt. But all affirmative precepts not limited to time are binding upon both men and women. And all negative precepts, whether limited to time or not limited to time, are binding upon both men and women; excepting, ye shall not round [the corners of your heads], neither shalt thou mar [the corners of thy beard], and, he shall not defile himself to the dead.

GEMARA: What is the meaning of ALL OBLIGATIONS OF THE SON UPON THE FATHER? Shall we say, all obligations which the son is bound to perform for his father? Are then women [i.e., daughters] exempt? But it was taught: [Every man, his mother and his father ye shall fear:] "Every man": I know this only of a man; whence do I know it of a women? When it is said "Every man, his mother and his father ye shall fear"—behold, two are [mentioned] here.—Said Rab Judah: This is the meaning: ALL OBLIGATIONS OF THE SON, [WHICH LIE] UPON THE FATHER to do to his son MEN ARE BOUND, BUT WOMEN [MOTHERS] ARE EXEMPT [BT Kiddushin 29a].

We thus learnt [here] what our Rabbis taught: the father is bound in respect of his son, to circumcise, redeem, teach him Torah, take a wife for him, and teach him a craft. Some say, to teach him to swim too. . . .

"To circumcise him." How do we know it?—Because it is written, *And Abraham circumcised his son Isaac.* And if his father did not circumcise him, Beth din [the court] is bound to circumcise him, for it is written, *Every male among you shall be circumcised.* And if Beth din did not circumcise him, he is bound to circumcise himself, for it is written, *And the uncircumcised male who will not circumcise the flesh of his foreskin, that soul shall be cut off.*

How do we know that she [the mother] has no such obligation?—Because it is written, [*"And Abraham circumcised his son . . .*] as God had commanded him": "him," but not "her" [the mother]. Now, we find this so at that time; how do we know it for all times?—The School of R. Ishmael taught: whenever "command" is stated, its only purpose is to denote exhortation for then and all time. . . .

"To teach him a craft": Whence do we know it?—Said Hezekiah: Scripture saith, *See to a livelihood with the wife whom thou lovest.* If "wife" is literal, [this teaches,] just as he [the father] is bound to take a wife for him, so is he bound to teach him a craft [for a livelihood]; if it is [a metaphor for] Torah, then just as he is bound to teach him Torah, so is he bound to teach him a craft. And some say, "[He must teach him] to swim in water too." What is the reason?—His life may depend on it. . . .

BUT ALL OBLIGATIONS OF THE FATHER UPON THE SON, etc., What is meant by "ALL OBLIGATIONS OF THE FATHER UPON THE SON?" Shall we say, all precepts which the father is bound to perform for his son—are then women bound thereby? But it was taught: "The father is obliged in respect of his son, to circumcise and redeem him": only the father, but not the mother?—Said Rab Judah, This is its meaning: All precepts concerning a father, which are incumbent upon a son to perform for his father, both men and women are bound thereby.

Source: BT Kiddushin 29a–30a.

Document 1–64

Maturity and Evil

A minor . . . is liable to observe the commandment of dwelling in a *sukkah*. . . .

[If] he knows how to shake [an object], he is liable to observe the commandment of the *lulab* [palm leaves, used on the holiday of Tabernacles]. [If] he knows to cloak himself, he is liable for the commandment of fringes.[83] [If] he knows how to speak, his father teaches him the *Shema*, Torah, and the Holy Language [Hebrew]. [If] he knows how to take care of his phylacteries, his father purchases phylacteries for him. [If] he knows how to take care of his person, they eat food preserved in a state of cultic cleanness depending upon the cleanness of his person. . . .[84] [If he can eat] an olive's bulk[85] of roast meat, they slaughter a Passover-sacrifice on his account. R. Judah says, "Under no circumstances do they slaughter a Passover-sacrifice on his account unless he knows how to distinguish good food from bad." Who knows how to distinguish good food from bad? Anyone to whom they give an egg, which he takes, and a stone, which he throws away.

Source: Tosefta Hagiga 1:2.

Document 1–65

Age of Learning

Elisha b. Abuyah said: "He that learns as a child, to what is he like? To ink written on a new paper. He that learns as an old man to what is he like? To ink written on a paper that has been blotted out." R. Jose b. Judah of Kefar ha-Babli said: "He that learns from the young to what is he like? To one that eats unripe grapes and drinks wine from his wine press. And he that learns from the aged, to what is he like? To one that eats ripe grapes and drinks old wine. Rabbi said: Look not on the jar but on what is in it; there may be a new jar that is full of old wine and an old one in which is not even new wine."

Source: Mishnah *Ethics of the Fathers*, 4:25.

Document 1–66

Maimonides Commentary

On the above passage, R. Moses Maimonides commented: "He is saying that what one learns when one is young remains and is not easily forgotten and what is learned in old age is the opposite and this is well known. R. Yose is saying that young people's wisdom is filled with doubts, unresolved questions and incomplete queries, because they have not had enough time to review their knowledge and banish their doubts. And Rabbi said, don't judge the wine by its vessel, for there is a new vessel with old wine and and old vessel that is empty, without anything in it. So too there are young people whose questions and knowledge are

[well] reasoned and without any confusion, like old wine which has separated, and there are old people who have no wisdom at all, moreover those who have confused and jumbled wisdom.

Source: *Mishnah with Moses Maimonides' Commentary*, edited by Joesph Kapah (Jerusalem: Mossad haRav Kook, 1965), 4:25 (twelfth century, Egypt).

Document 1–67

What Children Should Learn

At first, when a man hires a teacher for his son he should make sure he [the teacher] knows what he teaches, for if his children study Bible and the teacher knows Talmud and is ignorant in Bible, [they will not succeed] with what the boys need . . . that he should have a teacher who knows, even if he only learns Hebrew,[86] for he needs to understand what he learns. And when he teaches Bible he has to make the child understand; when he teaches the fear of God, for example, that he has to honor the Torah and he should teach him that the Creator [who] is in the sky is he who gives and who provides and he should show him that he [God] is in the heavens, and when he grows more he should teach him that there is heaven and hell, because children's hearts are like those of dreaming adults, they believe everything is true, and in this way your children believe all that you say is true, before bad friends get him used [to evil ways].

Source: *Sefer Hasidim*, 2nd edition, edited by Judah Wistentski (Frankfurt am Main: Mekizei Nirdamim Press, 1924), #820.

Document 1–68

Reviewing the Lessons

I have turned to the teacher—may God continue his honor—about the children—may God preserve their lives—and I asked him to take more interest in them and especially in Abu Manzur—what he learns orally and what he reads, and let him review on the Sabbath what he learns during the week so that he will make me happy before my death. However, up until now, this objective has not been achieved. I cannot believe that the teacher—may God continue his honor—would not keep this promise.

Source: Ms. Cambridge Or. 1081, 4c, published by Shlomo D. Goitein, *Sidrei Hinukh beYemei haGeonim uBeit haRambam* (Jerusalem: Ben Zvi Institute and Hebrew University, 1962), 35 (medieval Egypt).

Document 1–69

Seasonal Teaching

I have already requested from him to teach the little one the *Haftarah* and the *Parashah*[87] every week. And it is accepted and practiced among other teachers that the children are taught what is proper for each season—on Purim the Megilla [Book of Esther] and before Passover—Song of Songs and other matters that have to do with the holidays.

Source: TS, Arabic Box 30, #36, published by Shlomo D. Goitein, *Sidrei Hinukh beYemei haGeonim uBeit haRambam* (Jerusalem: Ben Zvi Institute and Hebrew University, 1962), 36.

Document 1–70

The Proper Order of Teaching

The proper order is to first teach them the Pentateuch accompanied with the explanation of the words, from the beginning of Genesis through "before the eyes of all Israel" (Exod. 34:12), and not like the instructors of our generation practice. . . . Once he has studied the entire Pentateuch and understood the commandments of God, he should be taught the Mishnah—first those Mishnayot practiced in our times, and later the tractates on sacrificial matters and purities and impurities. . . . And once he is taught all of this, then he may teach him Talmud. And if he is not capable, he should teach him the twenty-four books of the Bible instead; each day he should instruct him with words of ethics and the fear of God all day, unlike what the instructors in current generations do, for they only care to receive their pay, and suffice with fulfilling their minimum daily obligations by teaching them only an hour a day. They take no care to teach him neither the fear of God, nor ethics, nor proper comportment. Consequently, most boys, when they leave the confines [of the house of study] to go home, the earth splits open at their voice, for they show no honor to their elders, and have no respect for people. They only dance like calves in the streets of the city, bereft of culture and proper behavior. As a result, among some of them, these habits have become second nature, and when they grow up they will be rebels and thorns, kicking at their teachers and dishonoring the visage of their elders; for they have not learned this from their teachers in their childhood, for their instructors cared only for their salaries. This is an unceasing plague which most of our masses have failed to notice. They see and gape: why do we find such behavior more frequently among the youth of Israel than among all other nations? And the truth is that it stems from the sin of their rabbis. In addition, in most cases, the father spoils his children and spares the rod, for he relies on the teacher, but the teacher does not take heed of the true purpose at all. On the contrary: they mislead the fathers through flattery, praising them and saying: "this boy will be a great Torah scholar," so that the father will hire him as teacher. And when the boy is ready to study halakhah, he tells him that he is ready to learn the *tosefot* [commentary on the Talmud], and it's like passing an elephant through the eye of a needle. But the father is pleased with these words, and as a result he tries to climb mountains and valleys, teaching him what is far, far beyond his comprehension, and in the end he remains empty of all, like one who attempts to gather up the wind in the hollow of his hand (Prov. 30:6); for all he has studied was acquired in a single night and lost just as quickly.

Source: R. Ephraim b. Aaron Luntshits, *Amudei Shesh* (Prague: Moshe Katz, 1607), Musar 'Amudei HaTorah, 61b (sixteenth century, Poland).[88]

Document 1–71

Motivating Learning

When the child has grown and has been taught several verses, he should teach him the alphabet, and [he should be] entreated with kind words, and bought nuts so that he learns. Then he is bought a handsome belt and shoes and given some money, but not much, so that he not grow accustomed to sweets and games. And he is taught the abridged grace after meals "Blessed be the merciful one, etc." (BT Berakhot 40b). And the fringes should be attached to his garment, and if his hands are clean, he may bind the tefillin on his arm, and be shown how to treat them properly. And he should kiss the tefillin, so that the commandments become dear to him and that he become fastidious in performing them. For even if minors are not obliged to perform the commandments, in any case, they should become accustomed to reciting the blessings.

Source: R. Moses b. Henoch Altschul Yerushalmi, *Brantspiegel,* translated by Jackie Feldman (Basel: Konrad Waldkirche, 1602), 169b–179a (seventeenth century, Prague).

Document 1–72

Learning while Young

Train a lad in the way he ought to go, He will not swerve from it even in old age (Prov. 22:6). That is, that a man is required to train his children while they are still small to worship the Creator and develop good character traits. And he should not, as a result of his desire for them, encourage them in the stubbornness of their heart while they are small. It is the way of the world, that when a small child hits, curses, and reviles his parents and other important people, the fathers consider such acts as clever, and laugh at him, and thus encourage him to repeat such deeds. This is improper, for habit controls all things, and if the boy teaches himself through these ways from childhood, he will not leave those paths when he grows older. Rather, he should bestow fear upon them when they are very small for each and every thing, so that they bow to his authority when they grow up. He should, however, not make them fear excessively, especially in the case of small children with tender hearts. For if he make his yoke too heavy, they may run away somewhere, and may even, God forbid, commit suicide. For this one requires great wisdom and understanding as to how to behave.

And each person should judge the nature of his children for himself, and act with them according to their nature. . . .

He should teach his son Torah while he is still small—a little bit, as much as the boy can absorb. For the Blessed Name ignores the stutterings of the young children as they speak of the Torah. Even if they stutter, the Holy One blessed be He loves them, as it is written "'His banner over me' is love' (Song of Sol. 2:4). Do not read 'his banner' [diglo], but 'his mistakes' [dilugo]." Furthermore the numerical value [gematria] of v'diglo alai' [his banner over me] is the same as that of 'katan' [child]. What shall he do? When the child begins to speak he is taught, "Moses commanded us the Teaching" [Deut. 33:4], and the first verse of the Shema. Thus, it is fitting to educate children to say Shema Israel when they wipe their hands. And as they grow, we continue to teach them verses by heart. And when he reaches three years of age, we begin to teach him the alphabet. And he should console the children with what is appropriate for them and tell them, "here is honey, roasted grains and almonds," so that they go to school and study.

Source: R. Joseph Juspa b. Pinhas Hahn Neurligen of Frankfurt, *Sefer Yosef Omez* (Frankfurt am Main: Hermon, 1928), 42–43 (early seventeenth century).

Document 1–73

Daughters and Torah

Hence declared Ben Azzai, A man is under the obligation to teach his daughter Torah so that if she has to drink [the waters of bitterness], she may know that the merit suspends[89] its effect. R. Eliezer says: Whoever teaches his daughter Torah teaches her obscenity. R. Joshua says: A woman prefers one *kab*[90] and sexual indulgence to nine *kab* and continence.

Source: BT Sotah 20a.

Document 1–74

Teaching Girls the Commandments

A father is obligated to teach his daughters the commandments, including halakhic rules. This may appear to contradict the Talmudic ruling, "Whoever teaches a woman Torah it is as if he teaches her obscenity" (BT *Sotah* 20a). However, the rabbis were referring to deep immersion in Talmudic study, discussion of the reason behind the commandments, and mystical understandings of the Torah. These should never be taught to a woman or to a minor. But one must teach her practical laws because if she does not know the rules for the Sabbath, how will she observe the Sabbath?

The same goes for all the other commandments she must perform. This is how it was in the days of the biblical king, Hezekiah of Judah, when men and women, old and young, were all knowledgeable about the laws, even the laws of ritual purity and the Temple sacrifices (BT *Sanhedrin* 94b). It is not appropriate for an unmarried man to teach unmarried girls, however, even if the father stands there and keeps watch so the teacher won't be alone with them. For even this will not avail if the teacher's sexual desire overcomes him or her desire is too much for her. Moreover, according to the Talmud, "A woman's voice is a sexual incitement" (BT *Hullin* 11b). Rather, the father himself should teach his daughter and his wife.

Source: *Sefer Hasidim*, #313, quoted from Judith R. Baskin, "Women and Ritual Immersion in Medieval Ashkenaz," in *Judaism in Practice: From the Early Middle Ages through the Early Modern Period*, edited by Lawrence Fine (Princeton: Princeton University Press, 2001), 142.

Document 1–75

Teaching Girls Good Character

And if one has daughters, he should develop in them good character, so that they be shy of people already in their infancy. And if any of their flesh be exposed, it should be covered up. And when strangers enter the house, they should hide their faces from them and not stand opposite them and wink [??] in their faces. And when people speak with them, they should lower their eyes to the ground. One should also train them not to be gluttonous, and get used to all the household chores so that they may become helpful. Their clothes should be clean at all times, and they should dress properly at mealtimes and whenever they stay at home. They should eat and drink moderately. He should train them to be satisfied with what they are given and not look at what others have, and not think in their hearts that others always have more than they do. They should also not choose what they should eat, and not despise the food on the table, saying: "this dish is too salty, and this one lacks salt; this is smoked, and this one burnt, this too moist and that too dry, this one should be flavored with that spice, and to that one vinegar should be added." Rather, they should sit sagely and remain silent and everything should please them and be tasty to them. And if they wish that a particular dish be properly cooked, they need only enter the kitchen, taste the dish and adjust it to their taste.

They should respect their fathers and mothers as well as the elderly and serve them according to all their needs. And even if there be maidservants in the household, nevertheless, they should perform this commandment themselves. They should fear the rebuke of their father and mother. When they are taken to the dances or to mitzvah feasts, they should go with much respect and be modest in their ways. If they have handsome clothes, they should not wear them for their pleasure whenever they feel like, but only on the Sabbath and holidays, new moons and weddings for the glory of God and His Blessed Name. If she has a husband, she should adorn herself before him so that she be attractive to him—this too is a commandment—but not do so before strangers. When she dresses and adorns herself for the Sabbath or holidays, she should go to see her father and mother to make them joyful. This too is a commandment. And she should not wear Sabbath clothing on weekdays, nor Sabbath clothing on holidays or new moons, but should wear the appropriate clothes for each holiday, thus demonstrating that she is an orderly woman.

She should be trained to get up in the morning and make her own bed, or at least stand by her bed while it is being made, so that she see that there is no unclean thing there. She should be taught not to boast before her girlfriends and to speak with them words of endearment—not just idle talk—with a welcoming face. And rich and poor should be equal before her. She should take care not to scream or speak loudly and not be a gadabout, a liar, a gossiper or a jealous woman.

She should be given a small amount of money so that she can give it to charity. When poor women come to the house, she should not scream at them or embarrass them. And she should be trained to do all manners of work, for one never knows what will bring her benefit and be of use to her. For even if she be rich, it is good that she give charity from her handiwork [for example, by baking or cooking for the poor]. And when she is told to do something, she should not reply: "I don't want to." And in general, she should not say, "this I want to have, and this I don't want." While they are still small, they should do all for heaven's sake; even if they don't understand it well at present, they will understand when they grow up, and all their lives do everything for the sake of heaven.

The boys should also be taught a trade, so that one not worry lest they steal or rob people . . . but they should be taught the Torah before they are taught a trade, for as King Solomon already said, "it is more precious than rubies" (Prov. 8:11).

Source: R. Moses b. Henoch Altschul Yerushalmi, *Brantspiegel*, translated by Jackie Feldman (Basel: Konrad Waldkirch, 1602), 169b–179a (seventeenth century, Prague).

Document 1–76

Exceptional Daughters

Let me relate the life of my older daughter Bellette. She was thirteen years
old and as modest as a bride.

She had learned all the prayers and songs from her mother, Who was modest
and pious, "Pleasant," and wise.

The maiden followed the example of her beautiful mother; she prepared my
bed and pulled off my shoes each evening.

Bellette was busy about the house and spoke only truth; she served her
Creator and spun, sewed, and embroidered.

She was imbued with reverence and with love to her Creator; she was
without any flaw. Her efforts were directed to Heaven, and she sat to
listen to Torah from my mouth.

And she was killed with her mother and with her sister on the evening of the
twenty-second of Kislev, when I was sitting peacefully at my table.

Two despicable ones came and killed them before my eyes and wounded me
and my students and also my son.

Let me tell about the life of my younger daughter [Hannah]. She recited the
first part of the Sh'ma prayer every day.

She was six years old and spun and sewed and embroidered. She entertained
me and she sang.

Woe is me for my wife and for my daughters! I cry out in lamentation. How
much have my sins found me out!

Source: R. Eleazar b. Judah of Worms, *Eshet Hayil*, excerpted from Judith R. Baskin, "Dolce
of Worms: The Lives and Deaths of an Exemplary Medieval Jewish Woman and Her
Daughters," in *Judaism in Practice: From the Middle Ages through the Early Modern Period*,
edited by Lawrence Fine (Princeton: Princeton University Press, 2001), 436–437 (twelfth
century, Germany).

Document 1–77

A Daughter Who Knows the Bible

R. Petahya of Regensburg (1180–1175) went on a journey and visited many far
Jewish communities. This is part of his account regarding the Jews of Bagdad:

"And he [R. Samuel b. Eli, the head of the yeshiva] does not have sons, and
he has only one daughter and she is fluent in the Bible and the Talmud and she
teaches the Bible to the boys and she is enclosed in a building and she teaches
through the window, the students are outside and downstairs and do not see
her."

Source: R. Petahya of Regensburg, *Hut haMeshulash*, edited by Eleazar Grünhout (Jerusalem:
Luntz, 1905), 8.

Discipline

The question of how Jews disciplined their children in general and in schools
has not been thoroughly studied to date. However, by examining a number of
sources over time, one can see changes in attitudes toward this issue. The biblical
sources discuss excessive violence toward parents more than anything else. These
emphases are rarely treated in later sources and, as the excerpts below demonstrate, most later discussions of discipline focus on discipline in school.

Document 1–78

Exodus 21:15

He who strikes his father or his mother shall be put to death.

Document 1–79

Deuteronomy 21:18–21

If a man has a wayward and defiant son, who does not heed his father or mother and does not obey them even after they discipline him, his father and mother shall take hold of him and bring him out to the elders of his town at the public place of the community. They shall say to the elders of the town: This son of ours is disloyal and defiant; he does not heed us. He is a glutton and a drunkard. Thereupon the men of his town shall stone him to death.

Document 1–80

Deuteronomy 27:16

Cursed be he who insults his father or mother.

Document 1–81

Proverbs 13:24

He who spares the rod hates his son but he who loves him disciplines him early.

Document 1–82

Age of Discipline

Rab said to R. Samuel b. Shilath: Before the age of six do not accept pupils; from that age you can accept them, and stuff them with Torah like an ox. Rab also said to R. Samuel b. Shilath: When you punish a pupil, only hit him with a shoe latchet. The attentive one will read [to himself], and if one is inattentive, put him next to a diligent one.

Source: BT Baba Batra 21a.

Document 1–83

Severe Discipline

A man was very ill. When he cried they said to him: "Why are you crying? If it is for your little children, your brothers will take your place." He said: "My brothers will take care of their worldly needs. I am only crying because, had I lived, I would have reproached them and tormented them so that they could attain the world to come, by teaching them and directing them in the path of righteousness. The guardian he appointed for his son said: I will replace you [= be under you], and serve in your position." He said to him: "No. Serve, rather, to replace me [= be under me], but from your own position—[that is], if they were to cause you sorrow or steal from you, you would beat them so they do so no more. Thus, you will be in the place of their maker: educate them to perform the commandments, and if they sin toward the Creator, torment them and don't say 'how can I hit an orphan?' Rather, if they say: 'if our father were alive, he would have pity on us and would not allow us to be beaten,' tell them: '[Your father] would have hit you even more. It is he who commanded me to torment you . . . and they will be loyal like a dog, for a dog is beaten and he is loyal to his master, because he gives him food. So do to my children. Give my sons food and let your fear be upon them when they sin and show them love when they do the will of the Creator, as you command them."

Source: *Sefer Hasidim*, 2nd edition edited by Judah Wistentski (Frankfurt am Main: Mekizei Nirdamim, 1924), #302 (thirteenth century, Germany).

Document 1–84

Letter to a Brother on Educating Siblings

I inform your honor that I am not succeeding to educate this boy Abu Manzur and maybe you can help me. When I beat him, I beat him significantly. But when I do this, the teacher [female] jumps up and takes him away from me and dismisses him with four or five spanks. If he were not sick, I would kill him with beatings, although he does deserve some respite in light of his meager clothing and since he is with us for only a short time. He does not accept any explanations nor is he calm. From the moment he enters he does not cease to hit and curse, he and his sister[91] and especially when I am not at home. Perhaps you should threaten him with a few beatings and you should talk to him [lit., talk to his heart] so that he will be wiser and more polite and quieter. However, anything you think your father and mother would be angry at, don't do.

Source: Taylor-Schechter S. 8, J 28 f. 7 II, published by Shlomo D. Goitein, *Sidrei Hinukh beYemei haGeonim uBeit haRambam* (Jerusalem: Ben Zvi Institute and Hebrew University, 1962), 45 (medieval Egypt).

Children's Obligations toward Their Parents

An important component of parent-child relationships was not only obligations parents have toward their children, which has been a main focus of attention up to this point, but also the obligation, originating in the Bible, for children to honor and fear their parents. Traditional commentaries explored these verses and the relationship between them, pursuing both the difference between mothers and fathers and between honor and fear. This commandment also has its limitations. One was not commanded to obey one's parent when he or she demanded something immoral or not allowed by Jewish law. Loyalty to God takes precedence over filial honor (Doc. 1–94).

Document 1–85

Exodus 20:12

Honor your father and your mother, that you may long endure on the land that the Lord your God is assigning to you.[92]

Document 1–86

Leviticus 19:1–3

The Lord spoke to Moses saying: "Speak to the whole Israelite community and say to them: You shall be holy, for I, the Lord, your God, am holy. You shall each revere his mother and his father and keep my Sabbaths, I the Lord am your God."

Document 1–87

Commentaries on Children's Obligations

Our Rabbis taught: What is "fear" and what is "honor"? "Fear" means that he [the son] must neither stand in his [the father's] place nor sit in his place, nor contradict his words, nor tip the scales against him. "Honor" means that he must give him food and drink, clothe and cover him, lead him in and out. The Scholars propounded: At whose expense?

Rab Judah said: The son's. R. Nahman b. Oshaia said: The father's. The Rabbis gave a ruling to R. Jeremiah—others state, to R. Jeremiah's son—in accordance with the view that it must be at the father's expense. An objection is raised: It is said, *Honor thy father and thy mother*; and it is also said, *Honor the Lord with thy substance*: just as the latter means at personal cost, so the former too. But if you say, At the father's [expense], how does it affect him?—Through loss of time.

Source: BT Kiddushin 31b.

Document 1–88

Mishnah Commentary

It is stated . . . (Eduyot 2:9) in the Mishnah: "A father endows his son with the blessings of beauty, strength, riches, wisdom and length of years . . . and just as the father endows the son with five things so too is the son obliged in five things: to feed him and give him drink, to clothe him, to put his shoes on for him and lead him."

Source: PT Kiddushin 1:7, 61a, excerpted from Gerald Blidstein, *Honor Thy Father and Mother: Filial Responsibility in Jewish Law and Ethics* (New York: Ktav, 1975), 10.

Document 1–89

Honoring Parents

The mother of R. Tarfon went walking in the courtyard one Sabbath day and her shoe tore and came off. R. Tarfon came and placed his hands under her feet and she walked in this manner until she reached her couch. Once when he fell ill and the sages came to visit him, his mother said to them: "Pray for my son R. Tarfon, for he serves me with excessive honor." They said to her, "What did he do for you?" She told them what had happened. They responded, "Were he to do that a thousand times, he has not yet bestowed even half the honor demanded by the Torah."

Source: PT Pe'ah 1:1; excerpted from Gerald Blidstein, *Honor Thy Father and Mother: Filial Responsibility in Jewish Law and Ethics* (New York: Ktav, 1975), 44.

Document 1–90

Serving Parents

A man should realize that his mother and father are the cause of his being in the world and therefore it is truly proper that he render them all the honor and do them all the service he can. For they brought him into this world and they labored greatly on his behalf during his childhood. Once a man has assimilated this trait, he will ascend by it to recognize the good done him by the Lord, Who is the cause of his beginning and the cause of the existence of all his forefathers."

Source: *Sefer Hahinukh*, mitzvah 33, excerpted from Gerald Blidstein, *Honor Thy Father and Mother: Filial Responsibility in Jewish Law and Ethics* (New York: Ktav, 1975), 14.

Document 1–91

Worshiping God: Honoring Parents

Honor your father and your mother: Even though I said you should only honor and worship me, honor your father and your mother! And do not forget all his bounties [Ps. 103:2], for they brought you to this world and sustained [weaned] you well until you grew up. And they worry for you and all their efforts are only for you. And if you honor them and recompense them for their efforts, I will know that you will honor me.

Source: R. Joseph of Orleans, *Perushei Joseph Bekhor Shor al haTorah*, edited by Yoehoshafat Nevo (Jerusalem: Mossad HaRav Kook, 1992) Jethro, 20:12 (twelfth century, France).

Document 1–92

Honoring Fathers before Mothers

[R. Moses of Couçy rephrases the Talmudic distinction as follows:]

And when speaking of honor, [Scripture] mentioned the father's honor before the mother's, because his [the child's] heart is more prone to honor his mother because she cajoles him [with her] words. And the fear of the mother is mentioned before fear of the father, because [the child's] heart is more fearful of his father's scolding. This teaches us that both are equal in honor and in fear.

Source: R. Moses b. Jacob, *Sefer Mitzvot haGadol* (Venice, 1957), Aseh #112 (thirteenth century, France).

Document 1–93

The Extent of Honoring Parents

How far must one go to honor one's father and mother? Even if they took his wallet full of gold pieces and threw it into the sea before his very eyes, he must not shame them, show pain before them or display anger to them: but he must accept the decree of Scripture and keep his silence. And how far must one go in their reverence? Even if he is dressed in precious clothes and is sitting in an honored place before many people and his parents come and tear his clothes, hitting him in the head and spitting in his face, he may not shame them, but he must keep silent and be in awe and fear of the King of Kings Who commanded him thus!

Source: Moses Maimonides, *Mishneh Torah* Mamrim 6:7, excerpted from Gerald Blidstein, *Honor Thy Father and Mother: Filial Responsibility in Jewish Law and Ethics* (New York: Ktav, 1975), 46.[93]

Document 1–94

Limitations on Honoring Parents

Since one might have assumed that the honoring of one's father and mother should supersede the Sabbath, it was explicitly stated, "Ye shall fear every man his mother and his father and ye shall keep my Sabbaths" (Lev. 19:3), it is the duty of all of you to honor me.

Source: BT Yevamot 5b.

A Story about Children and Parents

We end the section and the entire chapter with a story about relations between parents and children as told in the seventeenth century by Glückel of Hamel. Glückel wrote the story of her life for her children, and scattered many morals for them throughout the book. This story opens her memoir.

Document 1–95

A Parent's Memoir

. . . Dear children, I must not go into further depths, for then another ten books would not be enough for me. . . . This I beg my dear children: Have patience. If God sends you an affliction, accept it meekly and do not cease to pray. Perhaps he will have mercy. Who knows what is best for us sinful folk? Who knows if it is good to live in great riches and have much pleasure, enjoying all that the heart desire in this transient world; or if it is better, if the heavenly Father holds much from us in this sinful world so that we can have our eyes always fixed on heaven. . . .

Almighty God did all this in his infinite mercy that parents should love their children and help them to do right. And then the children, seeing this from their parents, do the same to their children.

For example: There dwelt on the seashores a bird that had three fledglings. Once, seeing that a storm was coming and that the sea waves rose over the shore, the old bird said to the young ones, "If we cannot get to other side at once we shall be lost." But the birdlings could not yet fly. So the bird took one little one in his claws and flew it over the sea. When halfway across, the parent bird said to his young one, "What troubles I have to stand from you, and now I risk my life for you. When I am old, will you also do good to me and support me?"

On which the fledgling replied: "My dear beloved father, just take me across the sea. I will do for you in your old age all that you demand from me."

On this the old bird threw the birdling into the sea so that he was drowned and said: "So should be done with such a liar as you." He flew back and returned with the second one.

When they reached halfway across, he spoke to this one as he had to the first. The little bird promised to do all the good in the world. But the old bird took this one too and threw him into the sea. "You also are a liar."

He flew again to the shore and brought the third birdling. When he came midway, he said to him, "My child, see what hardships I undergo and how I risk my life for your sake. When I am old and cannot move any more, will you be good to me and support me in my old age, as I do you in your youth?" To which the little bird answered his parent, "My dear father, all that you say is true, that you take great care of me and my need. I am in duty bound to repay you, if it is possible;

but I cannot promise for certain. But this I can promise: when one day I have a birdling of my own, I will do for my young as you have done for me." On this the father said, "You speak well and are also clever. I will let you live and take you across the water."

From this we can see that God gave the unreasoning bird sense to bring up his young; and the difference: how parents toil for their children while they, if they had the trouble with their parents as they parents with them, would soon tire. . . .

That parents love their children is no surprise. We find the same among unreasoning creatures who have young and look after them until they are grown and can fend for themselves. And they are left to themselves. We humans are in this sense better. We seek to support our children till they are grown; not only when they are small but as long as we live.

Source: Glückel of Hamel, *Zikhronot,* excerpted from Paula Hyman, "The Life of Glikl of Hameln," in *Judaism in Practice: From the Middle Ages through the Early Modern Period,* edited by Lawrence Fine (Princeton: Princeton University Press, 2001), 487–490 (seventeenth century, Germany).

NOTES

I wish to express my thanks to my colleagues Dr. Amram Tropper, Prof. Menahem Ben-Sasson, and Dr. Miriam Frankel and to my research assistant Orit Kandel for their assistance and advice. I also thank the German-Israel Foundation, Grant # 6045, for supporting my research. All translations that are not attributed to a person or book are my own. I thank Dr. Jackie Feldman for his help with the translation of sources.

1. Louis Jacobs, "Judaism," *Encyclopedia Judaica* (Jerusalem: Hebrew University, 1973), 10: 371–379.

2. For the United States, see Lloyd Gartner, *Jewish Education in the United States: A Documentary History* (New York: Teacher's College Press, 1969); Norman Drachler, *A Bibliography of Jewish Education in the United States* (Detroit: Wayne State University Press, 1996); and recently, Melissa R. Klapper, *Jewish Girls Coming of Age in America, 1860–1920* (New York: New York University Press, 2005); Jack Wertheimer, ed., *Family Matters: Jewish Education in an Age of Choice* (Waltham: Brandeis University Press and AVI CHAI Foundation, 2007). For England, see David Mendelsson, "Between Integration and Separation: The History of Anglo-Jewish Education 1944–1988," Ph.D. dissertation, Hebrew University, 2002. For France, see Zosa Szajkowski, *Jewish Education in France 1789–1939,* Jewish Social Studies, monograph no. 2 (New York: Columbia University Press, 1980). For Yemen, see Bracha Cohen-Joseph, "Jewish Education under British Colonialism: "Hebrew Education in Aden in the Years 1900–1950," Ph.D. dissertation, Haifa University, 2004 (in Hebrew). For Eastern Europe, see Isidore Fishman, *The History of Jewish Education in Central Europe* (London: Edward Goldston, 1944); Aron Moskovits, *Jewish Education in Hungary (1848–1948)* (New York: Bloch, 1964); Elias Schulman, *A History of Jewish Education in the Soviet Union* (New York: Ktav, 1971); Jacob Taitelbaum, "Jewish High School Education between the Two World Wars 1919–1939," Ph.D. dissertation, Tel Aviv University, 1994 (in Hebrew).

3. All translations of biblical texts are based on the *JPS Hebrew-English Tanakh, The Tradi-*

tional Hebrew Text and the New JPS Translation (Philadelphia: Jewish Publication Society, 1999).

4. The obvious group against whom Jews were reacting was Christians, who advocated celibacy over family life. However, in the ancient world, before Christianity, there were also groups that preached against procreation. See David Herlihy, *Medieval Households* (Cambridge: Harvard University Press, 1985), 23–26.

5. See Jeremy Cohen, *"Be Fertile and Increase: Fill the Earth and Master It": The Ancient and Medieval Career of a Biblical Text* (Ithaca: Cornell University Press, 1989); Cohen explores many aspects of procreation throughout the book.

6. The Mishnah was codified around 200 CE and the Talmuds in the fifth and fourth centuries in Babylon and Palestine, respectively.

7. Most of the early studies that addressed this issue began with Ariès, *Centuries of Childhood: A Social History of Family Life,* translated by Robert Baldick (New York: Vintage, 1962). See, for example: Simha Goldin, "Die Beziehung der Jüdischen Familie im Mittelalter zu Kind und Kindheit," *Jahrbuch der Kindheit* 6 (1989): 211–256; Israel Ta-Shma, "Children in Medieval Germanic Jewry: A Perspective on Ariès from Jewish Sources," *Studies in Medieval and Renaissance History* 12 (1991): 263–280, and especially Ephraim Kanarfogel, *Jewish Education and Society in the High Middle Ages* (Detroit: Wayne State University Press, 1992).

8. For example, Moritz Güdemann, *Sefer haTorah veHeHayim beArzot Ashkenaz beYemei haBenayim,* 3 vols. (Warsaw: Hevrat Ahiasaf, 1897); Israel Abrahams, *Jewish Life in the Middle Ages* (1896; reprint Philadelphia: Jewish Publication Society, 1960), and Solomon Schechter, "The Child in Jewish Literature," in *Studies in Judaism* ser.1 (Philadelphia: Jewish Publication Society, 1896), 282–313; Joshua Trachetenberg, "Jewish Education in Eastern Europe at the beginning of the Seventeenth Century," *Jewish Education* 11 (1939): 1–17; Simha Assaf, *Mekorot leToldot ha-hinukh be-Yisrael,* reedited by Samuel Glick (Jerusalem: Jewish Theological Seminary, 2001–2006), 4 vols.

9. Although the Ariès theory was widely accepted when it was first presented, today few scholars accept it. For a survey of developments in this field, see Barbara Hanawalt, "Medievalists and the Study of Childhood," *Speculum* 77 (2002): 440–460, and more recently, Louis Haas and Joel T. Rosenthal, "Historiographical Reflections and the Revolt of the Medievalists," in *Essays on Medieval Childhood,* edited by Joel T. Rosenthal (Donington: Shaun Tyas, 2007), 13–28.

10. See Ivan G. Marcus, *Rituals of Childhood: Jewish Acculturation in Medieval Europe* (New Haven: Yale University Press, 1996); Elisheva Baumgarten, *Mothers and Children: Jewish Family Life in Medieval Europe* (Princeton: Princeton University Press, 2004); Roni Weinstein, "Yaldut veHitbagrut baHevra haYehudit beItalia beReshit haEt haHadasha," *Italia* 11 (1994): 77–98 (in Hebrew).

11. For the ancient period, see Nissan Rubin, *The Beginning of Life: Rites of Birth, Circumcision and Redemption of the Firstborn in the Talmud and Midrash* (Tel Aviv: HaKibbutz haMeuhad, 1995) (in Hebrew); Shaye J. D. Cohen, *The Jewish Family in Antiquity* (Atlanta: Scholar's Press, 1993); and most recently, the studies by Amram Tropper, "The Economics of Jewish Childhood in Late Antiquity," *Hebrew Union College Annual* 76 (2005): 189–233; "Children and Childhood in Light of the Demographics of the Jewish Family in Late Antiquity," *Jewish Studies Journal* 37.3 (2006): 299–343; and "On the History of the Father's Obligation to Maintain His Children in Ancient Jewish Law," *Zion* 72 (2007): 265–299. As all of these studies demonstrate, although the legal literature is fairly rich, it is difficult to produce a social history of childhood based on

these sources. For the modern period we await Tali Berner's doctoral thesis "Children and Childhood in Early Modern Ashkenaz," and see note 3 above.

12. Avraham Grossman, *Pious and Rebellious: Jewish Women in Medieval Europe* (Lebanon, N.H.: Brandeis University Press, 2004); Paula Hyman, *Gender and Assimilation in Modern Jewish History: The Roles and Representation of Women* (Seattle: University of Washington Press, 1995); Cohen, *The Jewish Family in Antiquity*, and Baumgarten, *Mothers and Children: Jewish Family Life in Medieval Europe*.

13. The medieval sources are evenly divided. For the early modern period, I have provided slightly more sources from Christian lands than from Muslim lands.

14. One of the difficulties inherent in writing about any group that was not part of the adult elite is their lack of voice and agency in the texts that have reached us, which do not necessarily represent the reality they lived in.

15. For Jews under Islam, see Shlomo D. Goitein, *A Mediterranean Society: The Jewish Communities of the Arab World as Portrayed in the Documents of the Cairo Geniza*, 6 vols. (Berkeley: University of California Press, 1967–1993), and Mordekhai A. Friedman, *Jewish Marriage Contracts in Palestine: A Cairo Geniza Study* (Tel Aviv: Tel Aviv University Press, 1980). For other diasporas, see n. 22.

16. JPS translates this word *yaldut* as youth.

17. Once again, I have veered from the JPS translations and translated the word *yaldutekha* as childhood.

18. It is important to note that in traditional Jewish exegesis, the sin is not that of sexual intercourse but rather the loss of innocence after eating from the tree of life.

19. All translations of the Babylonian Talmud are based on the Soncino edition, *The Babylonian Talmud,* edited by I. Epstein (London: Soncino Press, 1948). Hereafter BT = Babylonian Talmud.

20. This rite, as seen below, included the removal of a shoe.

21. Jacob Katz, "Levirate Marriage (Yibbum) and Halitzah in Post-Talmudic Times," reprinted in his *Halakhah veQuabbalah* (Jerusalem: Magnes Press, 1984), 127–174 (in Hebrew); Grossman, *Pious and Rebellious*, 90–101.

22. Many figures from the first centuries CE are named in the quotes from the Mishnah and Talmud, all of which report discussions that took place in the house of learning. I have only provided dates for the most famous and important of these figures.

23. David Berger, *The Jewish Christian Debate in the High Middle Ages, A Critical Edition of The Nizzahon Vetus, with an Introduction, Translation and Commentary* (Philadelphia: Jewish Publication Society, 1979), 70.

24. See Elimelekh Westreich, *Transitions in the Legal Status of the Wife in Jewish Law* (Jerusalem: Magnes Press, 2002).

25. About the tkhine literature, see Chava Weissler, *Voices of the Matriarchs: Listening to the Prayers of Early Modern Jewish Women* (Boston: Beacon, 1998). The two tkhines cited in this chapter were written in Eastern Europe during the seventeenth and eighteenth century and appear regularly in popular tkhine collections, as discussed by Tracy Guren Klirs, *The Merit of Our Mothers. A Bilingual Anthology of Jewish Women's Prayers* (Cincinnati: Hebrew Union College, 1992).

26. All translations of the Mishnah are based on *The Mishnah*, translated by Herbert Danby (London: Oxford University Press, 1933).

27. This text, like many, refers to sons, and that is indeed how they are referred to in the texts. However, this need not be interpreted as meaning male offspring, since the

Hebrew word for child in its single form is conjugated in male form. However, as we will see, as in many other cultures, boys were preferred.

28. Ron Barkai, "Greek Medical Traditions and Their Impact on Conceptions of Women in Gynaecological Writings in the Middle Ages," in *A View into the Lives of Women in Jewish Societies*, edited by Yael Azmon (Jerusalem: Merkaz Shazar, 1995), 115–142 (in Hebrew).

29. See, for example, *The Book of Legends*, edited by Haim Nahman Bialik and Yehoshua Hana Ravnitzky, translated by Willaim G. Braude (New York: Schocken Books, 1992), 575–576.

30. The blessing "He who is good and does good" (Mishnah Berakhot 9:2) was traditionally recited when one was told a child had been born to him. However, in many different Jewish localities additional blessings were added.

31. For Jews under Islam, see Goitein, *A Mediterranean Society*, and Mordekhai A. Friedman, *Jewish Marriage Contracts in Palestine: A Cairo Geniza Study* (Tel Aviv: Tel Aviv University Press, 1980). In other diasporas see n. 22.

32. See Eliezer Bashan, *Parents and Children as Reflected in the Literature of North African Rabbis* (Tel Aviv: Hakibbutz haMeuhad, 2005) (in Hebrew).

33. BT Shabbat 128b.

34. Lillith was considered a she-demon who harmed infants.

35. These three angels are mentioned many times in the medieval literature and are known as angels who can protect the parturient and the baby from Lilith.

36. The *windel* or *wimpel* is the cloth diaper used at the circumcision ceremony. It was made into a Torah binder. See Joseph Gutmann, *The Jewish Life Cycle* (Leiden: Brill, 1987), 6–8.

37. The meaning here is not entirely clear, but the author is describing the drawing of the circle around the parturient's bed until the correct amount of time has passed, as he continues in the lines that follow.

38. The *Sturz* and *Schleier* were both head coverings.

39. The *Röckli* (lit., little skirt) was the name for shrouds in Ashkenaz. In this case, the parturient is wearing shrouds over her clothing.

40. The four matriarchs are Sarah, Rebecca, Rachel, and Leah.

41. Miriam, Deborah, Hannah, and Hulda.

42. Jael.

43. For a broader picture of this genre and the period, see Sigrid Riedel, ed., *Moses Henochs Altschul-Jeruschalmi' "Brantspigel"* (Frankfurt am Main: Peter Lang, 1993); and recently Edward A. Fram, *My Dear Daughter: Rabbi Benjamin Slonik and the Education of Women in Sixteenth Century Poland* (Cincinnati: HUC Press, 2007)

44. I have shifted from the active to the passive voice, and occasionally from singular to plural, reflecting the source text.

45. The winter months.

46. This source is echoed in subsequent criticism of parents who grieve excessively.

47. See Rubin, *The Beginning of Life*.

48. See Baumgarten, *Mothers and Children*, 93–99.

49. Reference to his father.

50. On this custom, see Daniel J. Lasker, "Transubstantiation, Elijah's Chair, Plato and the Jewish-Christian Debate," *Revue des Études Juives* 143 (1984): 31–58.

51. This is a figure who is not the father who carries the infant into the synagogue and holds him on his lap during the circumcision. See Baumgarten, *Mothers and Children*, 65–77.

52. See Doc. 1–63.

53. He was R. Meir's student, who compiled the book of his teacher's rulings.

54. These verses are generally recited as part of the Saturday night prayer service.

55. For this ritual, see also Marcus, *Rituals of Childhood*.

56. See Roni Weinstein, "Yaldut veHitbagrut baHevra haYehudit beItalia beReshit haEt haHadasha," *Italia* 11 (1994): 77–98 (in Hebrew).

57. See, for example, Doc. 1–56.

58. See Ivan G. Marcus, *The Jewish Life Cycle* (Seattle: Washington University Press, 2004).

59. Every week, a different portion of the Pentateuch is read in synagogue, and seven men are called to bless the Torah during the reading.

60. Literally, "He who helps and protects," the beginning of a specific prayer said when calling people to the Torah.

61. In modern Hebrew one would say bnei mitzvah as the plural. The seventeenth-century German author does not do so but rather says "for boys who are bnei mitzvah."

62. In the center of the synagogue was a platform on which the ritual was conducted.

63. Lit., at the time of *minha,* the afternoon prayers.

64. For a detailed discussion, see Israel Z. Gilat, *The Relations between Parents and Children in Israeli and Jewish Law* (Tel Aviv: Choshen Lamishpat, 2000), 156 (in Hebrew).

65. See Elimelech Westreich, "A Father's Obligation to Maintain His Children," *Jewish Law Annual* 10 (1992): 177–212 .

66. Baumgarten, *Mothers and Children*, 119–153.

67. Usha was a town in the upper Galillee.

68. Mishnah Bava Mezia 12:12.

69. Gilat, *The Relations between Parents and Children,* discusses this issue at length.

70. For a fascinating discussion of this issue, see Tropper, "The Economics of Jewish Childhood in Late Antiquity."

71. Town in the south of Israel where the major academy was built after the destruction of the temple.

72. See, for example, BT Yevamot 62b.

73. Grossman, *Pious and Rebellious,* 32–48.

74. See above, Doc. 1–11.

75. This is referring to the work done in the temple by the priests and Levites.

76. All references to the Tosefta refer to *The Tosefta,* translated by Jacob Neusner (New York: Ktav, 1981).

77. All Jewish response literature calls the figures by hypothetical names such as Reuven, Simon, Rachel, and Leah, and the names do not reflect reality.

78. In other words, she was divorced as soon as she received the document from him, because he had no intention of returning.

79. In the Talmud.

80. I have not translated this literally.

81. As opposed to marriage and issues regarding marriage, in which age twelve remained central.

82. This text is a later addition to *Ethics of the Fathers*.

83. Worn by men on clothes, known as *zizit*.

84. See above, n. 75, referring to what was practiced in the time of the Temple.

85. Standard amount that was to be eaten from the Paschal lamb at the Temple.

86. The meaning is that he does not understand words but can teach the vowels—the basics of reading.

87. The weekly Torah reading.

88. Although he lived in Prague at the end of his life, his work is seen as representative of Polish Jewry.

89. Meaning that she understands the efficacy of these waters.

90. Metaphorical for scanty livelihood.

91. Note the brother and sister learning together.

92. In slight variation, Deut. 5:16.

93. Similar formulations can be found *Shulkhan 'Arukh*, Yoreh De'ah, standard editions, #240.

2

Christianity

MARCIA J. BUNGE AND JOHN WALL

The relation of Christianity to children and childhood is complex, diverse, and disputed. It is as old as the origins of Christianity itself in Jesus's own birth and childhood and in his relationship to children. Two thousand years of Christian history have produced multiple and even conflicting theological understandings of childhood and how actual children should be treated by adults and society. What is more, considerations of childhood have frequently shaped—and been shaped by—other fundamental Christian beliefs and practices. However, in part because of the actions and sayings of Jesus that are recorded in the gospels, Christians throughout almost their whole history have interpreted Christian faith and practice in one way or another in relation to "these little ones."

This rich Christian history is all too often forgotten today, both in Christian communities and among Christian theologians and ethicists. Even within the Church, the interpretation of the meaning of children's lives is generally left to educators, psychologists, and social scientists. Recovering the history of Christian beliefs and practices regarding children can therefore help strengthen contemporary Christian theological and ethical reflection on children as well as encourage Christians to be stronger advocates for children themselves. This history is also important for all those interested in world religions to better understand Christianity itself.

This chapter aims to illustrate the long and varied tradition of Christian understandings of children and childhood. Since so much of this tradition is based on biblical texts, this chapter includes a range of passages from the New Testament. Selections in the rest of this chapter are drawn by and large from significant figures within Christianity who continue to influence beliefs and practices today. Important passages regarding children from what Christians call the Old Testament can be found in the chapter on Judaism, and many of them are highlighted in this introduction as well as cited by authors in this chapter.

So much has been written about and for children in the history of Christianity, and forms of Christianity worldwide are so multifaceted and varied, that these documents are far from exhaustive.[1] This chapter includes primarily theological essays. It does not include other important and interesting sources, such as baptismal liturgies, first communion and confirmation rituals, catechisms, Sunday school materials, missionary tracts, parenting manuals, denominational social statements, encyclicals, church records, legal documents, Canon Law, biblical commentaries, fiction, memoirs, diaries, biographies, novels, poetry, or material from Bibles, hymns, prayers, liturgies, art books, and sermons written directly for or, in some cases, by children. Furthermore, this chapter cannot address important historical questions such as how these texts were received and used, how children were actually treated, or what practices were actually carried out with and by children. Because most Christian theologians in history were male, there are few texts by women. Finally, none of the newly emerging writings on children in Christianity from the last thirty years are included.[2] Trying to represent diverse contemporary theological trends, although they are discussed further below, is beyond the practical scope of the chiefly historical focus of this chapter.

Despite these and other limitations, the included selections do illustrate some of the important questions, theological understandings, and religious practices that Christians worldwide and in diverse cultural settings have pursued and continue to pursue concerning children and childhood. And many contemporary Christian thinkers and communities around the world are highly informed by and critically appropriate ideas represented in these classical sources. The selections also do include sources arising out of a variety of forms of Christianity. Above all, it is hoped that these selected texts can serve as a springboard for further exploration of children and childhood within past and present forms of Christianity.

Key Questions and Common Themes

Although Christian attitudes toward children vary and rarely follow straight lines of historical development, one can detect throughout the history of Christianity at least three enduring questions and several common themes. These questions and themes have animated centuries of lively and productive debate and continue to do so today.

One very basic question concerns children's nature: What is the being and status of children as they enter the world and in relation to society and to God? This question has been the subject of profound and contentious debate. Are children innocent, sinful, or some mixture of the two? Are they divine gifts, prerational brutes, or developing rational human beings? A host of additional issues, such as moral agency, conscience, spirituality, free will, distorted will, pride, embodiment, and sexuality have all been addressed in relation to basic theological issues about childhood's unique nature and meaning.

Despite different responses to these questions, many Christians, building on biblical texts and central tenets of Christian faith, have held in tension two central themes when reflecting on the nature of children. On the one hand, they believe that children are divine blessings, gifts of God, made in God's image, and even examples for adults (cf. Docs. 2-10, 2-11, 2-15, 2-19, 2-24, 2-26, 2-31, 2-34, 2-35). Although parents nurture children, they are not made in the image of their parents but in the greater image of God (Gen. 1:27). Children, like all human beings, are therefore worthy of respect from the start. The sense of the integrity of each person, including children, is also grounded in the view that God intimately knows the number of "even the hairs of your head" (Matt. 10:30), forms your "inward parts," and "knit" you together in the womb (Ps. 139:13). On the other hand, many Christians speak about children as in some way fallen or sinful (cf. Docs. 2-16, 2-17, 2-25, 2-29). Although definitions of the fallen nature of children are diverse and set within larger theological frameworks, viewing children as sinful is a significant theme among Christians and often provides the basis for speaking about children as moral agents who bear some degree of responsibility for their actions. This conviction is based on several biblical passages, such as the human will being "evil from youth" (Gen. 8:21); folly being "bound up in the heart" of children (Prov. 22:15); and "there is no one who is righteous, not even one" (Rom. 3:9-10; cf. 5:12).

Clearly, some Christians have held what might be called an especially "high" view of children as uncorrupted gifts from or images of God, exemplars of humanity's primordial goodness, or even models of faith and wisdom. Others have held a particularly "low" view of children as uncivilized brutes freshly incarnating Adam's original sin. However, most Christians have combined conceptions of children as images of God, gifts to the community, and even exemplars of faith with notions of children as fallen and in need of instruction.

A second question is one of ethics: What are the obligations and responsibilities of adults toward children and of children themselves? Related questions are: Which adults and social institutions hold which responsibilities for children? What does it mean to "discipline" or to "teach" children? What kinds of obligations to self and others should children themselves carry out? One's response to the theological question (above) of the ontological status of children makes a great deal of difference in how one answers these ethical questions, but it does not determine one's answers altogether. Some Christians have understood responsibilities toward children primarily in terms of the protection and cultivation of children's gifts. Others have spoken more about the obligation to train and to discipline children's potentially unruly natures. Thus, Christians in the past and still today have disagreed about the meaning of "discipline," the limits of parental authority, and the role of physical punishment in "training" a child. They have also debated how children are to honor their parents (Docs. 2-9, 2-15, 2-23, 2-36), obey the commandments (Docs. 2-10, 2-15), and develop their gifts and talents in service to the wider community (Docs. 2-18, 2-20, 2-21, 2-26, 2-29, 2-31, 2-32). Perhaps surprisingly to modern ears, the responsibility for child rearing throughout almost all of Christian history has fallen significantly upon fathers.

Throughout history, many Christians have emphasized the duties of parents to care for their children and to teach them the faith, and they have written extensively on education and child rearing. At the same time, Christians have claimed that children are the responsibility of not only parents but also the extended family, community, church, society, and state. These extrafamilial responsibilities have generally been understood as more extensive than they are today, and Christians have continually debated how family, church, and society should relate to and support one another. Christians across time and denominational lines have emphasized the need for adults to "train children in the right way" (Prov. 22:6), to bring them up "in the discipline and instruction of the Lord" (Doc. 2-9: Eph. 6:4; see also Doc. 2-31), and to "recite" and "talk about" the words of the Lord "when you are at home and when you are away, when you lie down and when you rise" (Deut. 6:7). They have attended to biblical commands to care for all children, including the poor and orphans (Docs. 2-5, 2-8, 2-27, 2-29, 2-33, 2-37, 2-38).

And they have often taken a positive attitude toward the adoption of orphans, and the establishment of institutions that address children's needs such as schools, colleges, orphanages, and pediatric hospitals. They have also reflected on the role of the state in protecting and educating children and providing them with resources they need to thrive (Docs. 2–22, 2–27, 2–28).

A third enduring question in Christianity is one of practice: What actual religious rituals, practices, and activities should be carried out with, on behalf of, and by children? Included here are questions such as: How should adults help protect children and nurture their moral and spiritual development? What practices, traditions, and institutions are most important in this task? What is the significance for children of their parents being married? How do children learn to participate fully in various realms of public life? And what role should children themselves play in religious communities? Responses to these and other questions of practice are obviously shaped by responses to the other two questions above. However, they also reflect debates about Christian practice as such.

Although faith practices clearly vary across history and among Christians today, there are some common activities and rituals that have played a strong role in the formation of children throughout the Christian tradition. Theologians have emphasized several religious practices that are to be carried out with children and incorporated into family and community life, albeit in different ways and with diverse justifications. Common practices include reading the scripture, praying, singing hymns, worshiping, and serving the poor (see, for example, Docs. 2–13, 2–14, 2–28, 2–30). Two of the most important religious rites carried out by almost all Christians are baptism and communion (Docs. 2–6, 2–12, 2–17, 2–18, 2–24, 2–25, 2–32), thought to have been commanded by Jesus (Doc. 2–6: Matt. 28:19; and Luke 22:17–20). However, Christians today and in the past have disagreed about who participates in these rites, at what age, and under what conditions.

Organization of the Chapter

The texts collected together in this chapter illustrate some of the more prominent responses to these kinds of fundamental questions over time. The selected texts are arranged chronologically and divided into seven rough historical periods: the New Testament, the early church, the Middle Ages, the Reformation, the early modern period of the seventeenth and eighteenth centuries, the late modern period of the nineteenth century, and the twentieth century. This division by historical periods serves to help readers navigate a large amount of material. By no means, however, is it meant to suggest that the complex history of Christian understandings of children can be neatly divided or presented as a smooth progression or regression of ideas. Each era contains great diversity and is filled with disputes and exceptions.

The New Testament

On the whole, the New Testament suggests that Jesus viewed children as not only important members of the Christian community but even models for entering the Kingdom. The gospels of Matthew, Mark, and Luke all report Jesus healing, blessing, and touching children and claiming that "unless you change and become like children, you will never enter the kingdom of heaven" (Doc. 2–2). Furthermore, Jesus's own birth is interpreted by Christians as the first and most powerful sign of God's grace and renewal of the world. Indeed, childhood serves throughout the New Testament as a potent symbol for faith and life in God, such as in Jesus being called the "Son of God" and his disciples worshiping their Father as "children of God" (Doc. 2–5). The gospel of John and some Pauline letters also speak of becoming children of God through a new or second "birth" into life in the Holy Spirit or through adoption as children of God. At the same time, the New Testament includes admonishments to "put an end to childish ways" (Doc. 2–7) and commands for children to obey parents (Doc. 2–9).

The Early Church

The generally high regard for childhood found in the New Testament persists by and large throughout the early church, and theologians of this period write about childhood frequently and extensively. A central theological conception arises of children as fresh images of God by virtue of their simplicity, lack of worldly desire and passion, and sexual purity. The widespread practice of infant baptism in early Christianity is not yet a means for redressing original sin (as it becomes for some Christians later) but rather a first step toward secure membership in God's community on earth. Furthermore, adult and particularly parental responsibilities revolve, for many theologians of the early church, around nurturing children's gifts into righteousness in this community. At the same time, given the rise of Christian asceticism, children are sometimes oversimplified or viewed as spiritual impediments (see Docs. 2–10 to 2–15).

The Middle Ages

The Middle Ages here loosely signifies the thousand-year period between the fifth and fifteenth centuries, when Western Christianity was dominated by the Roman Catholic Church. One of the most dramatic shifts in the theology of childhood occurs early in this period with the writings of Augustine, arguably the most influential theologian in Western Christianity throughout the Middle Ages and beyond. Augustine unites a sense of human sinfulness (informed in part by his interpretation of Paul) with Plato's view, articulated in his *Republic* and *Laws*, that children are primarily unruly and irrational animals in need of civilizing. Augustine thus defines infancy, childhood, and adolescence as prime (though not exclusive) exhibits of human original sin. Later medieval Christian theology is additionally influenced by the ancient Greek philosopher Aristotle, rediscovered via Islam, in a more complex view of the natural world and social relationships out of which childhood is thought to arise. For example, Thomas Aquinas, an Italian monk and the father of modern Roman Catholic theology, retains Augustine's conception of children as sinful, yet he also develops the idea from Aristotle's *Nicomachean Ethics* and *Politics* that children possess rational and moral potentialities that are increasingly developed through family and societal attachments (see Docs. 2–16 to 2–20).

The Reformation

The Renaissance and the Reformation spark significant social, economic, intellectual, and political changes in sixteenth-century Europe. Christianity before this time already experienced schisms between the Roman Catholic Church and the Eastern Orthodox Church, but the Reformation divides Western Christianity between Protestantism and Catholicism and sparks the emergence of many denominations within Protestantism itself. Heated debates emerge in this period about infant baptism, education, and faith formation. For example, several leaders of the Reformation, such as Martin Luther, initiate profound educational reforms that emphasize the responsibility of parents and the community to educate all children, including girls and the poor. In line with many humanistic reforms of the day, this period also emphasizes the importance of "going back to the sources" and providing children with a solid liberal arts education. Luther and John Calvin articulate new theological understandings of "calling" or "vocation" that lift up the spiritual value of marriage, parenting, professional and civic responsibilities, and educating children to read the Bible and to serve Church and society. Even though they disagree on issues of infant baptism, various strands of the Reformation also take seriously the role of parents in the faith formation of children, providing religious materials and catechisms for use by parents in the home (see Docs. 2–21 to 2–25).

Early Modernity

Education and the faith formation of children continue to be important concerns in the seventeenth and eighteenth centuries, prompting further reflection about children's nature, development, and spiritual life. There are many examples of theologians in this period who establish schools and orphanages, play a role in educational reforms, or work closely with poor children and orphans. This is also a period of colonization and missionary expansion, and thus European Christian ideas about education, schooling, and childhood are being spread around the world, mixing with those of indigenous peoples in diverse countries and cultures. Many theologians during this period focus attention on the religious and spiritual lives of children themselves. The American Calvinist Jonathan Edwards, for example, speaks in vivid terms about the sins of children and their need for radical conversion. In contrast, Horace Bushnell, an American Congregationalist, later rejects this notion of child conversion and believes children's faith should be nurtured gradually, primarily by their parents. Although their understandings of sin, pride, the will, discipline, baptism, and childhood conversion vary, Christian theologians and educators generally acknowledge significant complexity and integrity in children's moral and spiritual development and the need to nurture and to educate all children, regardless of gender, race, or class (see Docs. 2–26 to 2–29).

Late Modernity

The nineteenth century is a period of rapid industrialization and the development of new academic disciplines such as cultural anthropology, sociology, religious studies, and psychology. These and other significant political and intellectual developments profoundly reshape Christian attitudes and behaviors toward children and childhood. Theologians of this period also develop their ideas of childhood in conversation with the conceptions of childhood influential at this time, such as those of John Locke, Jean-Jacques Rousseau, William Wordsworth, and Immanuel Kant. The German theologian Friedrich Schleiermacher, for example, places great emphasis on the role of play in child development, and his work echoes elements of Rousseau's Romantic view of children (see Docs. 2–30 to 2–32).

Twentieth Century

Until recently, Christian theologians and ethicists in the twentieth century have generally paid little attention to issues of children and childhood. They have focused more attention on other, albeit related, issues, such as abortion, gender relations, contraception, and sexuality. The second half of the twentieth century saw a relative neglect in the theology of childhood, and for several reasons: a narrowing of childhood itself in industrialized countries to the private sphere; children's increasing sentimentalization; a social prioritization of adult-like autonomy over relational and communal dependencies; and the rising authority of the psychological, social, and natural sciences to describe and explain children's behaviors. However, as the selections here from the first half of the twentieth century illustrate, Christians have nevertheless continued to wrestle with New Testament texts on children and the enduring importance of children and childhood in Christian faith and practice, generally arguing for holding children in higher regard in society (see Docs. 2–33 to 2–38).

Contemporary Developments

The 1980s and especially the 1990s and 2000s have seen a growing concern for children among Christian thinkers and the beginnings of an increasingly vibrant field of contemporary inquiry. This gradual upsurge can be attributed in part to greater awareness of the suffering and marginalization of children in a world of powerful mass media, individualism, economic and cultural globalization, and weakening social and family institutions. Childhood has also come to be seen as confronting theology with profound questions of gender, spiritual development, social justice, and human rights. In short, Christianity is beginning to face once again the task of rethinking childhood in a time of great social transformation.

Among those within the Christian community who are offering fruitful theological and ethical reflection on children and childhood, we already see a range of creative questions, uses of sources, and approaches. For example, some Christian theologians are arguing for more intentional efforts on the part of parents and Christian communities in forming children's spiritual, moral, and social agency and capabilities. Others are recovering the gospel sayings of Jesus to turn attention to children's own unique gifts and positive influence on adults, religious communities, and societies. In discussions of global Christianity, new attention is being focused on the complex role of children in the history of missions and how indigenous perspectives on children have informed current Christian beliefs and practices in diverse cultural contexts.

In the light of more serious attention to children, several Christian theologians and denominations are also revisiting their understandings of central Christian doctrines and practices. Many mainline Protestant churches, for example, have reexamined their understanding of the sacraments and are offering communion to children at younger ages. Furthermore, the Roman Catholic Church is revisiting its perspectives on salvation and infant baptism, and in 1994 it eliminated from its Catechism the notion that children who die before they are baptized go to limbo. Other theologians around the world, such as those engaged in the Child Theology Movement, are exploring how attention to children and childhood might reshape a range of other central themes and doctrines, such as Christology, the Church, worship, creation, and eschatology.

Christian ethicists and church leaders across denominations are also joining discussions about international children's rights, in part in response to the 1989 United Nations Convention on the Rights of the Child. The Roman Catholic Church has been an especially outspoken advocate of children's rights. Catholic social teaching and papal documents, such as Pope John Paul II's *Familiaris Consortio* (1981), have also emphasized, especially through the principle of subsidiarity, the primary importance of families in children's lives and, at the same time, the role of public authorities and the state for ensuring that all families have the economic, political, educational, and cultural support they need to carry out their responsibilities. Other denominations criticize notions of children's rights but are active in responding to the needs of children around the world. In general, the discussion of children's rights within the academy and across denominations is drawing attention to the needs of children as well as generating fresh theological reflection about children's agency, voice, citizenship, best interests, and participation.

Conclusion

Students of Christian perspectives on children find themselves in an exciting time in history when ancient traditions are being rediscovered and formed into new and creative thinking and practices. Unlike women's studies, environmental studies, or even family studies, Christian childhood studies is still very much, so to speak, in its infancy. Contemporary religious scholars have not generally engaged issues of children to the same degree as have researchers in other disciplines such as psychology, sociology, anthropology, history, law, and the emerging interdisciplinary field of childhood studies. As is becoming increasingly clear, however, religious, theological, spiritual, and ethical perspectives are absolutely central to understanding childhood today. Christians will undoubtedly develop diverse responses to issues facing children, and they will see their understandings of Christianity shaped in different ways in the process. But it can at least be said that the years and decades to come will challenge Christian thinking about children in profound new ways and in turn, one hopes, help significantly improve children's lives.

New Testament

Composed around the second half of the first century CE, the New Testament includes the four gospels of Matthew, Mark, Luke, and John that tell the story of Jesus's life and teachings, and a number of letters, many written by or attributed to Paul, that present early theological interpretations of the faith. The writers of the New Testament grew up within the context of Judaism and often refer back to Jewish sources (see the chapter on Judaism). The following selections are from the New Revised Standard Version (NRSV) of the New Testament and include significant passages and themes regarding children on which Christian theologians later build.

Document 2–1

Jesus's Birth and Childhood

Matthew 1:18–25

Now the birth of Jesus the Messiah took place in this way. When his mother Mary had been engaged to Joseph, but before they lived together, she was found to be with child from the Holy Spirit. Her husband Joseph, being a righteous man and unwilling to expose her to public disgrace, planned to dismiss her quietly. But just when he had resolved to do this, an angel of the Lord appeared to him in a dream and said, "Joseph, son of David, do not be afraid to take Mary as your wife, for the child conceived in her is from the Holy Spirit. She will bear a son, and you are to name him Jesus, for he will save his people from their sins." All this took place to fulfill what had been spoken by the Lord through the prophet:

> "Look, the virgin shall conceive and bear a son, and they shall name him Emmanuel,"

which means, "God is with us." When Joseph awoke from sleep, he did as the angel of the Lord commanded him; he took her as his wife, but had no marital relations with her until she had borne a son; and he named him Jesus.

Luke 1:26–38

In the sixth month the angel Gabriel was sent by God to a town in Galilee called Nazareth, to a virgin engaged to a man whose name was Joseph, of the house of David. The virgin's name was Mary. And he came to her and said, "Greetings, favored one! The Lord is with you." But she was much perplexed by his words and pondered what sort of greeting this might be. The angel said to her, "Do not be afraid, Mary, for you have found favor with God. And now, you will conceive in your womb and bear a son, and you will name him Jesus. He will be great, and will be called the Son of the Most High, and the Lord God will give to him the throne of his ancestor David. He will reign over the house of Jacob forever, and of his kingdom there will be no end." Mary said to the angel, "How can this be, since I am a virgin?" The angel said to her, "The Holy Spirit will come upon you, and the power of the Most High will overshadow you; therefore the child to be born will be holy; he will be called Son of God. And now, your relative Elizabeth in her old age has also conceived a son; and this is the sixth month for her who was said to be barren. For nothing will be impossible with God." Then Mary said, "Here am I, the servant of the Lord; let it be with me according to your word." Then the angel departed from her.

Luke 2:40–52

The child grew and became strong, filled with wisdom; and the favor of God was upon him.

Now every year his parents went to Jerusalem for the festival of the Passover. And when he was twelve years old, they went up as usual for the festival. When the festival was ended and they started to return, the boy Jesus stayed behind in Jerusalem, but his parents did not know it. Assuming that he was in the group of travelers, they went a day's journey. Then they started to look for him among their relatives and friends. When they did not find him, they returned to Jerusalem to search for him. After three days they found him in the temple, sitting among the teachers, listening to them and asking them questions. And all who heard him were amazed at his understanding and his answers. When his parents saw him they were astonished; and his mother said to him, "Child, why have you treated us like this? Look, your father and I have been searching for you in great anxiety." He said to them, "Why were you searching for me? Did you not know that I must be in my Father's house?" But they did not understand what he said to them. Then he went down with them and came to Nazareth, and was obedient to them. His mother treasured all these things in her heart.

And Jesus increased in wisdom and in years, and in divine and human favor.

Document 2–2

Welcoming of Children and Greatness in the Kingdom

Matthew 18:1–7, 10–14

At that time the disciples came to Jesus and asked, "Who is the greatest in the kingdom of heaven?" He called a child, whom he put among them, and said, "Truly I tell you, unless you change and become like children, you will never enter the kingdom of heaven. Whoever becomes humble like this child is the greatest in the kingdom of heaven. Whoever welcomes one such child in my name welcomes me.

"If any of you put a stumbling block before one of these little ones who believe in me, it would be better for you if a great millstone were fastened around your neck and you were drowned in the depth of the sea. Woe to the world because of stumbling blocks! Occasions for stumbling are bound to come, but woe to the one by whom the stumbling block comes!" . . .

"Take care that you do not despise one of these little ones; for, I tell you, in heaven their angels continually see the face of my Father in heaven. What do you think? If a shepherd has a hundred sheep, and one of them has gone astray, does he not leave the ninety-nine on the mountains and go in search of the one that went astray? And if he finds it, truly I tell you, he rejoices over it more than over the ninety-nine that never went astray. So it is not the will of your Father in heaven that one of these little ones should be lost."

Matthew 21:15–16

But when the chief priests and the scribes saw the amazing things that he did, and heard the children crying out in the temple, "Hosanna to the Son of David," they became angry and said to him, "Do you hear what these are saying?" Jesus said to them, "Yes; have you never read,

'Out of the mouths of infants and nursing babies you have prepared praise for yourself'?"

Mark 9:33–37

Then they came to Capernaum; and when he was in the house he asked them, "What were you arguing about on the way?" But they were silent, for on the way they had argued with one another who was the greatest. He sat down, called the twelve, and said to them, "Whoever wants to be first must be last of all and servant of all." Then he took a little child and put it among them; and taking it in his arms, he said to them, "Whoever welcomes one such child in my name welcomes me, and whoever welcomes me welcomes not me but the one who sent me." [See also Luke 9:46–48.]

Mark 10:13–16

People were bringing little children to him in order that he might touch them; and the disciples spoke sternly to them. But when Jesus saw this, he was indignant and said to them, "Let the little children come to me; do not stop them; for it is to such as these that the kingdom of God belongs. Truly I tell you, whoever does not receive the kingdom of God as a little child will never enter it." And he took them up in his arms, laid his hands on them, and blessed them. [See also Matt. 19:13–15 and Luke 18:15–17.]

Document 2–3

Jesus's Healing of Children

Matthew 17:14–18

When they came to the crowd, a man came to him, knelt before him, and said, "Lord, have mercy on my son, for he is an epileptic and he suffers terribly; he often falls into the fire and often into the water. And I brought him to your disciples, but they could not cure him." Jesus answered, "You faithless and perverse generation, how much longer must I be with you? How much longer must I put up with you? Bring him here to me." And Jesus rebuked the demon, and it came out of him, and the boy was cured instantly. [See also Mark 9:14–29 and Luke 9:37–43.]

Mark 5:22–24, 35–43

[O]ne of the leaders of the synagogue named Jairus came and, when he saw him, fell at his feet and begged him repeatedly, "My little daughter is at the point of death. Come and lay your hands on her, so that she may be made well, and live." So he went with him. And a large crowd followed him and pressed in on him. . . .

[S]ome people came from the leader's house to say, "Your daughter is dead. Why trouble the teacher any further?" But overhearing what they said, Jesus said to the leader of the synagogue, "Do not fear, only believe." He allowed no one to follow him except Peter, James, and John, the brother of James. When they came to the house of the leader of the synagogue, he saw a commotion, people weeping and wailing loudly. When he had entered, he said to them, "Why do you make a commotion and weep? The child is not dead but sleeping." And they laughed at him. Then he put them all outside, and took the child's father and mother and those who were with him, and went in where the child was. He took her by the hand and said to her, "Talitha cum," which means, "Little girl, get up!" And immediately the girl got up and began to walk about (she was twelve years of age). At this they were overcome with amazement. He strictly ordered them that no one should know this, and told them to give her something to eat. [See also Matt. 9:18–26 and Luke 8:40–56.]

For additional healing stories, see Matthew 15:21-28, Mark 7:24-30, and John 4:46-53.

Document 2–4

Jesus's True Family

Mark 3:31–35

Then his mother and his brothers came; and standing outside, they sent to him and called him. A crowd was sitting around him; and they said to him, "Your mother and your brothers and sisters are outside, asking for you." And he replied, "Who are my mother and my brothers?" And looking at those who sat around him, he said, "Here are my mother and my brothers! Whoever does the will of God is my brother and sister and mother." [See also Matt. 12:46–50 and Luke 8:19–21.]

Luke 12:51–53

[Jesus said,] "Do you think that I have come to bring peace to the earth? No, I tell you, but rather division! From now on five in one household will be divided, three against two and two against three; they will be divided:

father against son and son against father, mother against daughter and daughter against mother, mother-in-law against her daughter-in-law and daughter-in-law against mother-in-law."

Luke 14:25–26

Now large crowds were traveling with him; and he turned and said to them, "Whoever comes to me and does not hate father and mother, wife and children, brothers and sisters, yes, and even life itself, cannot be my disciple."

Luke 18:28–30

Then Peter said, "Look, we have left our homes and followed you." And he said to them, "Truly I tell you, there is no one who has left house or wife or brothers or parents or children, for the sake of the kingdom of God, who will not get back very much more in this age, and in the age to come eternal life."

Luke 21:16–19

You will be betrayed even by parents and brothers, by relatives and friends; and they will put some of you to death. You will be hated by all because of my name. But not a hair of your head will perish. By your endurance you will gain your souls. [See also Matt. 10:34–38.]

Document 2–5

Childhood and Adoption as Symbols of Discipleship

Matthew 5:43–48

[Jesus said,] "You have heard that it was said, 'You shall love your neighbor and hate your enemy.' But I say to you, Love your enemies and pray for those who persecute you, so that you may be children of your Father in heaven; for he makes his sun rise on the evil and on the good, and sends rain on the righteous and on the unrighteous. For if you love those who love you, what reward do you have? Do not even the tax collectors do the same? And if you greet only your brothers and sisters, what more are you doing than others? Do not even the Gentiles do the same? Be perfect, therefore, as your heavenly Father is perfect." [See also Luke 6:27–28.]

Luke 20:34–36

Jesus said to [some Sadducees], "Those who belong to this age marry and are given in marriage; but those who are considered worthy of a place in that age and in the resurrection from the dead neither marry nor are given in marriage. Indeed they cannot die anymore, because they are like angels and are children of God, being children of the resurrection."

John 1:1–5, 10–13

In the beginning was the Word, and the Word was with God, and the Word was God. He was in the beginning with God. All things came into being through him, and without him not one thing came into being. What has come into being in him was life, and the life was the light of all people. The light shines in the darkness, and the darkness did not overcome it. . . . He was in the world, and the world came into being through him; yet the world did not know him. He came to what was his own, and his own people did not accept him. But to all who received him, who believed in his name, he gave power to become children of God, who were born, not of blood or of the will of the flesh or of the will of man, but of God.

John 14:18–20

[Jesus said,] "I will not leave you orphaned; I am coming to you. In a little while the world will no longer see me, but you will see me; because I live, you also will live. On that day you will know that I am in my Father, and you in me, and I in you."

John 20:17

[After his resurrection] Jesus said to [Mary], "Do not hold on to me, because I have not yet ascended to the Father. But go to my brothers and say to them, 'I am ascending to my Father and your Father, to my God and your God.' "

Romans 8:12–17

So then, brothers and sisters, we are debtors, not to the flesh, to live according to the flesh—for if you live according to the flesh, you will die; but if by the Spirit you put to death the deeds of the body, you will live. For all who are led by the Spirit of God are children of God. For you did not receive a spirit of slavery to fall back into fear, but you have received a spirit of adoption. When we cry, "Abba! Father!" it is that very Spirit bearing witness with our spirit that we are children of God, and if children, then heirs, heirs of God and joint heirs with Christ—if, in fact, we suffer with him so that we may also be glorified with him. [See also Gal. 4:1–7.]

Ephesians 1:3–14

Blessed be the God and Father of our Lord Jesus Christ, who has blessed us in Christ with every spiritual blessing in the heavenly places, just as he chose us in Christ before the foundation of the world to be holy and blameless before him in love. He destined us for adoption as his children through Jesus Christ, according to the good pleasure of his will, to the praise of his glorious grace that he freely bestowed on us in the Beloved. In him we have redemption through his blood, the forgiveness of our trespasses, according to the riches of his grace that he lavished on us. With all wisdom and insight he has made known to us the mystery of his will, according to his good pleasure that he set forth in Christ, as a plan for the fullness of time, to gather up all things in him, things in heaven and things on earth. In Christ we have also obtained an inheritance, having been destined according to the purpose of him who accomplishes all things according to his counsel and will, so that we, who were the first to set our hope on Christ, might live for the praise of his glory. In him you also, when you had heard the word of truth, the gospel of your salvation, and had believed in him, were marked with the seal of the promised Holy Spirit; this is the pledge of our inheritance toward redemption as God's own people, to the praise of this glory.

1 Thessalonians 5:2–5

You yourselves know very well that the day of the Lord will come like a thief in the night. When they say, "There is peace and security," then sudden destruction will come upon them, as labor pains come upon a pregnant woman, and there will be no escape! But you, beloved, are not in darkness, for that day to surprise you like a thief; for you are all children of light and children of the day; we are not of the night or of darkness.

Hebrews 12:4–10

In your struggle against sin you have not yet resisted to the point of shedding your blood. And you have forgotten the exhortation that addresses you as children—

> "My child, do not regard lightly the discipline of the Lord, or lose heart when you are punished by him; for the Lord disciplines those whom he loves, and chastises every child whom he accepts" [Prov. 3:11–12].

Endure trials for the sake of discipline. God is treating you as children; for what child is there whom a parent does not discipline? If you do not have that discipline in which all children share, then you are illegitimate and not his children. Moreover, we had human parents to discipline us, and we respected them. Should we not be even more willing to be subject to the Father of spirits and live? For they disciplined us for a short time as seemed best to them, but he disciplines us for our good, in order that we may share his holiness.

Document 2–6

Baptism and Rebirth

Mark 1:7–11

[John the Baptist] proclaimed, "The one who is more powerful than I is coming after me; I am not worthy to stoop down and untie the thong of his sandals. I have baptized you with water; but he will baptize you with the Holy Spirit."

In those days Jesus came from Nazareth of Galilee and was baptized by John in the Jordan. And just as he was coming up out of the water, he saw the heavens torn apart and the Spirit descending like a dove on him. And a voice came from heaven, "You are my Son, the Beloved; with you I am well pleased." [See also Matt. 3:11–17; Luke 3:21–22; John 1:26–34.]

Matthew 28:18–20

And Jesus came and said to [the disciples], "All authority in heaven and on earth has been given to me. Go therefore and make disciples of all nations, baptizing them in the name of the Father and of the Son and of the Holy Spirit, and teaching them to obey everything I have commanded you. And remember, I am with you always, to the end of the age."

John 3:4–8

Nicodemus said to [Jesus], "How can anyone be born after having grown old? Can one enter a second time into the mother's womb and be born?" Jesus answered, "Very truly, I tell you, no one can enter the kingdom of God without being born of water and Spirit. What is born of the flesh is flesh, and what is born of the Spirit is spirit. Do not be astonished that I said to you, 'You must be born from above.' The wind blows where it chooses, and you hear the sound of it, but you do not know where it comes from or where it goes. So it is with everyone who is born of the Spirit."

Document 2–7

Giving up Childish Ways

1 Corinthians 13:11–12

When I was a child, I spoke like a child, I thought like a child, I reasoned like a child; when I became an adult, I put an end to childish ways. For now we see in a mirror, dimly, but then we will see face to face. Now I know only in part; then I will know fully, even as I have been fully known.

Hebrews 5:12–14

For though by this time you ought to be teachers, you need someone to teach you again the basic elements of the oracles of God. You need milk, not solid food; for everyone who lives on milk, being still an infant, is unskilled in the word of righteousness. But solid food is for the mature, for those whose faculties have been trained by practice to distinguish good from evil.

Document 2–8

Orphans

James 1:27

Religion that is pure and undefiled before God, the Father, is this: to care for orphans and widows in their distress, and to keep oneself unstained by the world.

James 2:2–5

For if a person with gold rings and in fine clothes comes into your assembly, and if a poor person in dirty clothes also comes in, and if you take notice of the one wearing the fine clothes and say, "Have a seat here, please," while to the one who is poor you say, "Stand there," or, "Sit at my feet," have you not made distinctions among yourselves, and become judges with evil thoughts? Listen, my beloved brothers and sisters. Has not God chosen the poor in the world to be rich in faith and to be heirs of the kingdom that he has promised to those who love him?

Document 2–9

Household Codes

Ephesians 6:1–4

Children, obey your parents in the Lord, for this is right. "Honor your father and mother"—this is the first commandment with a promise: "so that it may be well with you and you may live long on the earth."

And, fathers, do not provoke your children to anger, but bring them up in the discipline and instruction of the Lord. [See also Col. 3:20–21.]

1 Timothy 3:4–5

[A bishop] must manage his own household well, keeping his children submissive and respectful in every way—for if someone does not know how to manage his own household, how can he take care of God's church?

The Early Church

The diverse group of Christian theologians in this section lived around the Mediterranean region from the second to fourth centuries CE. They interpret the meaning of Christianity in its formative period between the scattering of early Christians after the Roman destruction of the Jerusalem temple in 70 CE and the eventual establishment of Christianity as the official religion of the Roman Empire under Theodosius I around 380-394 CE. In the intervening three centuries, Christians experience persecution and martyrdom but also rapid growth, the beginnings of monasticism, and increasing church organization and theological coherency culminating in the Nicene Creed of 325 CE. Each of the thinkers below in a way challenges the strongly hierarchical Greco-Roman family values of their time through Jesus's command to "change and become like children."

Clement of Alexandria

Clement of Alexandria (153–217 CE) is an early theologian whose *Paedagogus* (The Instructor), excerpted below, uses childhood as a complex metaphor for all Christian discipleship.

Document 2–10

All Who Walk According to Truth Are Children of God

That, then, Paedagogy is the training of children, is clear from the word itself. It remains for us to consider the children whom Scripture points to; then to give the paedagogue charge of them. We are the children. In many ways Scripture celebrates us, and describes us in manifold figures of speech, giving variety to the simplicity of the faith by diverse names. Accordingly, in the Gospel, "the Lord, standing on the shore, says to the disciples"—they happened to be fishing—"and called aloud, Children, have ye any meat?"—addressing those that were already in the position of disciples as children. "And they brought to Him," it is said, "children, that He might put His hands on them and bless them; and when His disciples hindered them, Jesus said, Suffer the children, and forbid them not to come to Me, for of such is the kingdom of heaven." What the expression means, the Lord Himself shall declare, saying, "Except ye be converted, and become as little children, ye shall not enter into the kingdom of heaven"; not in that place speaking figuratively of regeneration, but setting before us, for our imitation, the simplicity that is in children. . . .

And that He calls us chickens the Scripture testifies: "As a hen gathereth her chickens under her wings." Thus are we the Lord's chickens; the Word thus marvellously and mystically describing the simplicity of childhood. For sometimes He calls us children, sometimes chickens, sometimes infants, and at other times sons, and "a new people," and "a recent people." "And my servants shall be called by a new name" (a new name, He says, fresh and eternal, pure and simple, and childlike and true), which shall be blessed on the earth. And again, He figuratively calls us colts unyoked to vice, not broken in by wickedness; but simple, and bounding joyously to the Father alone; not such horses "as neigh after their neighbours' wives, that are under the yoke, and are female-mad"; but free and new-born, jubilant by means of faith, ready to run to the truth, swift to speed to salvation, that tread and stamp under foot the things of the world. . . .

And that He also calls us lambs, the Spirit by the mouth of Isaiah is an unimpeachable witness: "He will feed His flock like a shepherd, He will gather the lambs with His arm,"—using the figurative appellation of lambs, which are still more tender than sheep, to express simplicity. And we also in truth, honouring the fairest and most perfect objects in life with an appellation derived from the word child, have named training *paideia*, and discipline *paidagogia*. Discipline (*paidagogia*) we declare to be right guiding from childhood to virtue. Accordingly, our Lord revealed more distinctly to us what is signified by the appellation of children. On the question arising among the apostles, "which of them should be the greater," Jesus placed a little child in the midst, saying, "Whosoever, shall humble himself as this little child, the same shall be the greater in the kingdom of heaven." He does not then use the appellation of children on account of their very limited amount of understanding from their age, as some have thought. Nor, if He says, "Except ye become as these children, ye shall not enter into the kingdom of God," are His words to be understood as meaning "without learning." We, then, who are infants, no longer roll on the ground, nor creep on the earth like serpents as before, crawling with the whole body about senseless lusts; but, stretching upwards in soul, loosed from the world and our sins, touching the earth on tiptoe so as to appear to be in the world, we pursue holy wisdom, although this seems folly to those whose wits are whetted for wickedness. Rightly, then, are those called children who know Him who is God alone as their Father, who are simple, and infants, and guileless, who are lovers of the horns of the unicorns. . . .

To those, therefore, that have made progress in the word, He has proclaimed this utterance, bidding them dismiss anxious care of the things of this world, and exhorting them to adhere to the Father alone, in imitation of children. Wherefore also in what follows He says: "Take no anxious thought for the morrow; sufficient unto the day is the evil thereof." Thus He enjoins them to lay aside the cares of this life, and depend on the Father alone. And he who fulfils this commandment is in reality a child and a son to God and to the world—to the one as deceived, to the other as beloved. And if we have one Master in heaven, as the Scripture says, then by common consent those on the earth will be rightly called disciples. For so is the truth, that perfection is with the Lord, who is always teaching, and infancy and childishness with us, who are always learning. . . . Then it is right to notice, with respect to the appellation of infant (*nhpios*), that *no nhpion* is not predicated of the silly: for the silly man is called *nhputios*: and *nhpios* is *nehpios* (since he that is tender-hearted is called *hpios*), as being one that has newly become gentle and meek in conduct. This the blessed Paul most clearly pointed out when he said, "When we might have been burdensome as the apostles of Christ, we were gentle (*hpioi*) among you, as a nurse cherisheth her children." The child (*nhpios*) is therefore gentle (*hpios*), and therefore more tender, delicate, and simple, guileless, and destitute of hypocrisy, straightforward and upright in mind, which is the basis of simplicity and truth. For He says, "Upon whom shall I look, but upon him who is gentle and quiet?" For such is the virgin speech, tender, and free of fraud; whence also a virgin is wont to be called "a tender bride," and a child "tender-hearted." And we are tender who are pliant to the power of persuasion, and are easily drawn to goodness, and are mild, and free of the stain of malice and perverseness, for the ancient race was perverse and hard-hearted; but the band of infants, the new people which we are, is delicate as a child. . . .

For since Scripture calls the infant children lambs, it has also called Him—God the Word—who became man for our sakes, and who wished in all points to be made like to us—"the Lamb of God"—Him, namely, that is the Son of God, the child of the Father.

Source: "All Who Walk According to Truth are Children of God," in *The Ante-Nicene Fathers: The Writings of the Fathers Down to AD 325*, edited by Alexander Roberts and James Donaldson, revised by A. Cleveland Coxe (Peabody, Mass.: Hendrickson, 1994), 2:212–215.

Origen

Origen (185–253 CE), an Alexandrian ascetic known for first synthesizing Christianity and Platonism, explains in the following commentary that children are the greatest in God's kingdom because they are free of sensual impulses.

Document 2–11

Commentary on Matthew 13:16

If anyone who is a man mortifies the lusts of manhood, putting to death by the spirit the deeds of the body, and "always bearing about in the body the putting to death of Jesus," to such a degree that he has the condition of the little child who has not tasted sensual pleasures, and has had no conception of the impulses of manhood, then such an one is converted, and has become as the little children. And the greater the advance he has made towards the condition of the little children in regard to such emotions, by so much the more as compared with those who are in training and have not advanced to so great a height of self-control, is he the greatest in the kingdom of heaven.

Source: "Commentary on Matthew," in *The Ante-Nicene Fathers: The Writings of the Fathers Down to AD 325*, edited by Allan Menzies (Peabody, Mass.: Hendrickson, 1994), 9:484.

Cyprian

Cyprian (200–258 CE), the great third-century bishop of Carthage and martyr, argues in the following excerpt from a letter that children and adults are equally images of God.

Document 2–12

On the Baptism of Infants

But in respect of the case of the infants, which you say ought not to be baptized within the second or third day after their birth, and that the law of ancient circumcision should be regarded, so that you think that one who is just born should not be baptized and sanctified within the eighth day, we all thought very differently in our council. For in this course which you thought was to be taken, no one agreed; but we all rather judge that the mercy and grace of God is not to be refused to any one born of man. For as the Lord says in His Gospel, "The Son of man is not come to destroy men's lives, but to save them," as far as we can, we must strive that, if possible, no soul be lost. For what is wanting to him who has once been formed in the womb by the hand of God? To us, indeed, and to our eyes, according to the worldly course of days, they who are born appear to receive an increase. But whatever things are made by God, are completed by the majesty and work of God their Maker.

Moreover, belief in divine Scripture declares to us, that among all, whether infants or those who are older, there is the same equality of the divine gift. Elisha, beseeching God, so laid himself upon the infant son of the widow, who was lying dead, that his head was applied to his head, and his face to his face, and the limbs of Elisha were spread over and joined to each of the limbs of the child, and his feet to his feet. If this thing be considered with respect to the inequality of our birth and our body, an infant could not be made equal with a person grown up and mature, nor could its little limbs fit and be equal to the larger limbs *of a man*. But in that is expressed the divine and spiritual equality, that all men are like and equal, since they have once been made by God; and our age may have a difference in the increase of our bodies, according to the world, but not according to God; unless that very grace also which is given to the baptized is given either less or more, according to the age of the receivers, whereas the Holy Spirit is not given with measure, but by the love and mercy of the Father alike to all. For God, as He does not accept the person, so does not accept the age; since He shows Himself a Father to all with well-weighed equality for the attainment of heavenly grace.

For, with respect to what you say, that the aspect of an infant in the first days after its birth is not pure, so that any one of us would still shudder at kissing it, we do not think that this ought to be alleged as any impediment to heavenly grace. For it is written, "To the pure all things are pure." Nor ought any of us to shudder at that which God hath condescended to make. For although the infant is still fresh from its birth, yet it is not such that any one should shudder at kissing it in giving grace and in making peace; since in the kiss of an infant every one of us ought for his very religion's sake, to consider the still recent hands of God themselves, which in some sort we are kissing, in the man lately formed and freshly born, when we are embracing that which God has made. . . .

But if anything could hinder men from obtaining grace, their more heinous sins might rather hinder those who are mature and grown up and older. But again, if even to the greatest sinners, and to those who had sinned much against God, when they subsequently believed, remission of sins is granted—and nobody is hindered from baptism and from grace—how much rather ought we to shrink from hindering an infant, who, being lately born, has not sinned, except in that, being born after the flesh according to Adam, he has contracted the contagion of the ancient death at its earliest birth, who approaches the more easily on this very account to the reception of the forgiveness of sins—that to him are remitted, not his own sins, but the sins of another.

Source: "Epistle LVIII. To Fidus, On the Baptism of Infants," in *The Ante-Nicene Fathers: The Writings of the Fathers Down to AD 325*, edited by Alexander Roberts and James Donaldson, revised by A. Cleveland Coxe (Peabody, Mass.: Hendrickson, 1994), 5:353–354.

Gregory of Nyssa

Gregory of Nyssa (335–395 CE), a monastic bishop and defender of the then new Nicene Creed, offers in this text some reflections on the death of infants and an early theory of children's development.

Document 2–13

Concerning Infants Who Have Died Prematurely

[F]or the observations of our old age to be inspiring which step by step examine the question posed by your foresight, we must inquire about [infants] who have died prematurely and how birth is related to death. . . . "In his wisdom, God has made all things" (Ps. 103.24). What is the significance of this wisdom? It brought man into existence through birth where he draws breath and sighs with lamentation over life's afflictions before he can enjoy its pleasures. At birth man's senses were sluggish, and his limbs were not fully formed; he was tender, vulnerable and lacked coordination. We may sum up these observations by saying that before coming to birth (if reason is man's natural gift, he is not yet capable of it), man had nothing more in his mother's womb except the capacity for drawing in air or was in the same state when he disintegrated, has been exposed, suffocated, or spontaneously ceased living due to some infirmity. . . .

If there is a reward for persons who have done good and if an infant who has died has done neither good nor evil, how can such an infant expect any reward? We respond to those who consider the consequence of this matter because the good proper to human nature is intelligence and is a reward in and by itself. . . . Just as at the first stage of life an infant is nourished at the breast by milk, so does a person consume food when he becomes an adult. Thus I believe that the different stages of growth share a certain order and sequence according to one's capacity as he advances to the stage where he can enjoy a life of blessedness. We have learned this from Paul who in one way nourishes persons who have grown through virtue and in another way an infant who has not yet grown up: "I have fed you with milk, not solid food since you were not yet ready for it" (1 Cor. 3.2).

But for those persons who have attained maturity he says, "Solid food is for the mature" (Heb. 5.14), referring to those who have trained their senses through practice.

Source: "Concerning Infants Who Have Died Prematurely," The Gregory of Nyssa Homepage, edited by David A. Salomon and Richard McCambly, translated by Richard McCambly, www.sage.edu/faculty/salomd/nyssa/nfrnyssa.html.

Jerome

Jerome (340–419 CE), best known as the translator of the Bible into the Latin Vulgate, writes in a letter excerpted below what it means to educate children toward God.

Document 2–14

Letter 107. To Laeta

[I]n answer to your prayers and those of the saintly Marcella, I wish to address you as a mother and to instruct you how to bring up our dear Paula, who has been consecrated to Christ before her birth and vowed to His service before her conception. . . . [A] soul [must] be educated which is to be a temple of God. It must learn to hear nothing and to say nothing but what belongs to the fear of God. It must have no understanding of unclean words, and no knowledge of the world's songs. Its tongue must be steeped while still tender in the sweetness of the psalms. Boys with their wanton thoughts must be kept from Paula: even her maids and female attendants must be separated from worldly associates. For if they have learned some mischief they may teach more. Get for her a set of letters made of boxwood or of ivory and called each by its proper name. Let her play with these, so that even her play may teach her something. . . . Offer prizes for good spelling and draw her onwards with little gifts such as children of her age delight in. And let her have companions in her lessons to excite emulation in her, that she may be stimulated when she sees them praised. You must not scold her if she is slow to learn but must employ praise to excite her mind, so that she may be glad when she excels others and sorry when she is excelled by them. Above all you must take care not to make her lessons distasteful to her lest a dislike for them conceived in childhood may continue into her maturer years. . . .

She must not . . . learn as a child what afterwards she will have to unlearn. The eloquence of the Gracchi is said to have been largely due to the way in which from their earliest years their mother spoke to them. Hortensius became an orator while still on his father's lap. Early impressions are hard to eradicate from the mind. . . . If then parents are responsible for their children when these are of ripe age and independent; how much more must they be responsible for them when, still unweaned and weak, they cannot, in the Lord's words, "discern between their right hand and their left"—when, that is to say, they cannot yet distinguish good from evil? . . . When Paula comes to be a little older and to increase like her Spouse in wisdom and stature and in favour with God and man, let her go with her parents to the temple of her true Father but let her not come out of the temple with them. Let them seek her upon the world's highway amid the crowds and the throng of their kinsfolk, and let them find her nowhere but in the shrine of the scriptures, questioning the prophets and the apostles on the meaning of that spiritual marriage to which she is vowed. . . . Never either in you nor in her father let her see what she cannot imitate without sin. Remember both of you that you are the parents of a consecrated virgin, and that your example will teach her more than your precepts. Flowers are quick to fade and a baleful wind soon withers the violet, the lily, and the crocus.

Source: "Letters," in *Nicene and Post-Nicene Fathers*, second series, edited by Philip Schaff and Henry Wace, translated by W. H. Fremantle (Peabody, Mass.: Hendrickson, 1994), 6:190–193.

John Chrysostom

John Chrysostom (347–407 CE), considered one of the founders of the Eastern Orthodox Church, argues in the following excerpts from his homilies and letters for children's original purity and openness and their joining their own earthly mother and father into "one flesh."

Document 2–15

Excerpts from Homilies and Addresses

And wherefore did the disciples repel the little children? For dignity. What then doth He? Teaching them to be lowly, and to trample under foot worldly pride, He doth receive them, and takes them in His arms, and to such as them promises the kingdom. . . . For this is the height of true wisdom; to be simple with understanding; this is angelic life; yes, for the soul of a little child is pure from all the passions. Towards those who have vexed him he bears no resentment, but goes to them as friends, as if nothing had been done. . . . And nothing more than necessary things doth he seek, but just to be satisfied from the breast, and then he leaves sucking. The young child is not grieved at what we are grieved, as at loss of money and such things as that, and he doth not rejoice again at what we rejoice, namely, at these temporal things. . . . Therefore He said, "of such is the kingdom of Heaven," that by choice we should practise these things, which young children have by nature.

Source: "Homily LXII" of "Homilies on the Gospel of Saint Matthew," in *Nicene and Post-Nicene Fathers*, first series, edited by Philip Schaff, translated by W. H. Fremantle (Peabody, Mass.: Hendrickson, 1994), 10:385.

Listen to what [Paul] says: "Children, obey your parents in the Lord, for this is the first commandment with a promise." He will not speak here about Christ, or other lofty subjects, but will direct his words to young minds . . . [n]or does he speak here about the kingdom to come, since children would not be able to understand. . . . Do you want your child to be obedient? Then from the beginning bring him up in the discipline and instruction of the Lord. Don't think that it isn't necessary for a child to listen to the Scriptures; the first thing he will learn from them will be, "Honor your father and your mother," and immediately you will begin to reap your reward. . . . It is necessary for everyone to know Scriptural teachings, and this is especially true for children. Even at their age they are exposed to all sorts of folly and bad examples from popular entertainments. Our children need remedies for all these things! . . . Let everything take second place to our care for our children, our bringing them up in the discipline and instruction of the Lord. If from the beginning we teach them to love true wisdom, they will have greater wealth and glory than riches can provide. . . .

[I]f artists who make statues and paint portraits of kings are held in high esteem, will not God bless ten thousand times more those who reveal and beautify His royal image (for man is the image of God)? When we teach our children to be good, to be gentle, to be forgiving (all these are attributes of God), to be generous, to love their fellow men, to regard this present age as nothing, we instill virtue in their souls, and reveal the image of God within them.

Source: "Homily on Ephesians 6:1–4," in *On Marriage and Family Life*, translated by Catharine P. Roth and David Anderson (Crestwood, N.Y.: St. Vladimir's Seminary Press, 1986), 65–71.

How do [married parents] become one flesh? As if she were gold receiving the purest of gold, the woman receives the man's seed with rich pleasure, and within her it is nourished, cherished, and refined. It is mingled with her own substance and she then returns it as a child! The child is a bridge connecting mother to father, so the three become one flesh, as when two cities divided by a river are joined by a bridge. And here that bridge is formed from the substance of each! . . . That is why Scripture does not say, "They shall be one flesh," but that they shall be joined together "into one flesh," namely the child.

Source: "Homily on Colossians 4:18," in *On Marriage and Family Life*, translated by Catharine P. Roth and David Anderson (Crestwood, N.Y.: St. Vladimir's Seminary Press, 1986), 76.

To each of you fathers and mothers I say, just as we see artists fashioning their paintings and statues with great precision, so we must care for these wondrous statues of ours. Painters when they have set the canvas on the easel paint on it day by day to accomplish their purpose. Sculptors, too, working in marble, proceed in a similar manner; they remove what is superfluous and add what is lacking. Even so must you proceed. Like the creators of statues do you give all your leisure to fashioning these wondrous statues for God.

Source: "An Address on Vainglory and the Right Way for Parents to Bring up Their Children," in *Christianity and Pagan Culture in the Later Roman Empire*, edited by M.L.W. Laistner (Ithaca: Cornell University Press, 1951), 96.

Middle Ages

The selections in this section include writings from the thousand-year period between the fifth and fifteenth centuries: from the Christianization of the Roman Empire to the era of scholasticism. Even though Augustine is only a few years younger than the early church theologians above, he is included here because he introduces significant shifts in theology and the theology of childhood that deeply influence the Middle Ages and beyond.

Augustine

The following selections from Augustine (354–430 CE), Bishop of Hippo in North Africa, come from his *Confessions*, the first known autobiography and a powerful theological treatise, and from a treatise on baptism. They explain, among other things, his influential view of children's original sin.

Document 2–16

Confessions

Book I, chapter 7. Hear me, O God! How wicked are the sins of men! Men say this and you pity them, because you made man, but you did not make sin in him.

Who can recall to me the sins I committed as a baby? For in your sight no man is free from sin, not even a child who has lived only one day on earth. Who can show me what my sins were? Some small baby in whom I can see all that I do not remember about myself? What sins, then, did I commit when I was a baby myself? Was it a sin to cry when I wanted to feed at the breast? I am too old now to feed on mother's milk, but if I were to cry for the kind of food suited to my age, others would rightly laugh me to scorn and remonstrate with me. So then too I deserved a scolding for what I did; but since I could not have understood the scolding, it would be have been unreasonable, and most unusual, to rebuke me. We root out these faults and discard them as we grow up, and this is proof enough that they are faults, because I have never seen a man purposely throw out the good when he clears away the bad. It can hardly be right for a child, even at that age, to cry for everything, including things which would harm him; to work himself into a tantrum against people older than himself and not required to obey him; and to try his best to strike and hurt others who know better than he does, including his own parents, when they do not give in to him and refuse to pander to whims which would only do him harm. This shows that, if babies are innocent, it is not for lack of will to do harm, but for lack of strength. . . .

Book I, chapter 12. [E]ven as a boy I did not care for lessons and I disliked being forced to study. All the same I was compelled to learn and good came to me as a result, although it was not of my own making. For I would not have studied at all if I had not been obliged to do so, and what a person does against his will is not to his own credit, even if what he does is good in itself. . . . [Y]ou used the mistake I made myself, in not wishing to study, as a punishment which I deserved to pay, for I was a great sinner for so small a boy. . . . For this is what you have ordained and so it is with us, that every soul that sins brings its own punishment upon itself. . . .

Book I, chapter 20. And yet, Lord, even if you had willed that I should not survive my childhood, I should have owed you gratitude, because you are our God, the supreme God, the Creator and Ruler of the universe. For even as a child I existed, I was alive, and I had the power of feeling; I had an instinct to keep myself safe and sound, to preserve my own being, which was a trace of the single unseen Being from whom it was derived; I had an inner sense which watched over my bodily senses and kept them in full vigor; and even in the small things which occupied my thoughts I found pleasure in the truth. . . . Should I not be grateful that so small a creature possessed such wonderful qualities? But they were all gifts from God, for I did not give them to myself. His gifts are good and the sum of them all is my own self. Therefore, the God who made me must be good and all the good in me is his. I thank him and praise him for all the good in my life, even my life as a boy. But my sin was this, that I looked for pleasure, beauty, and truth not in him but in myself and his other creatures, and the search led me instead to pain, confusion, and error. . . .

Book II, chapter 6. If the crime of theft which I committed [one] night as a boy of sixteen were a living thing, I could speak to it and ask what it was that, to my shame, I loved in it. [It] had no beauty because it was a robbery. It is true that the pears which we stole had beauty, because they were created by you, the good God, who are the most beautiful of all beings and the Creator of all things, the supreme Good and my own true Good. But it was not the pears that my unhappy soul desired. I had plenty of my own, better than those, and I only picked them so that I might steal. For no sooner had I picked them than I threw them away, and tasted nothing in them but my own sin, which I relished and enjoyed. If any part of one of those pears passed my lips, it was the sin that gave it flavour. . . .

What was it, then, that pleased me in the act of theft? Which of my Lord's powers did I imitate in a perverse and wicked way? Since I had no real power to break his law, was it that I enjoyed at least the pretense of doing so, like a prisoner who creates for himself the illusion of liberty by doing something wrong, when he has no fear of punishment, under a feeble hallucination of power? Here was the slave who ran away from his master and chased a shadow instead! What an abomination! What a parody of life! What abysmal death! Could I enjoy doing wrong for no other reason than that it was wrong?

Source: *Confessions*, translated by R. S. Pine-Coffin (New York: Penguin Books, 1961), 27–28, 32–33, 40–41, 49–50.

Document 2–17

A Treatise on the Merits and Forgiveness of Sins, and on the Baptism of Infants

It may therefore be correctly affirmed, that such infants as quit the body without being baptized will be involved in the mildest condemnation of all. That person, therefore, greatly deceives both himself and others, who teaches that they will not be involved in condemnation; whereas the apostle says: "Judgment from one offence to condemnation," and again a little after: "By the offence of one upon all persons to condemnation." When, indeed, Adam sinned by not obeying God, then his body—although it was a natural and mortal body—lost the grace whereby it used in every part of it to be obedient to the soul. Then there arose in men affections common to the brutes which are productive of shame, and which made man ashamed of his own nakedness. . . . Hence men are on the one hand born in the flesh liable to sin and death from the first Adam, and on the other hand are born again in baptism associated with the righteousness and eternal life of the second Adam. . . . They, therefore, who say that the reason why infants are baptized, is, that they may have the remission of the sin which they have themselves committed in their life, not what they have derived from Adam, may be refuted without much difficulty.

Source: "A Treatise on the Merits and Forgiveness of Sins, and on the Baptism of Infants," in *Anti-Pelagian Writings* translated by Peter Holmes and Ernest Wallis (New York: Christian Literature, 1886), 23.

Thomas Aquinas

The following documents are from Thomas Aquinas's (1224–1274) monumental *Summa Theologica*, which synthesizes Christian with Greek, and especially Aristotelian, thought. Particularly of note are his theories of family love and obligations and children's rational and moral development.

Document 2–18

Summa Theologica

Part II–II, Question 10, Article 12. There are two reasons for this custom [of Christians not baptizing infants against their parents' wishes]. One is on account of the danger to faith. For children baptized before coming to the use of reason, afterwards when they come to perfect age, might easily be persuaded by their parents to renounce what they had unknowingly embraced; and this would be detrimental to the faith.

The other reason is that it is against natural justice. For a child is by nature part of its father: thus, at first, it is not distinct from its parents as to its body, so long as it is enfolded within its mother's womb; and later on after birth, and before it has the use of its free-will, it is enfolded in the care of its parents, which is like a spiritual womb, for so long as man has not the use of reason, he differs not from an irrational animal; so that even as an ox or a horse belongs to someone who, according to the civil law, can use them when he likes, as his own instrument, so, according to the natural law, a son, before coming to the use of reason, is under his father's care. Hence it would be contrary to natural justice, if a child, before coming to the use of reason, were to be taken away from its parents' custody, or anything done to it against its parents' wish. As soon, however, as it begins to have the use of its free-will, it begins to belong to itself, and is able to look after itself, in matters concerning the Divine or the natural law, and then it should be induced, not by compulsion but by persuasion, to embrace the faith: it can then consent to the faith, and be baptized, even against its parents' wish; but not before it comes to the use of reason. Hence it is said of the children of the fathers of old that they were saved in the faith of their parents; whereby we are given to understand that it is the parents' duty to look after the salvation of their children, especially before they come to the use of reason.

II–II.26.9. [T]he degrees of love may be measured from two standpoints. First, from that of the object. In this respect the better a thing is, and the more like to God, the more is it to be loved: and in this way a man ought to love his father more than his children, because, to wit, he loves his father as his principle, in which respect he is a more exalted good and more like God.

Secondly, the degrees of love may be measured from the standpoint of the lover, and in this respect a man loves more that which is more closely connected with him, in which way a man's children are more lovable to him than his father, as the Philosopher [Aristotle] states. First, because parents love their children as being part of themselves, whereas the father is not part of his son, so that the love of a father for his children, is more like a man's love for himself. Secondly, because parents know better that so and so is their child than vice versa. Thirdly, because children are nearer to their parents, as being part of them, than their parents are to them to whom they stand in the relation of a principle. Fourthly, because parents have loved longer, for the father begins to love his child at once, whereas the child begins to love his father after a lapse of time; and the longer love lasts, the stronger it is, according to Ecclus. ix.14: *Forsake not an old friend, for the new will not be like to him.*

II–II.101.2. We owe something to our parents in two ways: that is to say, both essentially, and accidentally. We owe them essentially that which is due to a father as such: and since he is his son's superior through being the principle of his being, the latter owes him reverence and service. Accidentally, that is due to a father, which it befits him to receive in respect of something accidental to him, for instance, if he be ill, it is fitting that his children should visit him and see to his cure; if he be poor, it is fitting that they should support him; and so on in like instance, all of which come under the head of service due.

II–II.154.2. [E]very sin committed directly against human life is a mortal sin. Now simple fornication implies an inordinateness that tends to injure the life of the offspring to be born of this union. For we find in all animals where the upbringing of the offspring needs care of both male and female, that these come together not indeterminately, but the male with a certain female, whether one or several; such is the case with all birds: while, on the other hand, among those animals, where the female alone suffices for the offspring's upbringing, the union is indeterminate, as in the case of dogs and like animals. Now it is evident that the upbringing of a human child requires not only the mother's care for his nourishment, but much more the care of his father as guide and guardian, and under whom he progresses in goods both internal and external. Hence human nature rebels against an indeterminate union of the sexes and demands that a man should be united to a determinate woman and should abide with her a long time or even for a whole lifetime. Hence it is that in the human race the male has a natural solicitude for the certainty of offspring, because on him devolves the upbringing of the child: and this certainly would cease if the union of sexes were indeterminate.

This union with a certain definite woman is called matrimony; which for the above reason is said to belong to the natural law. . . . Wherefore, since fornication is an indeterminate union of the sexes, as something incompatible with matrimony, it is opposed to the good of the child's upbringing, and consequently it is a mortal sin.

III.68.9. As the Apostle says (Rom. v.17), *if by one man's offense death reigned through one,* namely Adam, *much more they who receive abundance of grace, and of the*

gift, and of justice, shall reign in life through one, Jesus Christ. Now children contract
original sin from the sin of Adam; which is made clear by the fact that they are
under the ban of death, which *passed upon all* on account of the sin of the first
man, as the Apostle says in the same passage (ver. 12). Much more, therefore,
can children receive grace through Christ, so as to reign in eternal life. But our
Lord Himself said (John iii.5): *Unless a man be born again of water and the Holy
Ghost, he cannot enter into the kingdom of God.* Consequently it became necessary
to baptize children, that, as in birth they incurred damnation through Adam,
so in a second birth they might obtain salvation through Christ. Moreover it
was fitting that children should receive Baptism, in order that being reared from
childhood in things pertaining to the Christian mode of life, they may the more
easily persevere therein; according to Prov. xxii.6: *A young man according to his
way, even when he is old, he will not depart from it.*

Supplement 43.2. The age of seven years is fixed reasonably enough by law
for the contracting of betrothals, for since a betrothal is a promise of the future,
as already stated, it follows that they are within the competency of those who
can make a promise in some way, and this is only for those who can have some
foresight of the future, and this requires the use of reason, of which three degrees
are to be observed, according to the Philosopher [Aristotle]. The first is when
a person neither understands by himself nor is able to learn from another; the
second stage is when a man can learn from another but is incapable by himself
of consideration and understanding; the third degree is when a man is both able
to learn from another and to consider by himself. And since reason develops in
man by little and little, in proportion as the movement and fluctuation of the
humors is calmed, man reaches the first stage of reason before his seventh year;
and consequently during that period he is unfit for any contract, and therefore
for betrothal. But he begins to reach the second stage at the end of his first seven
years, wherefore children at that age are sent to school. But man begins to reach
the third stage at the end of his second seven years, as regards things concerning
his person, when his natural reason develops; but as regards things outside his
person, at the end of his third seven years. Hence before his first seven years a
man is not fit to make any contract, but at the end of that period he begins to
be fit to make certain promises for the future, especially about those things to
which natural reason inclines us more, though he is not fit to bind himself by
a perpetual obligation, because as yet he has not a firm will. Hence at that age
betrothals can be contracted. But at the end of the second seven years he can
already bind himself in matters concerning his person, either to religion or to
wedlock. And after the third seven years he can bind himself in other matters also;
and according to the laws he is given the power of disposing of his property after
his twenty-second year.

Supplement 49.2. Matrimony is instituted both as an office of nature
and as a sacrament of the Church. As an office of nature it is directed by two
things, like every other virtuous act. One of these is required on the part of the

agent and is the intention of the due end, and thus the *offspring* is accounted a good of matrimony; the other is required on the part of the act, which is good generically through being about a due matter; and thus we have *faith*, whereby a man has intercourse with his wife and with no other woman. Besides this it has a certain goodness as a sacrament, and this is signified by the very word *sacrament. . . .* Offspring signifies not only the begetting of children, but also their education, to which as its end is directed the entire communion of works that exists between man and wife as united in marriage, since parents naturally *lay up* for their *children* (2 Cor. xii.14); so that the offspring like a principal end includes another, as it were, secondary end. [See also Supplement 49.3–5.]

Source: *Summa Theologica*, translated by Fathers of the English Dominican Province (New York: Benziger Brothers, 1947), 2:1223, 1301, 1632, 1816, 2405, and 3:2720, 2738.

Julian of Norwich

Julian of Norwich (1342–1416), a female mystic and one of the first women to publish in English, writes innovatively here of Jesus as Christians' spiritual "Mother."

Document 2–19

Revelations of Divine Love

The Mother's service is nearest, readiest, and surest: [nearest, for it is most of nature; readiest, for it is most of love; and surest] for it is most of truth. This office none might, nor could, nor ever should do to the full, but He alone. We know that all our mothers' bearing is [bearing of] us to pain and to dying: and what is this but that our Very Mother, Jesus, He—All-Love—beareth us to joy and to endless living?—blessed may He be! Thus He sustaineth us within Himself in love; and travailed, unto the full time that He would suffer the sharpest throes and the most grievous pains that ever were or ever shall be; and died at the last. And when He had finished, and so borne us to bliss, yet might not all this make full content to His marvellous love; and that sheweth He in these high overpassing words of love: *If I might suffer more, I would suffer more. . . .*

The mother may give her child suck of her milk, but our precious Mother, Jesus, He may feed us with Himself, and doeth it, full courteously and full tenderly, with the Blessed Sacrament that is precious food of my life; and with all the sweet Sacraments He sustaineth us full mercifully and graciously. . . . The Mother may lay the child tenderly to her breast, but our tender Mother, Jesus, He may homely lead us into His blessed breast, by His sweet open side, and shew therein part of the Godhead and the joys of Heaven, with spiritual sureness of endless bliss. . . . To the property of Motherhood belongeth natural love, wisdom, and knowing; and it is good: for though it be so that our bodily forthbringing be but little, low, and simple in regard of our spiritual forthbringing, yet it is He that doeth it in the creatures by whom that it is done. The Kindly, loving Mother that witteth and knoweth the need of her child, she keepeth it full tenderly, as the nature and condition of Motherhood will. And as it waxeth in age, she changeth her working, but not her love. And when it is waxen of more age, she suffereth that it be beaten in breaking down of vices, to make the child receive virtues and graces. . . .

But He willeth then that we use the condition of a child: for when it is hurt, or adread, it runneth hastily to the mother for help, with all its might. So willeth He that we do, as a meek child saying thus: *My kind Mother, my Gracious Mother, my dearworthy Mother, have mercy on me: I have made myself foul and unlike to Thee, and I nor may nor can amend it but with thine help and grace.* And if we feel us not then eased forthwith, be we sure that He useth the condition of a wise mother. For if He see that it be more profit to us to mourn and to weep, He suffereth it, with ruth and pity, unto the best time, for love. And He willeth then that we use the property of a child, that evermore of nature trusteth to the love of the mother in weal and in woe.

Source: *Revelations of Divine Love*, edited by Grace Warrack (London: Methuen, 1901), LX–LXI: 149–151, 154.

Christine de Pizan

Christine de Pizan (1365-1429), a French noblewoman and early female Christian theologian, develops a Christian Aristotelian perspective in her book *The Treasure of the City of Ladies* on the obligations and practices of mothers and fathers in households.

Document 2–20

The Treasure of the City of Ladies

The third teaching of Prudence to the wise princess is that if she has children she should watch over them and their upbringing diligently, even the sons, although it is the father's responsibility to seek a teacher for them and take on such governors as are good and suitable. Although the lady perhaps does not care for so much responsibility, as it is the nature of a mother commonly to be more involved with the care of her children, she ought to consider carefully everything that pertains to them, but more to that which touches discipline and teaching than to the training of the body.

The wise princess will take care how they are disciplined, and she will be very interested in those who have charge of them, and how they carry out their duties. She will not wait for a report from someone else, but she herself will often visit her children in their rooms. She will see them go to bed and get up and see how they are disciplined. It is no dishonour for a princess to do such things, for children are the greatest haven, security and ornament that she can have. It often happens that someone would greatly like to harm the mother but would not dare to do it out of fear of the children; she ought to hold them very dear. It is great praise to say that she is careful about them, for it is a sign that she is wise and good.

Therefore, the wise lady who loves her children dearly will be diligent about their education. She will ensure that they will learn first of all to serve God, and to read and write, and that the teacher will be careful to make them learn their prayers well. The wise lady will try to get the children's father to agree that they be introduced to Latin and that they understand something of the sciences. This instruction is very suitable for the children of princes and lords. When they grow older and have some understanding, she will also want them to be apprised of practical matters, government and everything princes should know about. She will want them to be told and shown all the precepts of virtue and taught the way to avoid vices. This lady will pay close attention to the behaviour and wisdom of the teacher and others who come in contact with her children. . . . She will want her children to be brought to her often. She will consider their appearance, actions and speech and she will correct them severely herself if they misbehave. She will make them respect her and she will want them to do her great honour.

Source: *The Treasure of the City of Ladies*, translated by Sarah Lawson (New York: Penguin Books, 2003), 41–42.

The Reformation

The selections in this section include texts from leaders of four major strands of Christianity during the period of the sixteenth-century Reformation and highlight their influential perspectives on education and religious formation.

Erasmus

Desiderius Erasmus Roterodamus (1466–1536), a Roman Catholic, was one of the leading humanists of his time. *De Copia* was a popular textbook on rhetoric throughout northern Europe, and this dedicatory letter of 1512 is written to his friend, John Colet (1467–1519), dean of St. Paul's Cathedral and founder of St. Paul's School in London.

Document 2–21

De Copia

I for one am bound to pay warm tribute, dear [John] Colet, to the remarkable and truly Christian goodness that leads you continually to devote all your efforts

and all your life's endeavors, not to serving your own advantage, but to bene-
fiting your country and your fellow-citizens as far as you possibly can. Equally
do I admire the wisdom you show in having chosen two particular fields for the
greatest possible achievement of this aim. First, you observed that the richest
rewards of charity lie in bringing Christ into the hearts of one's countrymen by
means of continual preaching and by holy instruction. . . . Second, and it was
next in importance in your opinion, you founded a school that far excels the rest
in beauty and splendor, so that the youth of England, under carefully chosen and
highly reputed teachers, might there absorb Christian principles together with
an excellent literary education from their earliest years. For you are profoundly
aware both that the hope of the country lies in its youth—the crop in the blade,
as it were—and also how important it is for one's whole life that one should be
initiated into excellence from the very cradle onwards. . . . [Y]ou assume the role
of a father, indeed more than a father, towards all your fellow-citizens' children
and indeed all your fellow-citizens. You rob yourself to enrich them, strip yourself in order to equip them, wear yourself out with hard work in order that your
offspring may prosper in the Lord. In short, you devote your entire energies to
winning them for Christ.

Source: Dedicatory letter to "Copia: Foundations of the Abundant Style," in *Collected
Works of Erasmus*, edited by Craig R. Thompson, translated and annotated by Betty I. Knott
(Toronto: University of Toronto Press, 1978), 24:284–285. Spelling slightly updated.

Martin Luther

Martin Luther (1483–1546), along with his friend and colleague, Philipp Melanchthon
(1497–1560), were university professors and leaders of the German Reformation. In
the first excerpt, a treatise written to German rulers and published in 1524, Luther
emphasizes the responsibilities of the whole community for educating children.
In the second excerpt, the *Large Catechism* (1529), written to help adults nurture
faith at home, he outlines the meaning of the commandment to "honor your father
and mother."

Document 2–22

To the Councilmen of All Cities in Germany
That They Establish and Maintain Schools

First of all, we are today experiencing in all the German lands how schools are
everywhere being left to go to wrack and ruin. The universities are growing weak,
and monasteries are declining. The grass withers and the flower fades, as Isaiah
[40:7–8] says, because the breath of the Lord blows upon it through his word and
shines upon it so hot through the gospel. For now it is becoming known through

God's word how un-Christian these institutions are, and how they are devoted only to men's bellies. The carnal-minded masses are beginning to realize that they no longer have either the obligation or the opportunity to thrust their sons, daughters, and relatives into cloisters and foundations, and to turn them out of their own homes and property and establish them in others' property. For this reason no one is any longer willing to have his children get an education. "Why," they say, "should we bother to have them go to school if they are not to become priests, monks, or nuns? 'Twere better they should learn a livelihood to earn." . . .

A second consideration is, as St. Paul says in II Corinthians 6[:1–2], that we should not accept the grace of God in vain and neglect the time of salvation. Almighty God has indeed graciously visited us Germans and proclaimed a true year of jubilee. We have today the finest and most learned group of men, adorned with languages and all the arts, who could also render real service if only we would make use of them as instructors of the young people. . . .

The third consideration is by far the most important of all, namely, the command of God, who through Moses urges and enjoins parents so often to instruct their children that Psalm 78 says: How earnestly he commanded our fathers to teach their children and to instruct their children's children [Ps. 78:5–6]. This is also evident in God's fourth commandment, in which the injunction that children shall obey their parents is so stern that he would even have rebellious children sentenced to death [Deut. 21:18–21]. Indeed, for what purpose do we older folks exist, other than to care for, instruct, and bring up the young? It is utterly impossible for these foolish young people to instruct and protect themselves. This is why God has entrusted them to us who are older and know from experience what is best for them. And God will hold us strictly accountable for them. This is also why Moses commands in Deuteronomy 32[:7], "Ask your father and he will tell you; your elders, and they will show you."

It is a sin and a shame that matters have come to such a pass that we have to urge and be urged to educate our children and young people and to seek their best interests, when nature itself should drive us to do this and even the heathen afford us abundant examples of it. There is not a dumb animal which fails to care for its young and teach them what they need to know; the only exception is the ostrich, of which God says in Job 31 [39:16, 14] that she deals cruelly with her young as if they were not hers, and leaves her eggs upon the ground. What would it profit us to possess and perform everything else and be like pure saints, if we meanwhile neglected our chief purpose in life, namely, the care of the young? I also think that in the sight of God none among the outward sins so heavily burdens the world and merits such severe punishment as this very sin which we commit against the children by not educating them. . . .

Ah, you say, but all that is spoken to the parents; what business is it of councilmen and the authorities? Yes, that is true; but what if the parents fail to do their duty? Who then is to do it? Is it for this reason to be left undone, and the children neglected? How will the authorities and council then justify their position, that such matters are not their responsibility?

There are various reasons why parents neglect this duty. In the first place, there are some who lack the goodness and decency to do it, even if they had the ability. Instead, like the ostrich [Job 39:14–16], they deal cruelly with their young. They are content to have laid the eggs and brought children into the world; beyond this they will do nothing more. But these children are supposed to live among us and with us in the community. How can then reason, and especially Christian charity, allow that they grow up uneducated, to poison and pollute the other children until at last the whole city is ruined, as happened in Sodom and Gomorrah [Gen. 19:1–25], and Gibeah [Judg. 19–20], and a number of other cities?

In the second place, the great majority of parents unfortunately are wholly unfitted for this task. They do not know how children should be brought up and taught, for they themselves have learned nothing but how to care for their bellies. It takes extraordinary people to bring children up right and teach them well.

In the third place, even if parents had the ability and desire to do it themselves they have neither the time nor the opportunity for it, what with their other duties and the care of the household. Necessity compels us, therefore, to engage public schoolteachers for the children—unless each one were willing to engage his own private tutor. But that would be too heavy a burden for the common man, and many a promising boy would again be neglected on account of poverty. Besides, many parents die, leaving orphans, and if we do not know from experience how they are cared for by their guardians it should be quite clear from the fact that God calls himself Father of the fatherless [Ps. 68:5], of those who are neglected by everyone else. Then too there are others who have no children of their own, and therefore take no interest in the training of children.

It therefore behooves the council and the authorities to devote the greatest care and attention to the young. Since the property, honor, and life of the whole city have been committed to their faithful keeping, they would be remiss in their duty before God and humanity if they did not seek its welfare and improvement day and night with all the means at their command. Now the welfare of a city does not consist solely in accumulating vast treasures, building mighty walls and magnificent buildings, and producing a goodly supply of guns and armor. Indeed, where such things are plentiful, and reckless fools get control of them, it is so much the worse and the city suffers even greater loss. A city's best and greatest welfare, safety, and strength consist rather in its having many able, learned, wise, honorable, and well-educated citizens. They can then readily gather, protect, and properly use treasures and all manner of property.

Source: "To the Councilmen of All Cities in Germany That They Establish and Maintain Christian Schools," in *Luther's Works*, vol. 45, edited by Walther I. Brandt (Philadelphia: Muhlenberg Press), pp. 348, 351–356. Translation slightly revised.

Document 2–23

The Large Catechism

You shall honor your father and mother.

To fatherhood and motherhood God has given the special distinction, above all estates that are beneath it, that he commands us not simply to love our parents but also to honor them. With respect to brothers, sisters, and neighbors in general he commands nothing higher than that we love them. Thus he distinguishes father and mother above all other persons on earth, and places them next to himself. For it is a much greater thing to honor than to love. Honor includes not only love but also deference, humility, and modesty, directed (so to speak) toward a majesty hidden within them. It requires us not only to address them affectionately and reverently, but above all to show by our actions, both of heart and of body, that we respect them very highly and that next to God we give them the very highest place. For anyone whom we are whole-heartedly to honor, we must truly regard as high and great.

Young people must therefore be taught to revere their parents as God's representatives, and to remember that, however lowly, poor, feeble, and eccentric they may be, they are their own father and mother, given them by God. They are not to be deprived of their honor because of their ways or their failings. Therefore, we are not to think of their persons, whatever they are, but of the will of God, who has created and ordained them to be our parents. In other respects, indeed, we are all equal in the sight of God, but among ourselves there must be this sort of inequality and proper distinctions. God therefore commands you to be careful to obey me as your father and to acknowledge my authority.

First, then, learn what this commandment requires concerning honor to parents. You are to esteem and prize them as the most precious treasure on earth. In your words you are to behave respectfully toward them, and not address them discourteously, critically, and censoriously, but submit to them and hold your tongue, even if they go too far. You are also to honor them by your actions (that is, with your body and possessions), serving them, helping them, and caring for them when they are old, sick, feeble, or poor; all this you should do not only cheerfully, but with humility and reverence, as in God's sight. He who has the right attitude toward his parents will not allow them to suffer want or hunger, but will place them above himself and at his side and will share with them all he has to the best of his ability.

In the second place, notice what a great, good, and holy work is here assigned to children. Alas, it is utterly despised and brushed aside, and no one recognizes it as God's command or as a holy, divine word and precept. For if we had regarded it as such, it would have been apparent to all that they who lived according to these words must also be holy men. Then there would have been no need to institute monasticism or "spiritual estates." Every child would have remained faithful to this commandment and would have been able to set his conscience right toward God, saying: "If I am to do good and holy works, I know of none better than to show all honor and obedience to my parents, since God himself has commanded it. What God commands must be much nobler than anything we ourselves may devise. And because there is no greater or better teacher to be found than God, there can also be no better teaching than his."

Source: "The Large Catechism," in *The Book of Concord*, translated and edited by Theodore G. Tappert (Philadelphia: Fortress), 379–380.

Dirk Philips

Dirk Philips (1504-1568) was an early Anabaptist theologian and colleague of Menno Simons (1496-1561), whose followers later became known as Mennonites. As stated in the *Schleitheim Confession* of 1527, the Anabaptists reject infant baptism, reshaping, in turn, their views of children, free will, and original sin, as we see here.

Document 2–24

Christian Baptism (1564)

That the kingdom of heaven belongs to the children we believe without a doubt, as we have already declared. But that the salvation of children lies in their baptism and is bound to it we do not believe and cannot concede. For Christ accepted the children, and promised them the kingdom of heaven through grace and mercy, and not because of baptism. He neither baptized them nor commanded them to be baptized but laid his hands on them and blessed them.

Christ also makes it sufficiently plain to us why children are acceptable to God, inasmuch as he sets forth the children as an example to us, and moreover admonishes us that we should become like them. For he speaks thus to his disciples: "Truly, I say to you, unless you turn around and become as the children, you will not enter the kingdom of heaven. Whoever now humbles himself as this child, he is the greatest in the kingdom of the heavens" (Matt. 3:4; 19:14).

Since therefore Christ sets the children before us as an example and says that we should become like children, and humble ourselves, it follows without contradiction: first, that children (so long as they are in their simplicity) are innocent and judged by God to be without sin; second, that there is still something good in children (although they have become partakers of the transgression and sinful nature of Adam), namely, a simple, unassuming, and humble bearing, which makes them pleasing to God (yet purely by grace through Jesus Christ) so long as they remain in it. For this reason also Christ sets children before us as an example that we should in these respects become like them. . . .

Since therefore children are saved, are in God's hand, and are included in his grace, the kingdom of heaven is theirs (Matt. 19:14). It is therefore a great folly to baptize infants that they may thereby be preserved and saved, and to damn those infants who die unbaptized. This is openly belittling and slandering the grace of God and the merits of Jesus Christ. For since through Jesus Christ the sin of Adam, indeed of the whole world, is atoned for and taken away (John 1:29), how can infants be damned on account of the sin of Adam, since no sin can be imputed to them except that which comes from Adam? Indeed, who will charge it to the children, for whom Jesus Christ shed his precious blood? Who would condemn the children to whom the Lord in his unfathomable grace and mercy has promised the kingdom? (Matt. 19:14). Who can repudiate the Holy Scripture which so explicitly declares that the sin of Adam (Rom. 5:18) and of the whole world is taken away? . . .

Hence we conclude with the apostles and the entire Holy Scripture, that original sin has been paid for and taken away by Jesus Christ to the degree the children may not be judged and condemned on account of Adam's trangression (Gen. 6:5; 8:21). We conclude that the tendency of the nature of children is toward evil; but that does not damn them. By the grace of God it is not accounted as sin to them. As long as they are simple and without the knowledge of good and evil, they are pleasing and acceptable to God through Jesus Christ. But why should many words be necessary? It is true and indubitable that children as well as adults—the children by their simplicity, the adults by their faith—are saved by the grace of our Lord Jesus Christ (Acts 15:11).

Source: "Christian Baptism," in *Anabaptism in Outline*, edited by Walter Klaassen (Kitchener, Ont.: Herald Press, 1981), 185–187.

John Calvin

John Calvin (1509-1564) was a leader of the Reformation in Geneva, and his theology significantly shapes a number of Calvinist or Reformed traditions. His most significant and influential work is the *Institutes of the Christian Religion*, first published 1536 (definitive version 1559). This selection from his affirmation of infant baptism illuminates much about his view of children.

Document 2–25

Institutes of the Christian Religion

Now, if we choose to investigate whether it is right to administer baptism to infants, shall we not say that a man is talking nonsense or indeed raving who would halt with the mere element of water and outward observance, but cannot bear to turn his mind to the spiritual mystery? If any account of this is made, it will be evident that baptism is properly administered to infants as something

owed to them. For in early times the Lord did not deign to have them circumcised without making them participants in all those things which were then
signified by circumcision.... For he expressly declares that the circumcision of
a tiny infant will be in lieu of a seal to certify the promise of the covenant. But
if the covenant still remains firm and steadfast, it applies no less today to the
children of Christians than under the Old Testament it pertained to the infants
of the Jews. Yet if they are participants in the thing signified, why shall they be
debarred from the sign? If they grasp the truth, why shall they be driven away
from the figure?....

   If anyone should object that the promise ought to be enough to confirm the
salvation of our children, I disregard this argument. For God views this otherwise;
as he perceives our weakness, so he has willed to deal tenderly with us in this
matter. Accordingly, let those who embrace the promise that God's mercy is to be
extended to their children deem it their duty to offer them to the church to be
sealed by the symbol of mercy, and thereby to arouse themselves to a surer confi-
dence, because they see with their very eyes the covenant of the Lord engraved
upon the bodies of their children. On the other hand, the children receive some
benefit from their baptism: being engrafted into the body of the church, they are
somewhat more commended to the other members. Then, when they have grown
up, they are greatly spurred to an earnest zeal for worshiping God, by whom they
were received as children through a solemn symbol of adoption before they were
old enough to recognize him as Father....

   They think that they are putting forward a very strong reason why children
are to be barred from baptism when they claim that children because of their
age are not yet able to understand the mystery signified in it, namely, spiritual
regeneration, which cannot take place in earliest infancy....

   But how (they ask) are infants, unendowed with knowledge of good or evil,
regenerated? We reply that God's work, though beyond our understanding, is still
not annulled. Now it is perfectly clear that those infants who are to be saved
(as some are surely saved from that early age) are previously regenerated by the
Lord. For if they bear with them an inborn corruption from their mother's womb,
they must be cleansed of it before they can be admitted into God's Kingdom, for
nothing polluted or defiled may enter there [Rev. 21:27]. If they are born sinners,
as both David and Paul affirm [Eph. 2:3; Ps. 51:5], either they remain unpleasing
and hateful to God, or they must be justified. And what further do we seek, when
the Judge himself plainly declares that entry into heavenly life opens only to
those who are born anew [John 3:3]?...

   For since we are born sinners, we need forgiveness and pardon even from the
time in our mother's womb. Now, since God does not cut off from childhood the
hope of mercy, but rather makes it sure, why should we take away the sign, much
inferior to the thing itself?... Infants receive forgiveness of sins; therefore, they
must not be deprived of the sign.... If Christ intends the washing with which
he cleanses his church to be attested by baptism, it does not seem fair that he

should not have his testimony in the little ones, who are rightly considered a part of the church, since they have been called heirs of the Kingdom of Heaven [Matt. 19:14]. . . .

Now, consequently, we must utterly reject the fiction of those who consign all the unbaptized to eternal death. Let us then fancy that, according to their assumption, baptism is administered to adults only. What will they say will become of a child who is duly and properly instructed in the rudiments of piety, and, when the day of baptism is at hand, happens to be snatched away by sudden death, contrary to the expectation of all? The promise of the Lord is clear: "Whosoever believes in the Son will not see death, nor come into judgment, but has passed from death into life" [John 5:24]. Nowhere do we find that he has ever condemned anyone as yet unbaptized. I do not want anyone on this account to think of me as meaning that baptism can be despised with impunity (by which contempt I declare the Lord's covenant will be violated—so far am I from tolerating it!); it merely suffices to prove that baptism is not so necessary that one from whom the capacity to obtain it has been taken away should straightway be counted as lost. . . .

Now I think no sober person will be in doubt how rashly they stir up Christ's church with their altercations and contentions over infant baptism. . . . For how sweet is it to godly minds to be assured, not only by word, but by sight, that they obtain so much favor with the Heavenly Father that their offspring are within his care? For here we can see how he takes on toward us the role of a most provident Father, who even after our death maintains his care for us, providing for and looking after our children. . . . For when we consider that immediately from birth God takes and acknowledges them as his children, we feel a strong stimulus to instruct them in an earnest fear of God and observance of the law. Accordingly, unless we wish spitefully to obscure God's goodness, let us offer our infants to him, for he gives them a place among those of his family and household, that is, the members of the church.

Source: *Institutes of the Christian Religion*, edited by John T. Mc Neill, translated by Ford Lewis Battles (Philadelphia: Westminster, 1960), 2:1327–1328, 1332, 1339–1340, 1345, 1349, 1358–1359.

Early Modernity

These selections from the seventeenth and eighteenth centuries are drawn from four influential European Protestants who worked closely with and on behalf of children. Their ideas about children, education, and faith formation spread to other parts of the world through their numerous publications and the growth of missionary activities.

John Amos Comenius

Johannes Amos Comenius (1592–1670), the innovative seventeenth-century Moravian bishop, theologian, and educator, emphasizes a holistic approach to education that includes moral and spiritual development. He is often called the "father of modern education," and his popular book, *The School of Infancy* (1633), points out the complex sensibilities and development of infants and young children and the need to nurture them at a very young age.

Document 2–26

The School of Infancy

Children, God's Most Precious Gift, and an Inestimable Treasure,
Claim Our Most Vigilant Attention
That children are a priceless treasure God testifies, saying: "Lo, children are the heritage of the Lord; the fruit of the womb His reward; as arrows in the hand, so are children. . . ."

Also, when God speaks of His love towards us, he calls us children as if there were no more excellent name by which to allure us. . . .

The Son of God when manifested in the flesh not only willed to become as a little child, but thought children a pleasure and a delight. Taking them in His arms as little brethren and sisters, He carried them about and kissed and blessed them. He severely threatened anyone who should offend them, even in the least degree, and commanded that they be respected as Himself.

If one seeks to learn why He is so delighted with little children, one will find many causes. First, if the little ones at present seem unimportant, regard them not as they now are, but as God intends they may and ought to be. You will see them not only as the future inhabitants of the world and possessors of the earth, and God's vicars amongst His creatures when we depart from this life, but also equal participants with us in the heritage of Christ: A royal priesthood, a chosen people, associates of angels, judges of devils, the delight of heaven, the terror of hell . . . heirs of eternity. . . .

If we consider even their present state, we see at once why children are priceless to God and ought to be so to parents. They are valuable to God first because being innocent, except for original sin, they are not yet the defaced image of God and are unable to discern between good and evil, between the right hand and the left.

Secondly, they are the purest and dearly purchased possession of Christ who saves all except those who shut themselves out by unbelief and impenitence. Since children have not yet so repelled Christ, "Theirs is the kingdom of heaven. . . ." Having not yet defiled themselves with the allures of sin, they follow the Lamb wherever He goeth. And that they may continue so to follow, they ought to be led, as with the hand, by a pious education.

Finally, God so embraces children with abounding love that they become a special instrument of divine glory. "From the lips of infants and sucklings thou has perfected praise. . . ." Why God's glory receives increase from children is certainly not at once clear to our understanding; but God, the discerner of all things, understands and declares it so.

That children ought to be dearer to parents than gold and silver, than pearls and gems, may be discovered from a comparison between both gifts of God; for:

Gold and silver and like things are inanimate, being only somewhat harder and purer than the clay which we tread beneath our feet; whereas infants are the living images of the living God. . . . Gold and silver are fleeting and transitory; children an immortal inheritance. Although they yield to death, they neither return to nothing, nor become extinct: they only pass out of a mortal tabernacle into an immortal one. . . . Gold and silver come forth of the earth, children from our own substance. Being a part of ourselves, they consequently deserve to be loved by us, certainly not less than we love ourselves. . . . Gold and silver pass from one to another as though they were the property of none, but common to all; whereas children are a peculiar possession of their parents, divinely assigned. . . . Gold and silver are gifts of God, yet they are not among those gifts that he promises angels to guard. Nay, Satan mostly intermingles himself with gold and silver to use them as nets and snares to entangle the unwary— drawing them as with thongs to avarice, pride, and prodigal ways. Whereas the Lord declares that little children are always committed to the guard of angels. Hence he who has infants within his house may be certain that he also has angels. He who takes little children in his arms may be assured that he takes angels. He who surrounded by midnight darkness rests beside an infant has the certain consolation that the spirit of darkness can not enter. What comfort here! What a priceless jewel bringing such gifts!

Gold and silver do not procure for us the love of God, nor, as infants do, defend us from His anger, for God so loves little children that for their sakes he occasionally pardons parents. . . . Finally, gold, silver, gems bring us no more instruction than do other created things, namely evidence of wisdom, power and beneficence of God. Yet infants are given us as a mirror in which we may behold humility, gentleness, benign goodness, harmony, and other Christian virtues. The Lord himself declares "Except ye be converted, and become as little children, ye shall not enter into the kingdom of heaven." Since God thus wills that children be our preceptors, we owe them the most diligent attention. . . .

In What Things Youth Ought to Be Exercised Gradually from Their Very Birth, So That They May Be Found Expert in Those Things in the Sixth Year of Their Age
Everyone knows that whatever disposition the branches of an old tree obtain they must necessarily have been so formed from its first growth, for they cannot

be otherwise. . . . Human beings therefore in the very first formation of body and soul should be molded so as to be such as they ought to be throughout their whole lives.

For although God can make an inveterately bad person useful by completely transforming him, yet in the regular course of nature it scarcely ever happens otherwise than that as a thing has begun to be formed from its origin so it becomes completed, and so it remains. Whatever seed one sows in youth, such fruit he reaps in age, according to the axiom, "The pursuits of youth are the delights of maturity."

Let not parents therefore give the instruction of their children alone to preceptors of schools and ministers of the church, since it is impossible to make the tree straight that has grown crooked. . . . But they ought *themselves* to know how to manage their own treasures that these may receive increases of wisdom and grace before God and humanity.

And inasmuch as every one ought to be competent to serve God and be useful to human beings, we maintain that he ought to be instructed in PIETY, in MORALS, in SOUND LEARNING, and in HEALTH. Parents should lay the foundations of these in the very earliest age of their children.

Source: *The School of Infancy*, edited and introduced by Ernest M. Eller (Chapel Hill: University of North Carolina Press, 1956), 59–70. Translation slightly revised.

August Hermann Francke

The German pietist August Hermann Francke (1663–1727) established a vast network of institutions for children, including a pediatric hospital, schools, and an orphanage, and his ideas about education spread to other countries through missionaries sent from his center in Halle, Germany. The following is from one of his most well-known sermons on helping the poor and needy.

Document 2–27

Duty to the Poor

I will believe that there is a true Christianity among us when I see that one uses the temporal goods among us not for pleasure and luxury, but rather in sincere love toward the poor. Since the "duty to the poor" is neglected when one does not think of the poor until they almost crawl on hand and foot to the door, likewise when one gives forced alms lovelessly out of ambition, or when one is devoted to excess in food, drink, and clothing so that the pomp may be preserved, the question arises, "How should we rightly observe and practice the duty to the poor?" . . .

"But if we would observe the duty well, we must 1) listen kindly to the poor and lament their misfortune" just as we gladly would that it should be done for us if we should fall into similar distress. . . . "Listen readily to the poor and answer him kindly and gently. Act toward the orphan like a father and toward their mother like a husband" (Wisdom of Sirach 4:1–10).

But it is not enough to listen to them kindly and feed them with mere words. Rather we should also much more 2) seek to help them. . . . From this we learn further 3) that our duty to the poor is this, that according to Isaiah 58, we "should break our bread with the hungry." . . . With this is further to be borne in mind that even if 4) the poor do not come to the door, but are "absent," one nonetheless "should do good unto them." If you sit at your table, for example, and see that perhaps a little is left over from your store, then consider if there are not the sick, poor orphans, poor widows, and the like here and there with whom you may be able to share. . . .

You should not depend on others asking you, but rather you should be disposed "motherly" toward the poor (Wisdom of Sirach 4:10). A mother does not let it come so far that her child falls into need, or if it is stuck therein, dying; rather she seeks to help her child as quickly as she can. . . .

We must also know further that we should not only help the poor in body, but because most men are "spiritually poor" and are ill-tended in their poor souls we should also think to help them get right also in their souls. Behold how some child goes astray who knows neither of God nor his Word, attends no school, is not instructed. There the eyes must be opened. You who have money and possessions, you must think how such a child may be wrested from the jaws of the devil. You should make it your concern how the child may be constrained to attend school, and should you pay the costs you make a good investment.

Source: "Duty to the Poor," in *God's Glory, Neighbor's Good: A Brief Introduction to the Life and Writings of August Hermann Francke*, edited by Gary Sattler (Chicago: Covenant Press, 1982), 171–175.

Nicolaus Ludwig von Zinzendorf

Nicolaus Ludwig von Zinzendorf (1700-1760) emphasizes the believer's intimate and heartfelt relationship with Jesus Christ, which is reflected in his religious education programs and the many forms of literature he wrote about and for children. The essay here on child nurture is written for adults, but Zinzendorf also wrote many sermons, hymns, litanies, and catechisms directly for children.

Document 2–28

Brief Essay on the Christian Nurture of Children

It is self-evident that a warrior of Jesus Christ, man or woman, will not trifle with children, will not entertain toward them any silly affection or attachment which would be harmful to them. It is equally self-evident that in all dealings with them one should act in accord with the promptings of the heart kindled by the love of Christ, not foolish or childish though childlike, not indulgent but loving and hearty, not indifferent but alert, not frivolous but friendly and cheerful. . . . What we love or hate in children must correspond in each case to what Jesus himself would love or hate no matter who is affected thereby. . . .

Children must be drawn to the Christian life lovingly, not by force. Our conduct, love of the Saviour, our faithfulness in all things great or small, the description of the Saviour, his attitude toward us, what he has done for us, what he desires to give to us, these things must attract them. They must know of no beauty, no wealth, no honor, no rest except such as the Saviour gives. . . .

The importance of loving Jesus, the beauty of his shame, his humility, his poverty, the lightness of his cross are impressed upon them with words and proofs lovingly and in a childlike spirit.

Source: "Brief Essay on the Christian Nurture of Children," in *Child Nature and Nurture According to Nicolaus von Zinzendorf*, edited by Henry Meyer (New York: Abingdon, 1928), 202–204.

John Wesley

John Wesley (1703–1791), the founder of Methodism, attended to the needs of children by establishing and supporting schools and orphanages, writing several documents directly on education, and publishing textbooks for use in the classroom. This sermon from 1783 addresses responsibilities for "training up" children by discussing human nature.

Document 2–29

On the Education of Children

In order to see distinctly what is the way wherein we should train up a child, let us consider, what are the diseases of his nature? What are those spiritual diseases which everyone that is born of a woman brings with him into the world?

Is not the first of these *atheism*? After all that has been so plausibly written concerning "the innate idea of God"; after all that has been said of its being common to all human beings, in all ages and nations; it does not appear that humanity has naturally any more idea of God than any of the beasts of the field: he has no knowledge of God at all, no fear of God at all, neither is God in all his thoughts. Whatever change may afterwards be wrought (whether by the grace of God, or by his own reflection, or by education) he is by nature a mere atheist.

Indeed, it may be said that every human being is by nature, as it were, his own god. He worships himself. He is, in his own conception, absolute Lord of himself. . . .

Another evil disease which every human soul brings into the world with him is *pride*—a continual proneness to think of himself more highly than he ought to think. Every human being can discern more or less of this disease in everyone—but himself. . . .

The next disease natural to every human soul, born with every man, is *love of the world*. Every human being is by nature a lover of the creature instead of the Creator; "a lover of pleasure" in every kind "more than a lover of God" (2 Tim. 3:4). . . .

Whether this be a natural disease or not, it is certain *anger* is. The ancient philosopher [Aristotle] defines it, "a sense of injury received, with a desire of revenge." . . .

A deviation from *truth* is equally natural to all the children of humanity. One said in his haste, "All human beings are liars" (Ps. 116:11); but we may say, upon cool reflection, All natural human beings will, upon a close temptation, vary from or disguise the truth. If they do not offend against *veracity*, if they do not say what is false, yet they frequently offend against *simplicity*. They use art; they hang out false colors; they practice either simulation or dissimulation. So that you cannot say truly of any person living, till grace has altered nature, "Behold an Israelite indeed, in whom is no guile!"

Everyone is likewise prone by nature to speak or act contrary to *justice*. This is another of the diseases which we bring with us into the world. All human creatures are naturally partial to themselves, and when opportunity offers have more regard to their own interest or pleasure than strict justice allows. Neither is any human being by nature *merciful* as our heavenly Father is merciful (Luke 6:36); but all more or less transgress that glorious rule of mercy as well as justice, "Whatsoever ye would that men should do unto you, the same do unto them" (Matt. 7:12).

Now if these are the general diseases of human nature, is it not the grand end of education to cure them? And is it not the part of all those to whom God has entrusted the education of children to take all possible care, first, not to increase, not to feed any of these diseases (as the generality of parents constantly do), and next, to use every possible means of healing them? . . .

But what can we do to cure their *self-will*? It is equally rooted in their nature, and is indeed the original idolatry, which is not confined to one age or country, but is common to all the nations under heaven. And how few parents are to be found even among Christians, even among them that truly fear God, who are not guilty in this matter? Who do not continually feed and increase this grievous distemper in their children? To let them have their own will does this most effectually. To let them take their own way is the sure method of increasing their self-will sevenfold. But who has the resolution to do otherwise? One parent in a hundred? Who can be so singular, so cruel, as not more or less to *humor* her child? "And why should you not? What harm can there be in this, which everybody does?" The harm is that it strengthens their will more and more, till it will neither bow to God nor man. To humor children is, as far as in us lies, to make their disease incurable. A wise parent, on the other hand, should begin to break their will the first moment it appears. In the whole art of Christian education there is nothing more important than this. The will of the parent is to a little child in the place of the will of God. Therefore studiously teach them to submit to this while they are children, that they may be ready to submit to his will when they are adults. But in order to carry this point you will need incredible firmness and resolution. For after you have once begun you must never more give way. You must hold on still in an even course: you must never intermit your attention for one hour; otherwise you lose your labor.

Source: "On the Education of Children," in *The Works of John Wesley*, edited by Albert C. Outler (Nashville: Abingdon, 1986), 3:350–354. Spelling and language slightly updated.

Late Modernity

These three selections from the nineteenth century are from German and North American theologians who are known not only for significantly shaping theological reflection in their day but also for writing extensively on education and child rearing.

Johann Gottfried von Herder

Johann Gottfried von Herder (1744–1803) was a German literary figure, Lutheran theologian, and educator who also significantly influenced the emerging historical consciousness of nineteenth-century Europe. His famous work, *Ideas toward a Philosophy of History* (1784–1791), emphasizes how human beings share one humanity yet are shaped by diverse linguistic, historical, geographical, religious, and cultural contexts.

Document 2–30

Ideas toward a Philosophy of History

As ready as human beings are to imagine that they are self-made, they are nevertheless dependent on others for the development of their capacities. . . . Just as human beings do not spring from their own wombs at birth, they themselves do not give birth to the use of their own mental powers. Not only is the seed of our internal disposition, like the structure of our body, genetic; but each development of this seed also depends on fate, which planted us in this or that place and supplied us according to time and circumstances with the means of our formation [*Bildung*].

Even the eye must learn to see, the ear to hear; and it should be no secret what skill is needed to acquire the principal instrument of our thought-language. Nature has obviously arranged our whole organism, including the character and length of our stages in life, for this external aid. An infant's brain is soft and still adheres to the skull; the strata of the brain are formed slowly; it grows firmer over the years, until at length it hardens and receives no more new impressions. It is the same with the bodily limbs and the instincts of a child. The limbs are fragile and develop through imitation. The instincts perceive what they see and hear with the aid of a wonderful, active attention and an inner life force. Thus, the human being is an organism that must be skillfully crafted. It is, to be sure, endowed with a genetic disposition and an abundance of life, but the organism does not work automatically, and even the most gifted person must learn how to work it. Reason is an aggregate of observations and exercises of the soul; it is the sum of the education of our race. The pupil, like a foreign artist, completes this education within the self according to given, external models. . . .

We are born almost without instinct, we become what we should and can be only through lifelong training toward humanity, and this is the reason our species is both perfectible and corruptible. It follows that the history of humanity is necessarily a whole, that is, from the first link to the last it is a chain consisting of social life and of the dynamic tradition that shapes us.

We can speak, therefore, of an education of the human race [*Erziehung des Menschengeschlechts*], for every individual becomes a human being only by means of education, and the whole human race lives solely within this chain of individuals. . . . An intellectual genesis, that is, education, connects the whole formation of an individual's humanity to that individual's parents, teachers, and friends, to all the circumstances in the course of that individual's life, consequently to that individual's people and their ancestors, and in the end to the whole chain of the human race, for some links of the chain are bound to influence one of the powers of that individual. . . .

All education exists only by means of imitation and training, that is, by means of the transmission of a model into an imitation. . . . Imitators must have powers, however, to receive what has and can be transmitted and to convert it, like the food whereby they live, into their own natures. . . .

What conclusions can be drawn from this well-grounded perspective, which is confirmed by the entire history of the human race? First, . . . whereas the human race is not self-made, and whereas there are dispositions in its nature that cannot be praised highly enough, the Creator must have appointed means for the development of these dispositions, and these means in turn reveal his most wise, paternal goodness . . . Second, as much as it flatters human beings that the deity has accepted them as assistants and left their formation here below to themselves, it is precisely this divinely chosen means of our formation that reveals the imperfection of our earthly existence, inasmuch as we *are* not yet human beings, but are daily *becoming* so. . . . Third, the philosophy of history that pays attention to the chain of tradition is, strictly speaking, the true history of humankind. . . . *The purpose of human nature is humanity [Humanität]; and with this purpose God has put the fate of our race in our own hands.*

Source: *Ideas toward a Philosophy of History*, in *Against Pure Reason, Writings on Religion, Language, and History*, translated and edited by Marcia Bunge (Minneapolis: Fortress, 1993), 48–55.

Friedrich Schleiermacher

The German theologian Friedrich Daniel Ernst Schleiermacher (1768-1834) wrote extensively and with remarkable psychological depth about children. His "Sermons on the Christian Household" (1818) provide a rich summary of his views on child rearing, and this excerpt reveals how his understandings of discipline, child obedience, and faith formation are informed by a high regard for children's play, intuition, and gifts.

Document 2–31

The Christian Household: A Sermonic Treatise

Text: Ephesians 6:4. "Fathers, do not provoke your children to anger, but bring them up in the discipline and instruction [admonition] of the Lord."
What, then, is included in and what is meant by the counsel that the young people who grow up among us should have the benefit of discipline from everything that we do with them, teach them, impose on them, give them and withhold from them? Now, before all else we must sort out what is the meaning of that term "discipline," where here sums up everything. My dear friends, discipline is definitely not the same thing as punishment, even though we tend to speak that way often in everyday life, but something entirely different. Punishment is a consequence of disobedience, while discipline presupposes obedience. Punishment simply has children undergo suffering, while discipline gives them something to do. Punishment more or less arbitrarily attaches something bitter and unpleasant to what is improper and blameworthy, while discipline aims at a praiseworthy exertion of a person's capacities so as to accomplish something or to exercise self-control, from which an inner joy automatically arises.

Moreover, just as the law never effects anything better than the knowledge of sin, and not the strength for good action, just as little can punishment produce anything but an external prevention of sin, and not any turning away of the heart from evil, for punishment derives its power from fear or from bitter experience. In contrast, the turning of the heart toward goodness can be effected only by a love that is to drive out all fear and, with it, the whole power of punishment.

Discipline, in fact, produces a wholesome knowledge concerning the power of the will and a presentiment of freedom and inner order, this by aiming to keep all stirrings of the mind and heart within limits and thoughtfully self-possessed, forcing the lower drives of nature under the dominion of the higher ones. . . .

While discipline is something contrary to punishment, it is far from being that inactive calmness in which people simply observe the free development of their children, as so many unfortunately think they ought to do. Such people do not consider that although the Lord God has indeed placed heaven before our eyes simply that we may contemplate it and enjoy the blessings that flow to us from its powers and inspirations, God put us into the human world on this earth not merely to be spectators but to be lords in God's name, to be instruments by which God will fulfill what God's grace has intended for the human race, by having the stronger ones guide and train the weaker ones, and chiefly by having people of mature age guide and train the young. Now, this lordship and training is put into practice through discipline. If we are inactive we thwart the divine promises. . . . Thus, the more we are removed from that enslaving, tyrannical wretchedness which wills to be satisfied with what can be accomplished by punishment, on the one hand, and, on the other, the more we can keep ourselves free from that destructive illusion which presumes that our children could become something all by themselves, especially in what mostly pertains to us, so much the more must we recognize and feel what great value lies in exercising discipline.

However, we should not practice discipline simply as something applied to isolated cases, whenever we notice an excessive behavior in our children that must be tamed or an insufficiency that must be removed. Rather, the apostle recommends that, with the exception of admonition, we raise our children only in discipline. Accordingly, the educating that we do will be correct only if all we do toward our children, and all activity we impose on them or permit, will benefit them for and as discipline, and nothing else will be imposed on them or permitted. . . . This may sound strange and overly strict, but it is as true as it is gentle and loving, as will be shown upon closer observation. . . .

If parents, without waiting to see what inclinations and talents will develop in their children, or without taking into account those which have already developed, insist, in a headstrong fashion, upon restricting the children to something that lies on the particular path of life that the parents have taken and want to implant in them as their sole way of life so that they will come to resemble their parents as much as possible, do we not then bitterly complain about exposing the young people to an unchristian use of authority? Further, must it not be a source of annoyance and consternation to the young people themselves, when they are old enough to understand the conduct of those who reared them, to feel how much selfishness was mixed into the love of their parents and caretakers?

Or consider the case where a direction toward some definite course of life is already assigned to young people through the type of instruction and practice employed and through its content—this because it offers tempting worldly prospects, because various benefits and advantages can make it seem easy and attractive in comparison with others, and because at its goal wealth and honor beckon more than would be true in other directions. In such a case, too, do we not complain about the grievous sins of a totally unenlightened despotism, which dares to turn the natural inclination of children away from that for which God has created it and to cripple it by sheer force for the sake of an uncertain worldly profit? As for the young people, must they not also be induced to treat things they might be constrained to do with indifference, to undervalue them, and to respect only worldly gain as the highest good? If not that, then they must suffer shipwreck, with no little injury to their souls, in their reverence toward those they are supposed to follow.

Again, take the case where parents may even carefully notice the traces of natural talents that develop in their children but then overstrain all their resources, as if in a race to reach the goal as quickly as possible. This they do in order to have the pleasure of their children's being seen to surpass their peers so that their good upbringing may shine before the world, whether in their strict conduct or in the treasures of art and sciences they have acquired. They do it even at the cost to their children of all the joys of life and at the risk of their failing to achieve any permanent success. Oh, how this grieves us in our inner-most soul! How we do lament that even the most noble gifts of young people guided in such a manner can only lead to a vain, ignoble way of life!

My dear friends, if we now look at all these misguided ways, we cannot but feel how difficult it is to keep a clear conscience in this important matter! And how shall we keep our conscience intact? Certainly, we will do so only if we neither set before ourselves any worldly goal in the instruction and training of our children nor draw their attention to something worldly and external by which the goal is to be attained. Rather, quite apart from any other result they should simply strive for their children to recognize and understand what means they possess with which they will be able at some point to advance the work of God on earth and to bring these faculties under the control of their will both by learning to overcome laziness and distraction and by protecting themselves against getting passionately engrossed in some particular thing. What else is this than exactly what the apostle wants? Conducted in this way, whatever instruction and exercises are done will contribute to their discipline, and only by becoming disciplined in this way will they acquire a genuine good, namely, a solid fitness for any work of God that may arise for them to do in the course of their life.

Look, now, at how far the realm of discipline extends! Even in the social inter-action with their peers that we allow our children, even in the joys corresponding to their age that we grant them, our first concern must be that these things should contribute to their discipline. Of course, this demand too may seem particularly harsh if it implies that even those things are to become discipline that are meant to be recreation and free play. Still, children are educated quite as much through companionship and play as they are through instruction and exercises. . . .

Thus, my dear friends, it seems to me that the apostle was right in stating that for all activities of young people we are responsible to supervise and regulate, no other rule is necessary than that everything contribute to their discipline. Accordingly, the more nearly complete the education of our children would be, the fewer the situations wherein we would not know how to guide them. In addition, the more that education occurs within the whole network of our common life, without our needing to alter or interrupt its natural course, surely the more pleasing to God the work of our love and wisdom for these young people is bound to be and the more favorable the outcome.

Source: *The Christian Household: A Sermonic Treatise*, translated by Dietrich Seidel and Terrence N. Tice (Lewiston, N.Y.: Edwin Mellen, 1991), 56–64.

Horace Bushnell

Horace Bushnell (1802–1876), an American Congregationalist theologian, devotes an entire book to the theme of *Christian Nurture*, challenging the notion of children's need for radical conversion and highlighting instead the importance of gradually and lovingly nurturing their moral and spiritual lives.

Document 2–32

Christian Nurture

Where and how early does the work of nurture begin? . . . The true, and only true answer is, that the nurture of the soul and character is to begin just when the nurture of the body begins. It is first to be infantile nurture—as such, Christian; then to be a child's nurture; then to be a youth's nurture—advancing by imperceptible gradations, if possible, according to the gradations and stages of the growth, or progress toward maturity.

There is, of course, no absolute classification to be made here, because there are no absolute lines of distinction. A kind of proximate and partly ideal distinction may be made, and I make it simply to serve the convenience of my subject—otherwise impossible to be handled, so as to secure any right practical conviction respecting it. It is the distinction between the age of *impressions* and the age of *tuitional influences*; or between the age of *existence in the will of the parent*, and the age of *will and personal choice in the child.* . . .

Now the very common assumption is that, in what we have called the age of impressions, there is really nothing done, or to be done, for the religious character. The lack of all genuine apprehensions, in respect to this matter, among people otherwise intelligent and awake, is really wonderful; it amounts even to a kind of coarseness. Full of all fondness, and all highest expectation respecting their children, and having also many Christian desires for their welfare, they seem never to have brought their minds down close enough to the soul of infancy, to imagine that any thing of consequence is going on with it. What can they do, till they can speak to it? What can it do, till it speaks? As if there were no process going on to bring it forward into language; or as if that process had itself nothing to do with the bringing on of intelligence, and no deep, seminal working toward a character, unfolding and to be unfolded in it. The child, in other words, is to come into intelligence through perfect unintelligence! to get the power of words out of words themselves, and without any experience whereby their meaning is developed! to be taught responsibility under moral and religious ideas, when the experience has unfolded no such ideas! In the first stage, therefore, which I have called the stage of impressions, how very commonly will it be found that the parents, even Christian parents, discharge themselves, in the most innocently unthinking way possible, of so much as a conception of responsibility. . . .

Just contrary to this, I suspect, and I think it can also be shown by sufficient evidence, that more is done to affect or fix the moral and religious character of children, before the age of language than after; that the age of impressions, when parents are commonly waiting, in idle security, or trifling away their time in mischievous indiscretions, or giving up their children to the chance of such keeping as nurses and attendants may exercise, is in fact their golden opportunity; when more is likely to be done for their advantage or damage, than in all the instruction and discipline of their minority afterward. . . .

By these and many other considerations that might be named, it is made clear, I think, to any judicious and thoughtful person, that the most important age of Christian nurture is the first; that which we have called the age of impressions, just that age, in which the duties and cares of a really Christian nurture are so commonly postponed, or assumed to have not yet arrived. I have no scales to measure quantities of effect in this matter of early training, but I may be allowed to express my solemn conviction, that more, as a general fact, is done, or lost by neglect of doing, on a child's immortality, in the first three years of his life, than in all his years of discipline afterwards. . . . .

But I must speak, in closing, of what appears to be a somewhat general misconception, as respects the *aim* of Christian teaching in the case of very young children. According to the view I am here maintaining, it is not their conversion, in the sense commonly given to that term. That is a notion which belongs to the scheme that makes nothing of baptism and the organic unity of the house; that looks upon the children as being heathens, or aliens, requiring, of course, to be converted. But according to the scheme here presented, they are not heathens, or aliens; but they are in and of the household of faith, and their growing up is to be in the same. Parents therefore, in the religious teaching of their children, are not to have it as a point of fidelity to press them into some crisis of high experience, called conversion. Their teaching is to be that which feeds a growth, not that which stirs a revolution. It is to be nurture, presuming on a grace already and always given, and, for just that reason, jealously careful to raise no thought of some high climax to be passed. For precisely here is the special advantage of a true sacramental nurture in the promise, that it does not put the child on passing a crisis, where he is thrown out of balance not unlikely, and becomes artificially conscious of himself, but it leaves him to be always increasing his faith, and reaching forward, in the simplest and most dutiful manner, to become what God is helping him to be. . . .

There is, for the little ones, a more quiet way of induction. Show them how to be good, and then, when they fail, how God will help them if they ask him and trust in him for help. In this manner they will be passing little conversion-like crises all the time. Rejoice with them and for them as they do, only do not put them on the consciousness, in themselves, of what you seem to see. Let them be accustomed to it as a fact of experience that they are happy when they are right, and are right when God helps them to be, and that he always helps them to be when they put their trust in him. The Spirit of God is nowhere so dovelike as he is in his gentle visitations and hoverings of mercy over little children.

What is wanted is, to train them by a corresponding gentleness, and keep them in the molds of the Spirit. No spiritual tornado is wanted that will finish up the parental duties in a day; but there is to be a most tender and wise attention, watching always for them, and, at every turn or stage of advance, contributing what is wanted; enjoying their bright and happy times of goodness and peace with them, helping their weak times, drawing them out of their discouragements, and smoothing away their moods of recoil and bitterness; contriving always to supply the kind of power that is wanted, at the time when it is wanted. Very young children religiously educated, it will be remembered by almost every grown up person, have many times of great religious tenderness, when they are drawn apart in thoughtfulness and prayer. The effort should be to make these little, silent pentecosts and gentle openings God-ward sealing-times of the Spirit, and have the family always in such keeping, as to be a congenial element for such times; and to suffer no possible hindrance, or opposing influence, even should they come and go unobserved. Under such kind of keeping and teaching, God, who is faithful to all his opportunities, as men are not, will be putting his laws into the mind and writing them in the heart, and the prophet's idea will be fulfilled to the letter; it will not be necessary to go calling the children to Christ, and saying, know the Lord; for they will know him, every one, the least as the greatest, and the greatest as the least, each by a knowledge proper to his age.

Source: *Christian Nurture*, introduction by John M. Mulder (1861; reprint, Grand Rapids: Baker Book House, 1979), 233–236, 248, 381–384.

Twentieth Century

The selections here are from major figures of early and middle twentieth-century Christianity who, while not well known for their attention to children and childhood, write a few texts that helpfully reflect on them.

Karl Rahner

The following excerpt, from a short essay written in 1966 by the highly influential twentieth-century Catholic theologian Karl Rahner (1904–1984), articulates the beginnings of a complex theology of childhood and has influenced contemporary Catholic approaches to religious education. The essay affirms children's full humanity and integrity and explores the meaning of being "children of God."

Document 2–34

Ideas for a Theology of Childhood

First and foremost the child is *a human being* [*Mensch*]. Probably there is no religion and no philosophic anthropology which insists so manifestly and so strongly upon this point as one of its basic presuppositions as does Christianity; the point namely that the child is already a human being, that right from the beginning he is already in possession of that value and those depths which are implied in the name of a human being. It is not simply that he gradually grows into a person [*Mensch*]. He *is* a person. As his personal history unfolds he merely realizes what he already *is*. He does not seek about in a void of indefinite possibilities ranging from all to nothing, to see what he can achieve by chance. He is equipped as a human being, given his allotted task and endowed with grace to perform it right from the very outset with all the inexpressible value and all the burden of responsibility which this entails. And this, because it comes from God and because his personal history, in spite of being inextricably bound up with the history of the cosmos and of the life principle as a whole, is related with absolute immediacy to God himself, to his original creative and inalienable design for him. The child is the human being whom God has called by a name of *his own*, who is fresh and unique in each individual instance, never merely a "case," a particular application in the concrete of a general idea, *always* having a personal value of his own and therefore worthy to endure for ever. He is not an element in a process advancing and receding incalculably like the tides, but the unique explosion in which something final and definitive is constituted. The child is the human being who is, right from the first, the partner of God; he who opens his eyes only to keep that vision before him in which an incomprehensible mystery is regarding him; he who cannot halt at any point in his course because infinity is calling him; who can love the smallest thing because for him it is always filled with the all; he who does not feel the ineffable as lethal to him, because he experiences the fact that when he entrusts himself to it without reserve he falls into the inconceivable depths of love and blessedness. The child is the human being, therefore, who is familiar with death and loves life, does not comprehend himself but knows this, and precisely *in* this (provided only that he commits himself to the incomprehensible one in trust and love) has precisely understood all, because thereby he has come into God's presence. The child is a human being; the one, therefore, who always lives in a spirit of fraternity, leads a life of infinite complexity, knows no law other than that of endlessly journeying on and of great love and of that adventure which he can only recognize that he has come to the end of when he stands before God in his absolute infinitude. This is how Christianity views the human being and it sees all this already present in the child. And for this reason it protects the child while it is still in its mother's womb. It takes pains to ensure that the sources of life are not poured away upon the trifles of the lowlands of mere lust and desire. It has reverence for the child, for the child is a human being.

The child is a human being *right at the very outset....*

Childhood is, in the last analysis, a *mystery.* It has the force of a beginning and a twofold beginning at that. It is a beginning in the sense of the absolute origin of the individual, and also the beginning which plunges its roots into a history over which the individual himself has no control. Childhood has the force of a beginning such that the future which corresponds to it is not simply the unfolding of some latent interior force, but something freely sent and something which actually comes to meet one. And it is not until this future is actually attained to that the beginning itself is unveiled in its significance, that it is actually given and comes to its own realization, as a beginning which is open to the absolute beginning of God who is utter mystery, the ineffable and eternal, nameless and precisely as such accepted with love in his divine nature as he who presides over all things....

We have now reached a stage at which we can take a [further] point as the object of our enquiry. In a theology of children something must also be said about what it means to be a *child of God....* For our existence to be sound and redeemed at all, childhood must be an intrinsic element in it. It must be a living and effective force at the roots of our being if that being is to be able to endure even in the depths of the mystery. Childhood as an inherent factor in our lives must take the form of trust, of openness, of expectation, of readiness to be controlled by another, of interior harmony with the unpredictable forces with which the individual finds himself confronted. It must manifest itself as freedom in contrast to that which is merely the outcome of a predetermining design, as receptivity, as hope which is still not disillusioned. This is the childhood that must be present and active as an effective force at the very roots of our being....

Childhood is openness. Human childhood is infinite openness. The mature childhood of the adult is the attitude in which we bravely and trustfully maintain an infinite openness in all circumstances and despite the experiences of life which seem to invite us to close ourselves. Such openness, infinite and maintained in all circumstances, yet put into practice in the actual manner in which we live our lives, is the expression of [humanity's] religious existence. Now this infinite openness of existence which we maintain, and which is childhood in the developed sense, can have its counterpart in our experience in the form of an infinite and loving self-bestowal on God's part. . . . Now it is this openness that constitutes the very essence of childhood in the mature sense, and it is nothing else than what is called in theological language childhood of God, the grace of divine sonship in the *Son*.

Source: "Ideas for a Theology of Childhood," in *Theological Investigations*, translated by David Bourke (New York: Seabury Press, 1977), 8:33–50. Translation and spelling slightly updated.

Hans Urs von Balthasar

In this excerpt from a book written shortly before his death, Hans Urs von Balthasar (1905–1988), a Swiss Jesuit priest, meditates on the meaning of becoming like children.

Document 2–35

Unless You Become Like This Child

Jesus' attitude toward children is perfectly clear. No one will enter the Kingdom of God, which has come close to us in Jesus, unless he makes a turnabout and returns to the mentality of his beginnings. "Amen I say to you: Whoever does not receive the Kingdom of God like a child will not enter into it" (Mark 10:15). . . . We are confronted at one moment with a child chosen in the street, a child which the disciples want to keep away from Jesus as being insignificant and bothersome. To this Jesus objects: "Let the children come to me and do not hinder them" (Matt. 19:14). And suddenly we take a leap from this child to the unique child that Jesus himself is. And Jesus does not see in this any leap over an abyss but, on the contrary, a direct continuity, for "whoever welcomes such a child in my name, welcomes me" (Matt. 18:5). A child, therefore, is not merely a distant analogy for the Son of God: whoever turns with loving concern "to such a child" (any one out of hundreds of thousands), and does this, consciously or unconsciously, in the name of Jesus, of one mind with him—that person is welcoming the archetypical Child who has his abode in the Father's bosom. And because this Child cannot be separated from his abode, whoever turns to the most insignificant of children is, in fact, attaining to the ultimate, to the Father himself: "Whoever welcomes me is not welcoming me but him who sent me"

(Mark 9:27). In the context of the Gospel, however, what is intended here is not a form of social welfare but a profound mystery, rooted in the very being of Christ, whose identity is inseparable from his being a child in the bosom of the Father. The mystery of Christ is inseparable as well from . . . the interior turning in the direction of spiritual childhood, toward what Jesus calls "birth from the spirit" or "rebirth from above" or, simply, "birth from God" (John 1:13). This is what he repeatedly stresses as being the express condition for entering into the Kingdom of God: "Whoever is not born again cannot see the Kingdom of God," "cannot enter into the Kingdom of God" (John 3:3, 5).

Source: *Unless You Become Like This Child*, translated by Erasmo Leiva-Merikakis (San Francisco: Ignatius, 1988), 9–11. Translation and punctuation slightly updated.

Karl Barth

The Swiss Reformed theologian Karl Barth (1886-1968) devotes a section of his greatest work, the *Church Dogmatics*, to issues regarding children and parents, reexamining the duty to honor and obey parents in relationship to his understanding of God.

Document 2–36
Church Dogmatics

When the command of God [to honor your father and mother] is heard in this sphere, it means that the children are directed to assume a very definite attitude of subordination in relation to their parents. But the fact that the latter are *parentes*, i.e., those who are responsible for their physical generation, is only the fact in consequence of which these are the two human beings who in the manner suggested are set over their children, and to whom the children are invited to adopt this attitude. It is not with this physical relationship as such that the command is concerned, but with a certain oversight and responsibility with regard to the children which this physical relationship implies for the parents. This oversight and responsibility does not belong to the physical but, broadly speaking, to the historical order. It consists in the fact that the parents are really the elders in relation to the children, and that they are their particular elders, those who have lived before and longer than they, and are therefore wiser and more experienced. And in relation to their children they do not merely represent their own knowledge and experience but that conveyed to them by their own predecessors. The command is concerned with this twofold distinction of the parents. That children must subordinate themselves to the latter means that they are to regard and comport themselves as those who are less experienced and less wise. They must give heed to them. They must learn from them as those who have greater knowledge. They are not by nature their property, subjects, servants or even pupils, but their apprentices, who are entrusted and subordinated to them in order that they might lead them into the way of life. The children must be content to accept this leading from their parents. In general outline, this is what the command of God requires of them. . . .

The necessity and divine compulsion of this demand is rooted in the fact that from the standpoint of children parents have a Godward aspect, and are for them God's primary and natural representatives. The superiority which entitles them to this specific respect from their children really consists in their mission, not in any quality inherent in them, nor in their character as physical *parentes* (which, although it gives rise to vital emotional relationship to them on the part of the children, has nothing to do with this respect), nor in any particular moral quality possessed by them (which may again produce a special attachment on the part of the children but not necessarily the respect required by the command). The superiority which demands this respect consists rather in the correspondence of their parenthood to the being and action of God. It does not belong to them either as a physical or as a moral quality. It is the brightness of a light which falls and rests upon them from outside, from above—the light of the free grace of the Creator turned towards them as parents. Because of this divine grace, their children are challenged to submit themselves to them. They would necessarily be resisting the grace of God if they refused to do this. We can clarify this basis of the command along various lines.

No human father, but God alone, is properly, truly and primarily Father. No human father is the creator of his child, the controller of its destiny, or its saviour from sin, guilt and death. No human father is by his word the source of its temporal and eternal life. In this proper, true and primary sense, God—and He alone—is Father. He is so as the Father of mercy, as the Father of His Son, of the Lord Jesus Christ. But it is of this Father's grace that, in correspondence to His own, there should exist a human fatherhood also. And the fact that the latter may symbolise the fatherhood of God in a human and creaturely form is what lends it its meaning and value and entitles it to respect. . . .

God alone is true Wisdom, and therefore the true Teacher, Guide and Educator. But the fact that He is this primarily and properly gives competence to earthly fathers and mothers who, with their modest and problematical experience, wisdom and knowledge, are set as "elders" over their children. They are charged to imitate God's action, and in so far as they do so in all honesty, the children are summoned to honor God by honoring their parents, by being content to accept this action of their parents. . . .

Without ceasing to be authority, [parental authority] is now for the first time brought into clear light by being measured against the authority of God in which it is rooted. What the true honoring of God is, as fulfilled in the honoring of parents, has now become a question which must be answered not merely by considering the relationship of the child to his parents, but also by considering his own immediate relationship to God. The honoring of parents is not abolished;

on the contrary it is now genuinely demanded. But it has acquired the character of a free and individual decision. It is now clear and operative that the authority of the parents is that of a spiritual power, and therefore that the obedience which children owe to them can consist only in a spiritual act and attitude.

Source: *Church Dogmatics*, edited by G. W. Bormiley and T. F. Torrance (Edinburgh: T. & T. Clark, 1961), vol. III/4, pp. 243–250. Translation and spelling slightly revised.

Howard Thurman

Howard Thurman (1900–1981) was a Baptist pastor, theologian, and educator, and the first African American to be the dean of Marsh Chapel at Boston University. His writings influenced Martin Luther King, Jr. and other leaders of the civil rights movement. In this short essay, he echoes the concern of many Christians since the early church for children as among the poor and vulnerable.

Document 2–37

Let Us Remember the Children

Let us bring before our spirits the children of the world! The children born in refugee camps where all is tentative and shadowy, except the hardness of the constant anguish and anxiety that have settled deep within the eyes of those who answer when the call is "Mommy" or "Daddy." . . . the numberless host of orphans corralled like sheep in places of refuge where the common conscience provides bread to eat, water to drink, and clothes to cover the nakedness and the shame . . . the inarticulate groan of those who are the offspring of hot lust held in its place by exploding shells and the insanity of war—these are the special wards of the collective guilt of the human race, the brood left behind when armies moved and the strategy of war made towns into a desolation. The illegitimate children of peacetime, who have no peg upon which to hang the identity of meaning, whose tender lives are cut adrift from all harbors of refuge and security—these are choked by a shame not of their making and who look upon their own existence with heartache and humiliation. The children in families where all love is perishing and they cannot even sense the awareness that their own lives are touched by love's gentleness and strength. The sick children who were ushered into the world as if their bodies were maimed and twisted by disaster which was their lot in some encounter before the fullness of time gave them birth among the children of men. Those who played and romped on the hillside but now will never walk again. Those who once enjoyed the beauty of sky and earth, who looked upon everything about them with unsullied wonder, but who are closed in darkness never to see again. The children of the halting, stumbling mind in whom some precious ingredient is lacking, leaving in its place the vacant mindless stare. The children of great and good fortune whose lives have been always surrounded by the tenderness of affection and the gentleness of understanding, across whose paths no shadows have fallen and for whom life is beautiful and free—

What we bring before our presence, our Father, we share with Thee in our time of quiet and prayer. We thank Thee for the gift to do this, the strange power inherent in our spirits. Grant that what we see in this way may not leave us untouched but may inspire us to be active, responsive instruments in Thy hands to heal Thy children, to bless Thy children, to redeem Thy children. Amen.

Source: "Let Us Remember the Children," in *A Strange Freedom: The Best of Howard Thurman on Religious Experience and Public Life*, edited by Walter Earl Fluker and Catherine Tumber (Boston: Beacon, 1998), 306–307.

NOTES

1. For studies on children and childhood in the Bible and history of Christianity, see, for example: O. M. Bakke, *Childhood in Early Christian Traditions*, translated by Brian P. McNeil (Minneapolis: Fortress, 2005); Marcia J. Bunge, ed., *The Child in Christian Thought* (Grand Rapids: Eerdmans, 2001); J. T. Carroll, "Children in the Bible," in *Interpretation* 55.2 (April 2001): 121–134; Danna Nolan Fewell, *The Children of Israel: Reading the Bible for the Sake of Our Children* (Nashville: Abingdon, 2003); vol. 17 (2002), entitled *Gottes Kinder*, of the *Jahrbuch für Biblische Theologie*; Philip Greven, *The Protestant Temperament: Patterns of Child-Rearing, Religious Experience, and the Self in Early America* (New York: Alfred A. Knopf, 1977); Peter Müller, *In der Mitte der Gemeinde: Kinder im Neuen Testament* (Neukirchen-Vluyn: Neukirchener Verlag, 1992); *The Child in the Bible*, edited by Marcia J. Bunge, Terence E. Fretheim, and Beverly Roberts Gaventa (Grand Rapids: Eerdmans, 2008); and Diana Wood, ed., *The Church and Childhood* (Oxford: Blackwell, 1994).

2. Recent studies in the areas of ethics and systematic and practical theology include, for example: Herbert Anderson and Susan B. W. Johnson, *Regarding Children* (Louisville: Westminster/John Knox, 1994); Pamela Couture, *Seeing Children, Seeing God: A Practical Theology of Children and Poverty* (Nashville: Abingdon, 2000); Marva Dawn, *Is It a Lost Cause? Having the Heart of God for the Church's Children* (Grand Rapids: Eerdmans, 1997); Dawn DeVries, "Toward a Theology of Childhood," *Interpretation* 55.2 (April 2001): 161–173; Kristin Herzog, *Children and Our Global Future: Theological and Social Challenges* (Cleveland: Pilgrim, 2005); Timothy P. Jackson, ed., *The Morality of Adoption: Social-Psychological, Theological, and Legal Perspectives* (Grand Rapids: Eerdmans, 2005); David H. Jensen, *Graced Vulnerability: A Theology of Childhood* (Cleveland: Pilgrim, 2005); Kathleen Marshall and Paul Parvis, *Honouring Children: The Human Rights of the Child in Christian Perspective* (Edinburgh: Saint Andrews Press, 2004); Joyce Ann Mercer, *Welcoming Children: A Practical Theology of Childhood* (St. Louis: Chalice, 2005); Bonnie Miller-McLemore, *Let the Children Come: Reimagining Childhood from a Christian Perspective* (San Francisco: Jossey-Bass, 2003); Jürgen Moltmann, "Child and Childhood as Metaphors of Hope," *Theology Today* 56.4 (2000): 592–603; Deusdedit R. K. Nkurunziza, "African Theology of Childhood in Relation to Child Labour," in *African Ecclesial Review* 46.2 (2004): 121–138; Trygve Wyller and Usha S. Nayar, eds., *The Given Child: The Religions' Contribution to Children's Citizenship* (Göttingen: Vandenhoeck & Ruprecht, 2007); Karen-Marie Yust, *Real Kids, Real Faith: Practices for Nurturing*

Children's Spiritual Lives (San Francisco: Jossey-Bass, 2004). We do not include here the wide Christian theological and ethical literature of the last thirty years on marriage and families, which often touches on children. For a fuller discussion of current trends, see Marcia J. Bunge, "The Child, Religion, and the Academy: Developing Robust Theological and Religious Understandings of Children and Childhood," and John Wall, "Childhood Studies, Hermeneutics, and Theological Ethics," both in the *Journal of Religion* 86.4 (October 2006).

3

Islam

AVNER GILADI

What exactly do we mean by *Islam* when referring to "The Child in Islam"? Do we mean the beliefs and practices of the about 213 million Muslims, who constitute 88 percent of the population of Indonesia, making it the largest Islamic country in the world? Or those of the about 380 million Muslims living in the Indian subcontinent (India, Pakistan, and Bangladesh)? Is it the religious world view of the 73 million Muslims in Egypt, of the 70 million Iranians, the 33 million Moroccans or the 65 million Muslims in Nigeria that we have in mind? Is it the Islam of the 26 million inhabitants of Saudi Arabia or that of the members of the Muslim communities in Great Britain (1.5–2 million), in France (between 3 and 6 million) or in the United States (between 5 and 8 million)? In other words, what, if any, is the common denominator uniting approximately 1.3 billion Muslims who are spread out today over five continents, and who between them reveal all the differences likely to be found between such disparate population groups as city dwellers, villagers, and nomads? In what way can we call *Muslim* communities that are geographically so remote from each other, have adopted Islam at different times and through different historical processes during more than 1,400 years of Islamic history, and often incorporated local social customs and cultural characteristics into their new faith?

The Arabic word *Muslim* refers to a person who by accepting *Islam* ("Obedience") surrenders himself/herself to "God One (*Allahu ahad*), God the everlasting Refuge,"[1] as revealed through the message and life of his Prophet Muhammad (570?–632 CE). It is this purely monotheistic concept that has become the cornerstone of the "Great Tradition" of Islam as it first emerged in Mecca and Medina (in northwest Arabia), in the seventh century CE, propounded by the Prophet of Islam and his adherents, and then, with the sweeping Islamic conquests that followed, developed in the new centers of religious learning in Iraq, Syria, Iran, Central Asia, Egypt, North Africa, and Spain throughout the classical period (the first three to four centuries) of Islamic history.

The Qur'an (lit., "recitation"), the Islamic scripture, is the foundation of this "Great Tradition." Preserved, according to Islamic theology, as the eternal word of God, in a "heavenly tablet"–the source of all monotheist sacred books–the Qur'an was revealed, in installments, in the Arabic language to the Prophet Muhammad through the mediation of the angel Jabra'il (or Jibril–Gabriel). It was then disseminated, still in the Prophet's lifetime, by way of recitation, among the inhabitants of the Arab peninsula, as they converted to Islam. With the spread of Islam in the Middle East and beyond, the Qur'an began to be taught to the newly converted as an essential part of their socialization into the new religion.

It was probably the Prophet Muhammad himself who initiated the assembling of individual Qur'anic revelations and the editing of their written texts. This task was accomplished, by the middle of the seventh century CE, under the supervision of his first successors (caliphs).

The Qur'an is composed of 114 chapters (sing. *sura*), each consisting of verses (sing. *aya*). According to the Islamic tradition, some ninety of the *suras* were revealed to Muhammad while he was preaching in Mecca, the city where he was born and raised; the rest–in Medina, where he settled after his emigration (*hijra*) from Mecca in 622 CE.

Heavily relying on biblical heritage, the Qur'an lays the foundations for later formulations of the Islamic creed and the emphasis it puts on the belief in one, eternal, and omnipotent God, merciful and compassionate; in Muhammad as "the seal of the [monotheist] prophets," God's last messenger to humankind, in general, and to the Arab people, in particular, and in the resurrection of the dead which leads to the Last Judgment and either eternal bliss in Paradise or everlasting torment in Hell.

The moral and legal rules the Qur'an contains form the basis for the Islamic law (*sharīʿa*) as it consolidated during the four centuries following the revelation of the Qur'an to Muhammad. A central part is taken up by the ethical rules of family life in the spirit of Islam, including the attitudes Muslims ought to adopt toward children.

When they found they needed to adjust the teaching of the Qur'an to different social, cultural, and historical circumstances after the death of Muhammad and began interpreting the holy text accordingly, Muslim scholars developed one of the most fertile branches of Islamic thought and writing, namely, Qur'an exegesis (*tafsir*). Tafsir emerged side by side with the literature of the tradition, the hadith, that brings together sayings attributed to the Prophet Muhammad and his close companions as well as descriptions of the Prophet's actions and of events that occurred during his lifetime. With the canonization of six collections of sound (*sahih*) traditions in the ninth century CE, they, particularly the two compiled by Muslim Ibn al-Hajjaj al-Naysaburi and Muhammad Ibn Isma'il al-Bukhari, became an integral part of the Islamic sacred books, ranking only one degree below the Qur'an, the word of God, itself.

Derived, in principle, from the Qur'an and hadith, it is the shari'a, the Islamic religious law, that sets out the rules and regulations governing the lives of Muslims. In fact, the interpretative activity of Muslim jurists, no doubt influenced also by pre-Islamic local, regional, and imperial systems of law, came to play an important role in the construction of the Islamic legal system. This process took place in various centers in the Middle East, in the classical period of Islamic history, within the circles of disciples of commanding jurists who all differed somewhat in their attitude toward the sources of Islamic law. Four of these circles of jurisconsults, namely, the Hanafis, Malikis, Shafi'is, and Hanbalis, became recognized as the authoritative schools of Sunni Islamic law.

Like Judaism, Islam is an *orthopraxis*, which means that the proper behavior and way of life of each believer is given priority over his or her *orthodoxy*, proper faith. Islamic religious law is therefore comprehensive: it covers all aspects of human behavior and it is in the heart of the life of individual Muslims, determining to a great extent the pace and nature of communal life, even for those members who do not fully subscribe to the beliefs and practices of the faith.

The spread of Arabic as the lingua franca of Islam, the foundation of certain common types of educational institutions (mainly the *kuttab* and the *madrasa* for elementary and advanced education, respectively), and the "journeys in search of knowledge" between the great centers of learning, a highly popular custom among medieval Muslim scholars, helped establish the "Great Tradition" and a corpus of written learned texts that it encompassed, in addition to the Qur'an: Qur'an exegesis, prophetic tradition and law, theology (*kalam*), mystical theories (*tasawwuf*), biography, and hagiography. In its diversity and complexity reflecting the contribution of thousands of individual thinkers, each, again, inspired by various sources of theory and practice, this "Great Tradition" emerged as a uniting force for Muslim scholars everywhere, and through them, for the masses of believers.

When, during the first centuries of Islamic history, selective borrowings from ancient Indian, Persian, and Greek sources in the domains of the arts, philosophy, and sciences were adapted and absorbed into the Islamic worldview, they added a further dimension to Islam as civilization.

Social historians and particularly historians of the family in medieval Islamic contexts find they are up against an almost total lack of archival sources, from which they would normally extract concrete aspects of every day life, or documents relating how people actually practiced their beliefs. Instead, they are left mainly with theoretical, normative, or purely literary texts. In this chapter we shall deal with concepts of childhood and attitudes toward children as we find them reflected in these sorts of texts, the distillation of the collective efforts of the spiritual-intellectual elites in urban centers of the Muslim Middle East in premodern times. Once incorporated into the "Great Tradition" of Islam, these texts served, on top of local traditions, as a source of inspiration for Muslims in various places and times, including, of course, our own.

To be sure, the ideas and images of childhood we encounter in these texts were not created in a vacuum but are the product of particular historical circumstances. At the same time, they manifest common literary conventions or strict rules of scholarly argumentation that make it difficult to ascertain the authenticity of the historical details they contain. And, of course, given the patriarchal nature of Muslim societies, these ideas and images of childhood were exclusively articulated by men. Therefore, their main importance for us lies in the normative-educational role they have played throughout Islamic history and still, to a certain extent, play today. Altogether this means that, while focusing on Islamic cultural elements in rearing and educating children in premodern Muslim societies, the picture that this chapter draws can only be partial: missing will be the huge variety of the more practical aspects of children's lives and adult-child relations in these societies.

Concepts and Images of Childhood in Islamic Culture

In Islamic ethics the principal purpose of marriage is the fathering, bearing, and rearing of children; its fulfillment is an obligatory religious mission (Docs. 3-2, 3-3, 3-4). In legal terms a child has the status of a minor, *saghir*, until the onset of physical maturity and the ensuing ability to control his or her own affairs. According to this criterion, Muslims as young as nine or ten years old could be regarded as adults. When a child is late to show signs of physical maturity, fifteen was generally regarded as the dividing line between majority and minority, for boys and girls alike (Doc. 3-26). Thus, theoretically, childhood was a fairly short period in comparison with childhood in industrial societies today. However, the popularity of the traditional beginners' school (*kuttab*) as a framework of elementary education in premodern Muslim societies (Doc. 3-24) may well have helped delay the initiation of children into the labor force for some years.

Despite the social marginality of small children and women in the patriarchal-patrilineal societies of the medieval Middle East (where the Islamic ideas of childhood first developed), Muslims in the past were familiar with the concept of childhood, which for them formed a distinct stage in the human life cycle, and they saw psychological bonds between parents and their offspring as universal. Childhood was seen as a unique period that had its own gradual process of development and that differed in physical and psychological terms from other periods in life. Arabic has a rich vocabulary to designate not only childhood but also the various subdivisions and the many phenomena that made up this gradual process. There were also specific terms that expressed ideas and rules of conduct to help channel parental instincts. Methods of childrearing, medical-hygienic treatment (Docs. 3-18, 3-19), and education (Docs. 3-21, 3-22, 3-23, 3-24) emerged together with a system of rites of passage through which children were incorporated into their own societies (Doc. 3-20). And laws were put in place to safeguard the lives of children, ensure their proper care and welfare, and secure their rights (Docs. 3-27, 3-28).

The great number of references to childhood in Arabic-Islamic sources, particularly the fact that the subject was often dealt with in special chapters and treatises, is in itself an indication of the attention Muslim thinkers paid to childhood and the importance they gave it. Concern for the welfare of children, their rights, and the treatment they deserve is mirrored in the Qur'an and hadith as well as in ethical and legal literature. Similarly, medical writings, some of them devoted to pediatrics and related topics, are based on a relatively rich and varied body of knowledge regarding the uniqueness of childhood, the physical development of children, the diagnosis and treatment of childhood diseases, and child psychology (Doc. 3-18).

These and other literary sources also reflect close psychological and emotional relations between parents and children. The fact that a genre of consolation treatises for bereaved parents flourished in the Muslim Middle East in the late Middle Ages, when so many children fell victim to the Black Death, may be seen in itself as a sign of the emotional intensity of such relationships (Docs. 3-41, 3-42). However, given the vestiges of pre-Islamic patriarchal concepts of childhood that Islam contains in its ethical and legal system, the picture is more complex. In general, attitudes toward childhood were not unambiguous. Children were regarded, on the one hand, as pure and innocent creatures; on the other, there existed an overall image of the child as an ignorant creature, full of desires and with a weak and vulnerable spirit, and of childhood as a period of suffering. Female children were discriminated against, not only in everyday life but also in theoretical (legal, educational) terms (Doc. 3-13). Even male children were sometimes counted as no more than a source of familial-tribal economic strength and political power (Doc. 3-8). Moreover, practices such as corporal punishment (Docs. 3-22, 3-24, 3-28) child marriage (Doc. 3-31), child labor, and slavery, although falling into line with Islamic worldviews (and those of other ancient and medieval cultures) strike us today as going against the child's well-being.

The majority of the sayings in Arabic-Islamic sources that show understanding and sympathy for children refer to male children, always more desirable in patriarchal-patrilineal societies than females. That female children were discriminated against from birth is shown, inter alia, by the efforts the Qur'an and later religious scholars made to counteract this practice, the latter, for instance, by praising fathers who are clearly devoted to their daughters and by denouncing the displeasure that led fathers to reject newborn females or even wish them dead (Docs. 3-11, 3-13). Occasionally, jurists made attempts to close (or, at least, to minimize) the gap between female and male children. Thus, for instance, while the common view was that the urine of only female children was unclean, and that therefore when an adult's clothes had been moistened by it they should be fully washed before prayer, Ibn Qudama, the Hanbali jurist and theologian (d. 1223 CE in Damascus), claimed that the urine of all children was impure. Statements, though admittedly rare, to the effect that the prayer of an intelligent girl is as valid as that of her male counterpart should also be mentioned here. Some scholars urged Muslims to grant their daughters a basic religious and moral training not only at home but also in special institutions where female children were given some form of elementary education.

Among the authors of consolation treatises for bereaved parents, 'Abd al-Rahman al-Sakhawi (d. in Cairo in 1497 CE)—who, by the way, included in his huge biographical collection a whole volume of women's biographies with no fewer than 1,075 entries—seems to have been particularly sensitive to the impact of female children's deaths and quotes an impressive number of narratives that pertain to bereaved mothers.

While following their fellow physicians in supporting equal physical treatment for girls, medieval Muslim scholars justified gender differences whenever questions of socioreligious nature, such as childhood rites, education, and child marriage, arose. Here, in spite of remarkable individual differences among orthodox authorities and the shifting boundaries they reflect between, on the one hand, ancient patriarchal norms and, on the other, Islamic moral, more egalitarian values, we find an overwhelming inclination to adjust to the social structure and the male dominance that is at the heart of it.

This survey as well as the selection of texts is based on the assumption that Islamic attitudes toward children are best expressed by the shari'a, the comprehensive Islamic system of law and ethics. Viewing children, on the whole, as vulnerable, dependent creatures, Islamic law supplies various rules for the protection of their bodies, their psychological well-being, as well as their properties. In some cases more attention is given to the child's benefit than to the interests of his or her parents.

Under Judeo-Christian influence and as a response to the challenges of structural changes in Arabic tribal society, the Qur'an shows a special sensitivity toward the vulnerable in society, including children. Here, too, with the normative-ethical significance they entail, Qur'anic statements about children came to underpin later Islamic morality and law. They mainly concern such issues as adoption (Doc. 3-16), breastfeeding (Doc. 3-27), orphans (or rather fatherless children) (Doc. 3-14), and prohibition of infanticide (Doc. 3-5, 3-6).

Compilers of hadith collections dedicated whole chapters, sometimes special treatises, to the themes of children and childhood. These include rites of passage (Doc. 3-20), child education (Doc. 3-21), the religious status of children, children's games, and the treatment of fatherless children (Doc. 3-15). Particularly interesting are those chapters which, through hadith reports, set examples for the psychological attitudes Muslims should adopt when dealing with children. Thus, we find chapters on the parents' duties to treat all their children with justice and equity and to behave well towards their daughters (Doc. 3-11). Others highlight sympathy, loving care, and compassion, and recommend close physical contact, for instance, by telling parents to carry children in their arms, and smell and kiss them; and instructing them how to dandle infants and play with them. The Prophet Muhammad is often shown as treating children properly (Docs. 3-9, 3-10). According to one of the most revealing traditions in this regard, quoted by Abu Hamid Muhammad al-Ghazali (d. 1111 CE), a caring father who in the middle of the night gets up to warm his children with his own clothes is more virtuous than a fighter in a holy war. No wonder, then, that Salah al-Din al-Ayyubi, who led the Muslim armies in the reconquest of Jerusalem from the Crusaders in 1187 CE, and the epitome of *jihad* (fight against infidels), is also depicted as a loving father to his seventeen children.

The collections of Islamic positive law discuss various aspects of children's status within the family and society as a whole. I briefly mention some of the legal and ethical themes that best reflect the jurists' concepts of childhood and their attitudes toward children.

Who Is a Muslim? Any child born to Muslim parents is regarded as Muslim. Since a prophetic tradition stipulates that Islam "overcomes" other religions, this is true also when only one parent is Muslim. According to another legal opinion, the child "always follows" his father's faith.

The Right to Paternity: From the child's right to an established paternity (*nasab*), crucial in patrilineal families, follow rights of inheritance, guardianship, and maintenance. Out of concern for the children's well-being, Islamic law placed few difficulties in the way of recognizing their legitimacy. Also, by instigating a "waiting period"—a period of abstention from sexual relations imposed on a widow or a divorced woman—Qur'anic law intended to help ascertain the biological father in cases of divorce or the father's death.

Adoption: Inspired by the Qur'an's negative attitude toward the formal adoption of children, the shari'a regarded this mechanism as one literally based on a "lie," that is, as an artificial tie between adults and children, devoid of any real emotional relationship, as a cause of confusion where lineage was concerned, and thus a possible source of problems regarding marriage between members of the same family and regarding inheritance.

Parents' Obligations toward Their Children: Fathers, whom Islam regards as ideally discreet and compassionate, retain the power of guardianship (*wilaya*) over their children, who are formally attributed to them, not to their mothers. This involves guardianship over their property and over their person, including overall responsibility for their physical care, socialization, and education. Mothers, viewed as ideally full of pity and gentle, are entrusted with the care and control of their children for the first few years of their life and, in case of dispute (e.g., after divorce), have the right to lactation and custody during these years. If a child's mother dies, the responsibility for raising him or her falls upon other female relatives, preferably—and exceptionally in Islamic law—in the mother's line (Doc. 3–28).

Childhood Rites: In Islam, as in other civilizations, birth and the subsequent transitions from one stage in life to another are marked by various ceremonies. The purpose of these ceremonies is "to enable the individual to pass from one defined position to another which is equally well-defined."[2] The first stages of incorporating the newborn child into the larger human society, and particularly into the Muslim community, are symbolized by a series of childhood rites, most of them of tribal, pre-Islamic origin that Islam adopted after having discarded the pagan elements they contained. By performing these rites, the father confirms his fatherhood in public and thus his responsibility toward the child (Doc. 3–20).

Child Education: According to medieval Muslim thinkers, character training should start in early childhood, when the child's soul is still pure and impressionable and good character traits can be engraved upon it as "upon a smooth stone." At this stage particularly, parents should protect children from harmful influences in their social environment. In writings inspired by Greek ethical thought, Islamic moral education is guided by the ideal of balancing the psychic forces of desire and anger (Docs. 3–22, 3–23). While fathers are called upon to inculcate the basic principles of faith as soon as the child starts talking, the "age of discernment" between good and evil (*tamyiz*), that is, six or seven years, was generally perceived as the appropriate time to begin systematic education, primarily toward performing the religious commandments, and to send children to the *kuttab* for their elementary education (Doc. 3-24).

Children and Ritual: Muslim jurists debate whether children, as long as they are not legally capable, should be obliged to pray, to fast during Ramadan (the ninth month of the Islamic calendar during which Muslims refrain, from morning to evening, from eating, drinking, smoking, and from having sexual relations), to pay legal alms, to make a pilgrimage to Mecca (*hajj*; incumbent on every adult believer, male and female, at least once in one's life), or even whether children may be allowed to serve as leaders (*imams*) in public prayer. Even though they are aware of the special religious status of children, there is no agreement among jurists on these questions. A common argument is that in the case of children the observance of religious commandments, particularly prayer and the fast of Ramadan, can serve an educational rather than a formal-religious function (Doc. 3-33).

Protection and Interdiction: As they are subject to legal disability or interdiction children, like the insane, do not have the capacity to sign a contract, do not owe full obedience to criminal law and, therefore, cannot be punished as Muslims who are sane and come of age (Doc. 3-28).

Children's Sexuality: From the Islamic legal point of view, the sexuality of infants had little significance. Male children, when young, could be dressed, for instance, in silk clothes more typical of girls, until adults noticed their budding sexuality. Similarly, hadith and law compilations recommend separating children in bed when they have reached the age of ten and having adults avoid washing children of the other sex as soon as they are seven years old. They even consider any form of physical contact between a mother and her six-year-old daughter a form of incest, reflecting an awareness of the latent sexuality of children approaching maturity (Docs. 3-29, 3-30).

Child Marriage: That Islamic law allows child marriage seems to contradict its general protective attitude toward children. The shari'a in this regard may have been following the social practice of the Muslim core countries in the seventh through tenth centuries CE. The minors involved were predominantly girls, and marriage contracts were made up for them while their ages ranged anywhere between birth and sexual maturity, although consummation of marriage was not allowed before the child reached the age of puberty (Doc. 3-31).

Children and War: The Prophet Muhammad is said not to have allowed the fourteen-year-old Ibn 'Umar to join the Muslim fighters in the battle of Uhud, near Medina (625 CE), but then, two years later, agreed to include him among the warriors of the Battle of the Trench (627 CE). While reaffirming the age of fifteen as the criterion of majority, this hadith reflects a general Islamic objection to the participation of children in war. The prohibition, attributed to the Prophet, against the killing of an enemy's children (and women) in time of war is also important here (Docs. 3–34, 3–35).

Contemporary Middle Eastern thinkers, as well as ethnographers and anthropologists, have drawn attention to the significance of Islamic and of local and customary attitudes toward children, of patterns of parent-child relations in patrilineal families, and of the traditional methods of formal education in Muslim countries as influential factors in their societies. This is in spite of the fact that from the first half of the twentieth century we see shari'a law and traditional educational systems being replaced in many Muslim countries by new ones in the emerging nation-states and under the impact of the West.

On the basis of ethnographic and anthropological works carried out in various regions of the Muslim Middle East in the twentieth century, Elizabeth Warnock Fernea observes the following general patterns of childrearing and education:

Early indulgence of babies and demand breast-feeding . . . plus a great deal of affectionate behavior toward the baby, primarily from the mother but also from the father, older siblings, and other relatives. . . . Physical closeness and indulgence are combined with early toilet training, before the age of one year; either long-term breastfeeding or abrupt weaning may occur, depending on when the next child is born into the family. The arrival of a new sibling usually signals the end of the period of indulgence for the older child.

Banishment from the mother's breast also means the beginning of socialization into specific gender roles, cultural values, and the division of a child's labor according to sex and age. . . .

Socialization for other important societal norms of behavior began almost as soon as a child was conscious of others. These included respect for food, for religion, for the kin group, hospitality to guests and, above all, respect for and obedience to the authority of the father. . . . Religion involved a respect for food as well as learning to pray and understand religious duties as Muslims. . . . The type of punishment varied from group to group. Some parents argued that corporal punishment was not condoned by the Qur'an, but most were in full accord with the "spare the rod and spoil the child" approach favored in some western times and places.

Ritual events in the life of the child also played a part in socialization. Primary among these were ceremonies surrounding birth and naming; circumcision, for all boys and some girls; graduation from Qur'anic school, particularly for boys; and finally marriage. . . .

Religious socialization took place not only in the home (for boys and girls) and in the mosque (for boys) but also in the Qur'anic school, or *kuttab*. A knowledge of the Qur'an was deemed necessary for a child's religious development. . . . Most parents, even the poorest, tried to send their sons and sometimes their daughters to a *kuttab* for some period of time. . . . Boys traditionally spent more time in Qur'anic schools than girls, but there were always exceptions.[3]

The awareness of the psychological and sociocultural significance of rearing and educating children and of their status in society is reflected, inter alia, in a relatively new tendency among Muslims writing their autobiographies to devote whole chapters, sometimes even entire works, to their childhood.

Pro-natal Attitudes

The pro-natal attitude of Islam is inspired by those Qur'anic verses describing God not only as responsible for the initial creation of the universe but also as continually involved in the origination of every single creature. Implicit in these verses is the idea that by fathering and giving birth to children Muslims contribute to the continued existence of the human race, the lord of creation.

The sample of Qur'anic verses is followed here by extracts from two later texts, which elaborate on the theme of the religious advantages of having children: first, *Kitab adab al-nikah* (The Book of the Etiquette of Marriage), one of the forty treatises comprising *Ihya' 'ulum al-din* (Revival of the Religious Sciences) by Abu Hamid Muhammad al-Ghazali, a prominent theologian, jurist, and mystic who was born in Tus in northeast Iran in 1058 CE and died there in 1111 CE; second, *Tuhfat al-mawdud bi-ahkam al-mawlud* (A Present for the Beloved on the Rules concerning the Treatment of Infants) by Muhammad Ibn Qayyim al-Jawziyya, a Hanbali theologian and jurist, who lived in Damascus and died there in 1350 CE. Dedicated exclusively to questions connected with children, this treatise deals particularly, from a legal-ethical point of view, with the rites carried out by Muslims on newborn children. As in many genres of Islamic religious writing, *Tuhfat al-mawdud*'s text is composed mainly of reports (hadiths) of the Prophet Muhammad's sayings and deeds. A short invocation of God by a Shi'ite scholar of the tenth century CE closes the section.

Document 3–1

The Qur'an on the Divine Creation

Sura 40: verse 67

It is He who created you of dust
then of a sperm-drop,
then of a blood-clot,
then He delivers you as infants,
then that you may come of age,
then that you may be old men—
though some of you there are who die before it—
and that you may reach a stated term;
haply you will understand.

Sura 42:49–50

To God belongs the Kingdom of the heavens and the earth;
He creates what He will;
He gives to whom He will females,
and He gives to whom He will males
or He couples them, both males and females;
and He makes whom He will barren.
Surely He is All-knowing, All-powerful.

Sura 7:189

It is He who created you out of one living soul,
and made of him his spouse
that he might rest in her.
Then, when he covered her, she bore a light burden
And passed by with it;
But when it became heavy
They cried to God their Lord, "If Though givest us
a righteous son, we indeed
shall be of the thankful."

Sura 16:72

God has appointed for you of yourselves wives,
and He has appointed for you of your wives
sons and grandsons, and He has provided you
of the good things. What, do they believe
in vanity, and do they disbelieve
in God's blessing?

Source: English translation by Arthur J. Arberry, *The Koran Interpreted* (London: George Allen & Unwin; New York: Macmillan, 1971).

Document 3–2

Al-Ghazali on the Purposes of Marriage

There are five advantages to marriage: procreation, satisfying sexual desire, ordering the household, providing companionship, and disciplining the self in striving to sustain them.

Procreation: The first advantage—that is, procreation—is the prime cause, and on its account marriage was instituted. The aim is to sustain lineage so that the world would not want for humankind. . . .

The eternal powers of the Almighty were not incapable of creating beings from the beginning without tilling or coupling. But wisdom decreed the ordering of causes and effects together with the lack of need to demonstrate the power of God to complete the wonders of creation and to fulfill what the Divine Will decreed beforehand; thereby the word was fulfilled as decreed by the pen (Qur'an 96:4).

To bring forth a child is a four-faceted intimacy which is the original reason for encouraging it even after being safe-guarded against excessive desire, so that no one wants to meet God as a celibate. The first: to conform to the love of God by seeking to produce the child in order to perpetuate mankind. The second: to earn the love of the Prophet of God by increasing those in whom he can be glorified. The third: to seek the blessing of the righteous child's invocation after him [i.e., after the death of the father]. The fourth: To seek intersession through the death of the young child should he precede his [father's] death.

As for the first facet: . . . God Almighty has created the pair; He has created the male organ and the two ovaries, as well as the sperm in the sheath; He has prepared for it [the sperm] in the ovaries, arteries and ducts, and created the womb as a depository for the sperm; He has endowed both the male and the female with desire. These deeds and instruments bear eloquent testimony to the design of their creator and declare their purpose unto those imbued with wisdom. This would be the case [even] if the Creator had not revealed the design through His prophet in the statement "Marry and multiply"; how [much more] if He had openly declared the matter and revealed the secret! Everyone who refrains from marriage neglects tilling, wastes away the seed, does not use the prepared instruments which God has created, and is a violator of the aim of nature as well as the wisdom implied in the evidences of creation foreordained upon these organs by divine writ, unexpressed in letters or voices—writ which can be read by every [person] who has divine insight to understand the intricacies of everlasting wisdom. . . .

The one who marries is seeking to complete what God has desired, and the one who abstains wastes away what God detests to have wasted.

Source: Abu Hamid Muhammad al-Ghazali, *Ihya' 'ulum al-din* (Cairo: Mu'assasat al-Halabi, 1967), 2:31–32. English translation by M. Farah, *Marriage and Sexuality in Islam: A Translation of al-Ghazali's Book on the Etiquette of Marriage from the Ihya* (Salt Lake City: University of Utah Press, 1984), 53–55.

Document 3–3

Ibn Qayyim al-Jawziyya on the Religious Advantages of Having Children

The desirability of wanting to have children

From Anas [Ibn (the son of) Malik]: "The Messenger of God, *may God bless and save him*, used to command the state of marriage and strongly forbid celibacy. He would say: 'Marry the fond and fertile women, for I will exceed through you in number the other prophets on the Day of Resurrection.'" . . .

From 'A'isha: "The Messenger of God, *may God bless and save him*, said: 'Marriage is part of my way of conduct (*sunna*), and whoever keeps away from my way of conduct is not of my followers. Marry! for I will exceed through you in number the other nations.'"

From Abu Hurayra, from the Prophet, *may God bless and save him*: "The believer will be promoted one level up [in Paradise]. He will then ask: 'O Lord, how is it that I deserve this?' and [God] shall reply: 'It is thanks to the prayers your child has prayed on your behalf, begging forgiveness for your sins, after your death.'"

From Mu'awiya Ibn Qurra, from his father: "A man used to come to the Prophet, *may God bless and save him*, along with one of his sons. Once, the Prophet asked him: 'Do you love your son?' The man replied: 'O Messenger of God, I wish God loved you as much as I love him.' After a while in which the Prophet, *may God bless and save him*, had not seen the child, he asked: 'How is the son of so and so?' and they told him: 'O Messenger of God, the child died.' The Prophet said to the father: 'Will not you be pleased to know that no matter which gate of Paradise you will arrive at, you will find your son waiting for you next to it?' Someone then asked: 'Does this apply to him alone, O Messenger of God, or to all of us?' The Prophet replied: 'To all of you.'"

. . . Related from Abu Sa'id al-Khudri: "The Messenger of God, *may God bless and save him*, addressed women and said: 'Any of you who will lose three children will have these children serving as a screen protecting her from the fire of Hell.' Then a woman asked him: 'What about [women who lose] two?' The Prophet, *may God bless and save him,* replied: 'Also [she who loses] two [will be protected]. . . . ' "

From Abu Hurayra: "A woman brought her son [to the Prophet] and said: 'O Prophet of God! Pray to God on his behalf, for I have already buried three!' The Prophet asked: 'Did you bury *three*?' She replied: 'Yes, I did.' Then he said to her: 'You have protected yourself greatly from the fire of Hell, for children benefit their parents both when they outlive their parents, and when they die before them.' "

. . . From Abu Hurayra: "The Prophet, *may God bless and save him*, said: 'When a man dies, all his deeds come to an end, except for three: an ongoing charity [an endowment that continues to produce revenue], a contribution to knowledge for the people's benefit, and a devout child who prays for him [after his death].' "

Source: Ibn Qayyim al-Jawziyya, *Tuhfat al-mawdud bi-ahkam al-mawlud* (Bombay: Sharafuddin & Sons, 1961), 5–8. English translation by Yaron Klein.

Document 3–4
A Plea for a Child

Sa'id Abu 'Abdallah: "Any of you who awaits a child for a long time should say: 'O my Lord, leave me not solitary, though Thou art the best of inheritors' (Qur'an 21: 89; trans. Arberry). My actual expression of gratitude to You falls short of my intentions. But if You give me an offspring of good nature, either male or female, who will keep me company away from loneliness, and with whom I will find refuge from solitude, then I will be able to express my gratitude for Your complete grace, O Giver, O Great-one, O Sublime.' "

Source: Abu Ja'far Muhammad al-Kulayni, *al-Furu' fi al-kafi* (Teheran: Dar al-Kutub al-Islamiyya, 1971), 6:7. English translation by Yaron Klein.

The Sanctity of Children's Lives

In pre-Islamic time children were seen by Arabs as the physical property of their father, for him to do with as he saw fit. The Qur'an totally rejects this view and instead asserts children have rights of their own, and regards their life as sacred. The Qur'an forbids infanticide as a grave sin, whether it was motivated by want and destitution, by the disappointment fathers felt at the birth of a daughter, or by the wish (of Arab pagans) to sacrifice their most beloved and precious children to their gods.

Though the Qur'anic verses that refer to infanticide are unclear on this point, it seems reasonable to assume that female infanticide was more common than male infanticide, not only in pre-Islamic Arabia but also later. Thus, Qur'an commentators like 'Abdallah Ibn 'Umar al-Baydawi of Shiraz (Southwest Iran, d. 1286 CE), quoted below, interpreted the relevant Qur'anic verses, even those that mention "children" in general as victims, in the light of this reality.

Document 3–5

Denunciation of Infanticide in the Qur'an

Sura 6:151

Say: "Come, I will recite what your Lord has
forbidden you: that you associate not
anything with Him, and to be good to your
parents, and not to slay your children
because of poverty; We will provide you and them;
and that you approach not any indecency
outward or inward, and that you slay not
the soul God has forbidden, except by right.
That then He has charged you with; haply you
will understand."

Sura 17:31

And slay not your children for fear of poverty;
We will provide for you and them;
surely the slaying of them is a grievous sin.

Sura 6:137

Thus those associates of theirs have decked out
fair to many idolaters to slay their children,
to destroy them, and to confuse their religion
for them.

Sura 6:140

Losers are they who slay their children in
folly, without knowledge, and have forbidden
what God has provided them, forging against God;
they have gone astray, and are not right-guided.

Sura 16:57–59

And they assign to God
daughters; glory be to Him!—

and they have their desire;
and when any of them is given the good tidings of
a girl, his face is darkened
and he chokes inwardly, as
he hides him from the people because of the evil
of the good tidings that
have been given unto him,
whether he shall preserve it in humiliation, or
trample it into the dust.

Sura 60:12

O Prophet, when believing women come to thee,
swearing fealty to thee upon the terms that
they will not associate with God anything,
and will not steal, neither commit adultery,
nor slay their children, nor bring a calumny
they forge between their hands and their feet,
nor disobey thee in aught honourable, ask God's
forgiveness for them; God is All-forgiving,
All-compassionate.

Sura 81:1–3, 8–9, 14

When the sun shall be darkened,
when the stars shall be thrown down,
when the mountains shall be set moving . . .
when the buried infant shall be asked for what sin she was
    slain . . .
then shall a soul know what it has produced.

Source: English translation by Arthur J. Arberry, *The Koran Interpreted* (London: George Allen & Unwin; New York: Macmillan, 1971).

Document 3–6

A Commentary on Qur'an 17:31

And slay not your children for fear of poverty: for fear of scarcity. When [this verse states that] they [that is, the unbelieving Arabs] killed their children, this means that they buried their [newborn] daughters out of fear of poverty. God now prohibits this and promises to them the necessities of life by saying:

We will provide for you and for them. Surely the slaying of them is a grievous sin: a grievous transgression, since through it is brought about the cessation of reproduction and the extinction of the species. . . .

Source: 'Abdallah Ibn 'Umar al-Baydawi, *Anwar al-tanzil wa-asrar al-ta'wil* (Cairo: Mustafa al-Babi al-Halabi, 1955), 1:290. English translation by H. Gätje, *The Qur'an and Its Exegesis: Selected Texts with Classical and Modern Muslim Interpretation* (Berkeley: University of California Press, 1976), 198.

Parental Love

Several Qur'anic verses, while highlighting the mother's role in bearing children and raising them, recognize and praise parental love in general. Others depict children, much like possessions, as a temptation for nonbelievers and believers alike.

Many hadith reports further elaborate on the theme of parental love. Thus, *Kitab al-'iyal* (The Book of the Family) by 'Abdallah Ibn Abi al-Dunya (born in Baghdad in 823 and died there in 894 CE), a prolific writer of edifying literature, devotes some twenty out of his work's thirty-five chapters to various aspects of childhood, including the psychological attitudes Muslims should adopt when dealing with children. *Anba' nujaba' al-abna'* (Reports on Sons of Noble Breed), a collection of anecdotes on the childhood of famous Muslims, by Muhammad Ibn Zafar (who lived most of his life in twelfth-century Sicily) also offers us much material in this regard.

Document 3–7

The Qur'an on Parental, Particularly Maternal, Love and Care

Sura 17:24

And lower to them [to your parents] the wing of humbleness
out of mercy and say,
"My Lord,
have mercy upon them,
as they raised me up
when I was little."

Sura 31:14

And We have charged man concerning his
parents—his mother bore him in weakness
upon weakness, and his weaning was in
two years—"Be thankful to Me, and to
thy parents; to Me is the homecoming." . . .

Sura 28:7–13

So We revealed to Moses' mother, "Suckle him,
then, when you fearest for him, cast him into
the sea, and do not fear, neither sorrow, for
We shall return him to thee, and shall appoint him
one of the Envoys."
So then the folk of Pharaoh picked him out
to be an enemy and a sorrow to them. . . .
Said Pharaoh's wife, "He will be a comfort
to me and thee. Slay him not; perchance he will
profit us, or we will take him for a son." . . .
On the morrow the heart of Moses' mother
became empty, and she wellnigh disclosed him
had We not strengthened her heart, that she might be
among the believers;
and she said to his sister, "Follow him,"
and she perceived him from afar, even while
they were not aware.
Now We had forbidden to him aforetime
to be suckled by any foster-mother; therefore
she said, "Shall I direct you to the people of a
household who will take charge of him for you,
and look after him?"
So We returned him to his mother, that she might be
comforted and not sorrow, and that she might know
that the promise of God is true; but most of
them do not know.

Source: English translation by Arthur J. Arberry, *The Koran Interpreted* (London: George Allen & Unwin; New York: Macmillan, 1971).

Document 3–8

The Qur'an on Children as an Earthly Temptation

Sura 3:116

As for the unbelievers, their riches shall not
avail them, neither their children, against God;
those are the inhabitants of the Fire,
therein dwelling forever.

Sura 8:28

. . . [A]nd know that your wealth and your children
are a trial, and that with God is
a mighty wage.

Sura 18:46

Wealth and sons are the adornment of the present world;
but the abiding things, the deeds of righteousness,
are better with God in reward, and better in hope.

Sura 19:77

Hast thou seen him who disbelieves in Our signs and says:
    "Assuredly
I shall be given wealth and children?"

Sura 34:37

It is not your wealth nor your children
that shall bring you nigh in nearness to Us,
except for him who believes, and does
righteousness; those—there awaits them
the double recompense for that they did,
and they shall be in the lofty chambers
in security.

Sura 63:9

O believers, let not your possessions
neither your children divert you from
God's remembrance; whoso does that,
they are the losers.

Sura 64:14–15

O believers, among your wives and children
there is an enemy to you; so beware of them.
But if you pardon, and overlook, and if you
forgive, surely God is All-forgiving,
All-compassionate.
Your wealth and your children are
only a trial; and with God is
a mighty wage.

Source: English translation by Arthur J. Arberry, *The Koran Interpreted* (London: George Allen & Unwin; New York: Macmillan, 1971).

Document 3–9

The Prophet Muhammad and Other Muslims
as Examples for Love and Care for Children

Narrated Ishaq Ibn Isma'il, from . . . Abu Hurayra: "Al-Aqra' Ibn Habis saw the Prophet, *may God bless and save him*, kissing [his grandson] Husayn. Al-Aqra' then said to him: 'I have ten children, and I have never kissed any of them.' The Prophet replied: 'He who has no mercy shall receive no mercy.'"

Narrated Sa'id Ibn Muhammad al-Jarami, from . . . 'Abdallah Ibn Burayda: "I heard Abu Burayda saying: 'While the Prophet, *may God bless and save him*, was preaching to us, [his grandchildren] al-Hasan and al-Husayn entered wearing red shirts, walking and stumbling. The Messenger of God got off the pulpit, picked them up, placed them in front of him and said: "God is right, *Your possessions and your children are a test* (Qur'an 8:28; trans. Arberry). I looked at these two children walking and stumbling, and I could not restrain myself until I interrupted my speech and picked them up."'"

Narrated 'Abd al-Rahman Ibn Salih, from . . . 'Abdallah: "It would happen that when the Prophet, *may God bless and save him*, was praying, [his grandsons] al-Hasan and al-Husayn would climb on his back. When he wanted to sit down, he would hold his hand like that behind his back, so that they would not fall."

Narrated Yusuf Ibn Musa, from . . . Ya'la al-'Amiri: "The Prophet, *may God bless and save him*, opened the mouth of al-Husayn and kissed it. Then he said: 'May God love whoever will love Husayn and Hasan, who both are the dearest grandchildren.'"

Narrated 'Uthman Ibn Abi Shayba, from . . . 'A'isha: "Usama [Ibn Zayd] stumbled over the doorstep and injured his face. The Messenger of God, *may God bless and save him*, said to me: 'Stop his bleeding,' but I was repelled by it, so the Messenger of God began sucking [the blood] and removing it from Usama's mouth. Then he said: 'If Usama was a girl, we would have adorned him and dressed him up beautifully so that people would want to marry him.'"

Narrated 'Ali Ibn Ya'qub, from . . . Abu Kamil, client of [the Umayyad Caliph] Mu'awiya: "I came in to Mu'awiya, together with Khalid Ibn Yazid Ibn Abi Sufyan, and there was Mu'awiya kneeling on all fours, a rope around his neck held by his son, playing with him as a child. We greeted him, and he was embarrassed because of me, and said: 'I heard the Messenger of God, *may God bless and save him*, saying: 'Whoever has a child should behave with him like a child.'"

Narrated 'Ali Ibn al-Ja'd, from . . . Abu 'Uthman al-Nahdi: "Al-Munsafaq saw [the second caliph] 'Umar Ibn al-Khattab, *God be pleased with him*, kissing his son and said: 'A caliph kisses his son? If I were a caliph I would not have kissed my son.' Then 'Umar said: 'It is not my fault that God, *blessed and exalted is He*, has taken compassion out of you. God, *to Him belong might and majesty*, is compassionate only to his compassionate slave.'"

Source: 'Abdallah Ibn Abi al-Dunya, *Kitab al-'iyal* (Al-Mansura: Dar al-Wafa, 1997), 178–179, 193, 195, 197, 199, 208. English translation by Yaron Klein.

Document 3–10

Anecdotes on Parental Love

From 'Ubaydallah Ibn 'Abbas, *may God be pleased with him*: "I was once in the residence of the Messenger of God, *may God bless and save him*, when his daughter Fatima, *may God be pleased with her*, came to him crying. The Prophet said to her, 'May your father be a ransom for thee, why are you crying?' and she replied: 'My children al-Hasan and al-Husayn went out, and I do not know where they spent the night.' He said: 'The one who created them is [even] more kind to them than you are.' Then he prayed, asking God to protect the two, and said: 'My Lord, whether they are in the sea or on land, please save and protect them.' Soon after, the angle Gabriel (Jibril), *may peace be upon him*, came and informed him that the two were in the enclosure of the Banu al-Najjar, and that God, *exalted is He*, had assigned an angel to guard them. The Prophet, *may God bless and save him*, got up and went to the enclosure, and there the two were sleeping hugging each other. The angel assigned to them had spread one of his wings and protected them with the other. The Prophet bent over and kissed them, until they woke from their sleep. He then took al-Hasan on his right shoulder and al-Husayn on his left shoulder and said: 'By God, I will treat you with honor as God, *blessed and exalted is He*, has.' [On his way back] Abu Bakr al-Siddiq [the future first caliph, successor of Muhammad] met the Prophet and said: 'O Messenger of God, hand me one of the boys, so I will lessen the burden from you.' The Prophet, *may God bless and save him*, said: 'What excellent mount they have! And what excellent riders they are! And their father ['Ali, the Prophet's cousin and son-in-law, the future fourth caliph] is even better than they are!' until he reached the mosque." . . .

I heard that Salma bint Sakhr, the mother of Abu Bakr al-Siddiq, *may God be pleased with him*, nursed her son for four whole years. When she finally wanted to wean him, she smeared her nipples with some juice pressed from an aloe tree. When Abu Bakr tasted it, he said: "Mother, wash your breasts!" She then replied: "My little son, my milk has gone sour, and its taste has become spoiled," to which the child responded: "I tasted this spoiled taste before I began sucking, so wash your breasts! However, if you have [decided to] become stingy with me regarding your milk, I hold myself back." She then hugged and kissed him, sucking in his saliva, and began to dandle him. . . .

Muhammad [Ibn Zafar], *may God forgive him*: "We were told that the parents of Abu Mahfuz Ma'ruf Ibn Fayruz al-Karkhi [a leading mystic, sufi, of the early ninth century CE in Baghdad], were Christian Persians. When Ma'ruf was a child, his parents sent him to someone to teach him their scripture. That person used to tell him: 'Say father, son and wife [sic].' But Ma'ruf would only say 'One God.' The instructor would beat him and then go back to teaching him, but Ma'ruf would not say anything but 'One God.'

One day the instructor had beaten him so severely that Ma'ruf ran away. His parents were unable to control themselves, and almost died from grief over him. They would say: 'If we would only find him, no matter what religion he adheres

to, we will follow him in his faith.' Meanwhile, still wandering around, Ma'ruf
met 'Ali Ibn Musa al-Radi [d. 818 CE, the eighth of the twelve imams recognized
by the Imami Shi'a], who was at that time a young man, and embraced Islam
because of him. Ma'ruf took him as his sponsor and served him for a long time,
until eventually he returned to his family. One night, he knocked on his parents'
door. They asked: 'Who is it?' Ma'ruf replied, 'It is Ma'ruf.' Before they opened
the door they asked him: 'What is your religion?' And he replied: 'I embrace the
religion of Islam.' Then they said: 'Come on in. We embrace your religion.' They
embraced Islam, and God reunited them to the right path."

Source: Muhammad Ibn Zafar, *Anba' nujaba' al-abna'* (Cairo: Dar al-Sahwa, n.d.), 66, 82,
85–86. English translation by Yaron Klein.

The Ethics of Childrearing

That Islamic law (shari'a) allowed male Muslims to marry up to four women simultaneously, to repudiate their wives at their will, and to beget children with their
own female slaves–this was bound to create, in past Muslim societies, situations
in which fathers would discriminate between children born to their different wives
or slaves. Moreover, the patriarchal-patrilineal structure of the family in these
societies put newborn female children in a lower position vis-à-vis males from
the moment of birth. Out of their sensitivity to the weaker members of society,
the Qur'an and in particular numerous hadith reports encourage Muslims to treat
children–males and females alike–with indiscriminate justice and impartiality, to
readily accept newborn girls and to support orphans and abandoned children. As
fathers served as their children's guardians, guaranteeing their social and economic
protection, it was the loss of a father, not of a mother, that Islamic ethics saw
as the main problem relatives and other Muslims should help solve. Islamic law
recommends adoption de facto as a possible solution without, however, its full
legal implications.

Document 3–11

Treating Children with Indiscriminate Justice and Impartiality

The example of the Prophet Muhammad and his companions
Narrated Ishaq Ibn Ibrahim from . . . al-Hasan: "Once, while the Messenger of
God, *may God bless and save him*, was talking to his companions, a child entered
and walked up to his father in the corner of the group. The father patted the

child on the head, and put him on his right leg. Shortly after, the daughter of the same man entered and walked towards her father. When she reached him, he patted her on the head, and sat her on the ground. Then the Messenger of God said: 'Why don't you seat her on your other leg?' The father picked her up and placed her on his other leg. The Messenger of God then said: 'Now you have acted indiscriminately.'"

Narrated 'Ali Ibn al-Ja'd, from . . . Ibrahim: "They [the Prophet's companions] would prefer to treat their children with equality, even in the number of kisses."

Narrated Ahmad Ibn Jami, from . . . 'A'isha: "A woman carrying her two daughters came to me begging, and I did not have anything except for a single date. I gave it to her, and she divided it between her two daughters without eating any of it herself. Then she got up and left. When the Prophet, *may God bless and save him*, came in I told him about the event and he said: 'Whoever suffers anything because of these girls, will be protected from the fire of Hell, for the girls will serve as a shield for him or her.'"

'Ali Ibn al-Ja'd, from . . . Abu Hurayra, from the Prophet, *may God bless and save him*: "The best of you in God's eyes is the best in terms of morality, and the best of you is the one who is most excellent to his daughters and wives."

Narrated Khalid Ibn Khidash from . . .—I think—Anas Ibn Malik: "The Messenger of God, *may God bless and save him*, said: 'Whoever supports two or three girls, or two or three sisters, on the Day of Judgment I and he will be like that,' and he stretched out his index finger together with the one next to it."

Source: 'Abdallah Ibn Abi al-Dunya, *Kitab al-'iyal* (Al-Mansura: Dar al-Wafa, 1997), 113, 138, 144, 145. English translation by Yaron Klein.

Document 3–12

Greeting Children

Religious scholars differ regarding the question of greeting children. Some of them argue that one should not salute them. . . . Others say: "It is better to greet them."

From Anas Ibn Malik: "I was once among children when the Messenger of God, *may God bless and save him*, appeared and greeted us."

Source: Muhammad Ibn Mahmud al-Asrushani, *Jami' ahkam al-sighar* (Cairo: Dar al-Fadila, n.d.), 1:213. English translation by Yaron Klein.

Document 3–13

Reprehensibility of People Being Displeasured with Having Girls

God, *exalted is He*, said: "To God belongs the Kingdom of the heavens and the earth; He creates what He will; He gives to whom He will females, and He gives to whom He will males or He couples them, both males and females; and He makes whom He will barren. Surely He is All-knowing, All-powerful" (Qur'an 42:49–50; trans. Arberry).

God, *exalted is He* . . . said that whatever is the [gender of the] child He has decided to grant any husband and wife, it is His decision. Suffice it [as punishment] for believers who display abhorrence with what God has given them [i.e., female offspring], to be subjected to God's hatred. Thus [in the above-mentioned verse], He has mentioned [newborn] females first. Some say that He did so in order to improve their fate, so that parents will welcome their position. Another, better, idea is that He mentioned girls first because, according to the context of the sentence, He does whatever He wants, not what parents want. Parents, more often than not, wish to have male offspring; God, *may He be praised,* informed them that He creates whatever He wills. Therefore He began with mentioning the kind [of child] that He wills and parents do not.

In my view there is another aspect involved here: God, *exalted is He,* has advanced the status of women by moving up those whom the Arabs before Islam [at the time of the Jahiliyya] had placed in the back, to the point that people used to bury their daughters alive at birth. [As though He is saying:] "Those who, according to your worldview, belong to this base group, are placed at the head by Me." Notice how He has made the females [in the verse] indefinite and the males definite. He redressed the disadvantageous position of femininity by giving it precedence [in the verse], and the disadvantage of [males] being put back by presenting them in the definite form. . . . Then, in the final part of the verse, when He mentioned the two kinds together He placed the males at the head, in order to give to each of the two genders its share in terms of position [in the verse].

The intention [here] is that being resentful for having female offspring belongs to the moralities of the pre-Islamic time, which God, *exalted is He,* had reproached saying: "When any of them is given the good tidings of a girl, his face is darkened and he chokes inwardly, as he hides him from the people because of the evil of the good tidings that have been given unto him, whether he shall preserve it in humiliation, or trample it into the dust. Ah, evil is that they judge!" (Qur'an 16:58–9; trans. Arberry). . . .

From Ibn 'Abbas: "The Messenger of God, *may God bless and save him,* said: 'Every Muslim who will have two daughters and shall be kind to them as long as he is with them and they are with him will enter Paradise on account of them.'"

God, *exalted is He*, said regarding women: ". . . [O]r if you are averse to them, it is possible you may be averse to a thing, and God set in it much good" (Qur'an 4:19; trans. Arberry). This applies to girls also. The believer may benefit from them both in this world and in the world to come. In disapproval of [parents'] dislike for them, it would be suffice to say that in this way they abhor that which God favors and has granted to his believer.

Salih Ibn Ahmad [Ibn Hanbal], said: "Whenever a girl was born to him, my father would say: 'The prophets themselves were fathers of girls.'"

Ya'qub Ibn Bakhtan, said: "Seven girls were born to me. Each time one of them was born, I went to Ahmad Ibn Hanbal. He would then say to me: 'O Abu Yusuf, know that the prophets themselves were fathers of girls.' His words would relieve my worries."

Source: Muhammad Ibn Qayyim al-Jawziyya, *Tuhfat al-mawdud bi-ahkam al-mawlud* (Bombay: Sharafuddin & Sons, 1961), 10–13. English translation by Yaron Klein.

Document 3–14

The Qur'an on the Treatment of Fatherless Children

Sura 2:83

And when We took compact with the Children of Israel:
"You shall not serve any save God;
and to be good to parents, and the near kinsmen;
and to orphans, and to the needy;
and speak good to men, and perform the prayer,
and pay the alms."

Sura 2:177

It is not piety, that you turn your faces
to the East and to the West.
True piety is this:
to believe in God, and the Last Day,
the angles, the Book, and the Prophets,
to give of one's substance, however cherished,
to kinsmen, and orphans,
the needy, the traveler, beggars,
and to ransom the slave,
to perform the prayer, to pay the alms. . . .

Sura 90:12–16

And what shall teach thee what is the steep?
The freeing of a slave,
or giving food upon a day of hunger
to an orphan near of kin
or a needy man in misery. . . .

Sura 107:1–3

Hast thou seen him who cries lies to the Doom?
That is he who repulses the orphan
and urges not the feeding of the needy.

Sura 4:2

Give the orphans their property, and do not
exchange the corrupt for the good; and devour
not their property with your property; surely
that is a great crime.

Sura 6:152

And that you approach not the property of
the orphan, save in the fairer manner, until
he is of age. . . .

Sura 4:8

And when the division [of an inheritance] is attended by
kinsmen and orphans and the poor,
make provision for them out of it,
and speak to them honourable words.

Sura 8:41

Know that, whatever booty you take, the
fifth of it is God's, and the Messenger's,
and the near kinsman's, and the orphans',
and for the needy, and the traveller. . . .

Source: English translation by Arthur J. Arberry, *The Koran Interpreted* (London: George Allen & Unwin; New York: Macmillan, 1971).

Document 3–15

The Prophet Muhammad on the Proper Attitude toward Fatherless Children

Narrated Ahmad Ibn Jamil, from . . . the Messenger of God, *may God bless and save him*: "Whoever wipes [caresses] the head of an orphan with his hand God shall wipe him [in the Hereafter]. Each hair his hand touches stores for him [a reward] for his good deeds. Whoever is kind to an orphan who is with him, I and he shall be in Paradise as these two," and he joined his two fingers.

Source: 'Abdallah Ibn Abi al-Dunya, *Kitab al-'iyal* (Al-Mansura: Dar al-Wafa, 1997), 341–342. English translation by Yaron Klein.

Document 3–16

The Qur'an on Adoption

Sura 33:4–5

God has not assigned to any man two hearts within
His breast; nor has he made your wives, when you
divorce, saying: "Be as my mother's back," truly
your mothers, neither has He made your adopted sons
your sons in fact. That is your own saying, the
words of your mouths; but God speaks the truth, and
guides on the way.
Call them after their true fathers; that is more
equitable in the sight of God. If you know not
who their fathers were, then they are your brothers
in religion, and your clients. There is no fault
in you if you make mistakes, but
only in what your hearts premeditate. God is All-forgiving,
All-compassionate.

Source: English translation by Arthur J. Arberry, *The Koran Interpreted* (London: George Allen & Unwin; New York: Macmillan, 1971).

Document 3–17

On the Treatment of Foundlings

"Foundling" [Arabic: *laqit*], designates a child who is found on the road, in the desert or at the threshold of a mosque, and whose parents are unknown. . . .

Unlike other articles found on the road, picking up a foundling is better than leaving it. [Moreover,] if one suspects that the child might die, one is obliged to pick him up.

A man who takes in a foundling, no one has the right to take it away from him, as he has established the right of keeping it by precedence. If someone else comes and takes the child away from him, it should be returned to him.

Source: Muhammad Ibn Mahmud al-Asrushani, *Jami' ahkam al-sighar* (Cairo: Dar al-Fadila, n.d.), 1:219–220. English translation by Yaron Klein.

Physical and Psychological Treatment of Children

Muslim doctors attached much importance to pediatrics and compiled special pediatric treatises, apparently not a common practice in the Hellenistic world and unknown in medieval Europe before the thirteenth century. Relying on Greek medical sources, in addition to their own experience, Muslim physicians possessed rich and

diversified knowledge that implied a keen understanding of some of the unique characteristics of children from both physical as well as psychological points of view.

Medical-hygienic writings and the child-rearing manuals by Muslim doctors
deal with a wide range of themes, from the diagnosis and the treatment of children's
diseases to the hygienic care of the newborn infant. Here feeding of children in
general and breast-feeding in particular constitute a central theme, as do questions
connected with wet nurses and the milk. This is in addition to instructions on how
to treat infants immediately after birth, how to prepare their cradle, how to wash
and swaddle them; advice on how to calm weeping children, on teething, on how
to treat children when they start walking and talking, and recommendations on how
to amuse them and introduce them to the company of other children.

Together with observations on how children develop psychologically, we find
authors discussing such theoretical issues as the relationship between innate
dispositions and acquired characteristics, how natural dispositions might change,
and the like.

Part of the material included in early Arabic pediatric writings, such as *Siyasat
al-sibyan wa-tadbiruhum* (The Book of Childrearing) by Ibn al-Jazzar of Qayrawan
(in today's Tunis), a famous physician of the tenth century CE, was later "Islamized,"
popularized, and adapted, as we see in *Tuhfat al-mawdud bi-ahkam al-mawlud* by
Ibn Qayyim al-Jawziyya.

Document 3–18

Arabic Pediatrics: Extracts from Ibn al-Jazzar's *Siyast al-sibyan*

Introduction
Child rearing and caring is a field of great value and importance. When I examined writings [by ancient Greek physicians], however, I could not find a single
work that was fully and comprehensively dedicated to the topic, although I did
come across [different bits of] valuable information on this subject scattered
throughout certain books in various places. As a result, some people have access
to only certain parts of the information and remain oblivious to other parts.
Other people are able eventually to arrive at full understanding, but the way they
do so is not the easiest and simplest.

Since the situation is as described, I decided to collect all [those different
bits of information] that lie scattered in the various works, and compile them in
this book, much like a craftsman arranges jewels together to create a magnificent crown, or strings them into a beautiful necklace. To the compiled material
I added whatever I knew of Galen's aphorisms on the subject. The book contains

twenty-two chapters. . . . I rounded the book off with the most important rules from the science of medicine, as it deals with how to maintain the well-being of healthy bodies and how to cure the illnesses of sick bodies. Thus I highlight how children's natural health can [best] be preserved and how to take care of them, and I describe what is the correct way for a nursing woman to take care of her body so that her milk will be of good quality and will easily be digested in their bodies. I further delve into the subject by outlining the symptoms of diseases that can appear in children from the moment they are born until they reach maturity, and how to cure them. . . . We ask God to make us successful and to direct us aright [in our endeavor] and for His help so that we may achieve our aim. He is our benefactor and worthy our praise.

From chapter 1: On taking care of children following their birth
We say: We should begin with the care of the child the moment he leaves the womb. The umbilical cord should be cut at a distance of four fingers from the umbilicus. [Immediately] after birth the child should be moderately covered with salt, so that the skin will become firm and strong. There are people who mix it [the salt] with *sadhij* leaves, *qust* wood, *sumac* berries, fenugreek grain, and wild thyme, all of which well pounded. . . . After the salt has been put on the child, one should rub it over his whole body, except for the mouth and nose. It should be left on his body until he becomes less dirty. Then he should be washed and cleaned with lukewarm water. His nostrils, mouth, and ears should be gently cleaned, his rectum should be opened with the small finger, and all that is in it should be removed. Then, a few drops of oil should be dropped into his eyes. His umbilicus should be tied and gently twisted together, and a shred immersed in oil should be put above it. The child should be wrapped well in clean tatters . . . to protect him from the cold. When the umbilicus comes off after three or four days, one should scatter over it ashes of burnt mole [?] and of a burnt calf's hamstring or burnt lead pulverized in a liquid, then coated on the place.

After care of the newborn has been initiated with the steps we have indicated, and he has been wrapped in a cloth as we have described, he should be fed with milk, for milk is the food that is best suited for him. God has made both nipples ready at the same time. . . . And if you put a nipple in the mouth of the newborn, you will find him squeezing it, using his lips to help it, and you will see his tongue upturning and drawing it, pushing the milk to his throat, as though he has learned and mastered [how to do this] a long time ago. . . .

Galen claimed that the mother's milk is the best milk, as long as she is not ill. This is because the milk of the mother is a substance to which the child is [already] accustomed, and through it he is molded and grows up.

Some of the physicians argue that it is not recommended for the mother to breastfeed until the child is three or four days old, and that he should be fed twice or three times a day only, as far as his stomach finds it tasty and is able to be fed, for too much lactation at that time is ineffective.

Following birth, a nurse should be taken for the child. She should be instructed not to rebuke him nor to cause him any grief. She should take special care with the place the infant sleeps in, putting him in a cradle that is both straight and not too soft so that the child will not turn over or bend his neck. Also, when put to sleep, the child's head should be placed higher than the rest of the body.

The nurse should be instructed to bathe the child in warm, sweet water, because child caring in general involves moistening the child's body so that it will remain wet for a long period of time. The water should be lukewarm, not too hot. This should be done in a mildly heated and slightly darkened room. The child should be bathed early in the morning, at noon, and in the evening.

The nurse should lay on her knees and thighs a soft cotton cloth, and put the child on it. She should then untie the rags, reveal his limbs, and bend his joints. All this she should do with gentleness and expertise. When bathing him the nurse should hold the child with her left hand, keeping his head and neck close [to herself] . . . while pouring water on him with her right hand. She should first daub and rub him gently. Then she should slowly pour the water so that he will not catch cold. She should gently cover his pubes so that he will urinate, and she should continue doing so until his entire body reddens. If she wants to turn the baby on his belly, the nurse should put her thumb under the baby's cheek so that his head will not bend toward the water. The nurse should bend every limb of his body correctly. Thus, the leg should be bent to the back and the hands to the front. If she does so she makes the joints move well in their places. She should level the head, legs, hands, and other members of his body. When the nurse finishes bathing him she should put him on her thighs, after having spread a soft cloth under it, dry and wipe him first. She should then lay him on his belly, then on his back, and in doing so lubricate him with one hand from underneath and the other from above. She should stretch his knees, tenderly clean his eyes with her thumb and straighten him out in every direction so that his blood vessels become wide, and his joints get used to be bent. Then, after having dried him, she should tie him with rags. This is how children should be bathed. . . .

From chapter 7: On the stages of childhood
At this point we shall discuss the symptoms children may show at all stages [of their development] and try to explain and clarify their reasons. . . .

The [Greek] physicians explained in many of their treatises that childhood is divided into four stages: [a] babyhood, when the child comes out of the womb; [b] childhood, when, after the stage of babyhood, teeth are growing; [c] the age of seven, and finally [d] fourteen, the age of sexual maturity. . . .

Source: Ibn al-Jazzar al-Qayrawani, *Siyasat al-sibyan wa-tadbiruhum*, edited by Muhammad al-Habib al-Hila (Tunis: al-Dar al-Tunisiyya li-al-Nashr, 1968), 57–58, 59–64, 86. English translation by Yaron Klein.

Document 3–19

A Religious Scholar on the Physical and Psychological Treatment
of Newborn Children

Chapter 16: On matters of child rearing that will benefit children in adulthood
Section [1]: In the two or three days after birth, the child should be nursed by a
woman other than his mother. This is because the mother's milk during these
first days is typically rough [of texture] and mixed [with other elements] and thus
different from the milk of a woman who has already started breastfeeding. All
Arabs share this concern. This is why they seek for their children Bedouin wet
nurses, as in the case of the Prophet, *may God bless and save him*, who was sent to
be nursed with the tribe of the Banu Sa'd.

Section [2]: It is desirable not to carry or walk around with infants until they
reach the age of three months, at least. This is because it is still close to the time
they were in their mothers' womb, and because their bodies are still weak.

Section [3]: It is desirable to feed them on milk alone until teething takes
place, because their stomachs are still weak and their ability to digest food is
poor. When the infant's teeth grow, his stomach becomes strong enough to
enable him to consume solid food. God, *exalted is He*, has delayed teething to
the time the baby needs solid food; this is due to His wisdom, benevolence, and
mercy upon the mother, as the child would otherwise bite her nipples with his
teeth.

Section [4]: It is desirable to proceed gradually with their nourishment. First,
children should be fed with milk, then bread dipped in hot water with fresh
[animal] milk. After that, [they should be given] cooked food and broths with no
meat. Then—very tender meat, well minced or chewed.

Section [5]: When children are close to the time they start speaking, and
their parents want to facilitate their first attempts to communicate, they should
rub honey and mineral salt on their tongue, because the two remove the heavy
moisture that impedes talking. When children start talking, one should instruct
them to say [the *shahada*—the Islamic profession of faith]: "There is no God but
Allah, and Muhammad is the Messenger of God," so that the first thing they hear
will be the knowledge of God, *exalted is He*, and His oneness. God is looking at
them from high above on His throne and hears what they say, since He is with
them wherever they are. The Children of Israel often called their sons by the
name Immanuel which means "God is with us." This is why God's favorite names
for children are 'Abd Allah [Servant of God] and 'Abd al-Rahman [Servant of the
Merciful], so that when the child gains consciousness and reason he understands
that he is the servant of God and that God is his lord and master.

Section [6]: When teething begins, the children's gum should be rubbed with
fresh and melted butter every day, and the nape of the neck should be anointed
intensively. At this time, one should be very careful with giving them hard food

substances, until the teeth are fully grown and firm. One should refrain from giving them such substances because of the danger that in this way they will damage their teeth, bend and crack them.

Section [7]: The baby's crying and screaming should not trouble his parents, especially when he is hungry and wishes to drink milk. The infant benefits a great deal from crying. It trains his limbs and stretches his intestines, widens his chest and heats his brain, warms up the mixture of the humors in his body, stirs up his innate heat, and helps nature in getting rid of excrement as well as of waste from the brain such as mucus and others.

Section [8]: One should not neglect the matter of [properly] swaddling the toddler and tying him, even if it might be difficult for him. This, until his body becomes strong, his members sturdy, and he is able to sit on the ground. At that point, he should be trained and accustomed, little by little, to move and stand up, until, having acquired these abilities to the point where they become a habit for him, he manages by himself.

Section [9]: One should keep the child away from any loud and frightening sounds that might upset him, as well as from hideous sights and disturbing movements. These might harm the strength of his mind, still fragile, so that he will not be able to benefit from it when he grows up. If such events do occur to him, one should lose no time, but repair the damage by [exposing him] to the opposite and amuse him with something that will make him forget it. The mother should immediately give him her breasts and quickly let him suckle, so that any trace of that alarming event will be eliminated, and none of it will be registered in his memory. One should gently rock the baby so that he falls asleep and forgets the event. It is not advisable to disregard the event, because by doing so, fear and anxiety settle in the [child's] heart. He will then grow with it, and it will be most difficult to remove it.

Section [10]: The state of the child changes at the time of teething. He is more prone to vomit and to high fever and bad temper. This is especially so when teething occurs with cold weather in winter, or an intensive heat in the summer. The most favorable times for teething are spring and fall. Teeth normally grow when the infant is seventh month old, though they might start growing earlier, after only five months [from birth], or later, after ten months. At this time, one should be very gentle in handling the baby. Bathe him frequently and nourish him with simple foods so that his belly will not be too full, which might lead to diarrhea. He should be wrapped with something that makes him feel good, such as a woolen dressing sprinkled with some tender cumin, celery, and aniseeds, and his gums should be rubbed with these [plants]. . . . There is nothing more harmful for the child than to have constipation of his stool, and nothing more profitable to him than to have easy stool. . . .

Section [11]: Regarding the proper time of weaning, God said: "Mothers shall suckle their children two years completely, for such as desire to fulfill the suckling. It is for the father to provide them and clothe them honorably. No soul is charged save to its capacity; a mother shall not be pressed for her child, neither a father for his child. . . . But if the couple desire by mutual consent and consultation to wean, then it is no fault in them. And if you desire to seek nursing for your children, it is no fault in you provide you hand over what you have given honorably; and fear God, and know that God sees the things you do" (Qur'an 2:233; trans. Arberry). The verse contains several rules. First, a whole nursing period constitutes of two years. This is the child's right, if he needs it. God emphasized two *full* years, so that it would be impossible to understand the [verse's] wording as meaning "a little more than a year." Second, if the parents want to wean the child earlier, and they consult each other and agree about it, they have the right to do so, provided no harm is caused to the child. Third: if the father wants to get a wet nurse for his son other than the child's mother, he has a right to do so, even if the mother objects. Only if there is harm involved for the mother and her child should his request be denied. It is permissible that the mother continues nursing for another six months after the two years, or even more. The best times for weaning are when the weather is temperate, and when the child's front teeth and molars have come out and are capable of chewing and handling the food. . . .

Section [12]: It is recommended that when the nursing woman decides to wean the child, she would do so gradually, and not inflict it upon him all at once. She should rather accustom the child to it and train him, because a sudden change from what one is used and accustomed to is harmful. . . .

Section [13]: Allowing children to stuff themselves and eat and drink in excess are among the bad practices of raising children. It is most beneficial to feed them up to a point where they are not fully sated, so that their digestion functions well, the humors of their bodies are even, their bodily wastes minimal, their bodies remain in good health and deceases occur seldom. . . .

Section [14]: Galen said: "I do not object categorically to children drinking cold water and I even approve it, especially after meals and in the hot days of the summer when they crave it. . . . "

Section [15]: It is advisable to be cautious with allowing the child to walk too early. This might result in deformation of the legs to which their weakness makes them still susceptible.

Be extremely careful not to stop him from vomiting, sleeping, eating, or drinking, as well as sneezing, urinating, or bleeding. Barring these have negative implications for the child as well as the adult. . . .

Source: Muhammad Ibn Qayyim al-Jawziyya, *Tuhfat al-mawdud bi-ahkam al-mawlud* (Bombay: Sharafuddin & Sons, 1961), 137–141. English translation by Yaron Klein.

Childhood Rites

While the Islamic risk-minimizing practices and rituals during pregnancy and child-birth focused on the physical well-being of mother and child and took place in an all-female environment, rituals of induction into the community stress the critical importance of reproducing the patriline and thus redirect the focus onto men. Central are rites performed on the seventh day after birth, when the prospects for the infant's survival look brighter. These are the first haircut, which separates the child from the all-female environment, the slaughter of a sheep or a goat, symbolically substituting for the child, to express gratitude for his or her birth ['aqiqa], and naming.

As in Judaism, male circumcision in Islam is regarded as a "'sign of union' with a particular deity and a mark of membership in a single community of the faithful."[4] Although not mentioned in the Qur'an, male circumcision has been strongly supported by Islamic tradition, and while some jurists define it as a recommendation only, there are others who regard it as a formal religious obligation. There are differences also with regard to the age in which male circumcision should take place: from the seventh day after birth to the age of seven or ten or even thirteen years (in the latter case, as a rite of passage to mark the beginning of adolescence and to prepare the child for marriage rather than as a childhood rite). While unanimously supporting male circumcision, Islamic authoritative sources are much more hesitant toward female circumcision.

Document 3–20

The 'Aqiqa Ceremonies

The *'aqiqa* is a sacrifice offered in place of the newborn, in the first days after he comes into the world, which benefits the newborn greatly. . . . It is a ransom through which the newborn is being redeemed, as God, *exalted is He*, redeemed Isma'il, "the slaughtered one," for a ram.[5] In pre-Islamic times people already used to perform this ceremony and called it *'aqiqa*. They would stain the head of the child with the animal's blood. The Messenger of God, *may God bless and save him*, affirmed the sacrificial ceremony but did away with the word *'uquq* and the practice of staining the head of the child with its blood. . . . He said: "Whoever wants to offer a sacrifice on behalf of his child—let him do so." . . . If we look at God's wisdom [as reflected] in His legislation and decree it is not impossible to regard the *'aqiqa* as the cause for the child's growing up in a favored manner, for being preserved and his health and his life prolonged, shielding him from the evil of the Devil. Every limb of the sacrifice is considered redemption for the equivalent limb of the child. This is why it is recommended that one will say [the same words] over the sacrifice that is customary to say over the sacrificial animals [in *'Id al-adha*, Sacrificial Feast, the major festival in Islam].[6]

Abu Talib said: "I asked Abu 'Abdallah: 'what should a man say while performing an *'aqiqa* ceremony?' He replied: 'He should say: *In the name of God*, then slaughter the animal [for the sake of God] with good intention, just as he does in *'Id al-adha*. He should [also] say: *This is the 'aqiqa of so and so* and: *God, this is from you, and [back] to you.*' All which is recommended regarding the slaughtered animal in *'Id al-adha*, in terms of alms giving and the distribution of the sacrifice's meat, is recommended for the *'aqiqa* as well." . . . The act of sacrificing [an animal on behalf of the child] combines several meanings: offering to God, gratitude [to Him], ransom [through which the newborn child is protected from danger], alms giving and the customary distributing of food in times of extreme happiness, as thanks to God for showing His grace [namely, granting offspring], which is the utmost purpose in matrimony.

Since he [the Prophet] sanctioned providing food on the occasion of a wedding, which itself is only a means to reach that grace [of having children], the permission [to do so] on the occasion of the desired purpose [of marriage] is even more suitable and appropriate. . . .

There is nothing better and more pleasant to the hearts of Muslims than this rule regarding the newborn. The customs surrounding wedding banquets and other celebrations similarly follow it. For this is an open expression of happiness and delight on the occasion of fulfilling the rules of Islam and of the coming into the world of a Muslim soul by which the Prophet, devoting himself to the service of God, will exceed [through his followers] in number, on the Day of Resurrection, the other religious communities and overcome his enemies.

When the Messenger of God, *may God bless and save him*, instituted the *'aqiqa* in Islam, emphasized its importance and announced that the child is held as a pledge for it [i.e., for the sacrificed animal], he forbade people to put blood on the head of the child. [Instead,] he prescribed them to replace it with saffron. This is because in pre-Islamic times they [the pagan Arabs] used to stain the head of the child with the blood of the *'aqiqa*, seeking a blessing in this way. They regarded the blood of the sacrificed animal as blessed to the point that they used to stain it on their gods in honor of and respect for them. [With the advent of Islam] they were ordered to stop this practice because it resembled that of the polytheists. They replaced it with something which is more beneficial to the parents, the newborn and the poor people alike, namely, shaving the head of the child, and giving alms at the weight of his hair in gold or silver. The Prophet prescribed them to stain the head with saffron, which has a pleasant odor and beautiful color, instead of the blood, which is unclean in its essence and has a bad odor. . . . Shaving the head removes harm from the child; it does away with his weak hair so that stronger and sturdier hair, more beneficial to the head, replaces it. At the same time it relieves the child and opens the pores of the head so that vapor is able to come out of it more easily, resulting in strengthening his vision and his sense of smell and of hearing.

The prophet, *may God bless and save him*, prescribed in the law that for a male child two sheep will be slaughtered [and for a female—one]. This is in order to show the male's eminence, and to affirm the place by which God has set him above the female, as He has given him preference over her in inheritance, blood-money and in testimony.[7] He also stipulated that the two sheep would be similar. . . .

[T]he sacrificed animal should be free of any of the blemishes that render an animal invalid as a sacrifice in *'Id al-adha* and other ritual slaughtering, lest it abrogates its status as a pledge for the newborn. For he is redeemed, as the Prophet, *may God bless and save him*, said, through his *'aqiqa*. . . .

God, *exalted is He*, made the sacrifice on behalf of the child to detach the latter from his pledge to the Devil, who clings to him from the moment he has come into the world . . . The *'aqiqa* is a ransom and a way to set [the child] free from the Devil's detention and from captivity in its prison. It frustrates the Devil['s efforts] to prevent the child from pursuing his best interests in the next world, to which he will return.

Source: Muhammad Ibn Qayyim al-Jawziyya, *Tuhfat al-mawdud bi-ahkam al-mawlud* (Bombay: Sharafuddin & Sons, 1961), 39–42. English translation by Yaron Klein.

Child Education

Muslim scholars were interested both in moral and in formal elementary education. Character training was to commence in early childhood. To be content with little, to be meek, and to show powers of endurance are traits the child should acquire through specific habits of eating, sleeping, and dressing, and social conduct.

Islamic sources from the Middle East, North Africa, and Spain indicate that the teaching level in the *kuttabs*, the institutions of elementary education, was at times low, that the curriculum, with the memorization of the Qur'anic text at its heart, was limited, and that the use of corporal, sometimes severe, punishment was common. On the whole, parents and teachers believed that the memorization of the Qur'an imbued children with obedience to God, filial piety, and good conduct. Thus they would be protected in this world as well as in the Hereafter. As there was no state educational system, teacher-pupil relations were legally based on a contract between the father (or the guardian) of the child and the teacher, stipulating such practical matters as the child's age of admission, the period of study, the curriculum, the methods of punishment, as well as the teacher's wages and work conditions. Since it was in their interest to make teachers adhere to the agreement, it is natural to assume that fathers must have been involved, at least to a certain extent, in the educational process in the *kuttab*. Thus, crowded as *kuttabs* may have been, they probably never became institutions of "mass education" in which the individual student was lost in anonymity. Moreover, by serving as a special institution for child education, the *kuttab* helped in prolonging the period of childhood for a while, particularly within prosperous urban households.

After they had completed their elementary education, the father was expected to help his male children choose an occupation in accordance with their talents and inclinations and train them toward their vocation.

In addition to texts by Ibn Abi al-Dunya, al-Ghazali, and Ibn Qayyim al-Jawziyya, this section features extracts from the *Muqaddima* (The Introduction to the Universal History) by 'Abd al-Rahman Ibn Khaldun, the outstanding historian, sociologist, and philosopher. Ibn Khaldun was born in Tunis in 1332, served at the courts of Fez, Granada, and Bougie (in today's Algeria), and then as a professor and judge in Cairo, where he died in 1406.

Document 3-21

Sayings of the Prophet Muhammad and His Companions on Moral Education at Home and the Beginning of Religious Education

Teaching one's wife and children and educating them
Narrated Khalid Ibn Khidash, from . . . Ibn 'Umar: "The Messenger of God, *may God bless and save him*, said: 'All of you are shepherds, accountable [in the Day of Judgment] for your flock. For every man is a shepherd taking care of his family, and is responsible for them.'"

Narrated Abu Bakr Ibn al-Mughira, and al-Qasim Ibn Hashim, from . . . Anas Ibn Malik: "The Messenger of *God, may God bless and save him*, said: 'Love your children and educate them well.'"

Narrated 'Abd al-Rahman Ibn Salih, from . . . Jabir Ibn Samura: "The Messenger of God, *may God bless and save him*, said: 'It is better for a man to provide good education to his child than to give a daily charity'" . . .

Narrated my father from . . . al-Hasan: "Whoever has an inner voice to warn him God will protect him, as God has mercy on whoever preaches to himself and his family and says: 'My family, be careful in your prayers and your almsgiving, pay attention to your neighbors and your poor so that God will have mercy on you on the Day of Judgment. For God has commended the believer who engages in such activities saying: 'He [Ishmael] bade his people to pray and to give the alms, and he was pleasing to his Lord (Qur'an 19:55; trans. Arberry).'"

Narrated Ishaq Ibn Ibrahim, from . . . 'Abdallah Ibn Bakr al-Muzani, from his father: "Luqman[8] said to his son: 'The beatings by a father of his son are like fertilizer to the field.' "

Narrated al-Husayn Ibn 'Abd al-Rahman: "Maslama Ibn 'Abd al-Malik [one of the most prominent Umayyad generals (d. 738 CE)], appointed a tutor for his children saying: 'I have connected your arm with mine and I consent to have you as a companion to my children. Take good care of their education so that their righteousness will redound to you. When punishing them, be lenient insofar as physical punishment is concerned. Teach them to speak nicely, prevent them from getting involved with vile people and forbid them from knowing what they should not know. Be to them like a gentle horse-groom and a tender tutor. Your kindness will gain you their love, affection and acceptance as well as praiseworthy future. By the influence you will imprint on them and by your good education of them you will gain not only my good opinion but also my generous and gracious repay.'

Teaching the young
Narrated al-Husayn Ibn Muhammad al-Sa'di from . . . Yazid Ibn Mu'ammar: "Studying at a young age is like engraving in stone."

Teaching children how to pray
Narrated Ishaq from . . . Muhammad Ibn 'Abd al-Rahman: "The Messenger of God, *may God save and bless him*, said: "When your children reach the age of seven command them to pray. When they reach the age of ten, punish them when they do not, and separate between them in their beds."

Teaching children the Qur'an
Narrated Ishaq Ibn Isma'il . . . : "Al-Dahhak Ibn Qays used to say: 'People, teach your family the Qur'an, because God sends to any Muslim, male or female destined by Him to paradise, two angels. They surround him or her and say to him or her: *Read, and thou shall ascend the steps of Paradise*, until they place him or her [in the appropriate section of Paradise] according to his or her knowledge of the Qur'an.'

Narrated al-Qasim Ibn Hashim, from . . . Sa'id Ibn al-'As: "If I teach my child the Qur'an, take him to perform the pilgrimage [*hajj*] and marry him, I have fulfilled my obligation toward him. Now he is left with his obligation toward me."

Narrated Harun Ibn 'Abdallah from . . . Malik Ibn Dinar: "It has come to my knowledge that God says: 'Whenever I am on the verge of punishing mankind, I look at those who study the Qur'an in company, at the dwellers of mosques, and at the young children of Islam, and my anger subsides.'"

Source: 'Abdallah Ibn Abi al-Dunya, *Kitab al-'iyal* (al-Mansura: Dar al-Wafa, 1997), 228, 231, 232, 233, 237, 338, 219, 225, 226. English translation by Yaron Klein.

Document 3-22

Al-Ghazali on Child Moral Education

An exposition of the way in which young children should be disciplined, and
the manner of their upbringing and the improvement of their character

Know that the way in which young children are disciplined is one of the most important of all matters. A child is a trust in the care of his parents, for his pure heart is a precious uncut jewel devoid of any form of carving, which will accept being cut into any shape, and will be disposed according to the guidance it receives from others. If it is habituated to and instructed in goodness then this will be its practice when it grows up, and it will attain to felicity in this world and the next; its parents too and all his teachers and preceptors, will share in its reward. Similarly, should it be habituated to evil and neglected as though it were an animal, then misery and perdition will be its lot, and the responsibility for this will be borne by its guardian and supervisor. . . . A father may strive to protect his son from fire in this world, but yet it is of far greater urgency that he protect him from the fires which exist in the Afterlife. This he should do by giving him discipline, teaching him and refining his character, and by preserving him from bad company, and by not suffering him to acquire the custom of self-indulgence, or to love finery and luxury, in the quest for which he might well squander his life when older and thus perish forever. Rather should he watch over him diligently from his earliest days, and permit none but a woman of virtue and religion to nurse and raise him. . . .

When the signs of discretion appear in him he should again be watched over carefully. The first of these is the rudiments of shame, for when he begins to feel diffident and is ashamed of certain things so that he abandons them, the light of the intellect has dawned in him, whereby he sees that certain things are ugly, and different from others, and begins to be ashamed of some things and not others. This is a gift to him from God (Exalted is He), and a good foretoken that his traits will be balanced, his heart pure, and his intellect sound when he enters upon adulthood.

The child who has developed the capacity for shame should never be neglected; rather this and his discretion should be used as aids in his education. The first trait to take control of him will be greed for food; he is to be disciplined in this regard, so that, for instance, he picks up food only with his right hand, says "In the name of God" when raising it, eats from that which is nearest to him, and does not start eating before others . . . and he should acquire the habit of sometimes eating nothing but bread so that he does not think that the presence of other kinds of food is inevitable. He should be made to dislike eating large quantities by being told that this is the practice of animals, and by seeing other children reproached for overeating or praised for being well-mannered and moderate. He should be made to enjoy giving the best food for others, and encouraged to pay little heed to what he eats and to be contended with its coarser varieties.

He should be encouraged to like white rather than colored or silk garments, and made firmly to believe that these latter are proper to women and to effeminate men, and that [true] men disdain them. . . . He should be protected from children who are accustomed to luxury and comfort, and to wearing expensive garments, and from mixing with all who would speak to him of such things and thereby make them seem fine in his eyes. For the child who is neglected in the early years of his growth will usually grow up to be ill-natured, dishonest, envious, obstinate, inclined to theft, backbiting, and excessive chatter and laughter, and slyness and immorality, from all of which things he can be protected through a sound upbringing.

Next he should be busy at school learning the Qur'an, the Traditions, and tales of devout men, so that love for the righteous may take root in his heart. He should be preserved from those varieties of poetry which treat of lovers and passion, and from the company of such men of letters as claim that things are part of an elegant and sophisticated nature, for this would implant the seeds of corruption in his heart. Whenever a good trait or action manifests itself in the child he should be admired and rewarded with something which gives him joy, and should be praised in front of others; likewise, when once in a while he does something bad it is best to pretend not to notice and not to bring it to the attention of others (but never to reveal to him that it is something which others might be bold enough to do), particularly if the child himself has diligently endeavored to hide his action, for the exposure of such deeds may cause him to grow emboldened, until he no longer cares when they are made public. Should he repeats the action, he should be privately reproached and made to feel that it was a very serious thing, and be told "Beware of doing anything like this again, or I shall tell others and you will be disgraced in front of them!" He should not be spoken to at length every time, for this would accustom him to being blamed for his misdeeds, and destroy the effectiveness such words have upon his heart. A father should rather preserve the awe in which the child holds his speech by reproaching him only sometimes: similarly the mother, when reproving him, should frighten him [threatening to mention the matter] to his father. He should not permitted to sleep by day, for this conduces to laziness, and should always be allowed to sleep at night, but not on a soft bed, which would prevent his members from growing tough. His body should not be allowed to grow fat, for this would make it hard for him to renounce self-indulgence; instead he should be habituated to rough bedding, clothing and food.

He should also be prevented from doing anything secretly, for he will conceal things only when he believes them to be ugly, and if he is left to continue these practices he will grow used to doing ugly things. He should acquire the habit of walking, moving about and taking exercise for part of the day so that he is not overcome by idleness, and should be taught not to uncover his limbs or walk fast and not to dangle his arms but to keep them close to his trunk. He must be forbidden to boast to his fellows about any of his parents' possessions, whether these be money or property, or about anything he eats or wears, or about his tablet and pen-case, and should become used to being modest, generous and mild in his speech to all with whom he associates. He should be prevented from accepting anything from other boys, if he is from a wealthy and powerful family, and be taught that it is honorable to give, and base and blameworthy to take; while if his parents are poor he should be taught that greed and taking from others is a disgraceful and humiliating practice fit only for dogs, which wag their tails hoping for a morsel.

Children should always be made to deem the love of gold and silver as unsightly thing[s], and should be warned in this regard even more vigorously than they are warned about snakes and scorpions, for the vice which consists in such a love is more dangerous to them (and to adults also) than poison.

A child should be put in the practice of not spitting, yawning or wiping his nose in the presence of others, and taught not to turn his back to anyone, or to cross his legs, or lean his chin and support his head on his hand, for these practices indicate the presence of sloth. He should be taught how to sit, and be forbidden to speak excessively, it being explained to him that this is a sign of impudence and the custom of children from low families. Making oaths of any sort, whether true or false, should be forbidden him, so that he never acquires this habit as a child. He should be put in the habit of never speaking before anyone else, and of speaking only in response to questions and in proportion to them, and of listening properly whenever an older person is speaking, and rising [when he enters], and making a place for him and sitting facing him. He should be forbidden to speak loosely, or to curse or insult anyone, or to mingle with those who do such things, for these habits will inevitably be acquired should he fall in with bad company, the preservation from which is the very root and foundation of the education of children. If the teacher strikes him he should not cry out and sob, or seek anyone's intercession, but should rather bear his punishment, and be told that to do so is a mark of courage and manhood, while to cry is the practice of slaves and women.

After school he should be allowed to play in a fashion which gives him some rest after his hard work in class, although he should not be allowed to grow exhausted. To prevent a child from playing, and to fatigue him with constant lessons, will cause his heart to die and harm his intelligence, and make life so hateful to him that he will cast around for some means of escape.

He should be taught to obey his parents and his teacher, and all people who are older than himself, whether relations or not, and to look upon them with respect and admiration and not to play in their presence. As he reaches the age of discretion he should not be excused the ritual ablution and the Prayer, and should be told to fast for a few days during Ramadan, and should be prevented from wearing gold, silk or embroidered clothes. He should be taught about the limits laid down by the Law, and put in fear of theft and unlawful gain, and also of lying, treachery, deceit, and all the other traits which tend to predominate among children. If he is brought up in this way, then as he approaches adulthood he will come to understand the reasons which underlie these things, and will be told that food is a means of maintaining health, and that its sole purpose is to enable man to gain strength for the worship of God (Great and Glorious He!), and that this world is without reality, since it will not endure, and that death must bring its pleasures to an end, and that it is a place through which we pass but in which we cannot abide, unlike the Afterlife, in which we must abide and through which we cannot pass, for death awaits us at every moment, and that therefore the intelligent and insightful man will lay up provisions in this world for his journey into the next so as to gain a high degree in the sight of God and abundant bliss in the Gardens of Heaven. If his upbringing was sound, then when he attains to maturity these ideas will have a powerful and wholesome effect which will leave an impress on his heart like an inscription on stone; had it been otherwise, so as the child had grown accustomed to play, boastfulness, rudeness and insolence, and greed for food, clothes and finery, his heart will shrink from accepting truth in the manner of a field where crops wither because of its dry soil.

It is the beginning which should be supervised carefully. For a child is a creature whose essence is receptive to both good and evil: it is only its parents who cause it to be disposed to one or the other. . . .

Source: Abu Hamid Muhammad al-Ghazali, *Ihya' 'ulum al-din* (Cairo: Mu'assasat al-Halabi, 1967), 3:92–95. English translation by *Al-Ghazali on Disciplining the Soul*, translated by T. J. Winter (Cambridge: Islamic Texts Society, 2001), 75–82.

Document 3–23

Ibn Qayyim al-Jawziyya on Child Moral Education

What the infant needs above all is that attention will be given to [the forming of] his character. For the child is raised on whatever his educator accustoms him to: enmity, anger, obstinacy, precipitancy, capriciousness, rashness, fury, or greed. When he grows up, it is difficult for him to eradicate these traits. Instead, they become characteristics and dispositions deeply rooted in him. Even if he is vigilant, they will appear at some point. This is why we find that the character of most people is deformed. This is so because of the upbringing they received. Also, when a child reaches the age of reasoning, he should refrain from attending congregations of amusement, futility, and singing and from being exposed to [words of] obscenity, heresy, and to bad language. Because these, once clung to the ears, are hard to get rid of in adulthood. . . . Changing one's habits is among the most difficult tasks. To do so, a person must develop a second nature. . . .

The child's guardian should keep him away from the habit of taking from people. This is because when the child gets used to taking from other people it becomes a second nature to him, and he grows up taking rather than giving. The guardian should accustom him to giving and granting. Whenever the guardian wants to give something [to anyone], he should do so through the child, so that the latter will get a taste of the sweetness there is in giving.

He should also keep the child away from deceit and deception, since they are more dangerous to him than deadly poison. This is because when dishonesty and deception become easy for him, the child loses both the happiness of this world and that of the Hereafter, and all good will be deprived from him.

The guardian should keep the child away from laziness and idleness, meekness and comfort. Moreover, he should take their opposites, and let his soul and body rest only for the sake of work. This is because laziness and idleness only lead to misfortune and remorse, while seriousness and toil lead to favorite circumstances, in this world, in the next one, or in both. . . .

The guardian should keep the child away from overindulgence in eating, talking, sleeping or hanging out with people, for there is much loss in all these, and they will cause the believer to lose the good of both this world and the next. He should do everything he can to keep the child away from harmful desires, both those related to the stomach and those related to the genitals. Because when they root in him, they corrupt the youth in a way that will be difficult to correct. How many fathers have made their children miserable in this and the next world by neglecting their education and assisting them to satisfy their desires! They believe that they treat them with respect, but in fact, they only bring shame upon them. They imagine that they act toward them with mercy, but in reality they only harm and deprive them. As a consequence, they lose the benefit they would have had from their children, and cause their children to miss their good fortune in this world and the next. When you examine the corruption of children, you usually find out that most of it is caused by their parents.

Be very careful that the child does not get used to consuming substances that might impair his mind, such as alcoholic beverages and the like, does not associate with any person who might corrupt him or his language, and does not take from his hand, for this is the ultimate [form of] devastation. . . . Children are as corrupt as the negligence and the inattention of their fathers. . . .

One should prevent the male child from dressing in silk, for it is harmful to him, and twists his nature in the same way that homosexuality, drinking wine, stealing, and lying do. The Prophet, *may God bless and save him*, said: "Silk and gold are forbidden for the men of my community and permissible for the women." As for a male child, even when he is not yet obliged to observe the percepts of religion, his legal guardian is, and the latter should thus not allow him to get used to practicing something illegal. . . .

The guardian should direct the child to a vocation that suits the latter's nature. . . . He should not make him take an unsuitable profession as long as he is legally authorized in this matter. For if the child is directed to a vocation he is not prepared for, he will not succeed in it, and he will lose whatever he is ready for. If the guardian finds the child possesses adequate understanding, sound perception, good memory, and attentiveness—[he should know that] these are the signs of the child's readiness for [theoretical] study. . . . If the guardian finds him entirely different than the aforementioned, namely, inclining to horsemanship and its related skills, such as riding, archery, and spear drills, having no acute discernment for [theoretical] studies, and he realizes the child is not created for them, then the guardian should enable him to attain the skills required for horsemanship and have him practice this. This would be best both for the benefit of the child and for the Muslim community in general. If the guardian finds him other than the aforementioned . . . but he notices the child's eyes open [in fascination] for a certain craft, and finds him fit and ready for that craft—as long as this craft is one which is permissible by law and beneficial to people—then the guardian should direct him to it. All this, after the guardian has taught the child all the essentials he needs to know about his religion.

Source: Ibn Qayyim al-Jawziyya, *Tuhfat al-mawdud bi-ahkam al-mawlud* (Bombay: Sharafuddin & Sons, 1961), 142–145. English translation by Yaron Klein.

Document 3–24

Ibn Khaldun on Elementary Education in the Lands of Islam

The instruction of children and the different methods employed in the Muslim cities
It should be known that instructing children in the Qur'an is a symbol of Islam. Muslims have, and practice, such instruction in all their cities, because it imbues hearts with a firm belief [in Islam] and its articles of faith, which are [derived] from the verses of the Qur'an and certain Prophetic traditions. The Qur'an has become the basis of instruction, the foundation of all habits that may be acquired later on. The reason for this is that the things one is taught in one's youth take root more deeply [than anything else]. They are the basis of all later [knowledge]. The first impression the heart receives is, in a way, the foundation of [all scholarly] habits. The character of the foundation determines the condition of the building. The methods of instructing children in the Qur'an differ according to differences of opinion as to the habits that are to result from that instruction. . . .

The fact that the people of Ifriqiyah [Tunis] and the Maghrib [northwest Africa] restrict themselves to the Qur'an makes them altogether incapable of mastering the linguistic habit. For as a rule, no [scholarly] habit can originate from the [study of the] Qur'an, because no human being can produce anything like it. Thus human beings are unable to employ or imitate its ways, and they also can form no habit in any other respect. Consequently, a person who knows [the

Qur'an] does not acquire that habit of the Arabic language. It will be his lot to be awkward in expression and to have little fluency in speaking. This situation is not quite so pronounced among the people of Ifriqiyah as among the Maghribis, because . . . the former combine instruction in the Qur'an with instruction in the terminology of scientific norms. Thus, they get some practice and have some examples to imitate. However, their habit in this respect does not amount to a good style [eloquence], because their knowledge mostly consists of scholarly terminology which falls short of good style. . . .

As for the Spaniards [i.e., the Muslims of Spain], their varied curriculum with its great amount of instruction in poetry, composition, and Arabic philology gave them, from their early years on, a habit providing for a better acquaintance with the Arabic language. . . .

Accepted custom gives preference to the teaching of the Qur'an. The reason is the desire for the blessing and reward [in the other world resulting from knowledge of the Qur'an] and a fear of the things that might affect children in "the folly of youth" and harm them and keep them from acquiring knowledge. They might miss the chance to learn the Qur'an. As long as they remain at home, they are amenable to authority. When they have grown up and shaken off the yoke of authority, the tempests of young manhood often cast them upon the shores of wrongdoing. Therefore, while the children are still at home and under the yoke of authority, one seizes the opportunity to teach them the Qur'an, so that they will not remain without knowledge of it. . . .

Severity to students does them harm
Severe punishment in the course of instruction does harm to the student, because it belongs among [the things that make for a] bad habit. Students, slaves and servants who are brought up with injustice and [tyrannical] force are overcome by it. It makes them feel oppressed and causes them to lose their energy. It makes them lazy and induces them to lie and be insincere. That is, their outward behavior differs from what they are thinking, because they are afraid that they will have to suffer tyrannical treatment [if they tell the truth]. Thus, they are taught deceit and trickery. This becomes their custom and character. They lose the quality that goes with social and political organization and makes people human, namely, [the desire to] protect and defend themselves and their homes, and they become dependent on others. Indeed, their souls become too indolent to [attempt to] acquire the virtues and good character qualities. Thus, they fall short of their potentialities and do not reach the limit of their humanity. As a result, they revert to the stage of "the lowest of the low." . . .

Thus, a teacher must not be too severe toward his pupil, nor a father toward his son, in educating them. . . .

One of the best methods of education was suggested by [the 'Abbasid caliph Harun] al-Rashid [r. 786–809 CE] to Khalaf Ibn Ahmar, the teacher of his son Muhammad al-Amin. Khalaf Ibn Ahmar said: "Ar-Rashid told me to come and educate his son Muhammad al-Amin, and he said to me: 'O Ahmar, the Commander of the Faithful is entrusting [his son] to you, the life of his soul and the fruit of his heart. Take firm hold of him and make him obey you. Occupy in relation to him the place that the Commander of the Faithful has given you. Teach him to read the Qur'an. Instruct him in history. Let him transmit poems and teach him the Sunnah of the Prophet. Give him insight into the proper occasions for speech and how to begin [a speech]. Forbid him to laugh, save at times when it is proper. Accustom him to honor the Hashimite dignitaries [that is, his 'Abbasid relatives] when they come to him, and to give the military leaders places of honor when they come to his salon. Let no hour pass in which you do not seize the opportunity to teach him something useful. But do so without vexing him, which could kill his mind. Do not always be too lenient with him, or he will get to like leisure and become used to it. As much as possible, correct him kindly and gently. If he does not want it that way, you must then use severity and harshness.'"

Source: 'Abd al-Rahman Ibn Khaldun, *al-Muqaddima,* edited by M. Quatremère (Paris, 1858), 3:260–266. English translation by Ibn Khaldun, *The Muqaddima, An Introduction to History,* translated by F. Rosenthal (Princeton: Princeton University Press, 1967), 3:300–307.

Document 3–25

The Low Image of Kuttab Teachers

Muhammad [Ibn Zafar], *may God forgive him:* "I was told that Sari Ibn al-Mughallas [al-Saqati, an important mystic of the second generation of *sufis* in Baghdad, d. 867 CE], recited to his teacher the verse: 'On the day that. . . We shall drive the evildoers into Gehenna [Hell] herding' (Qur'an 19:86; trans. Arberry), then asked his teacher: 'Master, what is the meaning of the word *herding*? To this he replied: 'I do not know.' Sari continued reciting the following verse: 'having no power of intercession, save those who have taken with the All-merciful covenant' (Qur'an 19:87; trans. Arberry) and asked: 'Master, what is the meaning of *the covenant*?' The teacher replied: 'I do not know.' Sari then stopped reciting and said: 'If you have no knowledge, why do you mislead people?' The instructor beat him up, then Sari said: 'Master, are ignorance and deception not enough that you add to them also injustice and harm?' The teacher accepted the admonition, and repented to God for his instruction. He turned to search for knowledge, and would say: 'Al-Sari manumitted me from the slavery of ignorance.'"

Source: Muhammad Ibn Zafar, *Anba' nujaba' al-abna',* edited by Ibrahim Yunus (Cairo: Dar al-Sahwa, n.d.), 192. English translation by Yaron Klein.

The Legal Status of Children

Religious law is at the core of Islamic thought and way of life. The shari'a, as a comprehensive system of law and ethics, instructs Muslims how to conduct their lives both in the private and the public sphere. Being one of the most elaborated themes in the Qur'an, family law in particular has become the subject of detailed, ramified legal discussions in writings of positive law and in collections of legal responsa (*fatawa*).

Recognizing childhood as a unique period in human life, Islamic law on the whole adopts a considerate attitude, its main aims being to ensure the physical and psychological well-being of children and to protect their property. At the same time, since they are regarded as mentally deficient, children's legal capacity is restricted and they are exempted from legal responsibility. Corporal punishment, child marriage, child labor and slavery, exceptional as they may seem to us today against the background of the dominant principles of Islamic family law, were sanctioned by Muslim legal authorities in the past, either under the pressure of socioeconomic needs or due to different religious-moral views.

Many of the legal texts in this section are taken from *Jami' ahkam al-sighar* (The Comprehensive Book of Legal Rules concerning Minor Children) by Muhammad Ibn Mahmud al-Asrushani (d. 1234 CE), a jurist of the Hanafi school of law from Asrushana, east of Samarqand (in today's Uzbekistan). This is a unique collection dedicated exclusively to legal questions connected with minor children. A single extract is taken from *al-Siyasa al-shar'iyya fi islah al-ra'i wa-al-ra'iyya* (Governance According to God's Law in Reforming both the Ruler and His Flock) by Taqi al-Din Ibn Taymiyya, the Damascene Hanbali theologian and jurist (d. 1328 CE).

Document 3–26

When Minority Comes to Its End

The earliest age in which a boy who has attained puberty is legally considered major is at the completion of twelve years. As for a girl who has reached puberty, the earliest age when the bleeding occurring to her is to be regarded as menstruation [and thus a criterion for legal majority] is nine years. . . .

Source: Muhammad Ibn Mahmud al-Asrushani, *Jami' ahkam al-sighar* (Cairo: Dar al-Fadila, n.d.), 1:34. English translation by Yaron Klein.

Document 3–27

The Qur'an on Parents' Legal Responsibility toward Their Children

Sura 2:233

Mothers shall suckle their children two years
completely, for such as desire to fulfil
the suckling. It is for the father to provide them
and clothe them honourably. No soul is charged
save to its capacity; a mother shall not be pressed
for her child, neither a father for his child.
The heir has a like duty. But if the couple
desire by mutual consent and consultation
to wean, then it is no fault in them.
And if you desire to seek nursing
for your children, it is no fault in you
provide you hand over what you have given
honourably; and fear God, and know that God sees
the things you do.

Source: English translation by Arthur J. Arberry, *The Koran Interpreted* (London: George Allen & Unwin; New York: Macmillan, 1971).

Document 3–28

The Shari'a on Parents' Legal Responsibility toward Their Children

Ranks of fostering parents

The person most worthy to rear the minor, whether his parents are
   married or separated, is the mother.
If the mother dies or remarries—then the mother of the mother.
If the latter dies or remarries—then the mother of the father.
If she dies or remarries—then a sister from both parents.
If she dies or remarries—then a sister from the mother's side.
If she dies or remarries—then a daughter of the sister from both parents
If she dies or remarries—then a daughter of the sister from the mother
   side. . . . (1:149)

Parents neglecting their child

[The Hanafi jurisconsult of the tenth century CE] Abu al-Layth [al-Samarqandi] wrote: . . . "A boy drowned or fell of a roof and died. If he could have looked after himself, no atonement is required of his parents. If he could not have looked after himself, atonement is required from the parents. For if he had the faculty to look after himself, he would have been regarded, for that matter, as legally major. If not, it was the parents' duty to look after him; by leaving him they caused him to perish. If [at the time of the accident] the child was under the supervision of both parents, atonement is required from both. If, on the other hand, the child was [at that time] under the supervision of one of them, only that person is required to atone...."

Abu al-Layth ruled that none of the parents are obliged to atone except if the child fell [directly] from the hands of one of them. This is because atonement is required only from the one whose actions are directly connected with the place of the action. . . . (2:146–147)

A child is injured as a result of negligence on the part of its parents

Narrated [the Hanafi jurist of the ninth century CE] Nasir [Ibn Yahya al-Balkhi], regarding a boy who drowned or fell off a roof and died: "If the child was around seven years old, there is nothing against the parents, since he was able to look after himself. But if he was not in full possession of his mental faculties or was very young, and died under such circumstances, atonement is required from the parents. If [at the time of the accident] the child was under the protection of one of them, atonement is required from that person only."

From [the Hanafi jurist of the tenth century CE] Abu Bakr al-Iskaf regarding parents who are negligent with their child who falls either from a high place or into a fire: "I do not think any atonement is required of the parents." (1:232–233)

A mother left her child with his father, who did not take a wet nurse for the baby, and he died

If a mother leaves her child with his father, then departs and the father refrains from hiring a wet nurse—although the child is willing to suckle from another woman—until he finally dies from hunger, the fault is with the father, and he is required to atone and repent. But if the child does not accept the breasts of a woman other than his mother, and the mother is aware of that, the guilt is on her, and she is the one who is required to atone. (2:147)

A father beats his son as a disciplinary punishment

A father hit his son as part of a disciplinary punishment and ended up injuring him. One should examine [the circumstances]: if he hit him for something one does not normally punish for, or if he hit him for something one does usually punish for but exceeded the norm—in both cases he is liable for indemnity for bodily injury as well as repentance; this is according to Abu Hanifa. According to Abu Yusuf and Muhammad [al-Shaybani], the father is liable in neither case. . . . (2:166)

A mother beats her son
According to Abu Hanifa, when a mother beats her small son as part of a disciplinary punishment, there is no doubt that she is liable. There are different views
among religious authorities about it. Some say that she is liable; others say that
she is not. (2:168)

The father's particular rights and obligations: Hiring out a child
It is permissible for a father, for a grandfather from the father's side, or for their
trustee to hire a boy out to do some kind of a work. This is because these people
have the legal power to make use of the boy, even without compensation, for
educational purposes and for training. However, it is better to compensate the
child [for his work]. (2:5)

The father's particular rights and obligations: A man hires someone
to inculcate in his child a certain kind of knowledge or a craft
The judge Fakhr al-Din wrote in his *Responsa* (*fatawa*): . . . "A man hires another to
teach his young slave or his child poetry, literature, handwriting, arithmetic, or
a vocation such as the art of sewing or the like; if he allocates for that a specific
time span, in the region of six months, it is permissible. As long as the teacher
dedicates himself to teaching, the man is required to pay the agreed fee regardless
of whether or not the child has learned [anything] during this period." (2:13)

The father's particular rights and obligations: Is it permissible
for the father or his warden to allow the child [to engage in commerce]?
Narrated Muhammad [Ibn al-Hasan al-Shaybani]: . . . "It is permissible for a man
to allow his son to conduct commerce, and to appoint the child as his representative, provided the latter fully understands the principles of buying and selling.
The same applies for his warden, i.e., he is permitted to allow a minor to engage
in commerce, as long as the child fully understands the principles of buying and
selling." (2:86)

The mother's particular rights and obligations in relation to her children:
In what conditions is the right of the mother and whoever is with her
to rear the child annulled?
The right to rear the child is annulled for those women only by their marriage
to a man outside the family. If they marry a related man with whom the child is
not allowed to marry, as in the case of a grandmother when her [new] husband is
the child's grandfather, or in the case of a mother when she marries the paternal
uncle of the child, the right of fostering remains valid. (1:150)

The mother's particular rights and obligations:
The end of the rearing [period] by women
Women have a legal priority to raise a [male] child as long as he needs help.

When he can do without assistance, in that he eats, drinks and get dressed on his own and, according to one transmission, wipes himself, then the father has the right over him. In the case of a girl, the mother has the right to foster her until she gets her first period or . . . until she reaches the age of sexual desire. (1:150–151)

The mother's particular rights and obligations: The place of nursing

Since the mother cannot be forced [to breast-feed her child] and in case the child has no property, it is the father's duty to provide a wet nurse to suckle the child in his mother's residence. The child should not be taken away from the mother, because Muslims agree that she has the right to hold the child in her bosom. However, it is not necessary for the wet nurse to stay in the mother's home, unless it is stipulated otherwise in the [hire] contract, and the child is able to dispense with the wet nurse in this situation [i.e., during her absence]. Rather, she has the right to nurse him and then return to her home. If it is not stipulated in the contract that she should nurse him at the mother's residence, she has the right to carry the child to her house, or ask for the child to be brought out to her, and nurse him in the courtyard of the [mother's] house. But [again], the wet nurse has to comply with a stipulation in the [hire] contract ordering her to stay with the [nursling's] mother. (1:127–128)

The mother's particular rights and obligations:
The migration of the mother along with her child

If a woman wants to migrate with her child from a [certain] town [back] to the village in which she got married she has the right to do so.

[On the other hand], the [twelfth-century Hanafi jurist] al-Baqali wrote in his responsa (fatawa) [collection]: "A mother does not have the right to migrate with her child from a city to a village under any circumstances. And she has no right to take away the child to an enemy territory, even if she got married there." [And he added]: "She has [only] the right to move the child to the outskirts of a city, even if the father cannot return home from visiting his son on the same day before darkness." . . .

A man married a woman in Basra and she bore him a son. Then, he took his little son to Kufa and divorced her. She took legal actions against him demanding him to return the child to her. Abu Yusuf ruled: "If the husband took the child to Kufa at her request—it is not incumbent upon him to return him, and she should be told: 'Go to him yourself, and take him.' But if the father took the child away against her consent, he should bring him to her." (1:154–155)

Legal protection for children and interdicting them from legal actions:
What is permissible for a child acting as a legal representative?

Since it is permissible for a boy to engage as a legally authorized representative in trade, he is considered to be in a status of a free person who is legally major in whatever falls under the category of legal representation. He is permitted to offer himself for hire, and to hire somebody for himself. He is also allowed to sell anything he had inherited, whether real estate or movable property, as it is permissible for any other free person who is legally major. If he acknowledges a debt created by his trade, his acknowledgment is valid. On the other hand, he is not permitted to manumit a slave by contract, nor can he release him from slavery for a fee. Also, he is not allowed to marry off his female slave. . . . (2:87–88)

Protection and interdiction: Interdiction of actions
with respect to certain categories of people
The circumstances which make interdicting actions [of certain categories of people] necessary are young age, slavery and insanity. A child cannot act according to his free will without the consent of his legal guardian just as a slave cannot act without the consent of his master. By no means is the insane, under a fit of madness, allowed to act according to his own judgment. (2:96)

Protection and interdiction: People committing theft while a child is among them
When people commit theft while among them is a child, an insane, a deaf or a kin, their hands should not be amputated [contrary to the fixed Qur'anic punishment on theft]; this is according to Abu Hanifa. . . . According to Abu Yusuf, if the one who took out the merchandise was a child, their hands should not be amputated but if it was an adult—they should be punished." (1:198)

Protection and interdiction: Highway robbers with a child among them
The same goes for highway robbers while among them are a child, an insane, an idiot or a deaf [person]; they are all exempt from the [Qur'anic] punishment [for robbery]. (1:198)

Source: From Muhammad Ibn Mahmud al-Asrushani, *Jami' ahkam al-sighar* (Cairo: Dar al-Fadila, n.d.). English translation by Yaron Klein.

Document 3–29

Children's Sexuality: The Qur'an on Children and Modesty

Sura 24:31
And say to the believing women, that they
cast down their eyes and guard their private
parts, and reveal not their adornment
save such as is outward; and let them cast
their veils over their bosoms, and not reveal

their adornment save to their husbands,
or their fathers, or their husband's fathers,
or their sons, or their husbands' sons,
or their brothers, or their brothers' sons,
or their sisters' sons, or their women,
or what their right hands own, or such men
as attend them, not having sexual desire,
or children who have not yet attained knowledge
of women's private parts. . . .

Source: English translation by Arthur J. Arberry, *The Koran Interpreted* (London: George Allen & Unwin; New York: Macmillan, 1969).

Document 3–30

Children's Sexuality: Dressing a Child with Gold and Silk

It is undesirable to dress boys with gold and silk. The reason is that the prohibition [to wear gold and silk] was directed to men. [Thus], just as wearing them is prohibited, dressing someone else in them is also prohibited. This is similar to [the case of] wine. Since drinking wine is forbidden, serving it is banned as well.

Source: Muhammad Ibn Mahmud al-Asrushani, *Jami' ahkam al-sighar* (Cairo: Dar al-Fadila, n.d.), 1:212. English translation by Yaron Klein.

Document 3–31

Child Marriage

Paternity of a ten-year-old child cannot be established
When a ten-year-old gets married and his wife gives birth to a child, the paternity of the child cannot be established, since the earliest age for one to be considered [legally] major is twelve years. Narrated 'Abdallah Ibn Mas'ud, *God be pleased with him*: "When I was ten years old, on a battle day, someone suggested to the Prophet, *may God bless and save him*, that I would go out to fight, but the Prophet refused. While I became twelve, I was presented to him again. This time he accepted me." The only reason for his initial rejection was his young age.

From Ibn 'Umar: "On the battle of Uhud [625 CE], when I was fourteen years old, my father suggested to the Prophet, *may God bless and save him*, that I go out to fight but the Prophet refused. Then, on the battle of the Trenches [627 CE], when I was [more than] fifteen, my father presented me again to the Prophet. This time the Prophet allowed me to take part in the battle."

Source: Muhammad Ibn Mahmud al-Asrushani, *Jami' ahkam al-sighar* (Cairo: Dar al-Fadila, n.d.), 2:137–138. English translation by Yaron Klein.

Document 3–32

Children's Conversion to Islam

[The prominent Hanafi jurist] Fakhr al-Islam 'Ali al-Bazdawi wrote [in the eleventh century CE]: "The embracing of Islam by an insane [person] is not valid. The embracing of Islam by an idiot is valid. . . . The minor after birth is like the insane, i.e., in lacking reason and discernment. However, when he reaches the age of reason, he resembles the idiot [and therefore] is allowed to adopt Islam as his faith."

Source: Muhammad Ibn Mahmud al-Asrushani, *Jami' ahkam al-sighar* (Cairo: Dar al-Fadila, n.d.), 1:112. English translation by Yaron Klein.

Document 3–33

Children and Ritual

Is it permissible for a boy to deliver a Friday sermon?
A boy delivers a Friday sermon reading from a written text, and an adult leads the people in prayer—this is permissible. . . .

Religious scholars differ regarding the issue of a Friday sermon delivered by a child. The disagreement assumes the child has full possession of his mental faculties.

Source: Muhammad Ibn Mahmud al-Asrushani, *Jami' ahkam al-sighar* (Cairo: Dar al-Fadila, n.d.), 1:41–42. English translation by Yaron Klein.

Document 3–34

Children and War: Al-Asrushani on Killing Children in Battle

Whenever the Messenger of God would send a body of troops [to battle] he used to say: "Do not kill a child, a woman or an elderly person [from among the enemy]." . . . These prophetic instructions refer to those [enemy] children who are not fit for battle, cannot shout when the ranks meet, and are not serving as military commanders. When they are, these children should be killed.

Source: Muhammad Ibn Mahmud al-Asrushani, *Jami' ahkam al-sighar* (Cairo: Dar al-Fadila, n.d.), 1:205. English translation by Yaron Klein.

Document 3–35

Children and War: Ibn Taymiyya on Killing Children in Battle

Since lawful warfare is essentially *jihad* [warfare against infidels] and since its aim is that the religion is God's entirely and God's word is uppermost, therefore, according to all Muslims, those who stand in the way of this aim must be fought. As for those who cannot offer resistance or cannot fight, such as women, children, monks, old people, the blind, handicapped and their likes, they shall not be killed, unless they actually fight with words [e.g., by propaganda] and acts [e.g., by spying and otherwise assisting in the warfare].

Some jurists are of the opinion that all of them may be killed, on the mere ground that they are unbelievers, but they make an exception for women and children since they constitute property for Muslims. However, the first opinion is the correct one, because we may only fight those who fight us when we want to make God's religion victorious. God, *Who is exalted*, has said in this respect: "And fight in the way of God with those who fight you, but aggress not: God loves not the aggressors" (Qur'an 2:190).

Source: Taqi al-Din Ibn Taymiyya, *al-Siyasa al-shar'iyya fi islah al-ra'i wa-al-ra'iyya* (Cairo: Dar al-Sha'b, 1971). English translation by Rudolph Peters in *Jihad in Classical and Modern Islam: A Reader* (Princeton: Markus Wiener, 1996), 49.

Document 3–36

Children of Non-Muslims

When a boy is captured in battle together with one of his [infidel] parents, and then dies in captivity, one should not pray over him. This is because he was a follower of his parents. The only exception is when the child has accepted Islam [before his death] while being in sound mind . . . or if one of his parents accepts Islam, since the child follows the parent who adheres to the better religion. If he was not captured along with one of his parents [and then died], one should pray over him, because in that case he, like a foundling, should be regarded as a Muslim due to the place of his residence [at the time of his captivity].

Source: Muhammad Ibn Mahmud al-Asrushani, *Jami' ahkam al-sighar* (Cairo: Dar al-Fadila, n.d.), 1:43. English translation by Yaron Klein.

Document 3–37

Children's Testimony

A boy testifies and the judge dismisses his testimony;
then he becomes of age and repeats his testimony
When a judge dismisses the testimony of a slave, a minor or an infidel, and they repeat their testimony after the slave has been manumitted, the minor has become of age and the infidel embraced Islam—their testimony is accepted. This is unlike the case of a sinner. When he testifies and his testimony is dismissed, this rejection holds even if he repents and testifies again. . . . (2:100)

Children's testimony regarding matters witnessed by children only
The testimony of children regarding what occurs in a playground is not accepted. . . . However, according to Malik [Ibn Anas], children's testimony regarding what is witnessed by children only is accepted. (2:100)

Determining the impurity of water by a statement of a child
The impurity of water could not be determined on the basis of a statement made either by a child or by an idiot. Their limited understanding may cause them to lie and make it impossible for others to determine whether they speak the truth or not. This is why an account by a child or an idiot is not acceptable [in court] in matters of law, and no child or idiot has ever transmitted any prophetic tradition from the Messenger of God. However, one should look into their claim and give one's judgment on it. If it is found that they were telling the truth, one should not [use the water to] perform ablution; if it is found that they were not, one can perform ablution with it. This applies to cases in which the child or the idiot have full possession of their mental faculties. If they do not, one should not pay attention to what they say at all. . . . (1:210)

Source: Muhammad Ibn Mahmud al-Asrushani, *Jami' ahkam al-sighar* (Cairo: Dar al-Fadila, n.d.). English translation by Yaron Klein.

Infant and Child Mortality

The frequency of infant and child deaths in medieval Muslim societies (as in other premodern societies), is the background against which Arabic-Islamic writings reacting to this reality should be read. Mortality rates were high in general, but particularly from the fourteenth century onward, when so many children fell victim to epidemics of the Black Death.

Two levels of reactions to infant and child mortality are worth mentioning here: Religious-theoretical, on the one hand, and emotional, on the other. While juridical and theological discussions dealing with the ways in which deceased infants and children should be treated and their fate in the Hereafter reflect the scholars' awareness of the uniqueness of children as well as the religious problems connected with their death, there are other genres that mirror the emotional confrontation with the phenomenon. They are mainly poems of lamentation and special treatises compiled to console bereaved parents.

The most intriguing themes of the consolation treatises are the tension they reveal between the emotional-spontaneous type of reaction and the religious-"rational" one, and the efforts they make to harmonize them. Among several types of parent-child relations, these writings bring to light strong psychological links between adults and children that result in moving emotional reactions in cases of death. However, in contrast with this type of reaction, other reports, equally reflected in many hadiths and anecdotes cited in the consolation treatises, call for restraint and control, to avoid any sort of protest against a divine decree, and even point out the religious "advantages" of children's death. Among the texts presented in this section are: *Man la yahduruhu al-faqih* (He Who Has No Scholar in His Proximity), one of the "Four Books" of the canonized Ithna-'ashari-Shi'ite collections of traditions compiled by Muhammad Ibn 'Ali Ibn Babuya (Arabized Ibn Babawayh) from Qumm in Iran (d. 991 CE); *Maqalat al-islamiyyin wa-ikhtilaf al-musallin* (The Muslims' Beliefs and Their [Theological] Disagreements) by Abu al-Hasan al-Ash'ari (died in Baghdad in 935 or 936 CE), the founder of the school of orthodox theology in Islam; *Tasliyat ahl al-masa'ib (fi mawt al-awlad wa-al-aqarib)* (Consolation for Those in Distress [over the Death of Children and Relatives]) compiled in north Syria by Abu 'Abdallah Muhammad Ibn Muhammad al-Manbiji, a fourteenth-century Hanbali scholar, to console Muslims who lost their relatives in the disastrous outbreaks of plague at the time; and another treatise of the same genre, *Sulwan al-musab bi-furqat al-ahbab* (Consoling Those Smitten by Calamity on the Separation from Their Beloved) by the Palestinian scholar Mar'i Ibn Yusuf al-Maqdisi (d. in Cairo in 1624 CE).

Document 3–38

Legal Considerations

Narrated 'Abd al-Rahman Ibn Waqid, from . . . Ibn Shawdhab: "A dead child was born to Qatada [an eighth-century scholar from Basra]. He named it Muhammad and prayed over it."

I asked Ahmad Ibn Hanbal: "When should one pray over an aborted fetus?" He replied: "When it is at least four months old, one should pray over it, and give it a name."

Narrated 'Ali Ibn Ja'd, from . . . Sa'id Ibn al-Musayyab: "I heard Sa'id Ibn Jubayr saying: 'One should not pray over a [dead] infant.'" Narrated 'Amr: "I mentioned this to Ibn Abi Layla, who said: 'I witnessed the remaining of the ansar[9] praying in their congregations over their dead-born children.'"

Narrated 'Ali Ibn al-Hasan, from . . . Ibrahim: "If a new-born child screams, then dies one should pray over him, and he should be entitled to inherit."

Source: 'Abdallah Ibn Abi al-Dunya, *Kitab al-'iyal* (Al-Mansura: Dar al-Wafa, 1997), 265–266. English translation by Yaron Klein.

It is agreed upon that one should not pray over a dead fetus. There are different opinions, however, regarding washing it. The preferred view is that it should be washed and buried wrapped in a cloth. It is mentioned in regard to foundlings. Muhammad [Ibn al-Hasan al-Shaybani] said: "And [the dead fetus] should also be named."

It is said in the *Dhakhira* [by the Hanafi jurist Mahmud Ibn Ahmad al-Bukhari (d. 1219 or 1220 CE)]: "When a dead child is born, one should not wash him or pray over him." In *Sharh al-Tahawi* [compiled in the tenth century CE]: "If most of the child's body has already come out while the child was alive, and only then did he die, one should pray over him, otherwise not. This is regardless of whether the baby comes out head first, or the legs come out before the head."

In [*Sharh Mukhtasar al-Tahawi* by] Ahmad Ji [d. sometime in the eleventh or twelfth century CE]: "A child can either be born alive or dead. If he is born alive [then dies] he should be washed, and a prayer should be said for him. He is entitled to receive heritage, inherit, and be named. If he is born dead he should not be washed. . . . One should also not pray over him nor give him a name; he cannot receive inheritance nor inherit." According to Muhammad [Ibn al-Hasan al-Shaybani] he should be named.

Source: Muhammad Ibn Mahmud al-Asrushani, *Jami' ahkam al-sighar* (Cairo: Dar al-Fadila, n.d.), 1:42–43. English translation by Yaron Klein.

Document 3–39

Theological Considerations: Al-Ash'ari on the Fate of Children in the Hereafter

The Rafidites [Ar. *Rawafid*, "rejectors," "abandoners," an abusive term used throughout the ninth century CE to designate the followers of the Shi'a] differ over the chastisement of children in the Hereafter. They can be divided into two groups: The first claims that God has the right either to torment children or to forgive them. . . .

The second group, the followers of [the Shi'te-Imami theologian] Hisham Ibn al-Hakam [d. 814 CE] . . . maintain that it is impossible for God to torment children, and that they are [all] in Paradise.

Most of the members of the Ibadiyya [one of the main branches of the Kharijites (Ar. Khawarij), the earliest religious sect in Islam, created in the seventh century CE] hesitated about whether the children of polytheists were caused pain in the Hereafter. They found it conceivable that God would inflict pain upon them in the Hereafter, for reasons other than revenge. They also thought it believable that He would admit them into Paradise as an act of grace. Others maintained that God inflicts pain on these children by necessity, not as a voluntary act.

The Kharijites hold three doctrines regarding children [in the Hereafter]: One group of them claims that the children of polytheists will be judged like their fathers [therefore destined] to be tormented in Hell. [They also claim] that the ruling in regards to the children of believers is likewise identical to that of their fathers [which means that they will follow them to Paradise]. This group disagrees as to those children whose fathers converted after their own [premature] death. Some of them are of the opinion that in that case, the children are converted [postmortem] along with their fathers and the ruling regarding them follows that of the latter. Others maintain that children who die are considered as being in the state their fathers were in on the day of their death, and that they do not convert [after their death] by their fathers' conversion.

The second group claims: It is possible for God to cause pain to the children of the polytheists in Hell not as a punishment, and it is possible that He will not do so. As for the children of believers, they will join their parents, according to God's promise: "And those who believed, and their seed followed them in belief, We shall join their seed with them" . . . (Qur'an 52:21; trans. Arberry). According to a third group (the Qadariyya), the children of both polytheists and believers are in Paradise.

There was a disagreement among the Mu'tazilites [lit., "those who keep themselves apart"; members of one of the theological schools in Islam (founded in the eighth century CE) known for relying on human reason to reach religious truths] with regard to children's pain [in this world]: . . . Some of them said that God torments children not [necessarily] for a [certain] reason. However, they rejected the idea that He compensates children [in this world] for the suffering He had inflicted upon them. They rejected [also] the possibility that He will punish them in the Hereafter.

Most of the Mu'tazilites claimed that God causes children pain as a lesson for those who are legally majors. He then compensates those children, for if not, by tormenting them He would have been committing injustice.

Another Mu'tazilite group argued that God torments children in order to compensate them although it is possible, and [indeed] more fitting, that He compensates children without having caused them suffering. However, He is not obliged to act according to the better option. . . . They also disagreed regarding the compensation that children deserve: is it perpetual or not? Some argued that the compensation they deserve is perpetual whereas others claimed that the perpetuation of the compensation is by way of grace, not by deservingness.

The Mu'tazilites agreed that it is inconceivable that God will cause suffering to children in the Hereafter and torment them.

Source: Abu al-Hasan 'Ali Ibn Isma'il al-Ash'ari, *Maqalat al-islamiyyin wa-ikhtilaf al-musallin*, edited by H. Ritter (Wiesbaden: Franz Steiner, 1980), 55, III, 125, 253. English translation by Yaron Klein.

Document 3–40

Theological Considerations: Ibn Babawayh on the Fate of Children in the Hereafter

Narrated Wahb Ibn Wahb, from . . . 'Ali: "The children of the polytheists are with their parents in Hell, and the children of the Muslims are with their parents in Paradise."

Narrated Ja'far Ibn Bashir, from 'Abdallah Ibn Sinan: "I asked Abu 'Abdallah what happens to the children of the polytheists who die before they reach the age in which they are accountable for their sins. He replied: 'They are infidels, and only God, *to Him belong might and majesty*, knows what they would have done [if they lived]. They will enter wherever their parents will.'"

Narrated Abu 'Abdallah: "Fire will set up for them [i.e., for the children of the polytheists], and they will be asked to jump into it. Those who will go into the fire will find it cool and harmless. As to those who will refuse, they will be addressed by God, *to Him belong might and majesty*, who will say to them, 'I have given you an order and you have disobeyed me.' Then God will order them to be sent to Hell."

Source: Ibn Babawayh al-Qummi, *Man la yahduruhu al-faqih* (Beirut: Dar al-Adwa', 1985), 3:317. English translation by Yaron Klein.

Document 3–41

Emotional Reactions to the Death of Infants and Children: Consoling Bereaved Parents in Times of Plague

Since calamities of various kinds—death or other misfortunes of time—are agonizing and tormenting disasters, terrifying and daunting events, the prophetic traditions include [descriptions of] the [high] ranks arranged [in Paradise] for those who were inflicted upon and glad tidings for the bereaved who endured these calamities and anticipate a reward in the Hereafter. One of the authorities of early times said: "If not for the calamities of this world, we would have arrived at the Day of Judgment empty handed."

This was beautifully expressed in a poem [by Abu Firas al-Hamadani]:

> "Man is a prisoner of never-ending calamities
> Until his body is laid in its eternal abode
> He whose [own] death is postponed encounters death in others
> While he whose death is hastened finds death in himself."

I wanted to compile a book that would bring consolation to the hearts of the bereaved, and would relieve the grief of those [whose heart is] burnt. I called it *Consolation for Those in Distress [on the Death of Children and Relatives].*

What prompted me to write this book is the plague that broke out in the year 775 AH [1374 CE] on the month of Rajab [the seventh in the Hijri calendar], and worsened at the end of the [tenth] month of Shawal, [the eleventh—] Dhu al-Qa'da, and [the twelfth—] Dhu al-Hijja. It decreased in the [first] month—Muharram—of the following year. During the plague, thousands of people died, and many homes were left empty. Many of these people were virtuous and pious believers. Thus, as so many excellent believers died, I designated the plague "the plague of the virtuous." But in fact, most of the casualties were children, to the point that several of my friends who had a number of offspring were left without any child.

I had already compiled, in the year 765 AH [1363 or 1364 CE], a book on the plague and the religious-legal rules connected with it. The book is a fine work, and I received nothing but praise for it. I included in it a large number of prophetic traditions and historical reports but not [a description of] what God has installed for the victims of plagues. I therefore dedicate this book as a comfort to whoever has been afflicted with the tragedies of this world; I have not seen nor have I heard of anyone who escaped some sort of affliction. . . .

From Usama Ibn Zayd: "We were in the home of the Prophet, *may God bless and save him,* when one of his daughters sent a messenger calling for him and informing him that one of her sons was dying. The Prophet said to the messenger: 'Go back and tell her that whatever God takes or gives is His possession, and all of His possession have a determined end. Tell her to show perseverance and to anticipate a reward in the Hereafter.' The messenger returned and said: 'She pleaded under oath that you would come to her.' The Prophet, *may God bless and save him,* rose along with [his companions] Sa'd Ibn 'Ubada, Mu'adh Ibn Jabal, Ubayy Ibn Ka'b, and Zayd Ibn Thabit, and I left with them. The boy was brought to the Prophet, clattering as someone near his death, and the Prophet's eyes were overflowing. [Looking at him] Sa'd Ibn 'Ubada, asked the Prophet: 'What is it, O Messenger of God?' And he replied: 'This is a sign of compassion that God has put in the hearts of His worshipers. God has compassion only on those worshipers of His who are themselves compassionate.'"

From Anas [Ibn Malik], *may God be pleased with him*: "The Messenger of God, *may God bless and save him,* said: 'A son was born to me, and I named him after my father, Ibrahim.'. . . Soon after we visited him, Ibrahim was about to pass away. The eyes of the Messenger of God began to shed tears . . . he put the boy in his arms and [while weeping] said: 'My little son, I have no ownership over you from God.' Then 'Abd al-Rahman Ibn 'Awf and Anas both asked: 'O Messenger of God, how is it that you cry while you forbid crying [on the dead]?' And the Prophet said: 'O Ibn 'Awf, this is compassion. Whoever has no compassion will receive no compassion.' Then he addressed them again and said: 'The eye sheds tears, the heart grieves, but we only say what pleases God. O Ibrahim, we are anguished by your departure. . . .'"

Abu al-Walid told us . . . from al-Bara' saying: "When Ibrahim, the son of the Prophet, *may God bless and save him*, died the Messenger of God said: 'He has a wet nurse in Paradise. . . . '" This was so, because Ibrahim died while he was still a suckling of seventeen or sixteen months old. . . .

Some of the transmissions report the Prophet saying: "My son died while still suckling. He has a wet nurse in Paradise." There is no indication that this arrangement was made for the Prophet's son alone. . . . [Indeed] this is a general right pertaining to all children of the believers, as is supported by a certain tradition that I do not have before me at the moment, but the content of which is: "In Paradise there is a tree carrying female breasts from which infants suck."

These are very glad tidings for the believers regarding their [dead] babies; they set the parents' minds at rest. . . .

Source: Abu 'Abdallah Muhammad Ibn Muhammad al-Manbiji, *Tasliyat ahl al-msa'ib* (Beirut: Mu'assasat al-Iman and Damascus: Dar al-Rashid, 1988), 8, 53, 54, 136. English translation by Yaron Klein.

Document 3–42

Emotional Reactions to the Death of Infants and Children:
Consoling Bereaved Parents

['Abd al-Rahman] Ibn al-Jawzi [d. 1200 CE] relates in his *al-Tawwabin* [The Repentants] that Malik Ibn Dinar [a preacher and moralist, died in Basra in 748 or 749 CE], being asked about his repentance, said: "Once, when I was a police officer, I bought an expensive slave girl. I was very fond of her, and she gave birth to a girl, whom I loved very much. When she would crawl on the ground, my heart went out for her even more. We were very close. When she was two years old, she died, and I grieved over her. Then, one night, on the Friday of the middle of the month of Sha'ban [the eighth month of the Islamic lunar year],[10] I saw in my dream as though the Day of Resurrection had occurred. The horn was blown,[11] the dead were raised from their graves[12] and gathered together, I being among them. Suddenly, I heard a sound. I turned and in front of me was a great sea monster colored black and blue. It opened its mouth and hastened towards me. I ran away from him terrified and shocked. On my way, I passed by an old man, wearing a clean garment and having [a] pleasant smell. I greeted him, and he greeted me back. I said: 'Oh old man, protect me from that sea monster, may God reward you.' The old man wept and said: 'I am weak and that one [the monster] is stronger than me. Go and make haste, perhaps God will lead you to something that will save you from it.' I turned away running, and mounted one of the high places of the resurrection site. The strata of Hell were close to me, and I almost fell into them out of fear. Then, a voice called: 'Go back! you are not of the people of Hell.' I trusted this voice and turned around, the sea monster following me. I reached [again] the old man and said: 'Master, I have asked you to save me from this sea monster, and you would not.' The old man cried and said: 'I am weak. But go to that mountain. It contains the deposits of the Muslims. If you have one in it, it will stand up for you.' I looked [and saw] a round silver mountain. It had openings carved into it with curtains hanging [in front]. On each opening there were two doors from red gold set with sapphire hemmed with pearls. When I saw the mountain I hurried towards it, the sea monsters behind me. The moment I got near it, one of the angels *prayers and peace be upon them*, called: 'Remove the curtains, and open the doors and look at him, perhaps this poor man has a deposit among you that will save him from his enemy.' When the doors opened, they rose to look at me, and I saw small children as [beautiful as] moons. The sea monster came ever close to me, and I did not know what to do. Then one of the children called: 'Woe unto you! rise and look at him all of you, for his enemy is approaching him.' Group after group they rose and looked at me, until suddenly my dead daughter appeared. She looked at me, wept and said: 'By God, this is my father!' Then she jumped in a palm of light, as fast as an arrow, reached me and put her left hand in my right hand, and held onto it. She pointed her right hand towards the sea monster, and he turned away running. Then, she seated me and sat in my lap, then she pointed her right hand towards my beard, and said: 'Dear father, "Is it not time that the hearts of those who believe should be humbled to the Remembrance of God?" . . . (Qur'an 57:16; trans. Arberry) I wept, and said: 'My dear daughter, you [children] know the Qur'an?' and she said: 'Dear father, we know it better than you [the living ones] do.' I said to her: 'Tell me about that sea monster that wanted to kill me.' She replied: 'It was your bad deeds. You made it strong. It wanted to drown you in the fire of Hell.' I said: 'And the old man?' She said: 'That was your good deeds. You made it weak to the point that it did not have the power to stand up against your bad deeds.' I said: 'My daughter, what are you doing on this mountain?' and she said: 'We, the children of the believers, reside in it waiting for you, until the Time [the Day of Resurrection] will come. On that day, you will come to us and we will intercede on your behalf.' Said Malik Ibn Dinar: 'I woke up frightened and in shock, I then broke the forbidden [musical] instruments, abandoned [the lifestyle I was living in], and repented to God. And God accepted my repentance.'"

Source: Mar'i Ibn Yusuf Ibn Abi Bakr Ibn Ahmad al-Qudsi al-Hanbali, *Sulwan al-musab bi-furqat al-ahbab* (Cairo: Dar al-Haramayn, 2000), 79. English translation by Yaron Klein.

NOTES

I am grateful to Yaron Klein, of Harvard University, whose cooperation throughout the work on this chapter proved essential. My deep gratitude goes also to my friend Dick Bruggeman for helping me edit the chapter.

1. Qur'an 112, 1–2, English translation by A. J. Arberry, *The Koran Interpreted* (London: George Allen & Unwin; New York: Macmillan, 1971), 2:361. Cited hereafter as (Qur'an, translation Arberry).

2. A. van Gennep, *The Rites of Passage* (London: Routledge and Kegan Paul, 1977), 3.

3. E. Warnock Fernea, "Introduction," in *Children in the Muslim Middle East,* edited by Elizabeth Warnock Fernea (Austin: University of Texas Press, 1995), 7–9.

4. Van Gennep, *Rites of Passage,* 72.

5. In Islamic tradition, the question whether Isma'il (Ishmael) or Ishaq (Isaac) was sacrificed by Ibrahim (Abraham) has remained open.

6. It is celebrated on the tenth through fourteenth of Dhu al-Hijja, the last month in the Hijri calendar, while the pilgrims to Mecca offer their sacrifice in the valley of Mina.

7. "And call in to witness two witnesses, men; or if the two be not men, then one man and two women, such witnesses as you approve of, that if one of the two women errs the other will remind her" (Qur'an 2:282; trans. Arberry).

8. A legendary figure featured in the Qur'an (sura 31) as a wise father giving pious admonitions to his son.

9. The people of Medina who welcomed the Prophet Muhammad and supported him after his escape from persecutions in Mecca and his immigration to their oasis.

10. According to Islamic tradition, in the night of the middle of Sha'ban God descends to the lower heaven and from there he calls the mortals in order to grant them forgiveness of sin.

11. See Qur'an 6:73.

12. See Qur'an 100:9.

4

Hinduism

LAURIE L. PATTON

Recent work on childhood in India has made the crucial point that the child is defined by what the child is *not*. As the classical literature on childhood has also argued, there are several ways we can think about the idea of the "child" and its opposite.[1] We can understand a child as a small homunculus, with lesser physical capacities than the adult, but with the same basic makeup. We can romanticize the child as a creature of innocence, closer to the sources of life (both "wild" and "divine") than adults. We can think of the child as a being yet to be formed psychologically and therefore faced with a variety of "developmental" challenges. We can mine the child as a potential source of labor. These various ways of conceptualizing childhood in India are not only ways of categorizing groups of children; rather, the figure of the child also has a role in the relationships between adult social groups. In the context of colonialism, the people "ruled" are also likened to children. Their "primitive" nature is likened to the childhood of humanity, and their innocent/ threatening qualities are the lenses through which the rulers view their subjects.

It is important to note at the outset that the term "Hinduism" as such is a construct, and does not reflect a singular entity, but rather a set of plural practices with some loose resemblance to one another. "Hinduism" as such was not used as a term until, at the very earliest, the tenth century in India, and only came into common parlance during the late Moghul and early British colonial periods. What is more, during the period of British rule, in a variety of interreligious polemics between colonial missionaries, colonial administrators, orthodox Hindu leaders, and less orthodox Hindu reformers, we see a grappling with the presence of multiple religions, and with the abstract idea of "religion" as such, and even more, "Hinduism" as such.

All of these dynamics are in play in the understanding of children within the complex and diverse set of traditions we now call "Hinduism." Two specific dynamics are most prominent with Hindu ideologies: first, the idea of the child as "ritually formed" as he or she goes through the various stages of becoming an adult; and second, the idea of the child as closer to the divine, especially in mythological and iconographic traditions. In many texts, there is an interaction between these two ideas, where the human child can contain some of the divine within, and gods can be depicted as very human children. Due to the general scope of this chapter, our discussion of these dynamics can be only representative and not exhaustive.

Early Texts

Beginning with the compositions of the Vedas, the earliest of which is dated by most scholars to around 1500 BCE, the idea of childhood, and of the overall life cycle, is bound up with a sacrificial ideology and way of life. "Veda" means knowledge, and the four Vedas constellate around the mechanics of sacrifice—*Rig-* (Verses); *Sama-* (Chants); *Yajur-* (Ritual procedures); *Atharva-* (Incantations) *Veda*. The *Rig Veda* is thus literally "Knowledge of the Verses," sacred mantras recited during sacrificial performance. Although the particular ways of life and prescriptions for conduct are no longer followed in contemporary India, the Vedas have created the basis for much of both classical and contemporary Hinduism. The ancient Vedic tribes, calling themselves "Aryan" or "noble," understood the daily, monthly, and yearly offerings to the gods as the "machinery" of the universe—that action which caused the world to be orderly, helped the seasons to turn, and the sun to rise and set as expected.

Thus, from the Vedas onward, the birth of a son is a crucial part of a prosperous life and lineage, and guarantees a good ritual death.[2] We can see this as early as *Rig Veda* 5.78, the hymn to Saptavadhri (Doc. 6-1). As legend has it, the sage Saptavadhri was called upon to help a king beget a child. When this event did not occur, the sage was thrown into the trough of a tree, and chanted a hymn to help himself both escape his arboreal prison and to help a child be born alive. The basic childhood rituals of the late Vedic period can be glimpsed in the domestic texts called Grihya Sutras.[3]

As the Aryan groups settled more permanently in the areas around the Gangetic Plain (900–400 BCE), a new way of living emerged in which sacrifice was not the only mode of ritual construction of the self and of the community. Rather, those thinkers who wanted to meditate upon the power behind the sacrifice moved away from the settled villages and into the forest to form schools. There, young students would gather around a teacher and discuss the nature of Brahman, the monistic force that animates all things in the universe. Childhood involved a period of celibate studentship (*brahmacarya*), living like the son of a teacher in the teacher's house. The conversations between student and teacher were recorded in texts called the Upanishads (900–300 BCE).[4] In the Upanishads, the idea of sacrifice was internalized, and seen as sacrifice within the body. Childhood development, then, involved gaining knowledge of Brahman through meditation and observation of one's own breathing body, and the identification of the smaller self with the larger "self" of Brahman. The *Chandogya Upanishad* (4.4–10) story of Satyakama Jabvala (Doc. 4–2) illustrates this idea beautifully. As a response to a test from his teacher, Satyakama goes to learn the nature of Brahman from the various elements in nature. The child gains wisdom from the natural world and the household of his teacher.

In addition to these rituals and educational guides, the more popular epics give us a rich account of the childhood of Kshatriyas, or the warrior or royal class. The classical world of India begins to emerge in the great Indian epic narratives, composed in verse form, between the second century BCE and the second century CE. The *Mahabharata* epic tells the story of the Pandavas, or sons of King Pandu, growing up with their cousins, the Kauravas, in Hastinapura—probably somewhere north of Delhi in the Gangetic plain.[5] The first book gives a vivid account of the childhood beginnings of the catastrophic jealousy that started the great and bloody war that is the main topic of the story (Doc. 4–3). The epic shows that the seeds of later social life, and the violence and loss to come, are sown in the so-called innocence of childhood games.[6]

While the *Mahabharata* injects a certain realism into our idea of ancient Indian childhood, a legal, or shastric, text called the *Laws of Manu* gives us the most idealized form of the right ways to grow up.[7] The shastras, or legal texts, of which the *Laws of Manu* is one, should not be seen as exact equivalents to legal treatises written in Enlightenment Europe. They are rather regional compendia of rules, rituals, and obligations for the conduct of life, and have also been translated as "custom" or "practice."

In the ritual formation of a child into an adult, *Manu* begins with the foetus and ends with the student. In *Manu*, offerings are given for the benefit of the foetus before it is even born. When the child is born and the umbilical cord is cut, the child is fed gold, honey, and ghee to the accompaniment of Vedic mantras. On the tenth or twelfth day, the child is given a name. The fourth month occasions the "walking around" of the child outside the house. The first cutting of the hair is given in the first or third year of childhood.

The initiation into the Veda, called the *upanayana*, or in *Manu*, "the tying of the *munja* grass girdle," is the most crucial rite of passage. It is literally a second birth, a birth from the Veda. A Brahmin is said to have three births—first from the mother; second, at this *upanayana*; and the third at the consecration of a sacrifice. At the *upanayana*, Savitri, the impeller, is said to be the child's mother, and his actual teacher is said to be the father, because he enables the student to perform rites. Until then he is not a "ritual" person, but a "preritual" person.

The timing of this ritual is dependent upon caste: one can perform an *upanayana* for a Brahmin child as young as eight years old (or even five if he is an ambitious student), and as late as sixteen years. For each of the lower castes (Kshatriya and Vaishya), the age range is moved up. The official period of childhood, if it is determined ritually, can end at either age five or at age twenty-four, depending upon both caste and ambition. Thus, while the early Indian ritual construction of childhood and adulthood might seem strictly determined, the actual system can be quite flexible.

What should the behavior of a student look like? *Manu* (2.225ff.) states that a young person's comportment should involve a respect for one's elders, because of the sacrifices they make for the child. Each of the elders is the embodiment of a god; obedience of a child toward a parent is said to be the highest form of ascetic toil.

Although the earlier Grihya texts imply that girls were able to have some Vedic learning, for the classical shastras, the major initiation rite for girls is marriage, which occurs usually after the onset of the first menstrual period. Manu states in 2.67 that the marriage ceremony equals the rite of consecration; serving the husband equals serving the teacher, and care of the house equals care of the sacred fires.[8] *Manu* (9.94-100) goes on to write that a thirty-year-old should marry a girl of twelve years of age. This marriage would also involve paying a bride price, but the groom's family should do so only if the goal was marriage and not the covert sale of a daughter. *Manu* 9.90 also argues that a girl shall wait after the onset of puberty for three years, and if she is not given in marriage, then she may find a husband on her own without incurring any fault. (However, she may not bring her own wealth into that liaison.) Many of the Vedic marriage rites also imply that the girl moves to the groom's home. Thus, for a girl, the end of childhood involves menstruation, marriage, and the move into a husband's home.

The shastric literature is not only concerned with initiation rites for children, however. In other passages about the behavior of Brahmins and kings, we see other statements about the power as well as the vulnerabilities of children. *Manu* 4.178 states that a Brahmin should foreswear arguments with children, among others. Here, children are understood to be rulers of "space," or the intermediate world, along with other vulnerable groups such as the aged, the feeble, and the sick. For Manu, "right relationship" is what constitutes the self, and children constitute a great part of a self's relationship. Similarly, *Manu* 9.45 argues that "wife, self and offspring" is the extent of "man"–thus he is defined legally by these relationships with his children. The son's identity is also defined by relationships. The son's ability to inherit as a full relative of two parents is circumscribed, depending on the caste and marriage status of those parents. To be a son is one thing, to be a son *and* heir is another (*Manu* 9.158–161).

So, too, children are considered vulnerable in their ability to inherit: *Manu* 8.27 argues that the king should protect the estate inherited by a child until he has returned home after his Vedic studentship and while he is a minor. Continuing this theme of vulnerability, *Manu* 11.202 also prohibits cohabiting with those who have killed children, women, and those who have come to them for protection. Yet vulnerability is also a complex category. It is worthy of honor as well as of protection; it is stated in *Manu* 8.395 that a king should honor Vedic scholars, the sick, and children, the aged, the poor, men from illustrious families and Aryas, or noble ones. Legal debates about the ownership of children, and their resulting identities, also occur in *Manu*, such as in 9.32.

Finally, children are also part of the cycle of purity and impurity associated with death. The impurity of the relatives after the death of a child depends upon a child's age. A child under two does not have bones collected after cremation, nor should any offerings of water be performed at the funeral rites. Rather, the body should be left behind in the wilderness "like a piece of wood" (*Manu* 5.68–70). Here, in stark detail, is the idea of a child being "less than a person," in the minimalism of the funeral rites.

The larger implications of these and other shastric laws are that the child learns the higher aims of humanity—the cultivation of sacred role or conduct (*dharma*), the regulation of desire (*kama*) and for some, the achievement of liberation (*moksha*). A child learns his or her own dharma through rituals, collectively known as *samskaras*, as well as the teachings of his caste (*varna*) and birth occupation (*jati*). Childhood is part of the larger cycle of the stages of life, which include early childhood (*balam*); studentship (*brahmacarya*); householdership (*grihasthana*); forest dwelling, semi-retirement (*vanaprastha*); and renunciation before death (*samnyasa*). Occasionally, for the upper castes, renunciation with an aim of achieving *moksha* could also occur during youth.

As Sudhir Kakar writes, dharma is a central concept that a child learns as a "life task" as well as part of a "life cycle." One has one's own dharma (*svadharma*), including family and social relationships, as well as dharma as a social force, that particular set of "right relationships" which keeps the order in society as a whole. One also has *ashramadharma*, the following of roles throughout the life cycle.[9] A child learns early on that the right way to cultivate dharma is through the conduct of ritual action, and right action more generally, also known as karma. Any action produces a tangible result, either in this life or the next, in the endless cycle of birth, death, and suffering we know as samsara (Doc. 4–5). Someone who is born in this life and commits violent or irresponsible acts will inevitably experience their results, or "fruits" at some point in the future. Through both daily and ritual activity, the child develops moral responsibility.[10]

Classical and Medieval Texts

The responsibilities and vulnerabilities of children are expressed in a markedly different way in the classical myths of Krishna. In these texts, the innocence and openness of the child is combined with divine strength. The Puranas (c. 400–1700 CE) are filled with theologically motivated narratives, whose purpose is to extol and explain the particular attributes of a god—particularly the gods of the classical Hindu pantheon Vishnu, Shiva, Devi the goddess, and Brahma, the creator god. Krishna is an avatar of Vishnu, the preserver who takes incarnation in order to save the world of a particular evil.

In a motif also found in the Greek and Christian traditions, the *Bhagavata*

Purana (ninth to the thirteenth century CE (Doc. 4–6) tells how Krishna's life is saved from an evil king's intentions by a miracle of "switching" at birth.[11] In the better-known tales of Krishna's childhood, the god grows up as a cowherd under the care of Yashoda and her husband. Krishna is known as a butter thief, a charming baby whose love of milk, cream, butter, and mischief gets him into a great deal of trouble. The most famous story of Krishna's eating concerns not dairy products, however, but dirt. When Yashoda hears that he has eaten dirt, she rushes over to him and commands that he open his mouth. When he does, she sees a vision of the universe—the wind, moon, stars, mountains, islands, all the elements and creatures within the known world. Yashoda has an experience of liberation through her child Krishna. Krishna also performs godlike feats as he moves into adolescence; the story of his trampling the serpent Kaliya is one example.

All of these legends of Krishna juxtapose the divinity of god with the vulnerability of a child. Unlike some other myths of childhood, however, the superhuman qualities of the child surprise and jolt people into a sense of true reality. The divine child is the coincidence of opposites that allows people to meditate upon the basic awesomeness of the universe, just when they are the least expecting it. The sixteenth-century poems of the devotional poet Sur Das explicitly plays with this tension (Doc. 4–7). The myths about the more mature Krishna explicitly dwell upon the less domestic themes of romantic and erotic love in separation, where Krishna's lover, the cowherdess Radha, becomes the archetypal devotee in her longing for Krishna. Even in his adult form, however, Krishna retains many of his childlike, playful aspects. He frequently trills whimsically on his flute, and in one *lila*, or moment of play, he appears to all of the cowherdesses together as if he were the sole lover of each one of them. Indeed, the creation of the entire universe is frequently likened to the childlike play of Krishna.[12]

This idea of the child-god's cosmic play is also enacted in the various communities associated with Krishna—particularly Brindavan and Mathura, in north India. On particular holidays, especially that of Krishna's birthday, dramatic plays (also called *lilas*) reenact the childhood events of Krishna's life. Here, a boy chosen from the community literally becomes the god Krishna as he enacts the part. He is understood by the audience to be an actual avatar of the god at that moment. The *lila* gives the boy divine status. This idea is crucial to Hindu notions of the child—that all children possess within them divine qualities and can act as gateways to god.

The medieval bhakti movements also provide an intriguing lens onto late medieval and early modern ideas about childhood. Many saints, such as Tukaram and Mirabai, have biographies with childhood miracles and great devotional feats attached to them.[13] In one rare document, we see the childhood narratives of seventeenth-century Bahina Bai (1628-1700) (Doc. 4-8), a Maharashtrian devotee of Saint Tukaram and a saint in her own right.[14] A childhood love of a calf was her first experience of bhakti—literally, intense longing and devotion to God. In the section included here, she narrates her experience of the loss of the calf, and how she comes to terms with it through devotion to Tukoba (Saint Tukaram.) She narrates some of the many difficulties of being a child bride, and the longing (both childlike and adult at the same time) to see the Shudra saint Tukaram in person, and the difficulties she has in persuading her husband and family to go to him.

In a later collection of poems, Ramprasad Sen, an eighteenth-century bhakti poet from Bengal, writes of the childhood of the mother goddess in complex imagery that provided the frame for this chapter (Doc. 4-9). In these poems, the mother is simultaneously child and adult; ferocious and tame. In poem 30, her play is similar to Krishna's *lila*—playing "tricks" of *maya*, or illusion, that can confound the world and make ordinary people confuse the divine and everyday reality. In poem 32, she is described as a pouting daughter, Uma, who is also called "Mother."

Colonial Dynamics

The mythology of childhood in Hinduism takes a very different hue when examined in the light of social life and British colonial legislation. Here, British and Indian (both Hindu and Muslim) views clashed severely as to the appropriate spheres for children and adults.[15] Satadru Sen writes convincingly of the colonial construction of childhood, which he sees as a "failed institutional attempt" to discipline and, even create, Indian children in the traditional European mode.[16] Using a Foucauldian perspective that links the prison, the hospital, and the school, he notes the doubleness that we have also noted in our introduction: that natives were already perceived as childlike, and thus the children of natives were doubly marginal. In addition to his legal analysis, Sen's work focuses on both reform schools, such as Matunga, as well as elite schools, such as Chief's College. Sen concludes that these institutions were short lived because in colonial eyes, the Indian child could never fully be a "child" in the European sense, and thus never able to gain the full authority of an adult, either.[17]

Much of the colonial debate about children centered on issues of the girl child. In times of social upheaval and change, the security of women, particularly young girls, becomes a large issue; this anxiety may be one of the many reasons for the Hindu community adopting earlier and earlier ages for child marriage during the Moghul and the colonial periods. The practice of child marriage led to a number of other social problems, such as child mothers, a high mortality rate among child wives and their children, and child widows. The first reform movements concerning this issue of child marriage occurred in the nineteenth-century colonial period, with women reformers like Pandita Ramabai leading the way. The issue of child marriage was conceptually linked to the questions of enforced widowhood and property rights for women, as well as the practice of dowry. Some reformers also argued that early marriage was also detrimental for boys, interfering as it did with their education and natural development, in addition to being physically detrimental for both girls and boys.[18]

Inspired by early voices such as the educator I. C. Vidyasagar, in the 1860s Keshub Chandra Sen and other members of the Reform Brahmo Samaj attempted a series of legislative acts to limit the marriageable age for girls. Laws were passed in 1872 and later. In October of 1929, under the pressure of many women's groups and reformers, the Marriage Bill (also called the Sarda Act) fixed the marriageable age for boys at eighteen and for girls at fourteen. However, while the Sarda Act raised the age of marriage, the bill did not make child marriage a punishable offense, and thus the practice of child marriage persisted, usually incurring the payment of a nominal fine. This act was finally given teeth after Independence in 1955, when, as part of the Marriage Restraint Act of the Hindu code, child marriage was made a punishable offense and the age of the girl was raised to fifteen. In many parts of India, the practice was dying out due not only to reformer's efforts but also due to economics; the expenses of weddings were such that many poor and middle-class families felt the need to delay daughters' weddings because of both World War Two and the effects of Partition. Finally, the higher marriage age was partly due to the better education of girls. Many efforts were succeeding around the education of girls; beginning with reform efforts in the nineteenth century, the number of educated girls rose in the years just before and after independence.[19]

This larger debate harks back to the issue of how we imagine a child: in the Hindu practice of child marriage, we can see the ways in which children can act as "miniature adults," assuming responsibilities at a young age with little time for such Western notions as "adolescence." In addition, we can see how children, particularly child brides, are understood in terms of economics: girls could be a burden to their natal families, but could also be a dowry resource or a source of household labor for the husband's family.

The period of colonialism in general was a time of conflicting messages and ideas for many Hindus, particularly from a child's point of view. In the autobiography of M. K. Gandhi (Doc. 4-10), we can see an intense ambivalence about the idea of "religion" per se; he attributes to Hinduism the pain of his early marriage (at the age of thirteen) to Kasturbai, and is grateful for frequent separation to strengthen their marriage later in life. Gandhi is an inheritor of the Reform idea that real religion is the Upanishadic idea of knowledge of atman, or the self. Writing slightly later in the late colonial period, Satyajit Ray (1921–1992) writes of his own interactions with the Brahmo Samaj—a Reform movement which some of the family followed and other parts of the family did not (Doc. 4-11). While Gandhi was repulsed by the glitter of traditional Hindu practices, Ray was attracted to it because it was forbidden to him. Ray's remarks are a compelling meditation on the subject of internal pluralism within Hinduism. Ray's own household is Brahmo Samaj, and thus does not practice the worship of images. His aunts and uncles who remained traditionally Hindus, therefore, were a source of fascination for him.

In both M. K. Gandhi and Satyajit Ray, we feel keenly the childhood experience of multiple religions, where there is a sense of "Hindu" even from an early age, and a distinction of "Hindu" from other religions. In addition, we see a sense of internal struggle within Hinduism, where different Hindu voices about the way to worship and the right Hindu principles are at stake. Childhood identity is confronted with pluralism from both within and without the Hindu world.

Contemporary Dynamics

Many of the tensions relevant to earlier Hindu times are carried to the contemporary period, reconfigured in new ways.[20] The idea of childhood is affected by the growing divide between urban and rural in post-independence India, the liberalization of the economy in the 1990s, and the growing presence of India on the global capitalist stage. Contemporary India brings with it the vexing issue of the relationship of children to the state; the issue of child labor in a society that is at once agricultural, industrial, and postindustrial technological; the question of human rights and children; and the persistence of discrimination against girl children (Doc. 4-14).[21] These Indian debates frequently take place within a "rights" perspective, catalyzed by the United Nations Conference on the Rights of Children.[22]

The contemporary debates around childhood in India also discuss whether childhood is a relative and culturally specific construct. For some, the Hindu (or Muslim, or Jain, or Christian) views of "the child" should be honored as such. For others, global processes have a profound affect on childhood that cannot and should not be reduced to cultural specificity. In India, as in almost all other parts of the globe, such global crises of resources and urbanization involve a view of children as commodities to be traded and used for adult pleasure. Yet some argue that such global shifts can also be influential in a positive way, increasing perceptions of gender equity in India, beginning in childhood.[23]

The omnipresence of children in many parts of contemporary Hindu life marks them as different from children in many contemporary Western cultures. As Trisha Tandon notes, in the Indian setting, there is no effort made to segregate children from adults in the family, so they normally witness adults interacting with each other in a variety of moods and tempers. Indeed there can be a relative absence of the Western emphasis on the separate role of the child.[24] As one Indian scholar working with a Western sociologist put it, "You bring up your children; we live with ours."

Sudhir Kakar (Doc. 4-13), in his well-known study *The Inner World*, writes that the traditional Indian extended family is usually organized in a way analogous to the caste system, where "superior and subordinate relationships have the character of eternal verity and moral imperative," and comprise a system of dependency and difference.[25] The determinants of authority tend to be age, sex, and generational status. As Kakar also notes, a son or daughter usually owes less formal deference to the mother than to the father; and an elder brother has greater authority over a younger sister than an elder sister over a younger brother. The authority of the father is usually more distant and absolute, and that of the mother is usually nurturing and positive in valence. In such an environment, personal talents and achievements can take on a lesser role than respect for tradition.[26] Thus, an "ideal"

Hindu childhood can subordinate one's ambitions and desires to the preferences of the extended family and *jati* (birth occupation) communities.[27]

But while the premise of these relationships is one of power and authority, their modality is usually one of nurturing love, built upon the model of the powerful mother figure of many Hindu childhoods. As Kakar puts it, maternal nurturing is expected on the part of the superior, filial respect and compliance on the part of the subordinate, and a mutual sense of highly personal attachment is expected of both.[28] This kind of ideal emotional tone of the family also extends to the tone of life-cycle rituals. Such rituals communicate that family ties are the most "moral and reliable of all social relations."[29]

To be sure, in much of rural Hindu India, traditions remain pronounced. For instance, although the practice has almost died out, some orthodox families still follow menstruation observances for a girl.[30] Others mark the initiation from childhood into adulthood with a new garment, such as a sari, gifts, garlands, and blessings for a girl after menstruation.[31] In rural north India, the patrilocal tradition remains strong, and a girls' leaving her mother's home is a poignant invocation of childhood as well as a leavetaking of it. In recent ethnographies, Gloria Raheja records such sentiments (Doc. 4-12).

These traditions aside, childhood in both urban Indian and diaspora families tend to be a more complex negotiation between so-called "Western" norms of separate identity and creativity and the more traditional Hindu norms of interdependence and family hierarchy.[32] Other earlier post-independence studies also show that educational values have shifted in addition to traditional family Hindu values. More access to education for girls has resulted in delayed marriage and childbirth, as well as training for professions outside the home.[33] To be sure, many teachers and children continue to draw on older, more "Hindu" pedagogic and cultural tradition, such as knowledge as received, verbal testimony (the Vedas) and the salience of memory in learning.[34] However, with the technological revolution in India at its apex, many urban children and young people are turning more to national and global media, as well as to their peer groups for role models. They rely less on the traditional forms of storytelling that are the models of their parents', and more, their grandparents' generations.

We can see this most poignantly in the recent novel of Hari Kunzru, *Transmission* (Doc. 4-15), where the protagonist's coming of age occurs when he is accepted as an apprentice in a multinational computer firm. In his leavetaking, he is inundated by his father's paternalistic admonitions, his mother's indulgence with sweets, and his little sister's adulations. The traditional Hindu family structure is still intact, but the prestige of Vedic learning in childhood is replaced with low-wage computer training in America.

And yet with all of these technological changes and shifts, the emphasis upon the divinity of the child still remains. In a recent article, Patricia Uberoi traces the representation of the child in calendar art and the longings of the Indian nation. Early calendar boys are represented as pure heroes, "little soldiers."[35] In post-liberalization India, however, the child is increasingly involved with commercial advertising—where Krishna is both god and the mischievous butter stealer for companies such as Gripe Water. One recent print by a Delhi company shows a playful infant, one hand on the computer monitor and another reaching out to the screen, in anticipation of Kunzru's story above.[36]

The Upanishadic story of Satyakama, the Puranic myths of Krishna, and the longings of child-bride and saint Bahina Bai give us the idea of children as closely connected to the divine, even at their most human moments. The Vedas, the Laws of Manu, and even some of the musings of Gandhi and Ray give us the sense of children as ritually constructed as well as spontaneously acting on their own behalf. The postmodern writings of experts on childhood as well as children themselves attest that all these identities are somehow part of the larger world of Hindu children in a global context. Transnational technological and industrial modes of social organization compete with traditional modes of family organization, and a Hindu child lives in the spaces in between, juxtaposing, challenging, accepting, and negotiating them all.

The Vedas

Dated from 1500–900 BCE, the Vedas are the earliest compositions known in the tradition we now call Hinduism. They argue for the centrality of sacrifice and offerings to a variety of gods, for the "goods" of ancient Indian life—cattle, fertility, rains, and offspring, particularly sons. Here, Soma is the sacred drink mentioned as an offering. Many Vedic hymns, such as this one, are based on narratives; in this hymn the sage Saptavadhri is thrown into a womblike trough of a tree for not being able to help a king produce a child. (The Sanskrit is ambiguous as to whether it is his child or the king's.) The sage's pleas for escape are also a metaphor for safe childbirth.

Document 4–1

Rig Veda 5.78 for a Safe Childbirth and the Begetting of a Son

1. You Ashvins, come here! Nasatyas, do not look away. Fly here like two geese to the Soma juice.
2. You Ashvins! Like two gazelles, like two buffaloes to the verdant field, fly here like two geese to the Soma juice.
3. You Ashvins, wealthy with gifts, accept our sacrifice fly here like two geese to the Soma juice.
4. As Atri descended into the pit and called out to you like a wailing woman, come with the fresh, auspicious speed of an eagle.
5. Open, O tree, like the womb of a woman in labor! Ashvins, hear my cry, and release Saptavadhri.
6. When the sage Saptavadhri was anxious and in misery, with your magic spells you Ashvins bend the tree together and apart.
7. Like the wind moves up a lotus pond all around, so let your embryo move, and come out when it is ten months old.
8. As the wind, the forest, and the ocean move, so may you, ten-month-old child, come down along with the afterbirth.
9. After the boy has lain in the mother, may he come out alive and unharmed, alive from the living woman.

Source: Translation is my own.

The Upanishads

Even though they also use the Vedic language of sacrifice, the Upanishads (700 BCE–100 CE) focus on the internal reality of the self, or atman, and its relationship to the power that animates the world–Brahman. Thus, the development of the self and the identity of children are viewed through a larger framework of an awareness of Brahman, particularly as it is taught through the wisdom of a teacher. As Satyakama does here, the child grows and develops as he gains meditative insight as a participant in the household of his teacher. One must be accepted into that household, and throughout one's young life, engage in a series of conversations that reveal the identity of the bodily processes and the cosmic processes. The teacher thus takes on the role of the parent of the child. Much of the Upanishads were understood as esoteric teachings, shared by those who had retired from the urban settlements emerging in the sixth to fourth centuries BCE, and who had moved to the forest to create ashramas, or dwelling spaces.

Document 4–2

Satyakama Jabala Comes of Age
(*Chandogya Upanishad* 4.4–4.9)

4.4. One day Satyakama Jabala said to his mother Jabala: "Mother, I want to become a vedic student. So tell me what my lineage is." She replied: "Son, I don't know what your lineage is. I was young when I had you. I was a maid then and had a lot of relationships. As such, it is impossible for me to say what your lineage is. But my name is Jabala, and your name is Satyakama. So you should simply say that you are Satyakama Jabala."

He went to Haridrumata Gautama then and said: "Sir, I want to live under you as a vedic student. I come to you, sir, as your student." Haridrumata asked him: 'Son, what is your lineage?'

And he replied: "Sir, I don't know what my lineage is. When I asked my mother, she replied: 'I was young when I had you. I was a maid then and had a lot of relationships. As such, it is impossible for me to say what your lineage is. But my name is Jabala, and your name is Satyakama.' So I am Satyakama Jabala, sir."

Haridrumata then told him: "Who but a Brahmin could speak like that! Fetch some firewood, son. I will perform your initiation. You have not strayed from the truth." So he initiated the boy and, picking out four hundred of the most skinny and feeble cows, told him: "Son, look after these." As he was driving them away, Satyakama answered back: "I will not return without a thousand!" He lived away for a number of years, and when the cows had increased to a thousand this is what happened.

4.5. The bull called out to him: "Satyakama!" He responded: "Sir?" The bull said: "Son, we have reached a thousand. Take us back to the teacher's house, and I will tell you one-quarter of Brahman."

"Please tell me, sir."

And the bull told him: "One-sixteenth of it is the eastern quarter; one-sixteenth is the western quarter; one-sixteenth is the southern quarter; and one-sixteenth is the northern quarter. Consisting of these four sixteenths, this quarter of Brahman is named Far-flung, my son.

"When someone knows this and venerates this quarter of Brahman consisting of four-sixteenths as Far-flung, he will become far-flung in this world. A man will win far-flung worlds, when he knows this and venerates this quarter of Brahman consisting of four-sixteenths as Far-flung."

4.6. The bull continued: "The fire will tell you another quarter." The next morning Satyakama drove the cows on, and at the spot where they happened to be around sunset he built a fire, corralled the cows, fed the fire with wood, and sat behind the fire facing the east.

The fire then called out to him: "Satyakama!" He responded: "Sir?"

"Son, I will tell you a quarter of Brahman."

"Please tell me, sir."

And the fire told him: "One-sixteenth of it is the earth; one-sixteenth of it is the intermediate region; one-sixteenth is the sky; and one-sixteenth is the ocean. Consisting of these four-sixteenths, this quarter of Brahman is named Limitless, my son.

"When someone knows this and venerates the quarter of Brahman consisting of these four-sixteenths as Limitless, there will be no limits for him in this world. A man will win limitless worlds, when he knows this and venerates the quarter of Brahman consisting of these four-sixteenths as Limitless."

4.7. The fire continued: "A wild goose will tell you another quarter." The next morning Satyakama drove the cows on, and at the spot where they happened to be around sunset he built a fire, corralled the cows, fed the fire with wood, and sat down behind the fire facing east.

A wild goose then flew down and called out to him: "Satyakama!" He responded: "Sir?"

"Son, I will tell you a quarter of Brahman."

"Please tell me, sir."

And the wild goose told him: "One-sixteenth of it is the fire; one-sixteenth is the sun; one-sixteenth is the moon; and one-sixteenth is lightning. Consisting of these four-sixteenths, this quarter of Brahman is named Radiant, my son.

"When someone knows this and venerates the quarter of Brahman consisting of these four-sixteenths as Radiant, he will become radiant in this world. A man will win radiant worlds, when he knows this and venerates the quarter of Brahman consisting of these four-sixteenths as Radiant."

4.8. The wild goose continued: "A water-bird will tell you another quarter." The next morning Satyakama drove the cows on, and at the spot where they happened to be around sunset he built a fire, corralled the cows, fed the fire with wood, and sat down behind the fire facing east.

A water-bird then flew down and called out to him: "Satyakama!" He responded, "Sir?"

"Son, I will tell you a quarter of Brahman."

"Please tell me, sir."

And the water-bird told him: "One-sixteenth of it is breath; one-sixteenth is sight; one-sixteenth is hearing; and one-sixteenth is the mind. Consisting of these four-sixteenths, this quarter of Brahman is named Abode-possessing, my son.

"When someone knows this and venerates the quarter of Brahman consisting of these four-sixteenths as Abode-possessing, he will have an abode in this world. A man will win worlds possessing abodes, when he knows this and venerates the quarter of Brahman consisting of these four-sixteenths as Abode-possessing."

4.9. Finally he reached his teacher's house. The teacher called out to him: "Satyakama!" He responded: "Sir?"

"Son, you have the glow of someone who knows Brahman! Tell me—who taught you?"

"Other than human beings," he acknowledged. "But, if it pleases you, sir, you showed it to me yourself, for I have heard from people of your eminence that knowledge leads one most securely to the goal only when it is learnt from a teacher." So he explained it to him, and, indeed, he did so without leaving anything out.

Source: *The Upanisads*, translated from the original Sanskrit by Patrick Olivelle (Oxford: Oxford University Press, 1996), 130–134.

Epic Narratives

The classical world of India begins to emerge in the great Indian epic narratives, composed in shloka, or verse, form, between the second century BCE and the second century CE. The complex idea of dharma, or sacred duty, is central to both the *Ramayana* and the *Mahabharata*. Dharma involves both one's varna, or caste, as well as duty toward family and society. In the *Mahabharata*, the Kshatriya dharma of going to war conflicts with the dharma of honoring one's family. The epic focuses on the cost of the great war between rivalrous cousins, the Pandavas and the Kauravas, whose childhood is described below. The idea of karma and destiny, as well as the "essential nature" of a person, are all present in childhood actions and dispositions, such as those of Bhima in the narrative below. Each of these actions has results, either in this life or the next life, as each individual continues to cycle around the endless round of birth and death called samsara.

Document 4–3

The *Mahabharata*: Book of the Beginning

The Pandavas received the sacraments that the Veda prescribes and grew up in their father's house, enjoying the pleasures of life. When they played in their father's house with the son of Dhrtarastra, the Pandavas excelled in all the games that children play. In racing, in hitting the target, in stuffing himself, in raising dust, Bhimasena beat all the boys of Dhrtarastra. Boisterously, he grabbed them by the hair above their ears as they were playing, held them by their heads, and set them to fight one another. The Wolf-Belly bullied them all, the one hundred and one powerful boys, alone and with little trouble. The strong Bhima would grab hold of their feet, topple them mightily in the dust, or pull the yelping children over the ground until their knees and heads and eyeballs were chafed. When he was playing in the water, he would catch ten of the kids in his arms and sit down under the water, letting go of them when they came close to drowning. And when they climbed the trees to pick fruit, Bhima would kick the tree to make it shake, and all shaken up they would tumble down with the fruit from the tree that shuddered from the kick, and fall down limply. Neither in fights nor speed nor drills did the princes ever get the upper hand when they were competing with Bhima. So Bhima became the bane of the sons of Dhrtarastra when he competed, not of out malice, but because he was a child.

When he had got to know Bhima's well-publicized strength, the high and mighty Duryodhana revealed his evil nature. Out of folly and ambition an ugly thought occurred to Duryodhana, who was loath of Law and looking for evil: "This Wolf-belly, strong among the strong, the middle son of Pandu by Kunti, must be brought down by trickery. Then I shall overpower his younger brother, and the eldest one, Yudhisthira, put him in fetters, and thereafter I shall sway the earth!"

Having made up his mind, the evil Duryodhana kept constantly watching for a chance to get at the spirited Bhima. For their water games he had large and colorful tents made of cloth set up at Pramanakoti on the Ganges, Bharata, just above the water line. When they all had stopped playing they would dress in fresh clothes and put on their ornaments and quietly feast on dishes that were opulent for all tastes. At nightfall the heroic Kuru princes, tired from their games, loved sleeping in their outdoor camp.

And so our powerful Bhima, always the first at sports but now tired from playing piggyback with the boys that had gone playing in the water, climbed up the bank at Pramanakoti to find a place for the night, and he fell asleep. He had put on a white cloth and, exhausted and befuddled with drink, slept like a corpse without stirring. Whereupon Duryodhana quietly tied him with fetters made from creepers and rolled him from the bank into the deep, dreadfully rushing river. Bhima woke up, broke his fetters, and the greatest of fighters rose from the water.

Another time when Bhima was sleeping, Duryodhana brought crazed, poison-fanged, virulent snakes and made them bite Bhima in all the weak spots of his body. But the fangs of the cobras, even when sunk in his weak spots, failed to cut through the skin, for the broadchested boy was too tough. Waking, Bhima ground all the snakes to death and struck his favorite charioteer with the back of his hand.

Again Duryodhana had poison thrown in Bhima's food, plant poison freshly collected, of a virulence to make one shudder. Vidura now told the Pandavas, for he wished them well. The Wolf-Belly ate it and digested it without any aftereffect. Even that virulent poison had no effect on him—Bhima, who was terribly tough, simply digested it. In this way Duryodhana, Karna, and Shakuni Saubala made various attempts to kill the Pandavas. The sons of Pandu, tamers of their foes, divined it all, but following Vidura's advice, did not bring it into the open.

(Then, seeing that the boys at play were getting too malicious, the king entrusted them to Gautama, so that they would be taught by a guru—Gautama Krpa, master of the precepts of the Veda, who had been born from a reed stalk.)

Source: *The Mahabharata: The Book of the Beginning*, translated by J.A.B. van Buitenen (Chicago: University of Chicago Press, 1973), I: 264–265.

Shastric Approaches

The shastras, or legal texts, of which the law of Manu is one, have also been translated as "custom" or "practice." They should not be seen as exact equivalents to universal legal treatises written in Enlightenment Europe, and are rather regional compendia of rules, rituals, and obligations for the conduct of life. Manu is one of the more complete compendia that we have, and certainly one of the most frequently cited in colonial and contemporary India. Here, we see the blossoming of the ritual construction of the person, beginning with the very clear childhood rites of the first five years, up to twenty years. These life-cycle rites, called *samskaras*, are also a powerful force in contemporary Hinduism in India and abroad. In Manu we also read about the vulnerability of children, and how they might be protected by rulers. We also see a continuation of the dharmic idea that the definition of children, and persons in general, is through right relationship to caste, family, and jati, or birth occupation.

Document 4–4

The Laws of Manu

Consecratory rites

2.26. The consecration of the body, beginning with the ceremony of impregnation, should be performed for twice-born men by means of the sacred vedic rites, a consecration that cleanses a man both here and in the hereafter.

2.27. The fire offerings for the benefit of the foetus, the birth rite, the first cutting of hair, and the tying of the Munja-grass cord—by these rites the taint of semen and womb is wiped from twice-born men.

2.28. Vedic recitation, religious observances, fire offerings, study of the triple Veda, ritual offerings, sons, the five great sacrifices, and sacrifices—by these a man's body is made "brahmic."

Childhood rites

2.29. The rule is that the birth rite of a male child must be performed before his umbilical cord is cut; he is fed gold, honey, and ghee to the accompaniment of vedic formulas.

2.30. One should see to it that the child's naming ceremony is performed on the tenth or the twelfth day after birth, on a day or at a time that is auspicious, or under a favorable constellation.

2.31.   For a Brahmin, the name should connote auspiciousness; for a Kshatriya, strength; for a Vaishya, wealth; and for a Shudra, disdain.

2.32.   For a Brahmin, the name should connote happiness; for a Kshatriya, protection; for a Vaishya, prosperity; and for a Shudra, service.

2.33.   For girls, the name should be easy to pronounce and without fierce connotations, have a clear meaning, be charming and auspicious, end in a long syllable, and contain a word for blessing.

2.34.   In the fourth month, one should perform the ceremony of taking the child out of the house; and in the sixth month, the feeding with rice, as also any other auspicious ceremony cherished in the family.

2.35.   The first cutting of the hair, according to the Law, should be performed for all twice-born children in the first or the third year, in accordance with the dictates of scripture.

Vedic initiation: time for initiation

2.36.   For a Brahmin, the vedic initiation should be carried out in the eighth year from conception; for a Kshatriya, in the eleventh year from conception; and for a Vaishya, in the twelfth year from conception.

2.37.   For a Brahmin desiring eminence in vedic knowledge, it should be carried out in the fifth year; for a Kshatriya aspiring to power, in the sixth year; and for a Vaishya aspiring to the spirit of enterprise, in the seventh.

Failure to be initiated

2.38.   For a Brahmin, the time for Savitri does not lapse until the sixteenth year; for a Kshatriya, until the twenty-second; and for a Vaishya, until the twenty-fourth.

2.39.   If, after those times, any of these three has not undergone consecration at the proper time, he becomes a Vratya, fallen from Savitri and spurned by Aryans.

2.40.   Even in a time of adversity, a Brahmin should never establish vedic or matrimonial links with such people, unless they have been cleansed according to rule.

Vedic study

2.164. A twice-born whose body has been consecrated following this orderly sequence should gradually amass the riches of ascetic toil consisting of vedic study while he resides with his teacher. A twice-born should study the entire Veda together with the secret texts . . . , as he carries out the various observances and special ascetic practices enjoyed by vedic injunctions. . . .

2.167. When a twice-born, even while wearing a garland, performs his vedic recitation every day according to his ability, he is surely practicing the fiercest ascetic toil down to the very tips of his nails.

2.168. When a Brahmin expends great effort in other matters without studying the Veda, while still alive he is quickly reduced to the status of a Shudra, together with his children.

2.169. According to a scriptural injunction, the first birth of a Brahmin is from his mother; the second takes place at the tying of the Munja-grass girdle, and the third takes place at the consecration for a sacrifice.

2.170. Of these, the one signaled by the tying of the Munja-grass girdle is his birth from the Veda. At this birth, the Savitri verse is said to be his mother, and the teacher his father.

2.171. The teacher is called the father because he imparts the Veda, for a man does not become competent to perform any rite until the tying of the Munja-grass girdle.

2.172. Such a man should not pronounce any vedic text, except when he offers a funerary oblation, for he is equal to a Shudra until he is born from the Veda.

Rules of conduct

2.219. A student may shave his head or keep his hair matted; or else he may keep just his topknot matted. He should never let the sun rise or set while he is asleep in a village.

2.220. If the sun should rise or set while he is asleep, whether deliberately or inadvertently, he should fast for one day while engaging in soft recitation.

2.221. If, after he had been asleep at sunrise or sunset, he does not perform the penance, he becomes saddled with a great sin.

2.222. After purifying himself by sipping water and becoming self-possessed, he should worship both twilights everyday, softly reciting the prescribed formula in a clean spot and according to rule.

2.223. If he sees a woman or a low-born man doing something conducive to welfare, he should do all of that diligently, or anything else that he is fond of.

2.224. Some say that Law and Wealth are conducive to welfare; others, Pleasure and Wealth; and still others, Law alone or Wealth alone. But the settled rule is this: the entire triple set is conducive to welfare.

Mother, father, teacher

2.225. Teacher, father, mother, and older brother—these should never be treated with contempt especially by a Brahmin, even though he may be deeply hurt.

2.226. The teacher is the embodiment of Brahman; the father is the embodiment of Prajapati; the mother is the embodiment of Earth; and one's brother is the embodiment of oneself.

2.227. The tribulations that a mother and a father undergo when humans are born cannot be repaid even in hundreds of years.

2.228. He should do what is pleasing to these two every day, and always what is pleasing to his teacher. When these three are gratified, he obtains the fullness of ascetic toil.

2.229. Obedient service to these three is said to be the highest form of ascetic toil. Without their consent, he should not follow any other rule of conduct.

2.230. For they alone are the three worlds; they alone are the three orders of life; they alone are the three Vedas; and they alone are called the three sacred fires.

2.231. The householder's fire is clearly the father; the southern fire, tradition says, is the mother; and the offertorial fire is the teacher—this is the most excellent triad of sacred fires.

2.232. A householder who does not neglect these three will win the three worlds; and, shining with his own body, he will rejoice in heaven like a god.

2.233. He obtains this world by devotion to his mother, and the middle world by devotion to his father; but he obtains the world of Brahman only by obedient service to his teacher.

2.234. When someone has attended to these three, he has attended to all his duties; should someone not attend to them, all his rites bear him no fruit.

2.235. So long as these three are alive, he should not follow another rule of conduct; taking delight in what is pleasing and beneficial to them, he should always render them obedient service.

2.236. Whenever he undertakes any mental, verbal, or physical activity for the sake of the next world without inconveniencing them, he should inform them of it.

2.237. When these three are gratified, a man has done all he has to do. This is the highest Law itself in person; all else is subsidiary Law.

Children's qualities resulting from nature of marriage

3.42. From irreproachable marriages are born children beyond reproach; from reproachable marriages are born children inviting people's reproach. Therefore, a man should avoid reproachable marriages.

3.262. The wife who is wedded according to the Law, devoted to her husband, and intent on worshipping the ancestors may eat the middlemost of those balls in the proper manner, if she wants to have a son.

3.263. She will give birth to a son endowed with long life, fame, intelligence, wealth, progeny, righteousness, goodness.

Family and social relations

4.179. Officiating priests; family priests; teachers; maternal uncles; guests; dependents; children; the aged; the sick; doctors; paternal, affinal, and maternal relatives;

4.180. father; mother; sisters; brother; son; wife; daughter; and slaves—he should not get into arguments with any of these.

4.181. By forswearing arguments with them, he is freed from all sins; and when he is conquered by them, the householder conquers all these worlds.

4.182. The teacher is the ruler of Brahman's world; the father of Prajapati's world; the guest, of Indra's world; the officiating priests, of the world of the gods;

4.183. The sisters, of the world of Apsarases; maternal relatives, of the world of the Vishvedevas; affinal relatives, of the world of the waters; and the mother and maternal uncles, of the earth.

4.184. The children, the aged, the feeble, and the sick are to be regarded as the rulers of space. His older brother is equal to his father, and his wife and son are his own body. His slaves are his own shadow, and his daughter is the object of supreme compassion. When he is assailed by any of these, therefore, he should always bear it without losing his temper.

Bodily purification: death or birth of a person belonging to the same ancestry

5.58. Someone who has teethed, someone younger, or someone who has had his first cutting of hair—when any of these dies, all his relatives become impure; the same is prescribed after the birth of a child.

5.59. A ten-day period of impurity following death is prescribed for those who belong to the same ancestry; alternatively, that period may last until the collection of bones, or for three days, or for a single day. . . .

5.67. When males die before the first cutting of their hair, tradition tells us, the impurity lasts a single night; but when they die after the cutting of their hair, purity is considered to be restored after three nights.

5.68. When a child under two dies, its relatives should decorate its corpse and lay it down in a clean spot outside the village; the ceremony of collecting bones is omitted.

5.69. Neither the consecration with fire nor the offering of water is done for such a child; after leaving it behind in the wilderness like a piece of wood, one should keep the observances for just three days.

5.70. Relatives should not offer libations of water for a child under three; they may do so optionally if it has teethed or if its naming ceremony has been performed.

Excursus: property of minors and women

8.27. The king should protect the estate inherited by a child until he has returned home after his studentship or until he is no longer a minor.

8.28. The same protection must be extended to barren women, women without sons or bereft of family, women devoted to their husbands, widows, and women in distress.

8.29. If their in-laws usurp their property while they are alive, a righteous king should discipline them with the punishment laid down for thieves.

To whom belongs a son?

9.32. It is acknowledged that a son belongs to the husband; but scripture is divided with respect to the sire—some argue for the man who fathered the child, others for the "owner of the field."

9.33. Tradition holds that the woman represents the field and the man the seed; all embodied beings spring from the union of field and seed.

9.34. Sometimes the seed is pre-eminent, at other times the female womb; but when both are equal, that offspring is greatly esteemed.

Marriage of daughters

9.88. When there is a suitor who is eminent, handsome, and of equal status, one should give the girl to him according to rule, even if she has not attained the proper age.

9.89. Even if she has reached puberty, a girl should rather remain at home until death; one should never give her to a man bereft of good qualities.

9.90. For three years shall a girl wait after the onset of puberty; after that time, she may find herself a husband of equal status.

9.91. If a woman who has not been given in marriage finds a husband on her own, she does not incur any sin, and neither does the man she finds.

9.92. A girl who chooses a husband on her own must not take with her any ornament coming from her father or mother or given by her brothers; if she takes, if is theft.

9.93. A man who takes a girl after she has reached puberty shall not pay a bride-price, for the father has lost his ownership of her by frustrating her menses.

9.94. A 30-year old man should marry a charming girl of 12 years, or an 18 year-old, a girl of 8 years—sooner, if his fulfilling the Law would suffer.

9.95. A husband marries a wife given to him by the gods, not from his own desire. He should always support that good woman, thereby doing what is pleasing to the gods.

9.96. Women were created to bear children, and men to extend the line; therefore, scriptures have prescribed that the Law is to be carried out in common with the wife.

9.97. If, after the bride-price has been paid for the girl, the man who paid the price dies, she should be given to the brother-in-law, if she consents to it.

9.98. Even a Shudra should not take a bride-price when he gives his daughter, for by accepting a bride-price, he is engaging in the covert sale of his daughter.

9.99. That after promising her to one man, she is then given to another—such a deed was never done by good people of ancient or recent times.

9.100. The covert sale of a daughter for a payment under the name "bride-price"—we have never heard of such a thing even in former generations.

Source: *The Law Code of Manu: A New Translation Based on the Critical Edition* by Patrick Olivelle (Oxford: Oxford University Press, 2005), 25–26, 36, 40–41, 46, 62, 78, 89, 125, 157, 161.

The Puranas

The Puranas are the texts which comprise the basis of classical theological Hinduism—where the gods Shiva, Vishnu, Brahma, and the Devi, or Goddess, are portrayed in full and elaborated detail. They span a large frame of time, from the earliest approximate date of the second century CE to the later date of the fourteenth and fifteen centuries CE. "Puranas" as such were being composed as late as the seventeenth and eighteenth centuries. They are compendia of lore, usually connected to a particular deity or to a particular temple or other sacred place. They also contain elaborate visions of the cosmos and our place within it, including many accounts of the four *yugas*, or ages, and the natural decay that occurs as the ages pass. In this schema, suffering is inevitable, both at the level of the cosmos and at the level of the individual. In the first, more pessimistic passage from the *Vishnu Purana*, childhood is described as the inauguration of inevitable karmic suffering, which lasts throughout a single lifetime and takes up the suffering of previous lifetimes. By the end of life, the person has changed so dramatically that childhood seems as if from another lifetime. The narratives of Krishna, introduced below, give a much more optimistic view of childhood, showing the diversity of theological and philosophical views on youth present within the classical period.

Document 4–5

Vishnu Purana 6.5.9–35: The Life Cycle, Beginning with Childhood, as Karmic Suffering

Suffering takes thousands of different forms, as it arises from conception, birth, old age, disease, death, and hell. The living creature that has a very delicate body becomes encased in abundant filth inside the embryo, where he is enveloped by the membrane and his back, neck, and bones are all twisted out of shape. As he grows, he suffers greatly from excessively acrid, bitter, spicy, salty, and burning hot food [that his mother has eaten]. He can't stretch out his own limbs or contract them or anything else, and he is squashed on all sides, lying there in the faeces and urine and slime. Though he is unable to breathe, he is conscious, and he remembers his hundreds of former births. Thus he sits there in the womb bound by his own karma, and very miserable.

As he is born, his face is smeared with faeces, blood, urine, and semen, and his bones and sinews are hurt by the wind of procreation. He is turned head downwards by the powerful winds of childbirth, and he comes out from his mother's stomach bewildered by pain. He faints, and when he is touched by the outside air, he loses his understanding, and is born. His body is hurt, as if pierced by thorns, as if split open by saws; he falls from his pustulent world like a worm upon the ground. Incapable of even scratching himself, or of turning over, totally without any control, he obtains food, such as the milk he drinks at the breast, by the will of another person. Lying asleep on a bed, unclean, he is bitten by insects' stings and other things, and can do nothing to ward them off.

There are many sufferings in birth, and many that come right after birth; and there are many that he encounters in childhood, inflicted by elemental factors and so forth. Covered over by the darkness of ignorance, a man's heart becomes stupefied; he does not know, "Where have I come from? Who am I? Where am I going? What am I made of? What bond is it that binds me? What is the cause, and what is not the cause? What is to be done, and what is not to be done? What is to be said, and what is not to be said? What is dharma, and what is against dharma? What does it consist in, and how? What is right to do, and what is not right to do? What is virtue and vice?"

Thus, confused like an animal, a man stumbles into the great misery that arises from ignorance, for he is primarily intent upon his penis and stomach. Ignorance is the source of inertia [tamas], and so the undertakings of ignorant men are deficient in good karma. But the seers say that hell is the reward for a deficiency in good karma, and so ignorant men suffer the most, both here and in the other world.

When old age shatters the body, gradually the limbs become loose; the old person's teeth decay and fall out; he becomes covered with wrinkles and sinews and veins; he can't see far, and the pupils of his eyes are fixed in space; tufts of hair appear in his nostrils, and his body trembles. All his bones become prominent; his back and joints are bent; and since his digestive fire has gone out, he eats little and moves little. It is only with pain and difficulty that he walks, rises, lies down, sits, and moves, and his hearing and sight become sluggish; his mouth is smeared with oozing saliva. As he looks toward death, all of his senses are no longer controlled; and he cannot remember even important things that he had experienced even at that very moment. Speaking takes great effort, and he repeats himself; he is wakeful and very tired because of his heavy breathing and coughing. An old man is lifted up by someone else, and dressed by someone else; to his servants, his own sons, and his wife he is an object of contempt. He has lost all his cleanliness, though he still has his desire for amusement and food; his dependents laugh at him and all his relatives are disgusted with him. Remembering the things that he did in his youth as if had experienced them in another birth, he sighs deeply and becomes very sad.

Source: *Textual Sources for the Study of Hinduism*, edited and translated by Wendy Doniger O'Flaherty with Daniel Gold, David Haberman, and David Shulman (Chicago: University of Chicago Press, 1988), 100–101.

Puranic Myths of Krishna

The Puranas also give us the very lengthy and intricate narratives of the birth, youth, and heroic and amorous exploits of Krishna. His birth is miraculous, in that he escapes the evil designs of the wicked king Kamsa and grows up idyllically in the pastoral town of Braj, in north India. Krishna is also known for his mischievous ways as a toddler, which alternate between misbehaving in typical toddler-like fashion, and revealing his cosmic strength and vision. As a youth he is also heroic, saving the town from evil serpents as he cavorts with his young fellow cowherds. Finally, the amorous Krishna is the object of desire for all the female cowherdesses, or gopis; their longing for him becomes the model of the relationship between devotee and god. In each of these episodes of childhood and youth, Krishna plays between reality and illusion; he is both an innocent suckling and someone who can kill the ogress posing as her nurse (and make her milk sweet in the process); he is both mischievous child and a being who reveals the entire universe in his mouth; he is both an amorous trickster and a teacher about attachment to worldly things, such as clothing.

Document 4–6

Four Episodes from the Bhagavata Purana

Infancy: Krishna kills the ogress Putana
When Nanda heard the speech of Vasudeva he thought, as he went on the road homewards, that this could not be false, and he sought refuge with Hari, for he feared some misfortune.

The horrible Putana ["Stinking"], a devourer of children, was sent by Kamsa. She wandered through the cities, villages, and pastures, killing infants. Wherever men do not recite the deeds of Krishna the Lord of the Satvatas, a recitation which destroys the Rakshasas, there evil demons work their sorcery. One day Putana came to Nanda's village, wandering at will, flying through the sky, and by her magic powers she assumed the form of a beautiful woman.[37] Jasmine was bound into her hair; her hips and breasts were full, her waist slender. She wore fine garments, and her face was framed by hair that shone with the luster from her shimmering, quivering earrings. She cast sidelong glances and smiled sweetly, and she carried a lotus in her hand. When the wives of the cow-herds saw the woman, who stole their hearts, they thought that she must be Shri incarnate, come to see her husband.[38] The infant-swallower, searching for children, happened to come to the house of Nanda, and she saw there on the bed the infant Krishna, whose true energy was concealed, like a fire covered with ashes. Though he kept his eyes closed, he who is the very soul of all that moves and all that is still knew her to be an ogress who killed children, and she took the infinite one onto her lap, as one might pick up a sleeping deadly viper, mistaking it for a rope. Seeing her, whose wicked heart was concealed by sweet actions like a sharp sword encased in a scabbard, his mother was overcome by her splendour, and, thinking her to be a good woman, stood looking on.

The horrible one, taking him on her lap, gave the baby her breast, which had been smeared with a virulent poison. But the lord, pressing her breast hard with his hands angrily drank out her life's breath with the milk. She cried out, "Let go! Let go! Enough!" as she was squeezed in all her vital parts. She rolled her eyes and thrashed her arms and legs and screamed again and again, and all her limbs were bathed in sweat. At the sound of her deep roar, the earth with its mountains and the sky with its planets shook; the subterranean waters and the regions of the sky resounded, and people fell to the ground fearing that lightning had struck. The night-wandering ogress, with agonizing pain in her breasts, opened her mouth, stretched out her arms and legs, tore her hair, and fell lifeless on the ground in the cow-pen, like the serpent Vritra struck down by Indra's thunderbolt. Then she resumed her true form, and as her body fell it crushed all the trees for twelve miles around; this was a great marvel. Her mouth was full of terrible teeth as large as plough-shafts; her nostrils were like mountain caves; her breasts were like boulders, and her hideous red hair was strewn about. Her eyes were like deep, dark wells; her buttocks were terrifying, large as beaches; her stomach was like a great dry lake emptied of water, her arms like dams. When the cow-herds and their wives saw her corpse they were terrified, and their hearts, ears, and skulls had already been split by the terrible roar.

When they saw the little boy playing on her breast fearlessly, the wives of the cow-herds were frightened and quickly took him away, and Yashoda and Rohini and the others protected the boy by waving a cow's tail on him and performing similar rites. They bathed the baby in cow's urine and cowdust, and with cowdung they wrote the names of Vishnu on his twelve limbs, to protect him. . . .[39] Thus the loving wives of the cow-herds protected him, and then his mother gave her son her breast to suck and put him to bed.

Meanwhile, Nanda and the other cow-herds returned to the village from Mathura, and when they saw the body of Putana they were astonished. "Indeed, Anakadundubhi has become a seer or a master of yoga," they said, "for he foresaw and foretold this whole calamity."[40] Then the villagers cut up the corpse with axes and threw the limbs far away, and they surrounded them with wood and burnt them. The smoke that arose from Putana's body as it burnt was sweet-smelling as aloe-wood, for her sins had been destroyed when she fed Krishna. Putana, a slayer of people and infants, a female Rakshasa, a drinker of blood, reached the heaven of good people because she had given her breast to Vishnu—even though she did it because she wished to kill him. How much greater, then, is the reward of those who offer what is dearest to the highest Soul, Krishna, with faith and devotion, like his doting mothers? She gave her breast to Krishna to suck, and he touched her body with his two feet which remain in the hearts of his devotees and which are adored by those who are adored by the world, and so, though an evil sorceress, she obtained the heaven which is the reward of mothers. What then is the reward of those cows and mothers whose breasts' milk Krishna drank? The lord, son of Devaki, giver of beatitude and all else, drank their milk as their breasts flowed because of their love for their son. Since they always looked upon Krishna as their son, they will never again be doomed to rebirth that arises from ignorance.

Childhood: Krishna's mother looks inside his mouth
After a little while, Rama and Keshava began to play in the village, crawling on their hands and knees.[41] They slithered about quickly, dragging their feet in the muddy pastures, delighting in the tinkling sound.[42] They would follow someone and then, suddenly bewildered and frightened, they would hasten back to their mothers. Their mothers' breasts would flow with milk out of tenderness for their own sons, whose bodies were beautifully covered with mud, and they would embrace them in their arms and give them their breasts to suck, and as they gazed at the faces with their innocent smiles and tiny teeth they would rejoice. Then the children began to play in the village at those boyish games that women love to see. They would grab hold of the tails of calves and be dragged back and forth in the pasture, and the women would look at them and forget their housework and laugh merrily. But the mothers, trying to keep the two very active and playful little boys from horned animals, fire, animals with teeth and tusks, and knives, water, birds, and thorns, were unable to do their housework, and they were rather uneasy.

After a little while, Rama and Krishna stopped crawling on their hands and knees and began to walk about the pastures quickly on their feet. Then the lord Krishna began to play with Rama and with the village boys of their age, giving great pleasure to the village women. When the wives of the cowherds saw the charming boyish pranks of Krishna, they would go in a group to tell his mother, saying, "Krishna unties the calves when it is not the proper time, and he laughs at everyone's angry shouts. He devises ways to steal and eat curds and milk and thinks food sweet only if he steals it. He distributes the food among the monkeys; if he doesn't eat the food, he breaks the pot. If he cannot find anything, he becomes angry at the house and makes the children cry before he runs away. If something is beyond his reach, he fashions some expedient by piling up pillows, mortars, and so on; or if he knows that the milk and curds have been placed in pots suspended in netting, he makes holes in the pots. When the wives of the cow-herds are busy with household duties, he will steal things in a dark room, making his own body with its masses of jewels serve as a lamp. This is the sort of impudent act which he commits; and he pees and so forth in clean houses. These are the thieving tricks that he contrives, but he behaves in the opposite way and is good when you are near." When his mother heard this report from the women who were looking at Krishna's frightened eyes and beautiful face, she laughed and did not wish to scold him.

One day when Rama and the other little sons of the cowherds were playing, they reported to his mother, "Krishna has eaten dirt." Yashoda took Krishna by the hand and scolded him, for his own good, and she said to him, seeing that his eyes were bewildered with fear, "Naughty boy, why have you secretly eaten dirt? These boys, your friends, and your elder brother say so." Krishna said, "Mother, I have not eaten. They are all lying. If you think they speak the truth, look at my mouth yourself." "If that is the case, then open your mouth," she said to the lord Hari, the god of unchallenged sovereignty who had in sport taken the form of a human child, and he opened his mouth.

She then saw in his mouth the whole eternal universe, and heaven, and the regions of the sky, and the orb of the earth with its mountains, islands, and oceans; she saw the wind, and lightning, and the moon and stars, and the zodiac; and water and fire and air and space itself; she saw the vacillating senses, the mind, the elements, and the three strands of matter. She saw within the body of her son, in his gaping mouth, the whole universe in all its variety, with all the forms of life and time and nature and action and hopes, and her own village, and herself. Then she became afraid and confused, thinking, "Is this a dream or an illusion wrought by a god? Or is it a delusion of my own perception? Or is it some portent of the natural powers of this little boy, my son? I bow down to the feet of the god, whose nature cannot be imagined or grasped by mind, heart, acts, or speech; he in whom all of this universe is inherent, impossible to fathom. The god is my refuge, he through whose power of delusion there arise in me such false beliefs as 'I,' 'This is my husband,' 'This is my son,' 'I am the wife of the village chieftain and all his wealth is mine, including these cow-herds and their wives and their wealth of cattle.'"

When the cow-herd's wife had come to understand the true essence in this way, the lord spread his magic illusion in the form of maternal affection. Instantly the cow-herd's wife lost her memory of what had occurred and took her son on her lap. She was as she had been before, her heart flooded with even greater love. She considered Hari—whose greatness is extolled by the three Vedas and the Upanishads and the philosophies of Sankhya and yoga and all the Satvata texts—she considered him to be her son.

Adolescence: Krishna subdues the serpent Kaliya

At the beginning of each month, all the serpents used to receive an offering under a tree, to prevent unpleasantness; this was agreed long ago by the people in the realm of the snakes. And each of the serpents, to protect himself, would give a portion of this offering to the noble Suparna at the beginning of each lunar fortnight.[43] But Kaliya, the son of Kadru, was full of pride because of the virulence of his poison, and he disregarded Garuda and himself ate that offering.[44] When the lord Garuda who is loved by the lord Vishnu learned of this he became angry and flew swiftly after Kaliya to kill him; and when the serpent, whose weapons were poison and fangs, saw him approaching swiftly he raised his many heads with their hideous tongues and hisses and fierce eyes and began to bite Suparna with his fangs. But Garuda the son of Tarkshya, the mount of the Chastiser of Madhu, became furious and swooped down upon him with a fierce attack and a great blast of speed, and struck the son of Kadru with his left wing, which shone like gold. When Kaliya was struck by the wing of Suparna he was greatly afflicted, and he entered a pool in the river Kalindi which Garuda could not enter or reach.

For in that very place Garuda had once eaten a fish that he wanted; even though the sage Saubhari had forbidden him to eat it, Garuda was so hungry that he ate it by force. And when Saubhari saw the poor fishes so miserable, their lord having been slain, he was overcome with pity and wished to protect and preserve the creatures there. "If Garuda enters here to eat the fishes," he said, "he will immediately part with his life's breath; this I swear." Kaliya knew of this, but no other serpent knew it; and so, because he feared Garuda, he dwelt there, until he was expelled by Krishna. . . .

One day as the lord Krishna was wandering about in Vrindavana without Rama, he went with his friends to the river Kalindi. The cows and cow-herds were oppressed by the heat of the summer and suffering from thirst, and they drank the polluted and poisoned water of the river. Their wits were overwhelmed by fate so that they touched that poisoned water, and they all fell lifeless on the bank. When Krishna, the lord of the lords of yoga, saw them in that condition, he revived his followers with a glance that rained ambrosia. They arose from the bank, their memories restored, and they looked at one another in amazement as they realized that their revival from death after drinking poison had been brought about by the favour of a glance from Govinda. . . .

There was a certain pool in the Kalindi into whose waters which boiled with the fire of Kaliya's poison, fell birds which were passing overhead and struck by blasts of air laden with drops from its poisonous waves; and breathing creatures, moving and still, who came to its banks died. When Krishna, who had become incarnate to restrain the wicked, perceived that the river had been polluted by that serpent whose poison was so virulent and swiftly active, he climbed a very high Kadamba tree, clapped his hands, girded his loins tightly, and plunged into the poisoned water. The mass of water in that pool of serpents was swelled by the poison emitted by serpents who were shaken by the blast caused by the vigorous dive of the Man, and it overflowed for a hundred bow-lengths on all sides with terrible waves tawny with poison, but this was nothing to him of infinite might.

When Kaliya heard the noise of the whirling of the club-like arms of Krishna, who was playing in the pool like a rogue elephant, and saw his own residence overwhelmed, he was unable to bear the sight and sound, and he slithered out. He enveloped angrily with his coils and bit in his vital spots that boy whose feet were like the inside of a lotus, who was bright as a cloud, beautiful to see in his youth, adorned with the Shrivasta, wearing the yellow garments, with a beautiful smile on his face, playing fearlessly. When Krishna's dear friends the cattle-tenders saw him caught up in the coils of the serpent, apparently motion-less, they were greatly distressed; since they had consigned themselves, their friends, their wealth, their families, and all their desires to Krishna, their minds were stupefied with grief, sorrow, and fear, and they fell down. The cows and bulls and calves lowed in their misery; gazing at Krishna in fear, they stood and seemed to weep.

Then there appeared in the village three kinds of violent great portent boding danger nearby: there were calamities on earth, in heaven, and in the body. When Nanda and the other cow-herds noted them they were terrified, knowing that Krishna had gone to tend the cows without Rama. Not knowing who he really was, they thought that his death had come, because of the evil portents; and since he was their very life's breath, and their hearts were set upon him, they were tortured by grief, sorrow, and fear. All of the cow-herds, the young, the old, and the women, went miserably out of the village, hoping to see Krishna. When the lord Bala saw them so discouraged he laughed, but he did not say a word, for he knew the powers of his younger brother.

As they searched for their beloved Krishna by following the path indicated by the footprints with the signs of the lord, they all came to the banks of the Yamuna. Hastening along on the path, they distinguished between the foot-prints of the cows and the footprints of the lord of all, for these were marked by the lotus, barley shoot, elephant goad, thunderbolt, and banner. When from a distance they saw Krishna in the pool, the watery abode, wrapped in the serpent's coils, and they saw the cow-herds stupefied and the cattle scat-tered and lowing, they became deeply alarmed and unhappy. The hearts of the cow-herds' wives were passionately devoted to the infinite lord, and they remembered his friendship, his smiles and glances and words; and when their dearest one was swallowed by the serpent they were burnt by great sorrow and saw the triple world as empty, for it was devoid of their beloved. They went to Krishna's mother, who was sorrowing for her child, and they sympathized with her and wept, for they shared their grief, and they told their favourite village stories, and fixed their gazes upon Krishna's face and seemed as if dead. When the lord Rama, who knew the true majesty of Krishna, saw that Nanda and the others, whose very life's breath was Krishna, were about to enter the pool, he prevented him.

Krishna, seeing that his own village, with its women and children, was so miserable because of him, and knowing that it had no refuge other than him, conformed to the way of the mortals and, staying for a moment, rose up from the serpent's grip. The serpent's hoods were tortured by the expanding body of Krishna, and he released him; he raised his hoods angrily and stood spitting venom through his hissing nostrils; he stared at Hari with is unblinking eyes that were like frying pans, and he licked the two corners of his mouth with his forked tongue, and his very gaze was full of the fire of a virulent poison. Playfully, Krishna circled about him, like Garuda, the lord of birds, and Kaliya also moved about, watching for an opportunity. When the serpent's strength was exhausted by moving about in this way, the First bent down the snake's raised shoulder and mounted upon his broad heads. Then the master of all musical arts danced, his lotus feet made bright red by their contact with the multitude of jewels on the serpent's head.[45] When the wives of the Gandharvas, Siddhas, divine Caranas, and gods saw that he was preparing to dance, they approached him joyfully with offerings of Mridanga, Panava, and Anaka drums, and musical instruments, and songs and flowers and praise.

He who bears a cruel rod of punishment trampled with his feet whatever head of the hundred-headed one was yet unbent, and the serpent, his life-span spent but still writhing, vomited clotted blood from his mouth and fell, suffering horribly. The Ancient Man danced on the serpent who still spewed poison from his eyes and hissed loudly in his anger, and he trampled down with his feet whatever head the serpent raised, subduing him as calmly as if he were being worshipped with flowers. Kaliya, his umbrella of hoods shattered by the gay dance of death, his limbs broken, vomited blood copiously from his mouths, remembered the guru of all who move and are still, the Ancient Man, Narayana, and he surrendered to him in his heart.

When Kaliya's wives saw that the serpent was sinking down under the burden of Krishna who is the very womb of the universe, and that his umbrella of hoods was crushed by the blows of Krishna's heels, then they were distressed, and their garments, ornaments, and hair-bindings became loose, and they sought refuge with the Primary One. Their hearts aching, the good women placed their children in front of them, prostrated their bodies on the ground, folded their palms together, bowed to the lord of creatures and sought refuge with him who gives refuge, for they wished to save their husband from harm and release him from sin.

The serpent's wives said, "Your punishment of this man who has sinned is proper, for you became incarnate to restrain the wicked. Viewing with an indifferent gaze your enemy or your sons, considering only the fruit of actions, you mete out punishment. You have favoured us, for your punishment of the wicked removes their impurity. Even your anger should be considered an act of grace, because our husband is embodied as a venomous reptile.[46] . . . You should endure the offence committed by our husband, committed by your own creature. As you have a peaceful soul, you should forgive the fool who did not know you. Lord, be gracious; the serpent is giving up his life's breaths. Grant life's breath to our husband, for we are women for whom good people will sorrow. Command us, your servants, for one who obeys your commands with faith is released from all danger."

When the lord was thus praised by the wives of the serpent, he released the unconscious Kaliya whose head had been smashed by the pounding of his feet. The wretched Kaliya gradually regained his senses and his life's breath, and breathing with difficulty he folded his palms together and said to Hari, Krishna, "We are evil from our birth, dark creatures whose anger endures. O lord, one's own nature is difficult to abandon, for it possesses people like an evil demon. Creator, this whole universe was created by you out of three strands, with various natures, powers, strengths, sources, seeds, hopes, and forms. And in it are we, O lord, serpents whose anger is far-reaching from birth. How can we ourselves, deluded creatures, abandon your delusion which is hard to abandon? You are the cause of this, omniscient one, Lord of the universe; ordain for us grace or punishment, as you think best."

Then the lord, who had taken human form, answered, "You must not stay here, serpent; go quickly to the ocean with your abundant kinsmen, children, and wives. Let this river be enjoyed by cows and men. Whatever mortal remembers my chastisement of you and recites it at dawn and sunset, he will have no fear of you. And whoever bathes in this pool where I have played and offers its waters to the gods and others, and fasts and remembers me and worships me, he will be released from all sins. Leave this pool and take shelter in the island Ramanaka. Suparna, whom you feared, will not eat you now that you have been marked by my foot." When Kaliya heard the words of the lord Krishna whose deeds are marvelous, he worshipped him in joy and ceremony, with his wives. He worshipped the lord of the universe, whose banner bears the Garuda, and propitiated him with excellent celestial garments, garlands, and jewels, with rich ornaments and with celestial perfumes and unguents, and with a great garland of lotuses; and he walked around him in reverence and bowed to him and happily received permission to leave. Then, with his wives, friends, and sons he went to the island in the ocean, and at that moment the Yamuna became free from poison, its water like ambrosia, by the grace of the lord who had taken human form for his sport.

Krishna steals the clothes of the girls of the village

In the first month of winter, the girls of Nanda's village performed a certain vow to the goddess Katyayani. They ate rice cooked with clarified butter; they bathed in the water of the Kalindi river at sunrise; they made an image of the goddess out of sand and worshipped it with fragrant perfumes and garlands, with offerings and incense and lamps, and with bouquets of flowers, fresh sprigs of leaves, fruits, and rice. And they prayed: "Goddess Katyayani, great mistress of yoga, empress of great deluding magic, make the son of the cow-herd Nanda my husband. I bow to you." Saying this prayer, the girls would worship her, and having set their hearts on Krishna, the girls performed this vow for a month; they worshipped Bhadrakali so that the son of Nanda would be their husband. Arising at dawn, calling one another by name, they would join hands and to bathe in the Kalindi everyday, singing loudly about Krishna as they went.

One day, when they had gone to the river and taken off their clothes on the bank as usual, they were playing joyfully in the water, singing about Krishna. The lord Krishna, lord of all masters of yoga, came there with his friends of the same age in order to grant them the object of their rites. He took their clothes and quickly climbed a Nipa tree, and laughing with the laughing boys, he told what the joke was: "Girls, let each one of you come here and take her own clothes as she wishes. I promise you, this is no jest, for you have been exhausted by your vows. I have never before told an untruth, and these boys know this. Slender-waisted ones, come one by one or all together and take your clothes." When the cow-herd girls saw what his game was, they were overwhelmed with love, but they looked at one another in shame, and they smiled, but they did not come out. Flustered and embarrassed by Govinda's words and by his jest, they sank down up to their necks in the icy water, and, shivering, they said to him, "You should not have played such a wicked trick. We know you as our beloved, son of the cow-herd Nanda, the pride of the village. Give us our clothes, for we are trembling. O darkly handsome one, we are your slaves and will do as you command, but you know dharma: give us our clothes or we will tell your father, the chieftain."

The lord said to them, "If you are my slaves and will do as I command, then come here and take back your clothes, O brightly smiling ones." Then all the girls, shivering and smarting with cold, came out of the water, covering their crotches with their hands. The lord was pleased and gratified by their chaste actions, and he looked at them and placed their clothes on his shoulder and smiled and said, "Since you swam in the water without clothes while you were under a vow, this was an insult to the divinity.[47] Therefore you must fold your hands and place them on your heads and bow low in expiation of your sin, and then you may take your clothes." When the village girls heard what the infallible one said, they thought that that bathing naked had been a violation of their vows, and they bowed down to Krishna, the very embodiment of all their rituals, who had thus fulfilled their desires and wiped out their disgrace and sin. Then the lord, the son of Devaki, gave their clothes to them, for he felt pity when he saw them bowed down in this way and he was satisfied with them.

Though they were greatly deceived and robbed of their modesty, though they were mocked and treated like toys and stripped of their clothes, yet they held no grudge against him, for they were happy to be together with their beloved. Rejoicing in the closeness of their lover, they put on their clothes; their bashful glances, in the thrall of their hearts, did not move from him. Knowing that the girls had taken a vow because they desired to touch his feet, the lord with a rope around his waist said to the girls, "Good ladies, I know that your desire is to worship me. I rejoice in this vow, which deserves to be fulfilled. The desire of those whose hearts have been placed in me does not give rise to further desire, just as seed corn that has been boiled or fried does not give rise to seed. You have achieved your aim. Now, girls, go back to the village and you will enjoy your nights with me, for it was for this that you fine ladies undertook your vow and worship." When the girls heard this from Krishna, they had obtained what they desired; and, meditating upon his lotus feet, they forced themselves to go away from him to the village.

Source: *Hindu Myths: A Sourcebook*, translated from the Sanskrit with an introduction by Wendy Doniger (New York: Penguin Books, 1975), 213–231.

Bhakti Writings and Writers

Beginning in the sixth century CE in south India, and continuing through the seventeenth century, and some would say even to the present day, the bhakti movement inaugurates an entirely new way of being religious. What we call the "movement" as such comprises a series of saints who give powerful testimony to a direct and passionate relationship to god. Bhakti goes against the idea of "priesthood," or indeed, any kind of mediated relationship to the divine, whether elite or popular. The bhakti saints, such as the ones included below, push against the "norm" by struggling, at times roughly, with their god. They speak and write out of the authority of their own experience. Many of the bhakti "saints," as they come to be called, are said to have childhood experiences that indicate the nature of their connection to the divine. Some of the bhakti writers, such as Sur Das, do not give accounts of their own life, but an imagined life, such as imagined scenes from the childhood of Krishna. Ram Prasad Sen, too, imagines the goddess as a pouting little girl whose larger, divine, powers are part of her childlike charm. Some of these narratives of childhood are unusual first-person testimonies, such as that of Bahina Bai. Her story allows us a glimpse into the complexity of childhood, where childlike longing and innocence occurs at the same time that she is negotiating the role of "child bride."

Document 4–7

The Writings of Sur Das

Krishna is coming outside from within
To walk into courtyard was easy, indeed;
at the doorway he's caught, though:
He trips and falls down—he just can't pass the threshold;
what labour to get him beyond it!
In only three steps he traversed the whole world;
but to move across his house takes him such time . . .
Deep within his soul Balaram has understood:
Krishna's just pretending to be helpless.
The countless glories of Sur's Lord
delight devotees' hearts. (743)

Watching Krishna walk gives joy to Mother Yashoda
On all fours now, close to the floor, Krishna flounders;
his mother sees the scene and points it out to all.
He makes it to the doorway then
comes back the other way again.
He trips and he falls, doesn't manage to cross—
which makes the sages wonder:
Ten millions of worlds he creates in a flash
and he can destroy them just as fast;
But he's picked up by Nanda's wife, who sets him down, plays games
     with him,
then with her hand supports him while he steps outside the door.
When they see Sur's Lord, gods, men, and sages
lose track of their minds. (744)

Yashoda, his mother, is teaching him to walk
He stumbles and then grabs her hand,
Unsteady, his feet have found the floor.
At times she looks at his beautiful face
And prays for his well being.
At times she beseeches her family gods:
"Let my boy Krishna have long life,"
At times she gives a shout to Balaram:

"Come play here with your brother in the yard."
Sur Das knows that this great glory of the Lord's play
Gives delight to Raja Nanda. (733)

Krishna's coming: crawling, crying joyfully
In the courtyard of Nanda, golden and jewel-studded,
Hari hurries to catch his reflection.
Now and then Hari, seeing his shadow,
gives it a grasp with his hands,
Then gleefully gurgles: two little teeth shine.
Hari repeatedly seized his image.
Hand-shadows, foot-shadows, on the golden ground
together all shine forth.
As if each hand and foot in every jewel on the earth
had come together in a lotus throne adorning Krishna.
Yashoda seeing the sweetness of childhood,
calls out to Nanda again and again.
Then hiding her son in the folds of her sari,
suckles Sur's Lord at her breast. (728)

Source: From Wendy Doniger O'Flaherty with Daniel Gold, David Haberman, and David Shulman, *Textual Sources for the Study of Hinduism* (Chicago: University of Chicago Press, 1988), 142–144).

"If you drink the milk of the black cow, Gopal,
you'll see your black braid grow.
Little son, listen, among all the little boys
you'll be the finest, most splendid one.
Look at all the other lads in Braj and see:
it's milk that's brought them their strength.
So drink: the fires daily burn in the bellies
of your foes—Kans, and Kesi, and the crane."
He takes a little bit and tugs his hair a little bit
to see if his mother's telling lies.
Sur says, Yashoda looks at his face and laughs
when he tries to coax his curls beyond his ear. (792)

Source: John Stratton Hawley and Mark Jurgensmeyer, *Songs of the Saints of India* (New York: Oxford University Press, 1988), 105.

Document 4–8

Bahina Bai the Child-Bride, Through Grief
for a Calf, Becomes a Bhakta

25.1. I began to experience great sorrow in my heart. Why, O Vitthal, have
you forsaken me, 2. I am all in a heat from the three fevers of life. What
matters it, let me die! 3–4. But just then on the seventh day, repeating
aloud the names and praises of God, Tukaram appeared in a vision before
my eyes, and said: "Remember the first lines (of the calf's *shloka*). 5. Do
not be troubled, I am beside you. Take from my hand this nectar. 6. When
a calf puts its mouth to the cow, stream of milk flows. This is excellent
nectar, drink it." 7. With this he placed his hand upon my head and
whispered a mantra in my ear. 8. I then placed my head on his feet. He
gave me a book called the *Mantra Gita*. 9. This vision in a dream occurred
through the Guru's favour on a Sunday, on the fifth day of the dark half of
the moon in the month of Kartika. 10. My heart rejoiced. It fixed itself on
Brahma, Pure Intelligence. I sat up astonished. 11. I recollected the mantra.
Tukoba, in the form of a vision, had manifested to me his abundant
mercy in this dream. 12. He had fed me with nectar, which to the taste was
unlike anything else. He only can appreciate this who experiences it. 13.
Says Bahini, "Such was the mercy of the *sadguru*. Tukaram had truly shown
it abundantly."

26.1. I was comforted by the Brahman's words. And I remembered the verses,
which I had heard in my dream. 2. Without having actually seen Tukoba, I
meditated on my mental image of him. 3. He whose verses give the mind
rest, he in his bodily form is Vitthal himself. 4. There seems no difference
between him and Vitthal. That was the witness my mind gave. . . .

27.1. [I have already related how] my husband had tied me up into a bundle,
and beaten me, unable to endure my grief [for the calf]. 2. How also on
the fourth day when I was on the point of dying, Vitthal performed a
miracle. 3. In the form of a Brahman, he came to me and awakened me
to consciousness. 4. My soul did awake, and my thought fastened itself
on Tukoba. 5. It was the seventh day after the calf had died, that Tukoba
had appeared in the dream, 6. comforted me, fed me with nectar, having
led the calf [me] to the cow [Tukaram]. 7. After feeding me with nectar
he whispered a mantra in my ear, which everywhere men repeat. 8. He
placed his hand on my head and blessed me. The favour he bestowed on
me, he alone could know its worth. 9. The greatness of such a blessing is
unlimited. It was what the calf declared in substance when it repeated the
latter half of the Sanskrit *shloka*. 10. On the eighth day I became physically
conscious, having drunk to the full the nectar Tukoba gave me. 11. Just
then I saw the cow directly before me. She looked at the point of death,

because of her calf's death. 12. But Tukoba said to me, "I have fed this nectar also to the calf. Never can death touch it. 13. The calf is here with me, immortal, its soul partaking gladly of the nectar." 14. Says Bahini, "After all the above had happened, the next events to take place will now be related in detail."

28.1.   Jayaram, the great, the ocean-of-wisdom, who could see things through his peculiar power of vision, 2. sent for Hirambhat, and asked him about my condition. 3. Hirambhat related to him all the events that had occurred at his house; 4. how a guru appeared to me in a dream, in the form of Tukoba; how he had enlightened me in the dream. 5. He told him, how the little girl awoke to consciousness, how she sat up, and how she had called the cow to her, caressed her, 6. and milked her while the cow was drinking water and eating the grass. 7. But he added that the character of the girl was changed. Her heart was now overflowing with emotion. 8. He told how her heart was absorbed in Tukoba. Her parents had chided her. 9. Her husband had become crazed against her, and was gazing at her not knowing what to do. 10. She was sitting in the house, absorbed in meditation, her thoughts being concentrated on Tukoba. 11. Such were the events Hirambhat related to Jayaram. He on his part rejoiced to hear them. 12.) Says Bahini, "Having heard these facts, Jayaram, did me a very kindly act."

29.1.   A very kindly feeling arose in Jayaram Svami towards me, and he came personally to see what my mental condition was. 2. When I saw him I felt very happy, and my throat was choked with the emotion of joy. 3. In my heart I performed the *arati* and chanted his praise. I bowed to him and, in my heart sincerely worshipped him. 4. Says Bahini, "Pandurang truly recognizes that love of his heart."

30.1.   He poured upon me his look of love, of affection, such as a mother would give. 2. Jayaram accepted my heart's worship, and with love for me returned to his lodging. 3. As he sat on his accustomed seat quietly, and with his mind brought to a state of peace, 4. suddenly a thing happened that had never occurred before. Tukaram appeared to him. 5. Jayaram joyfully made him a *namaskar* and embraced him. 6. To me also he gave a moment's vision of himself, and placed a morsel in my mouth. 7. He said to me, "I have come to visit Jayaram, but I recognize your desire also. 8. Do not remain any longer in this place. Do not let pass the opportunity for attaining self-knowledge and enlightenment." [9.] Says Bahini, "This is the second vision that Tukoba gave me through the working of my mind."

31.1.   The people thought all this as very strange, and came in crowds to see me. 2. My husband, seeing them, gave me much bodily suffering. 3. He could not endure seeing the people coming to see me. And moment by moment his hatred increased. 4. He exclaimed, "It would be well if this woman were dead. Why do these low people come to see her? 5. I wonder what next we shall see in her of demoniac possession! How is God going to supply her bodily needs?" 6. Says Bahini, "Such was the concern of my husband, but the Infinite One knew of it also."

32.1. My husband now began to say, "We are Brahmans. We should spend our time in the study of the Vedas. 2. What is all this! The shudra Tuka! Seeing him in a dream! My wife is ruined by all this! What am I to do? 3. Who cares for Jayaram, and who for Pandurang, My home has been destroyed! 4. What care I for singing the names and praises of Hari? Even in my dreams I know not bhakti. 5. Who cares for saints and *sadhus*! Who cares for the feelings of bhakti! Let us always be found in the order of the religious mendicants." 6. Says Bahini, "Thus did my husband think and discuss the matter in his own mind. 'Who cares to keep such a wife as she is!'" [7.] Says Bahini, "Thus did my husband talk, and I then began to think myself."

33.1. This is how my husband considered the subject in his own mind: "I will abandon her, and go into a forest, 2. for people are going to bow down to her, while she regards me as worth but a straw. 3. They will discuss with this woman the meaning of the *kathas*, but she herself will consider me a low fellow. 4. The people make regardful enquiries about her while I, who am a Brahman, have become a fool! 5. They are all calling her a Gosavin. Who will show me respect in her presence?" 6. Says Bahini, "Thus my husband discussed the matter in his own mind, and gave his own mind advice."

34.1. He said to himself, "This is my wife's condition. Do not remain here any longer. 2. Let me rather go to some sacred river, for asceticism is now my lot." 3. He made his *namaskar* to his mother-in-law and father-in-law saying, "My wife is advanced three months in pregnancy. 4. I am going on a pilgrimage to sacred places; my wife has become mad after God; look after her. 5. I do not wish to see her face any longer. Who is to make up to us our loss in reputation? 6. Who is going to stay here and suffer humiliation at her hands?"

35.1. What am I to do with my Fate? I must bear whatever comes to my lot. 2. I am not one who is possessed. My body is not subject to demoniac possession. 3. Therefore, holding to my own special duties, I will give my mind to listening to the Scriptures, and the winning of God. 4. My duty is to serve my husband, for he is God to me. My husband himself is the Supreme Brahma. 5. The water in which my husband's feet are washed has the value of all the sacred waters put together. Without that holy water, [all I do is] valueless. 6. If I transgress my husband's commands, all the sins of the world will be on my head. 7. The Vedas in fact say that it is the husband who has the authority in the matter of religious duties, earthly possessions, desires, and salvation. 8. This is then the determination, and the desire of my heart. I want my thought concentrated on my husband.

9. The supreme spiritual riches [*paramartha*] are to be attained through service to my husband. I shall reach the highest purpose of my life through my husband. 10. If I have any other God but my husband, I shall have committed in my heart a sin like that of the killing of a Brahman. 11. My husband is my *sadguru*. My husband is my means of salvation. This is indeed the true understanding and determination of my heart. 12. Says Bahini, "O God, Thou hast entered into my husband's heart and given it peace."

36.1.   Supposing my husband should go away to live the ascetic's life, then, O Pandurang, of what value would be my life among men? 2. Can the body attain to beauty when its life has left it? What is the night without the brightness of the moon? 3. My husband is the life; I am his body. In my husband lies all my well-being. 4. My husband is the water in which I am the fish. How can I live without him? 5. My husband is the sun, and I its brightness. How can these two be separated? 6. Says Bahini, "This is the conviction of my heart, and Hari knows these my thoughts." . . .

39.1.   My husband had made up his mind to leave us on the morrow, when 2. suddenly he was stricken ill and for seven days his body was burning with fever. 3. Even from those he knew, he accepted no advice. I was at his side day and night. 4. He rejected the medicines given to him. He suffered intense pain. 5. For more than month he rejected food, and endured excruciating pain. 6. The various gods and family deities were pleaded with in special ways, 7. but there was no cessation of his sufferings. He exclaimed, "I am about to die. 8. How I insulted Pandurang and Tukoba! and it was then that this suffering came to me. 9. If this pain is due to my having insulted Tukaram, then 10. O Tukaram, you who are honoured in all the universe, perform now a miracle. 11. Says Bahini, "My husband repented; Pandurang is the inner witness of this change."

40.1.   An oldish Brahman appeared and said to him, "Why is it you are wishing to die? 2. Why did it come to your mind to take up the ascetic's life? What are your reasons for wanting to desert your wife? 3. First, think in your own heart what wrong she has committed, and then if true, give yourself into the hands of anger. 4. If you wish to live, accept her. 5. If she has conducted herself without regard to her duties, then only you might abandon her, you idiot! 6. She is one who has no worldly desires. She is truly a *bhakta* of Hari. You should likewise be one also. 7. You will be blessed by it," said the Brahman, and my husband bowed down at his feet. 8. He explained all to the Brahman and exclaimed, "Give me now to-day the gift of life. 9. O my Svami, save me from this painful disease, and I will devote my life at your feet." 10. He did not speak at all to his wife, but with all his heart he pleaded with Hari for help. 11. He then arose and made a *namaskar* to the Brahman. The twice-born responded "You will be blessed." 12. I was listening to the conversation of the two, and I at once fell at the feet of my husband. 13. The Brahman immediately vanished out of sight and my husband regained his health and well-being. 14. Says Bahini, "If God bestows His favour, all the Siddhis stand at the door ready to serve."

Source: *Bahina Bai: A Translation of Her Autobiography and Verses*, by Justin E. Abbott, foreword by Anne Feldhaus (Delhi: Motilal Banarsidass, 1985), 18–24.

Document 4–9

Ramprasad Sen's Poems to the Mother Goddess in her Childlike Aspects

30

O Mother, who really
Knows Your magic?
You're a crazy girl
Driving us all crazy with these tricks.
No one knows anyone else
In a world of Your illusions.
Kali's tricks are so deft,
We act on what we see.
And what suffering—
All because of a crazy girl!
Who knows
What She truly is?
Ramprasad says: If She decides
To be kind, this misery will pass.

32

O Giri, I can't comfort
Your Uma anymore.
She cries and pouts,
Won't take the breast,
Won't touch Her *khir*,
And shoves away her cream.

When the moon lifts
In the night sky
She begs me to get
The moon for Her.
Her eyes are swollen,

Her face pale—
How can a mother
Stand it!
Crying, "Come, Mother,
Come," She holds my little finger
Wanting to go
I don't know where.
I ask Her—"Is there any way
To get the moon?"
And she flings
Her jewelry at me.
Giri sits up, lovingly
Takes Gauri on His lap
And smiling says: "Little mother, here
Is the moon," handing Her a mirror.
Seeing her face in the glass
She's happy,
And so shames
A million moons.
Shri Ramprasad says: He's a rich man
In whose house the Mother lives,
And saying this, he lays Her down
In Her small bed, fast asleep.

Source: Ramprasad Sen, *Grace and Mercy in Her Wild Hair: Selected Poems to the Mother Goddess,* translated by Leonard Nathan and Clinton Seely (Prescott, Ariz.: Hohm Press, 1999), 32, 34–35.

Hindu Writings from Colonial India

Colonial India gives us an intriguing glimpse into an India negotiating very complex realities. Beginning with the Muslim Mughal rulers onward, we see the beginning of a full-scale use of the idea of "Hinduism" as such; in public discourse, Hinduism emerges as a unifying construct in the minds of both ruler and, eventually, ruled. During the period of British rule, in a variety of interreligious polemics among colonial missionaries, colonial administrators, orthodox Hindu leaders, and less orthodox Hindu reformers, we see a grappling with the presence of multiple religions, and with the abstract idea of "religion" as such. Questions in the minds of people are: is Hinduism as such a religion that can stand on a par with Christianity, the religion of the rulers and missionaries? Can Hindu practices and legal codes make sense of and justify Hindu ways of life in the eyes of those who rule Hindus?

This issue becomes particularly salient when it comes to the issue of marriage at an extremely young age, otherwise known as "child marriage," and the related question of child widows.

Here we have two examples of childhood experiences in the late colonial period: the first from Gandhi's childhood in the late nineteenth century, and the second from the filmmaker Satyajit Ray just before independence. Gandhi was married to his wife, Kasturba, at a very young age. In addition, although he was from a more traditional Hindu family, Gandhi had many traditional and nontraditional Hindu acquaintances, which gave him a sense of the range of Hinduism. His childhood also involved inevitable exposure to Parsi, Muslim, and Christian views, something an earlier Hindu childhood would not have had. Satyajit Ray, on the other hand, is most concerned with the intra-Hindu relationships between traditional Hindus and Reform Hindus. He gives us a very intriguing portrait of the Brahmo Samaj, and how a child might experience the spare, mostly verbal ritual in the Brahmo community and its lack of images in the worship. His childhood assessment of Christianity is rather different from Gandhi's; the young Gandhi focuses on the missionary activity and the young Ray focuses on the commercial activity of colonial Christians in India.

Document 4–10

Gandhi's Autobiography

Glimpses of Religion

From my sixth or seventh year up to my sixteenth I was at school, being taught all sorts of things except religion. I may say that I failed to get from the teachers what they could have given me without any effort on heir part. And yet I kept picking up on things here and there from my surroundings. The term "religion" I am using in its broadest sense, meaning thereby self-realization of knowledge of self.

Being born in the Vaishnava faith, I had often to go to the *Haveli*. But it never appealed to me. I did not like its glitter and pomp. Also I heard rumors of immorality being practised there, and lost all interest in it. Hence I could gain nothing from the *Haveli*.

But what I failed to get there I obtained from my nurse, an old servant of the family, whose affection for me I still recall. I have said before that there was in me a fear of ghosts and spirits. Rambha, for that was her name, suggested, as a remedy for this fear, the repetition of *Ramanama*. I had more faith in her than in her remedy, and so at a tender age I began repeating *Ramanama* to cure my fear of ghosts and spirits. This was of course short-lived, but the good seed sown in childhood was not sown in vain. I think it is due to the seed down by that good woman Rambha that today *Ramanama* is an infallible remedy for me.

Just about this time, a cousin of mine who was a devotee of the *Ramayana* arranged for my second brother and me to learn *Ram Raksha*. We got it by heart, and made it a rule to recite it every morning after the bath. The practice was kept up as long as we were in Porbandar. As soon as we reached Rajkot, it was forgotten. For I had not much belief in it. I recited it partly because of my pride in being able to recite *Ram Raksha* with correct pronunciation.

What, however, left a deep impression on me was the reading of the *Ramayana* before my father. During part of his illness my father was in Porbandar. Here every evening he used to listen to the *Ramayana*. The reader was a great devotee of Rama—Ladha Maharaj of Bileshvar. It was said of him that he cured himself of his leprosy not by any medicine, but by applying to he affected parts bilva leaves which had been cast away after being offered to the image of Mahadeva in Bileshvar temple, and by he regular repetition of the *Ramanama*. His faith, it was said, had made him whole. This may or may no be true. We at any rate believed he story. And it is a fact that when Ladha Maharaj began his reading of the *Ramayana* his body was entirely free from leprosy. He had a melodious voice. He would sing the *Dohas* (couplets) and *Chopais* (quatrains), and explain them, losing himself in the discourse and carrying his listeners along with him. I must have been thirteen at that time, but I quite remember being enraptured by his reading. That laid the foundation of my deep devotion to the *Ramayana*. Today I regard the *Ramayana* of Tulasidas as the greatest book in all devotional literature.

A few months after this we came to Rajkot. There was no *Ramayana* reading here. The *Bhagavat*, however, used to be read on every Ekadashi [eleventh day of the bright and dark half of the lunar month] day. Sometimes I attended the reading, but the reciter was uninspiring. Today I see that the Bhagavat is a book which can evoke religious fervour. I have read it in Gujurati with intense interest. But when I heard portions of the original read by Pandit Madan Mohan Malaviya during my twenty-one days fast, I wish I had heard in my childhood from such a devotee as he is, so that I could have formed a liking for it at an early age. Impressions formed at that age strike roots deep down into one's nature, and it is my perpetual regret that I was not fortunate enough to hear more good books of this kind read during that period.

In Rajkot, however, I got an early grounding in toleration for all branches of Hinduism and sister religions. For my father and mother would visit the *Haveli* as also Shiva and Rama's temples, and would take or send us youngsters there. Jain monks also would pay frequent visits to my father, and would even go out of their way to accept food from us—non-Jains. They would have talks with my father on subjects religious and mundane.

He had, besides, Musalman and Parsi friends, who would talk to him about their own faith, and he would listen to them always with respect, and often with interest. Being his nurse, I often had a chance to be present at these talks. These many things combined to inculcate in me a toleration for all faiths.

Only Christianity was at the time an exception. I developed a sort of dislike for it. And for a reason. In those days Christian missionaries used to stand in a corner near the high school and hold forth, pouring abuse on Hindus and their gods. I could not endure this. I must have stood there to hear them once only, but that was enough to dissuade me from repeating the experiment. About the same time, I heard of a well-known Hindu having been converted to Christianity. It was the talk of the town that, when he was baptized, he had to eat beef and drink liquor, that he also had to change his clothes, and the thenceforth he began to go about in European costume including a hat. These things got on my nerves. Surely, I thought a religion that compelled one to eat beef, drink liquor, and change one's own clothes did not deserve the name. I also heard that the new convert had already begun abusing the religion of his ancestors, their customs and their country. All these things created in me a dislike for Christianity.

But the fact that I had learnt to be tolerant to other religions did not mean that I had any living faith in God. I happened, about this time, to come across *Manusmriti* which was amongst my father's collection. The story of the creation and similar things in it did not impress me very much, but on the contrary made me incline somewhat towards atheism.

There was a cousin of mind, still alive, for whose intellect I had great regard. To him I turned with my doubts. But he could not resolve them. He sent me away with this answer: "When you grow up, you will be able to solve these doubts yourself. These questions ought not to be raised at your age." I was silenced, but was not comforted. Chapters about diet and the like in *Manusmriti* seemed to me to run contrary to daily practice. To my doubts as to this also, I got the same answer. "With intellect more developed and with more reading I shall understand it better," I said to myself.

Manusmriti at any rate did not then teach me ahimsa. I have told the story of my meat eating. *Manusmriti* seemed to support it. I also felt that I was quite moral to kill serpents, bugs, and the like. I remember to have killed at that age bugs and such other insects, regarding it as a duty.

But one thing took deep root in me—the conviction that morality is the basis of all things, and that truth is the substance of all morality. Truth became my sole objective. It began to grow in magnitude every day, and my definition of it also has been ever widening.

Source: *Gandhi: An Autobiography* (Boston: Beacon, 1957), 31–35.

Document 4–11

Satyajit Ray's Childhood Days

My grandfather had four brothers. All but two of the brothers had become members of the Brahmo Samaj. The two who had remained Hindus were Sarada-ranjan and Muktidaranjan. The women in their houses wore sindoor in the parting of their hair, wrapped their sarees in a different way, and the men had amulets on their arms. The sound of bells and conch shells rang out from their puja rooms, and my aunts often fed me prasad at the end of a puja. None of this happened in my own home, but that never made me feel like an alien in their Hindu households. To tell the truth, the only difference between my grandfather and his brothers seemed to be religion. Their other interests in life were very similar. The Hindu brothers were as passionate about sports—including fishing—as the Brahmos. It was Saradaranjan who started playing cricket before anyone else, and gradually, almost everyone in the family took it up.

But it was really in the family of their sister that cricket took firm root. I called my grandfather's sister Shona Thakuma. She was married to a man called Hemen Bose, who was in the perfumery business. He used to advertise his products—hair oil, scent and paan masala—through a four-line rhyme. Every newspaper carried it:

> Rub in your hair Kuntaleen,
> On your hankie dab Delkhose;
> With your paan chew Tambuleen,
> And gratify Mister H Bose.

Growing up in a Brahmo household, there was only one thing that I minded. It was the lack of fanfare in the Brahmo annual festival, which was called Maghotsav. Devoid of the noise and excitement that were so much a part of a Hindu puja, Maghotsav simply consisted of devotional songs and long sermons that lasted for nearly two hours. We also had memorial services in our house every time there was a death in the family. Chairs and tables from our drawing room were removed, and a carpet spread on the marble floor. There were the inevitable songs and prayers. My mother was a good singer, so she sang each time. Sometimes, even those who could not sing all that well—such as Dhon Dadu Kakamoni—also took part. After sitting with my head bowed and staring down at the same carpet year after year, I came to know the designs and patterns on it by heart.

The other thing I could never forget were the Sanskrit prayers and hymns that were chanted, and their meaning in Bengali intoned by the acharyas [ministers] in a particular way. Each word was elongated for some reason. For instance, the first three lines of *Asato ma sadgamaya* were explained thus:

> Le-e-ad us from
> Untru-u-th into Tru-u-th

Le-e-ad us from Da-a-rkness into Li-i-ght
Le-e-ad us fro D-e-ath into E-e-ternal Li-i-fe!

Each acharya intoned these words in exactly the same way. Why no one ever thought of uttering them normally, I could never figure out.

There are two Brahmo temples in Calcutta, one in Cornwallis Street and the other in Bhowanipur. We continued to go to the former to celebrate Maghotsav even after moving to Bhowanipur. Although the festival took place in January, we had to get up at half past four in the morning to have a bath before going to the temple. The first hour was spent in Brahma keertan [praise for the Lord]. It was followed by more songs and prayers. We had to sit on straight-backed wooden benches so there was never any question of comfort.

Only on three days of the festival did we have any fun. On the first day, we could have *khichuri* after the prayers; on the second day, there was a picnic; and the third day was set aside for children. There were no prayers that day, and we were free to enjoy ourselves. Even so, this Brahmo festival lacked the pomp and gaiety of Durga or Kali puja. We did take part in the celebrations for Kali puja (Diwali) although the pleasure we got from our simple sparklers and crackers and bangers have now been drowned totally in the ear-splitting, heart-stopping racket that the festival has inevitably come to mean. But the fact remains that no Brahmo festival could ever hold the whole city together in a joint merrymaking. Perhaps that was the reason why we were keen to celebrate Christmas and make it a part of our lives.

Whiteway Laidlaw was the biggest shop in Calcutta in those days. It was like a modern department store. The office of the *Statesman* stood where the Metro cinema now stands in Chowringhee. Next to it, at the corner of Suren Banerjee Road, was Whiteway Laidlaw, a building with a clock on it. The entire first floor of this huge building turned into a toyland during the few days leading up to Christmas. Once my mother took me to see it.

At that time the British were still ruling our country. Whiteway was owned by them. The sales people, as well as most of the customers, were white. My eyes were dazzled by these glamorous people. We were supposed to go up to the first floor. But where was the staircase? There were no stairs immediately visible, but there was a lift. That was the first time I saw a lift. It is likely that the lift installed by Whiteway Laidlaw was the first one in Calcutta.

An iron cage which had been painted golden carried us up to the toyland. When I stepped into the store I felt as if I had arrived in a land of dreams. A large part of the floor was taken up by hills, rivers, bridges, tunnels, stations, signals and a toy train that went on a mini railway track. In addition to these there were balloons, paper chains, streamers, artificial flowers and fruits and Chinese lanterns. A Christmas tree stood in all its glory, covered with colorful balls and silver stars. But what impressed me the most was a massive fixture of Father Christmas: fat and rosy cheeks with a long white beard, a read coat and a red hat, and a big smile on his face.

The toys in the store were all foreign. I returned home with a box of crackers, which was the only thing we could afford to buy. One does not get to see crackers like those anymore. The noise they made was as impressive as the tiny gifts that popped out from them.

Most of the large and attractive stores were in Chowringhee. But there was an Indian shop near Whiteway called Carr & Mahalanabis. It sold gramophones and sports equipment. We knew one of its Bengali owners. I called him Bula Kaka. His shop had a special chair that was actually a weighing machine. None of us could pass Bula Kaka's shop without going in, sitting in that chair and getting ourselves weighed. . . .

As a result of moving from north to south Calcutta we lost touch with many relatives on my father's side. The two people who continued to visit us frequently were Chhoto Kaka (the judo enthusiast), and Dhon Dadu. Dadu was translating Conan Doyle into Bengali at the time. He used to dress like a pukka sahib: a suit made by the well-known tailor, Barkat Ali, with a tie if he went out in the evening. He came to our house at least three times a week.

It was Dadu who told me all the stories from the Mahabharat. We used to read a chapter a day. I made him tell me one particular story at least four times. It was the story of Jayadrath being killed in battle by Arjun. I thought it was the most thrilling story of all. Absolutely fascinated, I heard how, one day, Arjun vowed to kill Jayadrath before sunset and eventually did, with a bit of help from Krishna. But that was not all. The chopped head of Jayadrath could not be allowed to touch the ground, for Jayadrath's father's curse would then work on Arjun and Arjun's own head would be blown off. In a rather clever move, Arjun struck the head with six more arrows before it could reach the ground, and made it fly a great distance to land in the lap of Jayadrath's father. Startled, his father stood up, the chopped head fell on the ground, and his father's head was immediately blown to pieces.

Dadu told me stories from the Mahabharat, and Chhoto Kaka told me ghost stories. It is not easy to describe briefly what kind of person my uncle was, for I doubt very much if any other man could ever be found who was quite like him.

Source: Satyajit Ray, *Childhood Days: A Memoir*, translated from the Bengali by Bijoya Ray (New Delhi: Penguin Books, 1998), 15–20, 39–40.

Contemporary Voices

Postcolonial and post-Partition India, with its own constitutional and secular identity, comprises an 80 percent Hindu majority, an 18 percent Muslim minority, with the Sikhs, Christians, Jews, Parsis, and others making up the remainder. Although for the first fifty years of Independence, Hinduism was originally part of the social democratic state of Nehru, Hinduism as such has also been influenced by the liberalizing forces of the opening up of the India's economy to international investment in the early 1990s. With the BJP government of the 1990s, the communal identity of Hinduism also was on the rise; intercommunal riots between Hindus and Muslims, as well as Sikhs and Hindus, have been an unfortunate occurrence as a result of this return to communal consciousness within many traditions of India. In addition to being a majority religious tradition in India, Hinduism, and all the various "Hinduisms" of which it is composed, have become minority diaspora traditions in Trinidad, England, Europe, and the United States.

In this complex set of postcolonial "Hinduisms," the discourse around the child has become partly influenced by both social science and psychological models, originating in the West but taking on their own distinct hue in the Indian context as indigenous models interact with Western ones in a postcolonial, industrial, and increasingly technological context. As Pattnaik's comments included below indicate, issues of governmental policies on child labor, the human rights of children, and the domestic conditions for mothers and children are all deep concerns of contemporary Hindu societies, as well as the societies of other nonmajority religions in India. In a way, due to global influences, Hindu children share much in common with non-Hindu children in South Asia. Their issues form part of the public discourse between feminists, policy makers, and nonprofit NGOs (nongovernmental organizations.) These groups, too, argue whether childhood is universal or local, psychological or social, and how such conceptual views affect policy making on the practical level.

At the same time, many traditional ways of being a child remain part of the Hindu fabric, as the rural folks songs collected by Raheja in the 1990s show. As Sudhir Kakar notes below, the stresses between traditional ways of being a Hindu child and the larger impact of environmental changes of the last two centuries carry grave risks as well as possibilities. For a Hindu child, attempts at integration of the many different worlds—Hindu, Western, colonial, postcolonial, agricultural, industrial, and technological—may be more a matter of living awkwardly in the various multiplicities than achieving a grand sociopsychological synthesis. The humorous scene from Hari Kunzru's recent novel compellingly portrays these juxtapositions: many traditional Hindu family habits, such as the lighting of the aarti lamp and the placing of a tilak, or dot, on the forehead, accompany the very postmodern situation of a young Hindu computer student leaving Delhi to find his fortune in America.

Document 4–12

North Indian Girls' Folk Songs at the Time of Departure from the Childhood Home

Bidai Git 1

Refrain: [*Bride's natal kin*]
Dear girl, today you've left your father's house,
Today you've become "other" (*parayi*)
The streets in which you spent your childhood
Have today become *parayi*.
[*Bride speaking*]
My grandfather cries, my grandmother cries,
The whole family cries.
My younger brother cries,
Your sister born from the same mother (*ma jai*)
As left and gone away.

Bidai Git 3

Two water pots are on my head.
A beautiful golden pendant is on my forehead.
Call me back quickly, Mother,
Beg with folded hands.
My heart is not here in my husband's mother's house,
My heart is not here with this foreign man.
Call me back quickly, Mother,
Beg with folded hands.
We played with dolls together,
But then I went off to my sasural,
Call me back quickly, Mother,
Beg with folded hands.

Source: Gloria Raheja, "Women's Speech Genres: Kinship and Contradiction," in *Women as Subjects: South Asian Histories*, edited by Nita Kumar (Charlottesville: University Press of Virginia, 1994), 55, 57.

Document 4–13

A Hindu Psychoanalyst View from the 1970s

[W]ithout a more equitable balance between different kinds of reality and without an integration of the material and the instinctual with the "spiritual," Hindu culture may soon find itself entrapped in a field of critical environmental stresses. Like many other cultures which have lopsidedly overdeveloped only a part of man's nature and stressed only a part of his life experience, Hindu culture too may be caught up in contradictions and dead ends. This would indeed be a great loss since the many insights to be gleaned from the nature of traditional Hindu childhood and society are of vital importance for mankind's present position and its radical need for a holistic approach to man's nature.

Source: Sudhir Kakar, *The Inner World, A Psychoanalytic Study of Childhood and Society in India* (Delhi: Oxford University Press, 1978), 187–188.

Document 4–14

A Social Scientist's View from the Early 2000s

[T]here are diverse perspectives on childhood. However, . . . the ultimate test of these discourses lies in their impact on policies that protect children's rights and well being. This issue is very important in a period when globalization and imposition of neo-liberal economic models such as the structural adjustment programs imposed by the IMF [International Monetary Fund] as a condition for further lending has led to the reduction of governmental services (welfare, education, health, and nutrition) for [the] poor and lowered the living standards of poor families in South Asian countries.

From a policy perspective, the challenge remains, "How [do] we acknowledge and integrate these discourses into policy frameworks with a full understanding of genuine challenges that emerged from various discourses on childhood?" In addition, "How do we ensure successful implementation of these policies through comprehensive monitoring and evaluation so as to guarantee the human rights of all children?" These questions need to be addressed within their full complexities. Otherwise, as objects of the contested discourses on childhood and subjects of suffering from violations of human rights, South Asia's children will continue to stand at the cross-roads of divergent discourses and policies without making any significant progress toward a better future.

Source: Jyotsna Pattnaik, "Repositioning South Asia's Children within the Competing Discourses on Childhood," in Jyotsna Pattnaik, ed., *Childhood in South Asia: A Critical Look at Issues, Policies, and Programs* (Greenwich, Conn.: Information Age Publishing, 2004), 233–266.

Document 4–15

Arjun's Departure for an American Technology Company

The next day Mrs. Mehta woke early, and after a light breakfast spent her morning squeezing name-tagged woolens into a pair of new vinyl suitcases, already bursting with packages of sweets, nuts, homeopathic remedies and soft fruit. Arjun stayed in bed for as long as possible then diddled around desultorily with batteries and toothbrushes. Finally, unable to bear his mother's frenetic preparations, he locked himself in the bathroom. Only when it got too dark to see without switching on the light did he come out again.

The last supper was an ordeal. Various relatives were present, all in a state of high excitement, but Arjun was so nervous he could barely bring himself to eat. This upset his mother, who took it out on Priti, telling her off for toying with her food and for saying it would taste better on the Barbie, an Australian style of tandoori cooking. Only Mr Mehta was straightforwardly happy, marshalling helpings of rice and dal into his mouth with the air of a man for whom mealtimes had recently revealed themselves in a very positive light: as a celebration of family life, an expression of the joy of producing and managing successful and in their turn productive children, not worthless after all, who would soon be providing for one during a prosperous old age.

Finally it was time to leave for the airport. Uncle Bharat took photos and Cousin Ramesh panned a video camera across the scene as Mrs. Mehta performed aarti to bless the traveler, placing a lamp on a brass try and circling it high and low in front of Arjun as if he were a statue of God. Saying a prayer for his safety and swift return, she fed him sugar and placed a red tilak mark on his forehead with her thumb. Then, sniffling a little, she slipped a garland of marigolds round his neck. Arjun dipped down impatiently to touch her feet, then those of his father.

"Can we go now, Ma?" he pleaded.

"Beta, the plane will not fly off without you."

"Ma, actually it will."

"Don't be so silly."

Though his flight was not scheduled to depart until three in the morning, a total of eleven people were staying up to see him off. After a delay which he experienced as several millennia in duration, a convoy was finally assembled, engines running, outside the gates of the enclave. Mr Mehta settled himself in the driver's seat of the family Ambassador. The suspension groaned with the weight of people and luggage, the chowkidar saluted, and he swung the car imperiously into the road, forcing a cycle rickshaw to swerve and a bus-driver to stamp hard his vehicle's worn brakes. Two other cars followed behind.

The convoy sailed through the unlit Noida streets and Arjun rested his cheek against the cool glass of the window. On the other side the night was damp and broken, an underworld strafed by truck headlights and mottled by the orange glow of the bustee cooking fires. The traffic was heavy, and it took an hour to reach the airport. With their billboards promising denim and sports shows, the clothing outlets on the approach road beckoned like a premonition of the American future. The Mehta party shouldered its way through the crush of touts and drivers outsider the terminal, and all eleven relatives joined a long queue. At the check in desks airline employees handed out customs forms as red-uniformed porters manhandled luggage on to the conveyor belt and wildly overladen Indian families pushed trolleys against the ankles of disoriented foreigners, all dressed in the same characteristic mélange of factory made handicrafts, religious paraphernalia and hiking gear.

Little by little the line inched forward. As they neared the front, Mrs. Mehta started to sob in earnest, comforted by her next door neighbor and digitally recorded by Ramesh for posterity. Arjun handed over his documents, explaining that despite appearances he was traveling alone. He felt proud that in the eyes of his family he was finally doing something worth while. In a film the scene would be accompanied by music, and he would lead a crowd of long-haul passengers in a dance routine.

His father put his hands on his shoulders. "Son, we know you are going to be a great success. Don't disappoint us."

"I'll do my best, Babaji."

Priti tugged at his sleeve. "Come back a millionaire, Bro!" Relatives clustered round to add their good wishes. Mrs. Mehta's wailing rose in pitch. "God bless you, Beta!" she cried. "God Bless you!" Consumed with impatience, Arjun hardly took in what they were saying. Quickly, he took his boarding pass and hiked towards passport control. As soon as he was out of sight, he headed for the toilet, where he stuffed the garland into his bag and washed the paste from his forehead.

Source: Hari Kunzru, *Transmission* (London: Hamish Hamilton, 2004), 29–31.

NOTES

1. The bibliography on family and kinship structure is voluminous; I refer here only to representative works specifically focusing on cross-cultural issues in the study of the child, or the idea of the "child" per se in Hindu life. Philip Aries, *Centuries of Childhood: A History of Family Life* (New York: Alfred Knopf, 1962); Leigh Minturn and William W. Lambert, *Mothers of Six Cultures; Antecedents of Child Rearing* (New York, J. Wiley, 1964); S. Stephens, ed., *Children and the Politics of Culture* (Princeton: Princeton University Press, 1995); James A. Jenks and A. Prout, eds. *Theorizing Childhood* (Cambridge: Polity, 1998); more recently, D. K. Behera, *Children and Childhood in Contemporary Societies* (Delhi: Kamla Raj, 2001); H. Montgomery, Rachel Burr, and M. Woodhead, eds., *Changing Childhooods: Local and Global* (Milton Keynes: Open University Press, 2003); Urvashi Mishra, "Childhood: A Conceptual Construction," in *Contributions to Indian Sociology* 19.1:115–132; Krishna Kumar, "Study of Childhood and Family," in T. S. Saraswathi and Baljit Kaur, eds., *Human Development and Family*

Studies in India: An Agenda for Research and Policy (New Delhi: Sage, 1993), 67–76; Alan Roland,"Sexuality, the Indian Extended Family, and Hindu Culture," in *Cultural Pluralism and Psychoanalysis* (New York and London: Routledge, 1996),133–134; Ashis Nandy, "Reconstructing Childhood: A Critique of the Ideology of Adulthood," *Alternatives* 10.3 (September 1984): 359–375; revised version published in *Traditions, Tyranny, and Utopias* (New Delhi: Oxford University Press, 1987), 56–76; Jyotsna Pattnaik, ed., *Childhood in South Asia: A Critical Look at Issues, Policies, and Programs* (Greenwich, Conn.: Information Age Publishing, 2004); Patricia Uberoi, "The Family in India," in Veena Das, ed., *Handbook of Indian Sociology* (New Delhi: Oxford University Press, 2004), 275–307; Deepak Kumar Behera, *Childhoods in South Asia* (Delhi: Pearson Education, 2007).

2. *Atharva Veda* 6.2.3; 8.6.25; 6.9.10; 3.23.3, for starters; many of the Grihya Sutras focus almost entirely on male initiation rites. Although the Indian urban scene is changing, many contemporary rural practices and popular poems also attest to the preference for a boy. See my treatment of the story of Saptavadhri in "Mantras and Miscarriage: Controlling Birth in the Late Vedic Period," in *Jewels of Authority: Women and Textual Tradition in Hindu India* (New York: Oxford University Press, 2002), 51–69; Hans Peter Schmidt, *Some Women's Rites and Rights in the Veda* (Poona: Bhandarkar Oriental Institute, 1987); Stephanie Jamison, *Sacrificed Wife/Sacrificer's Wife* (New York: Oxford University Press, 1996).

3. Contrary to Western perceptions, some Grihya Sutras and later texts (such as *Manu* 2.66) allow these rites for girls as well as boys, but usually without the recitation of a mantra. See, for example, *Ashvalayana Grihya Sutra* 1.15.12; 1.16.6; 17. See my "If the Fire Goes Out, the Wife Shall Fast: Notes on Women's Agency in the *Ashvalayana Grihya Sutra*" in *Problems in Vedic Literature: Essays in Honor of G. U. Thite* (New Delhi: New Bharatiya, 2004), 294–305. In addition, *Ashvalayana Grihya Sutra* (1.7.4–6) has a rite that allows for a couple to choose whether they want only male children or female children, or both. The surprising thing here is that there would be mention of a desire for only female children.

4. The term *upanishad* has been traditionally understood to mean "to sit down near." Thus, even the names of these ancient texts imply a relationship between student and teacher, child and adult. Many references are made in the Upanishads to the correct way to become a pupil; *Chandogya Upanishad* 6.2.7 refers to visits by Shvetaketu and his father to Jaivali, and their subsequent discussion of the proper way to become a pupil; other mentions of this process are in the same Upanishad, 4.4.5; and the absence of such a ritual in 5.11.6. Children, particularly sons, are frequently mentioned as question-askers, or as receivers of wisdom: see *Brihadaranyaka Upanishad* 1.5.27; 21.4–5. 7–9, 13; 2.4.5; 3.5.1; 4.5.6; *Chandogya U.* 1.5.2–4; 3.11.4; 5.15.1; 5.17.1; 5.19–23, among many other citations.

5. A nice assessment of some of the early childhood issues in the *Mahabharata* are in Alf Hiltebeitel, *Rethinking the Mahabharata: A Reader's Guide to the Education of the Dharma King* (Chicago: University of Chicago Press, 2001). Irawati Karve's classic *Yughanta* also provides a discussion of characters' early years as part of their formation.

6. In contrast, the childhood of the brothers Rama, Lakshmana, and Bharata in the epic of the *Ramayana* is far more idealized and idyllic.

7. Among the voluminous literature on Manu, particularly relevant for our purposes would be those works concerned with the issues of women and inheritance, which also have to do with the child. These include J. Jolly, *Outlines of an History of the Hindu Law of Partition, Inheritance, and Adoption*, Tagore Law Lectures 1883 (Calcutta:

Thacker, Spink, 1885); H. W. Kohler, *Women in Manu: Sraddha in der vedischen und altbuddistischen Literatur* (thesis, Gottingen University, 1948), edited by K. L. Janert (Wiesbaden: Franz Steiner, 1973); Richard Lariviere, "Dharmasastra, Custom, 'Real Law' and 'Apocryphal' Smrtis," in *Recht, Staat, und Verwaltung im klassichen Indien*, edited by B. Koelver (Wiesbaden: Franz Steiner, 1997), 97–110; Julia Leslie, ed., *Rules and Remedies in Classical Indian Law*, Panels of the VII World Sanskrit Conference (Leiden: E. J. Brill, 1991); Kusuma Jaina and Sarla Kalla, eds., *Foundations of Classical Indian Law and Social Justice* (Jaipur: University of Rajasthan, 2003); Flavia Agnes, *Women and Law in India* (Delhi: Oxford University Press, 2004); Dwarka Nath Mitter, *The Position of Women in Hindu Law* (New Delhi: Cosmo, 2006).

8. Medhatithi, the shastric commentator, writes that "By reason of the marriage having taken the place of *upanayana*, it follows that just as in the case of men all the ordinance of the Srutis, Smritis, and custom become binding upon them after the *upanayana*, before which they are free to do what they like and are unfit for any religious duties, so for women also there is freedom of action before marriage, after which they all become subject to the ordinances of the Srutis and Smritis." Cited in R. M. Das, *Women in Manu and His Seven Commentators* (Varanasi: Kanchana, 1962), 72.

9. Sudhir Kakar, *The Inner World: A Psychoanalytic Study of Childhood and Society in India* (Delhi: Oxford University Press, 1978), 36–44.

10. And yet this becomes a tricky question: do actions in early childhood also sow seeds of karma? The Hindu tradition deals with this question also, in a variety of ways. The story of "Mandavya on the Stake" in the *Mahabharata* (1.101) addresses this question. In this story, a seemingly unjust punishment leads to the sage Mandavya pronouncing the deity Dharma himself unjust, deserving of rebirth in the womb of a Shudra. Mandavya declares that before the age of fourteen, karmic "fruits" will not be sown.

11. See Edwin Bryant's "Introduction" in his *Krishna: The Beautiful Legend of God* (Harmondsworth: Penguin Press, 2003), ix–xviii. Also see Daniel Sheridan, *The Advaitic Theism of the Bhagavata Purana* (Delhi: Motilal Banarsidass, 1986); and John Stratton Hawley, *Krishna, The Butter Thief* (Princeton: Princeton University Press, 1983)

12. See, among many others, Graham Schweig, *Dance of Divine Love: The Rasa Lila of Krishna from the Bhagavata Purana, India's Classic Love Story* (Princeton: Princeton University Press, 2005); and David Haberman, *Acting as a Way of Salvation: A Study of Raganuga Bhakti Sadhana* (New York: Oxford University Press, 1988).

13. See *Mirabai and Her Padas*, translated by Krishna P. Bahadur (New Delhi: Munshiram Manoharlal, 1998); Vaishnavi, *Women and the Worship of Krishna* (New Delhi: Motilal Banarsidass, 1996); A. J. Alston, *The Devotional Poems of Mirabai* (Delhi: Motilal Banarsidass, 1980); Hermann Goetz, *Mirabai Her Life and Times* (Bombay: Bharatiya Vidya Bhavan, 1966); S. M. Pandey, "Mirabai and Her Contributions to the Bhakti Movement," in *History of Religions* 5.1 (1965): 55–69; *In the Dark of the Heart: Songs of Meera*, translated by M. S. Subbalakshmi (New Delhi: Harper Collins India, 1994).

14. See Anne Feldhaus's treatment, "Bahina Bai: Wife and Saint," in *Journal of the American Academy of Religion* 50.4 (December 1982): 591–604.

15. Ruby Lal is currently at work on a book that addresses issues of domesticity and family through the lens of childhood, tentatively titled *Portraits of Respectability: Debates over Family and Childhood in Northern India, circa 1700–1900*. Among other things, it compares Hindu and Muslim views in this era, and we look forward to its results.

16. Satadru Sen, *Colonial Childhoods: The Juvenile Periphery of India, 1850–1945* (London: Anthem, 2005), 10–11, 211–213.

17. Ibid., 213.

18. For a full treatment of these and other issues, see, among many others, Monmayee Basu, *Hindu Women and Marriage Law: From Sacrament to Contract* (New Delhi: Oxford University Press, 2001), especially the chapter "Age of Marriage," 39–67, and also D. Promila Kapur, ed., *Girl Child and Family Violence* (New Delhi: Har Anand Publications); Namila Aggarwal, *Women and Law in India* (Delhi: New Century, 2002); Werner Menski, *Hindu Law: Beyond Tradition and Modernity* (New Delhi: Oxford University Press, 2004), especially his back-to-back chapters on "Hindu Marriage Law" and "Child Marriage," 273–374.

19. For an intriguing discussion of these dynamics in "schools for girls," see Nita Kumar's treatment of several colonial-era Varanasi schools in her article "Oranges for Girls: Or the Half-Known Story of the Education of Girls in Twentieth Century Banaras," in *Women as Subjects: South Asian Histories* (Charlottesville: University Press of Virginia, 1994), 211–233. Her assessment is in many ways parallel to that of Sen's, above: that such institutions were "failed experiments" due to the clashing constructions of childhood between ruler and ruled.

20. See, for example, Durganand Sinha, ed., *Socialization of the Indian Child* (New Delhi: Concept, 1981).

21. For a larger discussion of these tensions, see Jyotsna Pattnaik, ed., *Childhood in South Asia: A Critical Look at Issues, Policies, and Programs* (Greenwich, Conn.: Information Age Publishing, 2004).

22. See ibid., 244–257; xi–xiv.

23. See ibid., especially Pattnaik's "Repositioning South Asia's Children within Competing Discourses on Childhood: Implications for Policy," 233–266.

24. See, in particular, Trishna Tandon, "Process of Transmission of Values in the Indian Child," in Sinha, *Socialization of the Indian Child*, 11–30.

25. Kakar, *Inner World*, 117; and Tandon, "Process," 17.

26. See Kakar, *Inner World*, 117–118; and Tandon, "Process," 17, 21.One early study in that same volume, Shalini Bhogle, "Socialization among Different Cultures," noted a difference in child-rearing practices between caste Hindu mothers, rural "backward caste" Hindu mothers, and Muslim mothers—where the rural Hindu children were slightly more independent than caste Hindu children, and slightly less sociable than Muslim children.

27. Kakar, *Inner World*, 122–125.

28. Ibid., 119.

29. Ibid., 122.

30. See mention of this in Julia Leslie, "Sri and Jyestha," in *Roles and Rituals for Hindu Women* (Rutherford:Fairleigh Dickinson Press, 1991), 120; Frederique Apffel-Marglin, "The Sacred Groves: Menstruation Rituals in Rural Orissa," in *Manushi* (Delhi) 82 (1994): 22–32; G. Eichinger Ferro-Luzzi, "Food Avoidances at Puberty and Menstruation in Tamilnad: An Anthropological Study," 93–100 in J.R.K. Robson, ed., *Food, Ecology and Culture: Readings in the Anthropology of Dietary Practices* (New York: Gordon and Breach Science Publishers, 1980); Deborah Winslow, "Rituals of First Menstruation in Sri Lanka," in *Man*, New Series 15.4 (December 1980): 603–625.

31. Joyce Flueckiger has observed that Hindu pubescent rites tend to be more associated with south India; in many areas of the south, the category of "unmarried girl" vs. "married woman," and the songs, dances, and associated forms of *puja* show pubescence as a marked cultural category. See her *Gender and Genre in the Folklore of Middle*

India (Ithaca: Cornell University Press, 1996), 47–49. The question of the girl child
has been discussed in important recent work, in particular: Veena Das, "Voices of
Children" in *Daedalus* (Fall 1989); Sudhir Kakar, "Modernity and Female Childhood,"
in *Culture and Psyche: Psychoanalysis and India* (New York: Psyche Press, 1997); and
also his "Masculine/Feminine: A View from the Couch," in *Intimate Relations: Explor-
ing Indian Sexuality* (Chicago: University of Chicago Press, 1990); Margaret Trawick,
Notes on Love in a Tamil Family (Berkeley: University of California Press, 1992); Leigh
Minturn, *Sita's Daughters: Coming out of Purdah: The Rajput Women of Khalapur* (New
York: Oxford University Press, 1993); Susan Seymour, *Women, Family, and Child Care in
India* (Cambridge: Cambridge University Press, 1999).

32. Sunil Bhatt, "Acculturation, Dialogical Voices, and the Construction of the Diasporic
Self," *Theory and Psychology* 12.1 (2002): 55–77. Bhatt notes that children and adolescents are comfortable with the "multivocal" personality—an internal dialogue between
traditional Hindu values and Westernized ones. For Bhatt, childhood development
does not involve unifying these voices, but accepting their multiplicity. See also
Khyati Joshi's work, *New Roots in America's Sacred Ground: Religion, Race, and Ethnicity
in Indian America* (New Brunswick: Rutgers University Press, 2005). Also see Prema
Kurien, "Being Young, Brown, and Hindu: The Identity Struggles of Second Generation
Indian Americans," *Journal of Contemporary Ethnography* 34.4 (2005): 434–469.

33. Susan Seymour's work (1999) is quite comprehensive in this area. Also see the various
essays in Sinha, *Socialization of the Indian Child*, especially Trisha Tandon, "Process
of Transmission of Values in the Indian Child," 11–30; "Socialization, Family, and
Psychological Differentiation," 41–55; Amar Kumar Singh, "Development of Religious
Identity and Prejudice in Indian Children," 87–100. See in particular Padma Saranga-
pani, "Childhood and Schooling in an Indian Village," in Jacqueline Hirst and Lynne
Thomas, eds., *Playing for Real: Hindu Role Models, Religion, and Gender* (New Delhi:
Oxford University Press, 2004), 81–101.

34. Ibid., 99. See also Padma Sarangapani, *Constructing School Knowledge: An Ethnography of
Learning in an Indian Village* (New Delhi: Sage, 2003).

35. Patricia Uberoi, "Baby Iconography: Constructing Childhood in Indian Calendar Art," in
Sujata Patel, Jasodhara Bagchi, and Krishna Raj, eds., *Thinking Social Science in India:
Essays in Honour of Alice Thorner* (New Delhi: Sage, 2002), 264–282, especially p. 277.

36. Ibid., 279–280.

37. In the *Harivamsha*, Putana is a bird who defies the distinction between the species of
aves and mammals by giving Krishna her poisonous breast to suck.

38. Shri, "Prosperity," is Lakshmi, the wife of Vishnu and thus the wife of Krishna. She
carries a lotus, as Putana does here.

39. Here they chant a series of spells protecting him from various ogresses and diseases.

40. Vasudeva was called Anakadundubhi because at his birth the gods, foreseeing the birth
of Krishna, caused drums (*anaka* and *dundubhi*) to resound in heaven.

41. Rama in the *Bhagavata Purana* stories of Krishna always refers to Balarama, Samkarsana,
the brother of Krishna, and has nothing to do with the Rama of the *Ramayana*.

42. The commentator says that this is the sound of their own anklets and bangles.

43. "He who has beautiful feathers," an epithet of Garuda. Garuda is also called Tarkshya,
an epithet originally designating a horse.

44. Kadru, daughter of Daksha, wife of Kashyapa, was the progenitor of the race of nagas or
snakes. She once made a bet with Vinata, mother of Garuda and the birds, that the
horse Uccaihshravas had a black tail. Winning this bet by a ruse, she made Vinata

her slave, promising her freedom only if Garuda brought the ambrosia of the snakes. Garuda stole the ambrosia from the gods and placed it before the snakes on a bed of sharp kusha grass. The snakes freed Vinata and licked the grass, making their tongues forked, but Indra then stole back the ambrosia.

45. Great cobras are said to have rubies imbedded in their hoods.

46. That is, he is in a form from which your anger will soon release him, or a form which justifies your anger.

47. Because they had exposed their naked bodies to Varuna, god of the waters. Compare the sin of the Krttikas in exposing themselves to Agni by bathing naked, myth 43, p. 167 [in *Hindu Myths: A Sourcebook,* translated from the Sanskrit with an introduction by Wendy Doniger (New York: Penguin Books, 1975)].

5

Buddhism

ALAN COLE

Buddhist Doctrines and
Practices Related to Childhood

Like many religions, Buddhism was not created with an eye to its long-term viability as a social institution. Instead, Buddhism came into its full institutional presence in a gradual manner, with much of the "architecture" of Buddhist thought and practice fashioned long after the death of the Buddha. This seems particularly true for the range of Buddhist positions on children and childhood, positions that emerged slowly and for a variety of different reasons. Thus, if we can trust accounts of the Buddha's career (all of which were written hundreds of years after his death in the sixth or fifth century BCE), it would seem that he, like many contemporaneous mendicants, simply taught a way to avoid future rebirth in samara—the cycle of life and death—with little attention paid to legislating rules for family life.

Despite this otherworldly focus, after the Buddha's death a number of inventive steps were taken to codify his teachings and to build up various institutional bodies dedicated to preserving his teachings. In fact, a complex framework of monasticism emerged, with detailed rules for running a celibate community, but also with dictates for interacting with the community at large and families, in particular. Thus, though Buddhism was, and still is, rightly depicted as a religion organized around winning nirvana, this in no way inhibited the development of all sorts of life-managing doctrines and practices.

That said, I think it fair to offer the following generalization: Buddhism, by and large, has little to say about children directly. Likewise child-directed rituals are few: there are no birth-purification rites or infant baptisms, nor are there rites of circumcision or even clear rulings on childrearing; similarly, there are no Sunday school–like entities until the colonial era. Nonetheless, we can find a range of fascinating child-related issues in the vast corpus of Buddhist writing and practice.

To bring some order to this material, I have created four categories of child-related issues for Indian Buddhism, and then four for East Asian Buddhism. As for Indian Buddhism, in the first category I detail the various aspects of the Buddha's childhood—as invented in a variety of biographic forms in the centuries after his death. In the second category, I survey a range of narratives that shed light on how the Buddhists thought about children—their place in the family, in the Buddhist religion, and in the cycles of birth and rebirth. In the third and fourth categories, I explore the ways that children and childhood figure allegorically in a range of doctrinal statements. More exactly, category three, with reliance on the recent work of Reiko Ohnuma, details how Buddhist notions of universal compassion were often presented through examples of mother-son love which, naturally, had to be much revised to function in this global form. Category four relates how a kind of Buddhist paternity—being a "son of the Buddha"—structured a range of Mahayana statements regarding authentic Buddhist identity in the phase of Buddhist history that began roughly in the first century bce. This question of Buddhist sonship also played out in later Tantric formulations—beginning roughly in the seventh or eighth century ce—that created Buddhist "families" around a living guru who was likened to the Buddha and treated as a kind of padrone generating Buddhist disciples.

As for East Asian Buddhism, the first category covers the effort by the Chinese to create a kind of filial piety for Buddhism. These efforts took several forms before and during the Tang dynasty (618–907 ce), and became prominent in defining Buddhist thought and practice in China and the other East Asian countries—Japan, Korea, Vietnam—which received Chinese styles of Buddhism. The second category explores a kind of Buddhist fertility cult that took form in the medieval period in China and Japan, and is still prevalent today. The third category turns to a set of twentieth-century myths—from Japan and, less so, Taiwan—regarding abortion, which treat the unborn fetus as a fully developed individual who, once aborted, is imagined to be immensely important in organizing the family's relationship to Buddhism. The fourth category concerns the metaphoric use of the child in defining monastic identities, with special attention given to the role of the Chan (Zen) disciple as a filial son of the master.

As this introduction suggests, Buddhism is a rather flexible tradition. Even in its earliest phases, it is clear that Buddhist doctrines, rituals, and institutional arrangements had a high degree of fluidity and were often reorganized or redesigned to suit shifting political, cultural, or economic realities. This is not to say that there is no continuity behind various Buddhist positions—there is—but it is also true that without a Rome-like center and with a very open-ended canon, especially for Mahayana and Tantric Buddhism, Buddhism maintained itself by allowing, if unadmittedly, for a kind of plasticity in the development of a range of doctrines and practices to suit changing circumstances.

As is true for all successful religions, Buddhism both explained the nature of the world and articulated a way of living in it—to echo Clifford Geertz's useful definition of culture—and this meant figuring out ways to induct children into solid patterns of action and thought—forms of *habitas*, to use Pierre Bourdieu's terminology. Or put otherwise, in durable religious cosmologies there is a paradoxical connection between otherworldly doctrines of salvation—often presented as noncorporeal, legalistic, and patriarchal—and the altogether this-worldly process of making new adherents, that is, the world of women, reproduction, and childhood. Buddhism certainly fits this mold, and in ways that have been little appreciated in scholastic and popular discussions. Though it is changing, it is probably fair to say that the twentieth century saw a steady effort to recreate Buddhism as a rarefied philosophical-religion not at all akin to Christianity or Judaism, when in fact a more historically grounded account of Buddhism suggests that in many ways there are significant parallels. That said, let us consider how the Buddha's childhood was constructed in various Buddhist narratives.

Images of Children in Indian Buddhism: The Buddha's Childhood

The most important fact to appreciate about the Buddha's life story, as found in the various biographic accounts, is that the Buddha was supernatural in a variety of ways, including his conception, his birth, and his childhood. In fact, in many of the accounts he does not have a proper childhood since he is conscious before his birth and is delivered from his mother's side, already walking and talking. Thus, though well-known biographies such as Ashvaghosa's *Buddhacarita* or the

Lalitavistara (chapter 12, in particular) delight in reciting the Buddha's education and mastery of various cultural skills, the overall point of these biographies is to show that the Buddha came into the world as a most preternatural child. To catalogue these details we can point to six fundamental aspects of the Buddha's childhood. Though these aspects are unique to the Buddha's life, and not offered to Buddhists to emulate, they warrant careful attention because they format a range of templates for how the Buddhists would think and write about childhood.

First, it is usually said that the Buddha chose his parents and thus was a fully conscious agent before his conception and birth. Second, he was conceived magically and immaculately. Though this topic has been underplayed in modern accounts, it is clear that many Buddhist authors (Indian and East Asian) wanted to emphasize that the Buddha's existence on earth was *not* the result of sex. Instead it is usually stated, or implied, that his mother Maya practiced Buddhist-styled ethics, alone, and received the Buddha in a dream, in the form of a six-tusked elephant. This piece of mythology was far from being merely a scholarly position since it was regularly rendered in the art that decorated popular pilgrim sites and reliquaries throughout India. Third, Indian authors gave a lot of thought to detailing the Buddha's parturition, again with a notable emphasis on purity. Thus, it is regularly claimed that during gestation he was nestled in a jeweled box inside his mother's womb and in no way came in contact with her body, and especially not any fluids connected with the reproductive process. In keeping with these purity concerns, his birth supposedly occurred when he emerged from his mother's side and not through the birth canal. Once born, it is said that the Buddha immediately took seven steps and declared himself the master of the world. Fourth, as the Buddha enters adolescence, the biographies insist on the Buddha's uncanny ability to master all known forms of intellectual and physical training with effortless ease. With these details in view, it probably would be fair to say that the Buddha's biographers have more or less "stolen" his childhood in order to make his adult identity as cosmic master-of-truth appear as a preordained eventuality.

I should add that there is, too, a strain of triumphalism in the Buddha's biographies. Thus, there are accounts of how he vanquished rivals, demons, and enraged elephants, or upset traditional authority figures who did not recognize his cosmic stature. For instance, there is the famous account of the Buddha's father taking him as a very young child to worship the family gods, but once in their presence, they bow to him, acknowledging his vastly greater eminence.[1] The point of this mini-narrative is simply to show that the Buddha, though a child, upset all known hierarchies and found his rightful place at the top of the pyramid of religious powers.

The fifth fundamental aspect of the Buddha's childhood involves his early marriage and life in the harem. Despite the prominent themes of sexuality and marriage, this phase still seems "preadult" because it is designed to serve as the backdrop for the Buddha's "coming of age" awakenings, which often receive the lion's share of attention in these biographies. Treated as a sequence of trips from the organized delights of the palace into the disturbing public space of the city, it is here that the Buddha confronts the four figures on the road that will shape his future: an aged man, a sick man, a corpse, and a meditating mendicant. In the course of these sightings, the Buddha is jolted out of his complacent hedonism and begins to question the reality of being a creature condemned to suffer the vagaries of time and being. At this point we find a very interesting turn in narrative strategy: while the supernatural details regarding the Buddha's conception and birth are designed to underscore his absolute uniqueness, here the Buddha's gradual awakening to the dark side of life seems portrayed as a model that could be emulated by the reader or listener. Thus at this point the narratives' account of the Buddha's coming of age seems to function as a kind of universal bildungsroman in which the reader/listener is invited to identify with the Buddha's career, and see his own life depicted in clear and unflinching terms. Catching sight of these two aspects of the Buddha's childhood–the uniqueness and the universality–is crucial, since it shows that the authors needed first to secure the Buddha's identity as the unique site of authority and then use that authority to present a believable account of human life in its most universal forms.

Actually this tension between uniqueness and universality has another facet to it: it is regularly claimed that the Buddha's life, from conception to birth to enlightenment, fulfills a timeless cosmic template that all the previous buddhas and all the future buddhas mimic exactly. Thus in the selection below (Doc. 5-1), from the *Mahapadana* (The Great Lineage), we see that the Buddha's life is but a replica of these deeper biographic patterns responsible for the life-production of the perfect sage. In this light, there is no real drama here or potential for tragedy: the Buddha's birth, childhood, and awakening were prescribed in a thoroughly cosmic and indelible manner.

In forging the Buddha's life in reference to previous buddhas, there is one popular story that gives particular importance to his actions as a child in a previous life (Doc. 5-2). In this story, well known in several Indian sources and frequently rendered in popular art, the Buddha is shown as the youthful Sumati in the city of Dipavati preparing to worship the Buddha Dipamkara, who preceded the Buddha Sakyamuni of our era, and was on this occasion about to visit Sumati's hometown. The story links our Buddha to this invisible family of buddhas by creating a transmission moment when Dipamkara predicts Sumati's future as the Buddha Sakyamuni, as Sumati throws down his youthful locks so that Dipamkara need not tread on the mud. Presumably, the story can also be read as a reminder of the importance of encouraging children to participate in Buddhist worship. The point seems to be that, given that we don't know our karmic histories—only buddhas know these things—we ought to worship buddhas at every opportunity, and this practice should be encouraged for children as well. I should also point out that by giving Sumati a girlfriend of sorts in this story, the narrative also links the Buddha's spiritual career to family reproduction, since that childhood romance enacted in front of the Buddha Dipamkara is said to have repeated itself because the woman whom the Buddha marries, Yasodhara, is said to be none other than that girl with whom he worshiped Buddha Dipamkara in that past lifetime.

There is one more type of story regarding the Buddha's childhood that needs to be mentioned. Here the Buddha, though adult and enlightened, and with his teaching career in full swing, is depicted interacting with both his mother and his stepmother, Mahaprajapati, who raised him after his mother died a week after his birth. In the case of his birth mother, he takes a summer off from teaching and travels to heaven to teach her the Dharma in order to repay her for birthing him. All during the teaching, she is said to spontaneously lactate, with the milk looping across space and into the Buddha's mouth.[2] The second story, too, works around debts to one's mother, though this time the Buddha reluctantly consents to admitting women into the Buddhist order, but only when it is his stepmother who makes the request, and does so by reminding the Buddha that it was she who breast-fed him when he was an infant.[3] In both cases, the Buddha's sonship to either woman is imagined to continue into his adult identity, and, equally important, it seems that the stories are designed to show how, ironically, the Buddha's otherworldliness does not absolve him from recognizing these very intimate and very somatic connections that he had with his mother and stepmother.

Parents and Children in Buddhism

Early on in the formation of Buddhism, Buddhist authors collected several sets of stories—some adapted from generic Indian folk tales, others newly minted—which contained narratives about children, parents, and the Buddhist establishment. For the sake of bringing some clarity to this grab-bag collection of stories, I believe we can divide them into four different thematic categories: 1. losing a child and consequently turning to Buddhism; 2. children learning to care for their parents, alive or deceased; 3. children and parents at odds over supporting Buddhist clerics; and 4. disobedient children and their horrible fates.

As for the first type of story, there are several well-known narratives that focus on women coming to learn about the horrors of life and death, and then turning to the Buddha for an explanation and for advice on how to live with this knowledge. Key to notice here is that while it is true that most stories explaining male entrance into the Buddhist order emphasize the act of renunciation—renouncing family, home, sex, wealth, and so on—this mini-genre based on child-loss is almost exclusively focused on women. Thus, for instance, we have the case of Patacara, who loses her husband and then her two children, and then decides to turn to the Buddha for consolation (Doc. 5-3). Similarly, in another famous story, Kisa Gotami, having lost her child, becomes inconsolable and carries the dead child around until the Buddha promises to revive the child if Kisa Gotami will collect mustard seeds from every family that hasn't had a death in the family. In the course of trying to find these mustard seeds, she comes to realize how universal death is and joins the Buddhist order.[4] In either case, the stories are designed to highlight the riskiness of reproduction, and to provide women with some kind of recourse when faced with such devastating loss.

One of the more important stories in this category of child-loss is that of the goddess Hariti. Hariti, it seems, was an ancient Indian goddess-ogre known for devouring other people's children in order to feed her own. It seems, too, that she was connected to smallpox, as many Indian goddesses are. Apparently, the Buddhists reinvented her identity from these non-Buddhist stories and thus, below (Doc. 5-4), Reiko Ohnuma provides an account of Hariti's conversion to Buddhism which was effected, oddly it must be admitted, by the Buddha kidnapping one of her five hundred children. In facing the loss of this one child, despite her other four hundred and ninety-nine, Hariti comes to understand the pain that she has been causing other families as she takes and consumes their children. This Buddhist form of Hariti would spread all over Asia and is still prominent in East Asian mythology. As Richard Cohen has argued, this myth worked well not only to create a Buddhist fertility goddess but also to connect Buddhism with local goddess cults.[5]

While stories of this type focus on the vagaries of family reproduction and the tragedies that lurk therein, many other Buddhist stories highlight the value and desirability of continuity in family reproduction. Thus, in this second category of tales, there are many accounts of how a couple gained lasting fertility by offering the Buddhists gifts and transferring the merit won thereby to their deceased parents. Here the point is that children have to learn that their own fates are a function of a twofold submission defined as service to their parents and generosity to the Buddhist establishment. In this style of narrative, the emphasis is put on revealing that the Buddha, though a world-renouncer, is also in control of the goods in the universe, and will, in essence, distribute them when correctly propitiated.

Next to these stories that work to show how Buddhism can find a useful place in family reproduction, it is not surprising to find a set of stories—the third category of family-related tales—that explore the resistance that might develop in a family when resources are directed outside the family sphere to the Buddhist establishment. Here it is often the child's generosity which triumphs as the narrative explains that the child perseveres against stingy and unbelieving parents, and in the end is also able to thereby save these stubborn parents from long stays in hell. And, it so happened, that one of these stories—the story of Uttara's mother (Doc. 5–6)—was gradually rewritten into a narrative that would be crucial for defining East Asian forms of Buddhist filial piety.

In the last category of parent-child narratives, there are quite a few accounts explaining what happens to unfilial children. These cautionary tales usually detail how the smallest form of resistance or impertinence on the child's part will result in horrifying punishments in hell. Of course, here the theme is surely intent on producing docile children who will accept their parents' directives and work to maintain a status quo that the Buddhists have generally been in favor of throughout history. (Such stories are reasonably straightforward and thus, for reasons of space, I have not included an example.)

Besides these four themes, I should add that there is a famous text from the Pali canon (Sri Lankan Buddhism), the *Sigalaka Sutta*, in which the Buddha explains to a son who has just lost his father how he ought to organize his family life (see below, Doc. 5–7). In this story it is evident that the Buddhists were hoping to forge a reliable set of ethics for householders, and organized the delivery of these ethics with the trope of the Buddha figuring as a kind of paternal supplement.

Children as Symbols in Buddhist Literature

Next to these straightforward, folksy Buddhist tales there is another body of literature that also evokes a range of issues related to childhood. What distinguishes these instances, though, is a tendency to treat childhood as a useful allegory for defining preferred identities and attitudes in adult believers. For instance, Reiko Ohnuma has recently pointed out that one stock rhetorical figure for explaining the Buddha's love for sentient beings is a comparison of the Buddha to a mother who has only one son.[6] The trope works by arguing that the singular love that such a mother would have for her son is no different in intensity from what the Buddha feels for each and every sentient being. Here, as so often happens in religion, the private realm of family emotions is being deployed to construct its opposite: the world of invisible public religion, peopled by nonfamily members and their institutional representatives. Thus, with the Buddha depicted as a kind of super-mother, one is made to understand that at least some of one's love for real family members should be redirected toward the Buddha in order to reciprocate the mother-love that he has been directing to each of us.

In Mahayana Buddhism, which appears roughly at the beginning of the Common Era and develops in various modes, this relocation of mother-son emotions is found in the way that bodhisattvas (buddhas-to-be) are defined as having so much love for sentient beings that they postpone their exit from samsara in order to continue serving all sentient beings. Generating this bodhisattva attitude is, in fact, practiced in Tibetan Buddhism by meditating on the way that all sentient beings have been, in lifetimes past, one's mother. Thus, a bodhisattva is supposed to recollect the specific forms of kindness that his or her mother lavished on him or her in this life—breast-feeding, education/advice, love, and so on—and then transpose that intensity on to all sentient beings thinking: just as my mother cared for me so too did these creatures, and thus I ought to have limitless compassion for them and work for their welfare tirelessly. Here, clearly, mother-child emotions are being exported and universalized in order to create something like a higher order of family in which Buddhists locate themselves and act accordingly.

The final parent-child motif in Indian Buddhism—a metaphoric sonship to the Buddha—takes form in several prominent texts in Mahayana literature.[7] For instance, in a crucial sequence in the *Lotus Sutra* the narrator has the Buddha explain to his leading disciple, Sariputra, that Sariputra has always been a son of the Buddha even if he has not quite understood what this sonship involved. In fact, in older strata of Buddhist literature Sariputra *had* thought he was a figurative son-of-the-buddha—an identity that he here again lays claim to—but the Buddha convinces him that this was an initial form of sonship, a form that had to be expanded in order for Sariputra to win his full "inheritance," generated by what is called a birthing from the Buddha's mouth.[8] Following this conversion, the narrative then gives two extended parables that construct bodhisattvahood as a kind of lost or misrecognized sonship to the Buddha (Docs. 5–8 and 5–9). In one, the famous parable of the burning house, the Buddha qua father compassionately tricks his sons to leave a burning house by promising them different kinds of carts, representing the different forms of Buddhism, when in fact there is only one cart: the Mahayana. In the next parable, a distraught father seeks to lead his wayward son back home. Here, the basic motif is the same: all sentient beings are essentially sons of the Buddha even if they don't yet recognize this and have to be gently brought back "home."

In a different take on Mahayana sonship-to-the-Buddha, the *Tathagatagarbha Sutra* (and other texts, as well) asks readers to accept that within themselves there is a "buddha-fetus" (*tathagatagarbha*) which will in time be turned into a real buddha. Clearly, the idea is that Buddhist sonship is already substantially present in each being and simply needs to be cultivated into a working replica of the Buddha-father.[9] A slightly different version of this motif is offered in a set of claims in which Buddhist believers are likened to the Buddha's "biological son," Rahula. Here, as Richard Cohen has argued, the Buddhist clergy sought to identify itself as a kind descent group deriving "directly" from the Buddha, just as his son Rahula did.[10] In these various examples, the point is still basically that Buddhist identity is being structured in a parent-child form, with the believer playing the role of the child vis-à-vis the Buddha.

In Tibetan Buddhism, as in more developed tantric forms of Indian Buddhism, one also finds a kind of parent-child template in place explaining the relationship between a neophyte and his or her guru. In some tantric initiations, it is even the case that the neophyte is inducted into the guru's spiritual lineage/family by receiving a drop of semen on his or her tongue which is believed to effect this kind of rebirthing. Arguably, this sort of ritual works to make "visible" much of the father-son logic that had been generated in the earlier strata of Mahayana sutras, such as the *Lotus Sutra*.

Images of Children in East Asian Buddhism

As mentioned in my introductory comments, East Asian Buddhism presents four basic discourses involving children or relying on child-based motifs: 1. Buddhist forms of filial piety; 2. Buddhist management of the cycle of life and death, with a focus on fertility and the welfare of deceased children; 3. modern myths regarding abortion; and, 4. the use of father-son models in monastic settings.

In the first discourse, East Asian authors developed a kind of Buddhist filial piety that focused on getting sons and daughters to recognize that their existence was fully dependent on their parents and the only proper way to repay them was to make offerings to the Buddhist monasteries. On this front, it was roughly in the sixth century that various accounts of Mulian, who travels to hell to save his mother, begin to appear and define a new form of Buddhist family values that has lasted down to the present in East Asian countries. Key to understanding this story is that Mulian is both a monk and son, with these two roles being successfully combined such that Mulian's career as a Buddhist monk is motivated by his desire to care for his mother, and less pressingly, his patriline. In fact, in the various versions of this popular narrative, it was explicitly said that one could only truly be filial to one's parents by being Buddhist. Buddhist authors pushed this symbolic overhaul of traditional Chinese family values by coining the term "Great Filial Piety" (*da xiao*) and coming up with narratives such as the one below (Doc. 5–11) in which perfect sons fulfill their filial duties by participating in annual Buddhist rituals in which they transfer funds and goods from the sphere of the household to the monastics.

Second among the East Asian themes is a kind of Buddhist fertility cult that focused on the bodhisattva Guanyin, the Chinese translation of the Bodhisattva Avalokitesvara who appears prominently in chapter twenty-five of the *Lotus Sutra*.

In that chapter, it is clear that the Indian sutra offers women the hope that if this bodhisattva is worshiped, they can expect to become pregnant and even select the sex of their child. It seems that this chapter of the *Lotus Sutra* circulated separately throughout the medieval period, as it still does in Taiwan, and appears to have been important in the expansion of a cult of fertility based on Guanyin.[11] In fact, Guanyin's identity shifted from being male to being female; and, likewise, she gained a fertility-promising epithet: Child-granting Guanyin (*Songzi Guanyin*).

Along with Child-granting Guanyin, another bodhisattva, Ksitigarbha (Chinese: Dizang) became central in a cult of fertility and children.[12] In one textual statement, found in a sutra that appears to have been fabricated in China roughly in the tenth or the eleventh century, a narrative is developed explaining how a daughter named "Bright Eyes" (*Guangmu*) saves her wayward mother from eons of punishment in hell by propitiating the Buddhists (Doc. 5-12). By the end of the saga we learn that this filial daughter turned into Dizang, who is presented henceforth as a blend of bodhisattva and hell warden who, if treated correctly by believing Buddhists, will spare those who arrive in the netherworld. A focus on fertility is also evident in this narrative since Bright Eyes's mother is sent to hell for eating eggs and, in effect, interrupting the cycle of reproduction, an interruption that the story seeks to rectify.

Somewhat later in Japan, roughly in the fourteenth century, there is clearer evidence of a cult around Dizang (Japanese: Jizo), who now is presented as the special guardian of deceased children, even as he appears equally in charge of delivering fertility and ensuring the health of children. As the selection below (Doc. 5-13) suggests, this form of Jizo functions a bit like the Indian deity Hariti (Doc. 5-4) insofar as he is in charge of dead children, but he is also worshiped as their protector.

As for the third discourse on children, these various strands of East Asian Buddhist thought on filial piety, fertility, and deceased children took a somewhat different turn in the twentieth century. Starting in Japan in the 1970s, and then spreading more recently to Taiwan, there emerged a Buddhist cult based on caring for aborted fetuses. Built around "rites for the water child" (*mizukokuyo*), a sizable number of Japanese monasteries began offering intensive monthly and annual services for mothers, and families, who wished to propitiate their aborted fetuses. Below I have included a modern tract (Doc. 5-14) that shows how the doctrines around "water children" were not simply about resuturing the connection between the monastery and private life of the family—a trope that has a very long tradition in East Asia back to Mulian (Doc. 5-11)—but also that "water children" become the focus for new forms of Buddhist family values that are directed toward increasing fertility, wealth, and family well-being.[13]

Next to these narratives and practices designed to suture the family's life cycle to the Buddhist monastery is the fourth set of rhetorical practices that involve children in East Asian Buddhism. Early on in the history of Chan (Zen), the masters' disciples were categorized as little filial sons (*xiao xiaozi*). Thus in the earliest Chan monastic rules—the *Chanyuan qinggui* of 1103—the funeral of an abbot qua master is described with mourning roles given to his chosen "descendents" who are to don customary Confucian funeral garb and treat the abbot, their master, as though he was their father.[14] Admittedly this is a highly conscious and metaphoric use of sonship, but it raises important issues about how identity in the monastery was designed. On one level, it is obvious that the Chan monastic system borrowed the at-home model of patriarchal rule and then applied it in rather ingenious ways to structure authority in a durable manner in the large public monasteries. On another level, it raises the question of how participants thought of themselves: was sonship to the master understood and practiced in a manner that mimicked a son's obedience to his father, with the adult monk inhabiting a kind of adult-sonship vis-à-vis his master? And what of the master as father—what was implied by combining these two templates for monastic leaders?

Among the many Chan/Zen stories that work around this theme of monkish filial piety, there are two that are particularly vivid. First, there is the story of monk Huike (ca. late sixth century) cutting off his arm and giving it to the Indian monk Bodhidharma in an act of self-sacrifice performed in order to receive transmission from the master. While this might seem like a story simply intent on proving the zeal and ardor demanded of a Chan/Zen monk, it seems equally likely that this story mimicked a rather standard Confucian paradigm in which the loyal and filial son offers himself totally, sometimes even slicing off his flesh, in order to prove his genuine submission and love for his parents.[15]

A second example works in a similar manner: in various documents related to master Huineng (no date: it seems likely that he was invented in the mid-eighth century), we find a sequence in which a young disciple named Shenhui (d. 758) asks him a range of questions (Doc. 5-15). Though Shenhui is said to be only thirteen years old, in the conversations that develop Shenhui is shown holding his own against the old master. Most notable in the early accounts of this exchange is the beating that Huineng gives Shenhui. This corporal punishment seems to accomplish three things. First, the beating reveals that Shenhui is Huineng's main disciple; that is, the beating signals an intimate relationship between the master and this particular disciple. Second, the beating is presented in the context of making Buddhist truth appear to be like Confucian legacies that are passed on in this father-to-son manner, with the master taking on all the disciplinary privileges that an at-home father would have. Third, the beating seems included to prove both Shenhui's forebearance and to setup a template for future disciples, who likewise ought to cultivate a willingness to suffer at the hands of the stern master. Arguably, this early story shaped later disciplinary models in Chan and Zen, which both emphasize corporal punishment for trainees and a rather austere role for the father-abbot.

With these various themes and tropes in view it ought to be clear how important and multifaceted the image of the child was in the various forms of the Buddhist tradition.

Indic Sources

A Perfect Childhood That Matches All Other Perfect Childhoods

In this well-known account of a past buddha's life–Vipassi–we learn that every aspect of every buddha's biography is preordained, and matches the lives of various other buddhas. Within this pattern of repeating buddha-lives, we see a range of statements in which this era's buddha comes into being in a manner that highlights his purity during conception and partuition, and then his absolute ability to master all aspects of childhood and early adulthood. Clearly, the point of this narrative is to depict the Buddha of our era as a perfect human being whose existence did not rely on normal biological functions, just as it was not limited by the normal exigencies of childhood and coming of age. Against this message of perfection, the narrative takes a turn as it sets about depicting a buddha's gradual awakening to death and other aspects of life that he encounters during the four trips from the palace. In this phase of his maturation, he finally leaves his childhood and his cozy place in the harem in order to become the "best of men," as one of his common epithets puts it. The text is narrated by the Buddha of our era explaining to his monk-disciples this universal template for the lives of buddhas.

Document 5–1

The Mahapadana Sutta in the Dighanikaya

"It is the rule that when a Bodhisatta [Bodhisattva] descends from the Tusita heaven into his mother's womb, there appears in this world with its devas, maras and Brahmas, its ascetics and Brahmins, princes and people an immeasurable, splendid light surpassing the glory of the most powerful devas. And whatever dark spaces lie beyond the world's-end, chaotic, blind and black, such that they are not even reached by the mighty rays of sun and moon, are yet illumined by this immeasurable splendid light surpassing the glory of the most powerful devas. And those beings that have been reborn there recognise each other by this light and know: "Other beings, too, have been born here!" And this ten-thousand fold world-system trembles and quakes and is convulsed. And this immeasurable light shines forth. That is the rule.

"It is the rule that when a Bodhisatta has entered his mother's womb, four devas come to protect him from the four quarters, saying: 'Let no man, no non-human being, no thing whatever harm this Bodhisatta or this Bodhisatta's mother!' That is the rule.

"It is the rule that when a Bodhisatta has entered his mother's womb, his mother becomes by nature virtuous, refraining from taking life, from taking what is not given, from sexual misconduct, from lying speech, or from strong drink and sloth-producing drugs. That is the rule.

"It is the rule that when a Bodhisatta has entered his mother's womb, she has no sensual thoughts connected with a man, and she cannot be overcome by any man with lustful thoughts. That is the rule.

"It is the rule that when a Bodhisatta has entered his mother's womb, she enjoys the fivefold pleasures of the senses and takes delight, being endowed and possessed of them. That is the rule.

"It is the rule that when a Bodhisatta has entered his mother's womb, she has no sickness of any kind, she is at ease and without fatigue of body, and she can see the Bodhisatta inside her womb, complete with all his members and faculties. Monks, it is as if a gem, a beryl, pure, excellent, well cut into eight facets, clear, bright, flawless and perfect in every respect, were strung on a blue, yellow, red, white or orange cord. And a man with good eyesight, taking it in his hand, would describe it as such. Thus does the Bodhisatta's mother, with no sickness, see him, complete with all his members and faculties. That is the rule.

"It is the rule that the Bodhisatta's mother dies seven days after his birth and is reborn in the Tusita heaven. That is the rule.

"It is the rule that whereas other women carry the child in their womb for nine or ten months before giving birth, it is not so with the Bodhisatta's mother, who carries him for exactly ten months before giving birth. That is the rule.

"It is the rule that whereas other women give birth sitting or lying down, it is not so with the Bodhisatta's mother, who gives birth standing up. That is the rule.

"It is the rule that when the Bodhisatta issues from his mother's womb, devas welcome him first, and then humans. That is the rule.

"It is the rule that when the Bodhisatta issues from his mother's womb, he does not touch the earth. Four devas receive him and place him before his mother, saying: 'Rejoice, Your Majesty, a mighty son has been born to you!' That is the rule.

"It is the rule that when the Bodhisatta issues from his mother's womb he issues forth stainless, not defiled by water, mucus, blood or any impurity, pure and spotless. Just as when a jewel is laid on muslin from Kasi the jewel does not stain the muslin, or the muslin the jewel. Why not? Because of the purity of both. In the same way the Bodhisatta issues forth stainless. . . . That is the rule.

"It is the rule that when the Bodhisatta issues forth from his mother's womb, two streams of water appear from the sky, one cold, the other warm, with which they ritually wash the Bodhisatta and his mother. That is the rule.

"It is the rule that as soon as he is born the Bodhisatta takes a firm stance on both feet facing north, then takes seven strides and, under a white sunshade, he scans the four quarters and then declares with a bull-like voice: "I am chief in the world, supreme in the world, eldest in the world. This is my last birth, there will be no more re-becoming." That is the rule.

"It is the rule that when the Bodhisatta issues from his mother's womb there appears in this world . . . an immeasurable, splendid light. . . . This is the rule.

"Monks, when Prince Vipassi [a former buddha] was born, they showed him to King Bandhuma and said: 'Your Majesty, a son has been born to you. Deign, Sire, to look at him.' The king looked at the prince and then said to the Brahmins skilled in signs: 'You gentlemen are skilled in signs, examine the prince.' The Brahmins examined the prince, and said to King Bandhuma: 'Sire, rejoice, for a mighty son has been born to you. It is a gain for you, Sire, it is a great profit for you, Sire, that such a son has been born into your family. Sire, this prince is endowed with the thirty-two marks of a Great Man. To such, only two courses are open. If he lives the household life he will become a ruler, a wheel-turning righteous monarch of the law, conqueror of the four quarters, who has established the security of his realm and is possessed of the seven treasures. . . . But if he goes forth from the household life into homelessness, then he will become an Arahant, a fully-enlightened Buddha, one who draws back the veil from the world. . . .'

"Then King Bandhuma, having clothed those Brahmins in fresh clothes, satisfied all their wishes.

"And King Bandhuma appointed nurses for Prince Vipassi. Some suckled him, some bathed him, some carried him, some dandled him. A white umbrella was held over him night and day, that he might not be harmed by cold or heat or grass or dust. And Prince Vipassi was much beloved of the people. Just as everybody loves a blue, yellow or white lotus, so they all loved Prince Vipassi. Thus he was borne from lap to lap.

"And Prince Vipassi had a sweet voice, a beautiful voice, charming and delightful. Just as in the Himalaya mountains the *karavika*-bird has a voice sweeter, more beautiful, charming and delightful than all other birds, so too was Prince Vipassi's voice the finest of all. . . .

"Then King Bandhuma caused three palaces to be built for Prince Vipassi, one for the rainy season, one for the cold season, and one for the hot season, to cater for all the fivefold sense-pleasures. There Prince Vipassi stayed in the rainy-season palace for the four months of the rainy season, with no male attendants, surrounded by female musicians, and he never left that palace.

"Then, monks, after many years, many hundreds and thousands of years had passed, Prince Vipassi said to his charioteer: 'Harness some fine carriages, charioteer! We will go to the pleasure-park to inspect it.' The charioteer did so, then reported to the prince: 'Your Royal Highness, the fine carriages are harnessed, it is time to do as you wish.' And Prince Vipassi mounted a carriage and drove in procession to the pleasure-park.

"And as he was being driven to the pleasure-park, Prince Vipassi saw an aged man, bent like a roof-beam, broken, leaning on a stick, tottering, sick, his youth all vanished. At the sight he said to the charioteer: 'Charioteer, what is the matter with this man? His hair is not like other men's, his body is not like other men's.'

"'Prince, that is what is called an old man.' 'But why is he called an old man?'

"'He is called old, Prince, because he has not long to live.'

"'But am I liable to become old, and not exempt from old age?' 'Both you and I, Prince, are liable to become old, and are not exempt from old age.'

'Well then, charioteer, that will do for today with the pleasure-park. Return now to the palace.' 'Very good, Prince,' said the charioteer, and brought Prince Vipassi back to the palace. Arrived there, Prince Vipassi was overcome with grief and dejection, crying: 'Shame on this thing birth, since to him who is born old age must manifest itself!'

"Then King Bandhuma sent for the charioteer and said: 'Well, did not the prince enjoy himself at the pleasure-park? Wasn't he happy there?' 'Your Majesty, the prince did not enjoy himself, he was not happy there.' 'What did he see on the way there?' So the charioteer told the King all that had happened.

"Then King Bandhuma thought: 'Prince Vipassi must not renounce the throne, he must not go forth from the household life into homelessness—the words of the Brahmins learned in signs must not come true!' So the King provided for Prince Vipassi to have even more enjoyment of the fivefold sense-pleasures, in order that he should rule the kingdom and not go forth from the household life into homelessness. . . . Thus the prince continued to live indulging in, and addicted to, the fivefold sense-pleasures.

"After many hundreds of thousands of years Prince Vipassi ordered his charioteer to drive to the pleasure-park. . . .

"And as he was being driven to the pleasure-park, Prince Vipassi saw a sick man, suffering, very ill, fallen in his own urine and excrement, and some people were picking him up, and others putting him to bed. At the sight he said to the charioteer: 'What is the matter with this man? His eyes are not like other men's, his head is not like other men's.'

"'Prince, that is what is called a sick man.' 'But why is he called a sick man?'

"'Prince, he is so called because he can hardly recover from his illness.'

"'But am I liable to become sick, and not exempt from sickness?' 'Both you and I, Prince, are liable to become sick, and not exempt from sickness.'

"'Well then, charioteer, return now to the palace.' Arrived there, Prince Vipassi was overcome with grief and dejection, crying: 'Shame on this thing birth, since he who is born must experience sickness!'

"Then King Bandhuma sent for the charioteer, who told him what had happened.

"The king provided Prince Vipassi with even more sense-pleasures, in order that he should rule the kingdom and not go forth from the household life into homelessness. . . .

"After many hundreds of thousands of years Prince Vipassi ordered his charioteer to drive to the pleasure-park.

"And as he was being driven to the pleasure-park, Prince Vipassi saw a large crowd collecting, clad in many colours, and carrying a bier. At the sight he said to the charioteer: 'Why are those people doing that?' 'Prince, that is what they call a dead man.' 'Drive me over to where the dead man is.' 'Very good, Prince,' said the charioteer, and did so. And Prince Vipassi gazed at the corpse of the dead man. Then he said to the charioteer: 'Why is he called a dead man?'

"'Prince, he is called a dead man because now his parents and other relatives will not see him again, nor he them.'

"'But am I subject to dying, not exempt from dying?' 'Both you and I, Prince, are subject to dying, not exempt from it.'

"'Well then, charioteer, that will do for today with the pleasure-park. Return now to the palace. . . . Arrived there, Prince Vipassi was overcome with grief and dejection, crying: 'Shame on this thing birth, since to him who is born death must manifest itself!'

"Then King Bandhuma sent for the charioteer, who told him what had happened.

"The king provided Prince Vipassi with even more sense-pleasures. . . .

"After many hundreds of thousands of years Prince Vipassi ordered his charioteer to drive to the pleasure-park.

"And as he was being driven to the pleasure-park, Prince Vipassi saw a shaven-headed man, one who had gone forth, wearing a yellow robe. And he said to the charioteer: 'What is the matter with that man? His head is not like other men's, and his clothes are not like other men's.'

"'Prince, he is called one who has gone forth.' 'Why is he called one who has gone forth?'

"'Prince, by one who has gone forth we mean one who truly follows Dhamma, who truly lives in serenity, does good actions, performs meritorious deeds, is harmless and truly has compassion for living beings.'

"'Charioteer, he is well called one who has gone forth. . . . Drive the carriage over to where he is.' 'Very good, Prince,' said the charioteer, and did so. And Prince Vipassi questioned the man who had gone forth.

"'Prince, as one who has gone forth I truly follow Dhamma, . . . and have compassion for living beings.' 'You are well called one who has gone forth. . . .'

"Then Prince Vipassi said to the charioteer: 'You take the carriage and drive back to the palace. But I shall stay here and shave off my hair and beard, put on yellow robes, and go forth from the household life into homelessness.' 'Very good, Prince,' said the charioteer, and returned to the palace. And Prince Vipassi, shaving off his hair and beard and putting on yellow robes, went forth from the household life into homelessness.

"And a great crowd from the royal capital city, Bandhumati, eighty-four thousand people, heard that Prince Vipassi had gone forth into homelessness. And they thought: 'This is certainly no common teaching and discipline, no common going-forth, for which Prince Vipassi has shaved off hair and beard, donned yellow robes and gone forth into homelessness. If the Prince has done so, why should not we?' And so, monks, a great crowd of eighty-four thousand, having shaved off their hair and beards and donned yellow robes, followed the Bodhisatta Vipassi into homelessness. And with this following the Bodhisatta went on his rounds through villages, towns and royal cities.

'Then the Bodhisatta Vipassi, having retired to a secluded spot, had this thought: 'It is not proper for me to live with a crowd like this. I must live alone, withdrawn from this crowd.' So after a while he left the crowd and dwelt alone. The eighty-four thousand went one way, the Bodhisatta another.

"Then, when the Bodhisatta had entered his dwelling alone, in a secluded spot, he thought: 'This world, alas, is in a sorry state: there is birth and decay, there is death and falling into other states and being reborn. And no one knows any way of escape from this suffering, this ageing and death. When will deliverance be found from this suffering, this ageing and death?'"

Source: *The Long Discourses of the Buddha: A Translation of the Dighanikaya*, translated by Maurice Walshe (Boston: Wisdom, 1987), 203–213.

The Power of Gifts, Even When Given by Children

The following is an account of a past life of the Buddha of our era, Sakyamuni Buddha, in which as a youth named Sumati he encounters a past buddha, Dipamkara. Besides anchoring Sakyamuni in a lineage of previous buddhas, this story also serves to show the power of gifts to buddhas, even those gifts given by the youthful. Of particular interest is the way that this account gives the buddha-to-be, Sumati, a girlfriend who acts in a parallel manner. By the end of the story we learn that when the Buddha Sakyamuni was born in our era, his wife was the reincarnation of just this past girlfriend. Presumably making this point underscores the power of Buddhist devotion, even as it humanizes the Buddha.

Document 5–2

The Story of Sumati and Dipamkara in the Divyavadana

[Then the Buddha, recalling his former life, said to the monks: At that time,] there appeared in the world a Blessed Buddha named Dipamkara, completely enlightened as to knowledge and conduct, a Perfected One, knowing the world, the unsurpassed guide of those who are to be converted, a teacher of gods and humans.

Wandering here and there in the land, the Buddha Dipamkara came to the royal capital of Dipavati. There, ruled a king named Dipa, who spread prosperity, abundance, peace, and plenty among the people. And King Dipa invited the Buddha Dipamkara to enter the city with a resolute mind.

Now in a neighboring kingdom there was another king, named Vasava. He proclaimed a twelve-year sacrifice, at the end of which he put on display five great presents: a golden water jar with a handle, a golden food bowl, a couch made of four kinds of gems, five hundred pieces of gold, and a maiden adorned with all her jewelry. These, he declared, would be given to whatever brahmin was most accomplished in knowledge of the Vedas.

Not too far away, dwelt two youths who had studied the Veda. Knowing that it was the custom to give their preceptor a preceptor's fee and their teacher a teacher's fee, they were wondering how they would do this when they heard what King Vasava had proclaimed. "Those presents are as good as ours," they thought, "for who is there more learned and knowledgeable than us?" With this in mind, they set out for the great city of King Vasava.

In the meantime, the king had a vision of a divinity, who said to him: "Your Majesty, of the two youths who are coming, Sumati and Mati, give the offerings to Sumati. You have carried out a sacrifice for twelve years; from the meritorious fruit of that act, you can now make a great offering to the youth Sumati, who is of the highest rank. . . ."

When the king saw the two youths approaching, filled with grace and charm, . . . he thought he should do what was recommended by the gods, so he went up to the first youth and asked, "Sir, are you Sumati?"

Sumati replied, "I am."

Then King Vasava seated young Sumati on the highest seat, regaled him with food, and presented him with the five presents. The young Sumati accepted the first four of them, but he did not accept the gift of the maiden. "I am celibate," he explained.

The girl, seeing how gracious and charming young Sumati was, was filled with desire and love and pleaded with him, saying, "Brahmin, take me."

But he replied, "I cannot take you."

Now since King Vasava had given away that girl as a present, he could not take her back again, . . . so she went away to Dipavati, the city of King Dipa. Upon arrival there, she removed all of her jewelry and gave it to a garland maker, asking him, in return, to provide her every day with blue lotuses so that she could worship the gods.

In the meantime, Sumati took the four presents he had accepted and went and gave them to his teacher. His teacher agreed to accept three of them, but he gave the five hundred gold pieces back to Sumati. That very night, Sumati had ten dreams: he dreamed that he drank the great ocean; that he flew through the air; that he touched and clasped with his hand both the sun and the moon; that he harnessed the chariot of the king; and that he saw ascetics, white elephants, geese, lions, a great rock, and mountains. He then woke up and thought, "Who can clarify for me the meaning of these dreams?"

Not far from there lived an ascetic endowed with five supernatural powers. Accordingly, the young Sumati went to him . . . and asked him to interpret his dreams.

The ascetic said: "I cannot clarify the meaning of these dreams for you, but go to the royal city of Dipavati. King Dipa has invited the Buddha Dipamkara there, . . . [and] he will be able to interpret your dreams. . . ."

Now, in the royal city of Dipavati, King Dipa had requisitioned all the flowers from all the flower merchants in the land, thinking that in seven days, he would welcome the Buddha Dipamkara into the city. . . . And when all the flowers had been gathered by the king, the girl, who was now a devout worshipper of the gods, went to her garland maker and said, "Give me some blue lotuses; I wish to carry out the service of the gods."

But the garland maker replied, "Today, the king has taken all of the blossoms for Dipamkara's entrance into the city."

She said, "Go back again to the lotus pool and see if, through my merit, you cannot find some blue lotus flowers that have not been taken away."

The garland maker went there and saw that, through the power of her merit, seven blue lotuses had appeared in the pool.

"Please pluck them," she asked.

The garland maker replied: "I cannot pick them; I will be blamed by the king's men. . . ."

But she insisted: "Pluck these blossoms and give them to me; they have appeared on account of my merits."

"How will you get them into the city without the knowledge of the king's men?"

"Pluck them, sir, and I will enter the city with them hidden in a water pot"

Thus reassured, the garland maker plucked the blossoms and gave them to her. She took them, hid them in a jar, filled the jar with water, and set out for the city. Now, just at that time, young Sumati arrived in that place, and he reflected: "I should pay homage to the Blessed Buddha when I see him, but with what?" So he went from one garland maker's house to another, inquiring everywhere after flowers, but he did not find a single blossom. . . .

Then, in his search, he came to that garden and met the girl just as she was leaving. Out of the power of her merit, the blue lotuses suddenly emerged from her water pot.

Seeing them, Sumati said to her, "Give me five of those lotuses, and in exchange I will give you five hundred pieces of gold."

The girl said to Sumati: "Formerly you wanted to have nothing to do with me; now, you ask me for my lotuses. I will not give them to you." But then she went on: "What will you do with them?"

Sumati replied, "I wish to honor the Blessed Buddha."

Thereupon, the girl said: "I too wish to give flowers to the Buddha. So what am I to do with these gold pieces? But I will give you these lotuses on one condition: if you, at the time of your offering them to the Buddha, make a formal, earnest wish to have me as your wife in life after life, saying, 'May she become my spouse in repeated existences.'"

To this Sumati agreed, . . . and the girl gave him five lotuses and retained two for herself. . . .

Then, starting at the city gate, King Dipa had the road cleared of all stones, gravel, and potsherds. He had flags, banners, and archways put up, bands of cloth fastened, and perfumed water and sandalwood powder sprinkled about. . . . And taking a hundred-ribbed umbrella, the king set out to meet the Buddha Dipamkara. And so did King Vasava [who had come to the city] and all of their ministers. And King Dipa fell at the feet of the Blessed Buddha and declared: "Blessed One, take possession of this place."

Then the Blessed One, at the head of the community of monks, proceeded to enter into the city with proper mental preparation. And King Dipa held a hundred-spoked umbrella for the altogether enlightened Dipamkara, and so did his ministers, and so did King Vasava and his ministers, but through his supernatural power, the Blessed One made it so that each and everyone of them felt "I am holding the umbrella over: the Blessed One!" . . .

And there in the royal city of Dipavati, hundreds of thousands of living beings paid homage to the Buddha Dipamkara with flowers and incense and perfumes. Sumati and the girl also followed the Blessed One, holding their lotuses, but they were not able to get near him, surrounded as he was by the great crowd of people intending to worship him.

But the Blessed One then reflected: "This young Sumati is to become a great source of merit to this large crowd of people." So he magically fashioned a tumultuous rainstorm. In that way, the crowd dispersed, and now that there was more room, Sumati was able to see the entrancing sight of the Blessed One, and great faith was engendered in him. Filled with faith, he tossed his five lotuses toward the Buddha Dipamkara; just as they fell, the Blessed One magically fashioned them into a canopy of flowers the size of a wagon wheel, which, suspended in the air, followed him when he moved and remained stationary when he stopped.

When the girl saw this, faith was engendered in her also, and she tossed her two lotuses to the Blessed One. And again, just as they fell, they were magically fashioned into canopies the size of wagon wheels and took up their position on either side of the Buddha's head.

Now, in that place, a lot of mud had been created by the heavy downpour. So the young Sumati went up to the Blessed Buddha, and on the muddy ground in front of him, he spread out his long hair and spoke this verse:

"If I am to become a Buddha, awakened to enlightenment, may you tread with your feet on my hair—on my birth, old age, and death."

And the Buddha Dipamkara trod upon the young Sumati's locks . . . and he made a prediction about him: "Freed from human existence, you will become an effective Teacher, for the sake of the world. Born among the Sakyas, as the epitome of the Triple World, the Lamp of all Beings, you will be known as Sakyamuni."

When young Sumati had received this prediction from the Buddha Dipamkara, he, at that very moment, rose up into the air to the height of seven palm trees. And his hair fell out, and other even better hair appeared in its place. And a great many people, seeing him aloft in midair, made this firm resolve: "When this one attains to the highest knowledge, may we become his disciples."

And the girl too made a vow: "When you fulfill your resolve to become a Buddha, a guide, then I would be your wife, your constant companion in the Dharma. When you become completely enlightened, a most excellent trainer of the world, then I would, at that time, become your disciple. . . ."

[What do you think monks? asked the Buddha.] He who was in that time King Vasava, he is now King Bimbisara; and those who were his eighty thousand ministers are now eighty thousand deities; . . . and she who was the girl, is now Yasodhara; and he who was Sumati—that was myself, practicing the bodhisattva path.

Source: John S. Strong, trans., *The Experience of Buddhism* (Belmont, Cal.: Wadsworth Thomas, 2002), 19–23.

The Loss of One's Children

In this well-known tale, the ill-starred Patacara learns of the uncertainties of family life as she loses not just her husband and two sons, but her natal family, as well. With her bereavement amply dramatized, the story comes to closure by demonstrating that even such monstrous losses, and especially the loss of sons, can be countenanced by turning to the Buddha, who is shown sagely offering a teaching that renders these dark truths about life acceptable.

Document 5–3

The Conversion of the Nun, Patacara

At the time of the birth of the Buddha, a certain girl was born in Sravasti in the household of a guild master. When she had come of age, she secretly became sexually intimate with a workman in her household. In due time, however, her parents decided that she was to marry into a family of the same caste as her own. In desperation, she said to her lover: "Starting tomorrow, a hundred guards will prevent you from seeing me; if you are up to the task, take me away with you right now!"

"All right," he replied, and taking a certain amount of movable wealth, he went with her three or four leagues from the city, where they took up residence in a village. In time, she became pregnant, and when she was about to give birth, she said: "Husband, we are without resources in this place, let us go back and have this child in my family's home."

But he only said: "Shall we go today? Shall we go tomorrow?" Unable to decide, he let time pass.

Seeing him procrastinate in this way, she thought, "This fool will never take me." So, when he was out of the house, she set off on her own, thinking, "I will return home by myself!"

When her husband got back to the house, he did not find her anywhere. He asked the neighbors where she was, and they told him she had gone home. "Because of me, this daughter of a good family has become destitute," he thought, and he set out after her and caught up with her.

There on the road, she went into labor and gave birth. Thus, the very purpose for which they had set out had become accomplished in mid-journey. And thinking, "Why do we now need to go on?" they returned to the village.

Once again, she became pregnant, and everything repeated itself just as it had happened before. This time, however, when she went into labor and gave birth in the middle of the road, great clouds arose in all four directions. She said to her husband: "Husband, unseasonably, storm clouds have arisen all around; try to make me a shelter from the rain."

"I will do so," he replied, and built a hut out of sticks. Then, thinking he would get some grass for the roof, he went off to cut some at the foot of an anthill. But a black snake who lived in the anthill bit him on the foot, and he fell to the ground in that very place.

She spent the whole night, thinking: "He will come back now! He will come back now!" Then she thought: "Surely, he thinks I am a destitute woman, so he has abandoned me on the road and gone away." But when it became light the next day, she followed his tracks and saw him fallen, dead, at the foot of the anthill.

"My man has perished because of me!" she lamented, and taking her younger child on her hip and holding the elder by the hand, she went along the road until she came to a river flowing across her path.

"Now I cannot carry both children across at once," she reflected. "I will leave the elder on this bank, carry the younger one across to the other bank, put him down on a piece of cloth, come back again to get this one, and go on." So she entered the river and carried the baby across. But when, on her way back, she reached the middle of the stream, a hawk, thinking, "Here is a piece of meat," arrived to peck at the infant left on the bank. She waved her hand in order to scare the bird away. Seeing her gesture, the elder boy thought, "She is calling me" and went down into the river. He fell into the stream and was carried away by it. The hawk then carried off the infant, just before she could reach it. Overwhelmed by great sorrow, she went down the middle of the road, wailing this song of lament:

> Both my sons are gone
> and my husband is dead upon the road!

Thus lamenting, she arrived in Sravasti and went to the well-to-do neighborhood where she had lived, but . . . she was not able to find her own home.

"In this place, there is a family of such and such a name," she said. "Which one is their house?"

"Why do you ask about that family? The house where they dwelt was blown down by a great gust of wind, and all of them lost their lives. They are now, young and old, being burned right there, on a single funeral pyre. Look, you can still see the smoke."

Hearing this, she cried: "What are you saying?" And unable to bear even the clothes her body was dressed in, she stripped them off and, crying with outstretched arms the way she had at birth, she went to her family's funeral pyre and gave voice to this lament of total grief:

> Both my sons are gone
> and my husband is dead upon the road!
> And my mother and father and brother
> burn on a single pyre!

Again and again she tore off the garments that people gave her and threw them away. . . .

One day, when the Buddha was preaching the Dharma to a great crowd of people, she entered the monastery and stood at the edge of the assembly. The Master, spreading out his pervasive loving-kindness, said to her: "Sister, regain awareness, acquire mindfulness."

As soon as she heard the words of the Master, she became profoundly ashamed and fearful, and she sat down right there on the ground. A man standing nearby threw her his outer garment. She put it on and listened to the Dharma. With reference to her conduct, the Master then recited this verse from the *Dhammapada*:

> Neither sons, nor parents, nor kinfolk are a refuge.
> Relatives offer no shelter for one seized by Death.
> Knowing this situation, the wise, exercising moral restraint,
> can quickly clear the way that leads to nirvana.

At the end of the verse, even as she stood there, she was established in the fruit of stream-winner [the first level of Buddhist sainthood]. She approached the Master, venerated him, and asked to be ordained. He agreed to her ordination, telling her to go to the home of the nuns and wander forth there. She was ordained, and it was not long before she obtained arhatship, and grasping the word of the Buddha, she became a master of the book of the discipline (Vinaya). Subsequently, when the Master was seated at the Jetavana and assigning statuses to each of the nuns, he established Patacara as the foremost of those knowing the Vinaya.

Source: John S. Strong, trans., *The Experience of Buddhism* (Belmont, Cal.: Wadsworth Thomas, 2002), 56–58.

The following story, in the category of child loss, represents a good example of how the Buddhist tradition found a way to incorporate a long-standing set of pan-Indian myths about infant-eating goddesses, myths that coalesced around the figure of Hariti. Because the narrative is unusually long, I have chosen to use Reiko Ohnuma's summary of it; and, since her interlinear comments are useful in interpreting the details, I have included them as well. Key to understanding the Buddhist interest in turning this story into part of the Buddhist "canon" is that Hariti not only submits to the Buddha but that the Buddha institutes a ritual by which monks mollify such malevolent forces as they take their daily meals.

Document 5–4

Hariti, The Infant-Eating Demoness

The fullest version of her story can be found in the Chinese translation of the Mulasarvastivada Vinaya, the monastic disciplinary code for the Mulasarvastivada school. Here, we are told that Hariti is a *yaksini* (female demon) who lives in the city of Rajagrha at the time of the Buddha. She is married to the male demon Pancika, and together, they have five hundred sons, the youngest of whom is Priyankara, who is the favorite of his mother. Although Hariti comes from a family of virtuous and benevolent demons, because of "a criminal vow formed in a previous existence," she (with the help of her sons) engages in the habit of stealing and devouring all of the human children of Rajagrha. As more and more of their children die, the people of Rajagrha finally turn to the Buddha for help. He responds by going to Hariti's abode while she is out and hiding her youngest son Priyankara under his begging bowl. When Hariti returns and cannot find her youngest child, she is overwhelmed with grief. "Beating her breast, shedding tears of sorrow, her lips and mouth dry and burning, her spirit troubled and lost, her heart torn by suffering," she searches the entire kingdom but cannot find him. She rips off her clothes, lets her hair fly loose, crawls around on her knees and elbows, and then searches the entire world, the four quarters of the universe, the heavens, and the hells. She finally ends up at the abode of the god Vaisravana, who takes pity on her miserable condition and tells her to go to the Buddha, for only he can restore her son.

The story, up to this point, bears a striking resemblance to the stories of the Therigatha [a collection of songs by women who have become Buddhist nuns]. Once again, we have a mother who loses her child and is plunged into grief. Much like Patacara and Vasitthi, she rips off her clothes and lets her hair fly loose, and much like Kisa Gotami, she is finally led to the Buddha by someone who takes pity on her. The Buddha, moreover, once again brings the bereaved mother to her senses by encouraging her to universalize her grief (though in less doctrinal terms than we find in the Therigatha). "Hariti," he says, "because you no longer see one of your five hundred sons, you experience such suffering; so what will be the suffering of those whose only child you take and devour?" When she admits that their suffering must be even greater than her own, he replies: "Hariti, you know well now the suffering of being separated from what one loves. Why, then, do you eat the children of others?" In another version of the story, he further points out that "others love their children, just as you do," and they, too, "go along the streets and lament just like you." And in yet another text, he states: "It is because you yourself love your own son that you eagerly run around, demanding to see him. Why, then, with such cruelty, do you continually devour the children of others? Realize . . . that your feelings are instructing you: No longer kill, no longer torment." Hariti takes the Buddha's words to heart, understands the inherent connection between her own, particular grief and the suffering experienced by others, and, as a consequence, promises to give up her child-snatching ways. Like the nuns of the Therigatha, Hariti succeeds in universalizing her grief and is spiritually transformed in the process.

In spite of these similarities to the stories of the Therigatha, however, the remainder of Hariti's story goes in a significantly different direction. For once Hariti has made the transition from particularistic grief to universal insight, the Buddha *restores her beloved son to her*, and she becomes a loving mother once more—taking refuge in the Three Jewels [the Buddha, the Dharma, and the Sangha—the Buddhist community] and accepting the five precepts, and thereby becoming a laywoman rather than a celibate nun. Continuing to show a mother's concern for her own children, moreover, she then asks the Buddha how she will feed her five hundred children if they can no longer devour human babies, whereupon the Buddha strikes her a bargain: Every day, throughout all of the monasteries of India, Buddhist monks will make food offerings to her and her children after finishing their own meal. They will keep her and her children fed, but in exchange for this, she must agree to do two things: protect all Buddhist monasteries from harm, and respond to the pleas of childless parents by allowing them to have offspring. The ritual cult of Hariti described in these texts does, indeed, seem to have existed throughout India; the Chinese pilgrim I-ching (who traveled throughout India in the late seventh century CE) tells us that "the image of Hariti is found either in the porch or in a corner of the dining-hall of all Indian monasteries," and "every day an abundant offering of food is made before this image." Surviving shrines dedicated to Hariti have been found at various Buddhist monastic sites, with Hariti generally depicted as a benevolent mother-figure holding one baby in her arms and having another three to five children around her knees.

Source: Summarized by Reiko Ohnuma in her "Mother-Love and Mother-Grief: South Asian Buddhist Variations on a Theme," forthcoming in *Journal of Feminist Studies in Religion*; the narrative is found in the Chinese translation of the Mulasarvastivada Vinaya, translated into French by N. Peri in his "Hariti, la mère-de-demons," in *Bulletin de l'École Français d'Extrême-Orient* 17 (1917): 1–102.

The Buddha as Source of Fertility

In the famous story of Sujata, supposedly the first female to convert to Buddhism, the Buddha's spiritual success is again linked to family concerns, and fertility in particular. On the night of his enlightenment, Sujata offers him a bowl of rice-milk, and it is due to this rich meal that the Buddha is able to achieve enlightenment. However, around this simple act, the story develops several layers of complexity. First, Sujata is said to make her offering to the Buddha through misrecognizing him as a tree-spirit whom she thinks responsible for granting her the birth of her son,

Yasa. This error in no way ruins her offering, either for her own karmic account or for the Buddha's enlightenment that follows. In fact, this erroneous offering opens the door to another cycle of action that more closely links the Buddha's enlightenment to Sujata's family, since once Yasa has grown up, he, just as the Buddha supposedly had done, one day finds his harem disgusting and leaves. Thus, the son that Sujata "mistakenly" thanked the Buddha for turns out to behave just like the Buddha. And, since the story offers no explanation for this odd parallel, one might be tempted to read Yasa's action as proof that in some way the Buddha's identity was passed on to him due to his mother's gift to the Buddha. However one chooses to read that section of the narrative, the connections between this family and the Buddha are more amply developed when Yasa's father comes to the Buddha to find out what happened to his son—presumably a point of conflict that the story wants to negotiate—and the Buddha magically hides Yasa while he gives the father a Dharma lesson. This lesson results in both Yasa and his father awakening to the status of arhants, free forever from samsara. However, the story is not over until Yasa, as a monk, returns one day to beg from his homestead only to use the opportunity to preach Dharma to his mother who, too, achieves arhant status.

Thus in a cleverly wrought narrative, the story mediates the conflict between family and Buddhist renunciation, and even suggests that Dharma can, in reverse, work its way back into the family, in this case via Yasa's renunciation, so that his mother and father are indirectly saved as the result of their son's exit. Better still, all this is implicitly effected through the mother's unwitting gift to the Buddha that aided him at the crucial final moment before achieving enlightenment and also set in motion the cycle of events that would result in her entire family finding Buddhist salvation.[16]

Document 5–5

The Story of Sujata

Long ago, at the time of the past Buddha Padumuttara, a woman was born into a good family in Hamsavati. One day, after listening to the Master preach the Dharma and witnessing his establishment of a laywoman as "foremost of those taking refuge," she made a formal resolution, aspiring to attain that same status herself.

For one hundred thousand aeons, she was repeatedly reborn in samsara, in the realms of gods and humans, until just before our own Master Gotama's birth [the buddha of our era], she was reborn in the house of the landlord Senani in the village of Senani in Uruvela. Once she had come of age, she made this promise to the god of a banyan tree: "If, once I am married to someone of the same caste, my first child is a son, I will, every year, make a food offering to you."

Her wish was successful and a son, Yasa, was born to her. Then, on the full moon day of the month of Visakha, when coincidentally the six years of the bodhisatta's practice of extreme asceticism were just about over, she got up early in the morning and milked her cow before dawn, thinking, "Today, I will make that food offering!" The cow's calves had not yet suckled, but as soon as a new pot was put under the udder, the milk flowed out of its own accord. Marveling at this, Sujata took the milk in her own hand and directed it into the new pot, and she herself put it on the fire to cook. And when that milk-rice started to boil, great bubbles appeared, and auspiciously turned to the right. So that in bursting they would not splash over the sides, the god Brahma held an umbrella [as a lid over the pot], . . . while Indra regulated the fire, and the gods of the four directions added a divine nutritive essence to the milk-rice.

Beholding all these marvels, Sujata said to her servant Punna: "It has been a long time since I have seen so many good omens; go quickly and prepare the place of the god!"

"Yes, mistress," she answered, and as told, she hurried to the foot of the banyan tree.

Now the bodhisatta [the Buddha] had gotten up early, and waiting for the time of the begging round, he was sitting under that tree. And Punna, arriving at that pure place, mistook him for the tree god. She went back to Sujata and said: "The divinity is seated at the foot of the tree!"

Sujata replied, "Ah! If what you say is true, then it was he who gave me my son!" And putting on all of her ornaments she piled the milk-rice on a golden plate worth a hundred thousand pieces of gold, enclosed it in another golden bowl, wrapped it in a white cloth, added wreaths of sweet-smelling garlands, picked it up, and set forth. When she saw the Great Man [the Buddha], there arose in her an overpowering gladness, and she bowed down very low in front of him, touching her head to the ground. Uncovering the dish of milk-rice, she offered it to the Blessed One [the Buddha] with her own hand, saying, "Just as my wish has been fulfilled, so may yours be accomplished." Then she went away.

The bodhisatta went to the bank of the Neranjana River and put the golden dish down there on the shore; he bathed, got out, fashioned the milk-rice into four balls, and ate it. He then washed the dish in the river, and in due course he went to the seat of enlightenment, attained omniscience, spent seven times seven days contemplating his enlightenment, and set in motion the excellent wheel of the Dharma at the Deer Park of Isipatana.

In the meantime, Sujata's son, Yasa, had grown, and the Buddha, realizing that he had within him the conditions necessary for enlightenment, went and sat down under another tree planning to encounter him. Young Yasa, finding the door to his harem open at midnight, was suddenly full of restlessness. Muttering:

"How depressing! How distressing [is this life of sensual pleasure]!" he left his house, went out of the city, happened across the Blessed One, heard from him the teaching of the Dharma, and attained the first three fruits of the path.

Then his father, searching for him, followed his tracks until he too came to the Blessed One. He asked what had happened to his son. The Master, however, concealed young Yasa by making him invisible and preached the Dharma to his father. At the end of the sermon, Yasa's father attained the fruit of entering the stream, and Yasa [who, though invisible, had been listening], became an arhat. The Blessed One then ordained Yasa simply by saying, "Come, monk," and as soon as he heard those words, the characteristics of a layman in him disappeared and he became like a great elder, bearing a begging bowl and all the requisites of a monk, which had been magically created.

Yasa's father invited the Buddha to their home. The Blessed One, taking young Yasa as his novice disciple, went to their house, ate a meal, and preached the Dharma. At the end of the sermon, Yasa's mother, Sujata, . . . also attained the fruit of entering the stream, . . . and at the same time uttered the formula of the threefold refuge. Subsequently, when the Master was assigning statuses to the laywomen, he established her as the foremost laywoman among those taking refuge.

Source: John S. Strong, trans., *The Experience of Buddhism* (Belmont, Cal.: Wadsworth Thomas, 2002), 48–49.

Good Children Who Save Their Parents with Buddhism

One of the standard tales in the Buddhist repertoire is the account of the filial and loving child who converts to Buddhism and then sets about the task of saving one or both of his parents from unsavory postmortem lives. In the following story of Uttara Saving His Mother, this motif is more tightly focused to make this perfect Buddhist son the redeemer of his wayward and particularly anti-Buddhist mother. Such a story of a perfect Buddhist son saving his unworthy mother seems to have had some widespread appeal in India but it was not until Buddhism went to China that this trope developed more fully in the cycle of tales regarding Mulian that appeared in the fifth and sixth centuries. In fact, it seems that the stories about Mulian saving his mother (see the selection below entitled "The Ghost Festival") were bolstered with details from just this account of Uttara and thus we ought to count the following story as particularly potent in establishing one image of the child in Buddhism. I have included my interlinear notes to help the reader appreciate the logic of the story.

Document 5–6

The Story of the Monk Uttara Saving His Mother

Once there was a pure believer named Uttara who respected the Buddha, delighted in the Dharma, and revered the Sangha. Each month he performed the six vegetarian offerings (*zhai*), took the eight precepts, renounced violence and practiced benevolence. All living beings protected his life and he was called *Zhen Zhong* (Precious Heavy One). Fame and glory could not turn his mind. Voluptuous women and state funds could not disturb his will. He was chaste, honorable, and hard to sway. He did not drink, and he was filial and obedient with regard to his obligations. He would not eat after the [proper] time and, with his mind empty, was endowed with the Way. He did not adorn his body with fragrant flowers or [decorative] pastes. Soldiers with violent weapons could not smash his virtue. He was distant from stupidity and close to rectitude.

After this flattering profile it is said that Uttara, through the agency of Buddhist magical powers, has come to learn of his mother's sinfulness. It seems that she believed in non-Buddhist heterodox teachings and was stingy and greedy. No more is said about her sins or her relationship with her son, other than a sentence noting that he became a monk after her death. The scene then shifts ahead twenty years or more, when Uttara is described—much like the Buddha—sitting under a tree surveying the ten directions and training his mind on nirvana. While he is in this typically Buddhist pose, we are told that he is thinking about his deceased mother and the kindnesses she showed in bearing and raising him:

> With his mind on nirvana, he sat upright under a tree scanning the ten directions, always thinking to himself, "My mother has been dead more than twenty years now; I should try to find where she is because I want to repay the kindness she showed in giving birth to me and raising me (*yu bao shengyang zhi en*)."

That the text says "always thinking to himself" suggests that Uttara has long been preoccupied with the problem of finding and repaying his mother, even though the repayment ritual, soon to be described, only occurs twenty years after her death. While he is in the midst of his apparently regular search for his mother, she suddenly appears to him:

> At that moment a hungry ghost showed up, looking hideous, black, and really disgusting. Her hair was long and tangled about her body; it twisted around her feet, which were dragging dirt. Squatting and staggering forward and back, crying inconsolably, she came to the monk [Uttara] and said, "I

took up with stupid, evil people and did not believe in Buddhism. With a licentious tongue I said whatever I wanted, and now I am a hungry ghost. For twenty-five years I have not seen a monk. Today we have met. Since I died, I am stricken with hunger and thirst. Oh, that heaven would moisten me, mercifully give me some water. Save me, what's left of my life!"

In this initial encounter, the history of the hungry ghost's relationship to the monk is not revealed, although the parallel of twenty-some years implies that the ghost could be the monk's dead mother. As she grovels before him, begging for the simplest of things, he says to her, "The great oceans have pure water, why isn't that enough for you to drink?" She explains that water turns to blood and pus before she can drink it, and that food turns into flaming coals before she can get it into her mouth. Hence she contaminates whatever she wants to ingest. She also complains about evil ghosts who come to beat and skewer her in wanton acts of violence. Answering her, Uttara gives a diagnosis of her past karma to explain why she is suffering so. The ghost admits everything but adds that she had a son who was a perfect Buddhist in every way. She begins to wail, and Uttara tries to console her by asking what merit needs to be made to end her suffering. Most interestingly, it is she who knows what needs to be done, even though she is the heretic and he the keen Buddhist:

> The ghost said, "With a jar full of water that has a poplar twig set in the middle, or with Dharma robes, make offerings to the monks. Also offer them food and use my name in the dedication of merit, making [the monks] say, 'May she have clothes and food, and soon end her life as a hungry ghost.'" Everything was done accordingly . . . and she was reborn where there was a great lotus pond, and she had five hundred attendants.

Source: Alan Cole trans., from Baochang, *Details on Sutras and Vinayas*, of 516, printed in the *Taisho shinshu daizokyo*, T. 53.107b.2ff., in *Mothers and Sons in Chinese Buddhism* (Stanford: Stanford University Press, 1998), 57–60; see 247–248 for more bibliographic information.

Buddhist Advice for Being a Good Son

In this important text that appears to have been well known in Southeast Asia and East Asia, the Buddha is shown supplementing a father's advice to his son. At the moment of the discussion, the son is, in accordance with his deceased father's instructions, performing prostrations in the six directions–the four cardinal directions plus up and down–without assigning any particular meaning to this daily gesture. The Buddha intervenes and explains to the boy, in detail, how to organize these ritual observances so that they function to articulate and reaffirm all his familial and social obligations, even as the Buddha explains how to set all these responsibilities within a wider Buddhist context. The Buddha first—and this section seems rather unrelated and has been omitted here—explains lists of four and six items relevant to Buddhist ethics and practice that presumably could be correlated with the four and six directions. Then, in the second half of the work, the Buddha takes up the more germane topic of mapping the bowing in the six directions onto the boy's social world. Thus, beginning with a bow to the east, he is to honor his mother and father, followed by a bow to the south representing his teachers, then to the west for his wife and children, to the north for his friends, with the nadir reserved for his servants, and the zenith position, not surprisingly, held by ascetics. By supposedly advocating this handy ritual design, the Buddha is shown both fulfilling what the boy's biological father had failed to transmit to him, and giving the boy (and the reader) the structure and content to create a hierarchical, and yet integrated, map of familial, social, and religious obligation.[17]

Document 5–7

The Sigalaka Sutta: In the Dighanikaya

Thus have I heard. Once the Lord was staying at Rajagaha, at the Squirrels' Feeding Place in the Bamboo Grove. And at that time Sigalaka the householder's son, having got up early and gone out of Rajagaha, was paying homage, with wet clothes and hair and with joined palms, to the different directions: to the east, the south, the west, the north, the nadir and the zenith.

And the Lord, having risen early and dressed, took his robe and bowl and went to Rajagaha for alms. And seeing Sigalaka paying homage to the different directions, he said: "Householder's son, why have you got up early to pay homage to the different directions?" "Lord, my father, when he was dying, told me to do so. And so, Lord, out of respect for my father's words, which I revere, honor and hold sacred, I have got up thus early to pay homage in this way to the six directions." "But, householder's son, that is not the right way to pay homage to the six directions according to the Ariyan discipline." "Well, Lord, how should one pay homage to the six directions according to the Ariyan discipline? It would be good if the Blessed Lord were to teach me the proper way to pay homage to the six directions according to the Ariyan discipline." "Then listen carefully, pay attention, and I will speak." "Yes, Lord," said Sigalaka, and the Lord said: . . .

"And how, householder's son, does the Ariyan [Buddhist] disciple protect the six directions? These six things are to be regarded as the six directions. The east denotes mother and father. The south denotes teachers. The west denotes wife and children. The north denotes friends and companions. The nadir denotes servants, workers and helpers. The zenith denotes ascetics and Brahmins.

"There are five ways in which a son should minister to his mother and father as the eastern direction. [He should think] 'Having been supported by them, I will support them. I will perform their duties for them. I will keep up the family tradition. I will be worthy of my heritage. After my parents' deaths I will distribute gifts on their behalf.' And there are five ways in which the parents, so ministered to by their son as the eastern direction, will reciprocate: they will restrain him from evil, support him in doing good, teach him some skill, find him a suitable wife and, in due time, hand over his inheritance to him. In this way the eastern direction is covered, making it at peace and free from fear.

"There are five ways in which pupils should minister to their teachers as the southern direction: by rising to greet them, by waiting on them, by being attentive, by serving them, by mastering the skills they teach. And there are five ways in which their teachers, thus ministered to by their pupils as the southern direction, will reciprocate: they will give thorough instruction, make sure they have grasped what they should have duly grasped, give them a thorough grounding in all skills, recommend them to their friends and colleagues, and provide them with security in all directions. In this way the southern direction is covered, making it at peace and free from fear.

"There are five ways in which a husband should minister to his wife as the western direction: by honoring her, by not disparaging her, by not being unfaithful to her, by giving authority to her, by providing her with adornments. And there are five ways in which a wife, thus ministered to by her husband as the western direction, will reciprocate: by properly organizing her work, by being kind to the servants, by not being unfaithful, by protecting stores, and by being skilful and diligent in all she has to do. In this way the western direction is covered, making it at peace and free from fear.

"There are five ways in which a man should minister to his friends and companions as the northern direction: by gifts, by kindly words, by looking after their welfare, by treating them like himself, and by keeping his word. And there are five ways in which friends and companions, thus ministered to by a man as the northern direction, will reciprocate: by looking after him when he is inattentive, by looking after his property when he is inattentive, by being a refuge when he is afraid, by not deserting him when he is in trouble, and by showing concern for his children. In this way the northern direction is covered, making it at peace and free from fear.

"There are five ways in which a master should minister to his servants and workpeople as the nadir: by arranging their work according to their strength, by supplying them with food and wages, by looking after them when they are ill, by sharing special delicacies with them, and by letting them off work at the right time. And there are five ways in which servants and workpeople, thus ministered to by their master as the nadir, will reciprocate: they will get up before him, go to bed after him, take only what they are given, do their work properly, and be bearers of his praise and good repute. In this way the nadir is covered, making it at peace and free from fear.

"There are five ways in which a man should minister to ascetics and Brahmins as the zenith: by kindness in bodily deed, speech and thought, by keeping open house for them, by supplying their bodily needs. And the ascetics and Brahmins, thus ministered to by him as the zenith, will reciprocate in six ways: they will restrain him from evil, encourage him to do good, be benevolently compassionate towards him, teach him what he has not heard, and point out to him the way to heaven. In this way the zenith is covered, making it at peace and free from fear." Thus the Lord spoke.

And the Well-Farer [the Buddha] having spoken, the Teacher [the Buddha] added:

> Mother, father are the east,
> Teachers are the southward point,
> Wife and children are the west,
> Friends and colleagues are the north.
> Servants and workers are below,
> Ascetics, Brahmins are above.
> These directions all should be
> Honoured by a clansman true.
> He who's wise and disciplined,
> Kindly and intelligent,
> Humble, free from pride,
> Such a one may honour gain.
> Early rising, scorning sloth,
> Unshaken by adversity,
> Of faultless conduct, ready wit,
> Such a one may honour gain.
> Making friends, and keeping them,
> Welcoming, no stingy host,
> A guide, philosopher and friend,
> Such a one may honour gain.
> Giving gifts and kindly speech,
> A life well-spent for others' good,
> Even-handed in all things,
> Impartial as each case demands:
> These things make the world go round
> Like the chariot's axle-pin.
> If such things did not exist,
> No mother from her son would get

Any honour and respect,
Nor father either, as their due.
But since these qualities are held
By the wise in high esteem,
They are given prominence
And are rightly praised by all.

At these words Sigalaka said to the Lord: "Excellent, Reverend Gotama, excellent! It is as if someone were to set up what had been knocked down, or to point out the way to one who had got lost, or to bring an oil-lamp into a dark place, so that those with eyes could see what was there. Just so the Reverend Gotama has expounded the Dhamma in various ways. May the Reverend Gotama accept me as a lay-follower from this day forth as long as life shall last!"

Source: *The Long Discourses of the Buddha: A Translation of the Dighanikaya*, translated by Maurice Walshe (Boston: Wisdom, 1987), 461–469.

Buddhist Identity as Sonship to the Buddha

In the following two selections we find extended parables in which Mahayana Buddhist identity is promoted as a kind of sonship. These two narratives, drawn from the *Lotus Sutra*, demonstrate that at the beginning of the Common Era an image of perfect Buddhist identity was proferred to readers in such a way that they were asked to identify themselves as sons of the Buddha and to find a likeness of themselves in the sons presented in these two parables, sons who seem less than wise about the ways of Buddhism, even though in the course of the narratives they gain some insight into the Buddha's paternal strategies for delivering them from the suffering of samsara.

Document 5–8

The Parable of the Burning House
from Chapter 3 of the *Lotus Sutra*

"Moreover, Sariputra, I too will now make use of similes and parables to further clarify this doctrine. For through similes and parables those who are wise can obtain understanding.

"Sariputra, suppose that in a certain town in a certain country there was a very rich man. He was far along in years and his wealth was beyond measure. He had many fields, houses and menservants. His own house was big and rambling, but it had only one gate. A great many people—a hundred, two hundred, perhaps as many as five hundred—lived in the house. The halls and rooms were old and decaying, the walls crumbling, the pillars rotten at their base, and the beams and rafters crooked and aslant.

"At that time a fire suddenly broke out on all sides, spreading through the rooms of the house. The sons of the rich man, ten, twenty, perhaps thirty, were inside the house. When the rich man saw the huge flames leaping up on every side, he was greatly alarmed and fearful and thought to himself, I can escape to safety through the flaming gate, but my sons are inside the burning house enjoying themselves and playing games, unaware, unknowing, without alarm or fear. The fire is closing in on them, suffering and pain threaten them, yet their minds have no sense of loathing or peril and they do not think of trying to escape!"

Sariputra, this rich man thought to himself, I have strength in my body and arms. I can wrap them in a robe or place them on a bench and carry them out of the house. And then again he thought, This house has only one gate, and moreover it is narrow and small. My sons are very young, they have no understanding, and they love their games, being so engrossed in them that they are likely to be burned in the fire. I must explain to them why I am fearful and alarmed. The house is already in flames and I must get them out quickly and not let them be burned up in the fire!

"Having thought in this way, he followed his plan and called to all his sons, saying, 'You must come out at once!' But though the father was moved by pity and gave good words of instruction, the sons were absorbed in their games and unwilling to heed him. They had no alarm, no fright, and in the end no mind to leave the house. Moreover, they did not understand what the fire was, what the house was, what danger was. They merely raced about this way and that in play and looked at their father without heeding him.

"At that time the rich man had this thought: The house is already in flames from this huge fire. If I and my sons do not get out at once, we are certain to be burned. I must now invent some expedient means that will make it possible for the children to escape harm.

"The father understood his sons and knew what various toys and curious objects each child customarily like and what would delight them. And so he said to them, 'The kind of playthings you like are rare and hard to find. If you do not take them when you can, you will surely regret it later. For example, things like these goat-carts, deer-carts, and ox-carts. They are outside the gate now where you can play with them. So you must come out of this burning house at once. Then whatever ones you want, I will give them all to you!'

"At that time, when the sons heard their father telling them about these rare playthings, because such things were just what they had wanted, each felt emboldened in heart and, pushing and shoving one another, they all came wildly dashing out of the burning house.

"At this time the rich man, seeing that his sons had gotten out safely and all were seated on the open ground at the crossroads and were no longer in danger, was greatly relieved and his mind danced for joy. At that time each of the sons said to his father, 'The playthings you promised us earlier, the goat-carts and deer-carts and ox-carts—please give them to us now!'

"Sariputra, at that time the rich man gave to each of his sons a large carriage of uniform size and quality. The carriages were tall and spacious and adorned with numerous jewels. A railing ran all around them and bells hung from all four sides. A canopy was stretched over the top, which was also decorated with an assortment of precious jewels. Ropes of jewels twined around, a fringe of flowers hung down, and layers of cushions were spread inside, on which were placed vermilion pillows. Each carriage was drawn by a white ox, pure and clean in hide, handsome in form and of great strength, capable of pulling the carriage smoothly and properly at a pace fast as the wind. In addition, there were many grooms and servants to attend and guard the carriage.

"What was the reason for this? This rich man's wealth was limitless and he had many kinds storehouses that were all filled and overflowing. And he thought to himself, There is no end to my possessions. It would not be right if I were to give my sons small carriages of inferior make. These little boys are all my sons and I love them without partiality. I have countless numbers of large carriages adorned with seven kinds of gems. I should be fair-minded and give one to each of my sons. I should not show any discrimination. Why? Because even if I distributed these possessions of mine to every person in the whole country I would still not exhaust them, much less could I do so by giving them to my sons!

"At that time each of the sons mounted his large carriage, gaining something he had never had before, something he had originally never expected. Sariputra, what do you think of this? When this rich man impartially handed out to his sons these big carriages adorned with rare jewels, was he guilty of falsehood or not?"

Sariputra said, "No, World-Honored One [the Buddha]. This rich man simply made it possible for his sons to escape the peril of fire and preserve their lives. He did not commit a falsehood. Why do I say this? Because if they were able to preserve their lives, then they had already obtained a plaything of sorts. And how much more so when, through an expedient means, they are rescued from that burning house! World Honored One, even if the rich man had not even given them the tiniest carriage, he would still not be guilty of falsehood. Why? Because this rich man had earlier made up his mind that he would employ an expedient means to cause his sons to escape. Using a device of this kind was no act of falsehood. How much less so, then, when the rich man knew that his wealth was limitless and he intended to enrich and benefit his sons by giving each of them a large carriage."

The Buddha said to Sariputra, "Very good, very good. It is just as you have said. And Sariputra, the Thus Come One [the Buddha] is like this. That is, he is a father to all the world. His fears, cares and anxieties, ignorance and misunderstanding have long come to an end, leaving no residue. He has fully succeeded in acquiring measureless insight, power and freedom from fear and gaining great supernatural powers and the power of wisdom. He is endowed with expedient means and the paramita of wisdom, his great pity and great compassion are constant and unflagging; at all times he seeks what is good and will bring benefit to all.

"He is born into the threefold world, a burning house, rotten and old, in order to save living beings from the fires of birth, old age, sickness and death, care, suffering, stupidity, misunderstanding, and the three poisons; to teach and convert them and enable them to attain anuttara–samyak–sambodhi [limitless enlightenment].

"He sees living beings seared and consumed by birth, old age, sickness and death, care and suffering, sees them undergo many kinds of pain because of the five desires and the desire for wealth and profit. Again, because of their greed and attachment and striving they undergo numerous pains in their present existence, and later they undergo the pain of being reborn in hell or as beasts or hungry spirits. Even if they are reborn in the heavenly realm or the realm of human beings, they undergo the pain of poverty and want, the pain of parting from loved ones, the pain of encountering those they detest—all these many different kinds of pain.

"Yet living beings, drowned in the midst of all this, delight and amuse themselves, unaware, unknowing, without alarm or fear. They feel no sense of loathing and make no attempt to escape. In this burning house which is the threefold world, they race about to east and west, and though they encounter great pain, they are not distressed by it.

"Sariputra, when the Buddha sees this, then he thinks to himself, I am the father of living beings and I should rescue them from their sufferings and give them the joy of the measureless and boundless Buddha wisdom so that they may find their enjoyment in that."

Source: Kumarajiva's Chinese version of the *The Lotus Sutra*, translated by Burton Watson (New York: Columbia University Press, 1993), 56–59.

The second father-son story in the *Lotus Sutra* is told from the point of view of four of his disciples who address the Buddha, here titled "World Honored One," and recount the case of the misguided son who ran away from his fearsomely rich father and was only slowly coaxed to return to the homestead by his wily father's various ploys.

Document 5–9

The Parable of the Burning House
from Chapter 4 of the *Lotus Sutra*

"World-Honored One, we would be pleased now to employ a parable to make clear our meaning. Suppose there was a man, still young in years, who abandoned his father, ran away, and lived for a long time in another land, for perhaps ten, twenty, or even fifty years. As he grew older, he found himself increasingly poor and in want. He hurried about in every direction, seeking for clothing and food, wandering farther and farther afield until by chance he turned his steps in the direction of his homeland.

"The father meanwhile had been searching for his son without success and had taken up residence in a certain city. The father's household was very wealthy, with immeasurable riches and treasures. Gold, silver, lapis lazuli, coral, amber, and crystal beads all filled and overflowed from his storehouses. He had many grooms and menservants, clerks and attendants, and elephants, horses, carriages, oxen, and goats beyond number. He engaged in profitable ventures at home and in all the lands around, and also had dealings with many merchants and traveling vendors.

"At this time the impoverished son wandered from village to village, passing through various lands and towns, till at last he came to the city where his father was residing. The father thought constantly of his son, but though he had been parted from him for over fifty years, he had never told anyone else about the matter. He merely pondered to himself, his heart filled with regret and longing. He thought to himself that he was old and decrepit. He had great wealth and possessions, gold, silver, and rare treasures that filled and over-flowed from his storehouses, but he had no son, so that if one day he should die, the wealth and possessions would be scattered and lost, for there was no one to entrust them to.

"This was the reason he constantly thought so earnestly of his son. And he also had this thought: If I could find my son and entrust my wealth and posses-sions to him, then I could feel contented and easy in mind and would have no more worries.

"World-Honored One, at that time the impoverished son drifted from one kind of employment to another until he came by chance to his father's house. He stood by the side of the gate, gazing far off at his father, who was seated on a lion throne, his legs supported by a jeweled footrest, while Brahmans, noblemen, and householders, uniformly deferential, surrounded him. Festoons of pearls worth thousands or tens of thousands adorned his body, and clerks, grooms, and menservants holding white fly whisks stood in attendance to left and right. A jeweled canopy covered him, with flowered banners hanging from it, perfumed water had been sprinkled over the ground, heaps of rare flowers were scattered about, and precious objects were ranged here and there, brought out, put away, handed over and received. Such were the many different types of adornments, the emblems of prerogative and marks of distinction.

"When the impoverished son saw how great was his father's power and authority, he was filled with fear and awe and regretted he had ever come to such a place. Secretly he thought to himself: This must be some king, or one who is equal to a King. This is not the sort of place where I can hire out my labor and gain a living. It would be better to go to some poor village where, if I work hard, I will find a place and can easily earn food and clothing. If I stay here for long, I may be seized and pressed into service! Having thought in this way, he raced from the spot.

"At that time the rich old man, seated on his lion throne, spied his son and recognized him immediately. His heart was filled with great joy and at once he thought: Now I have someone to entrust my storehouses of wealth and possessions to! My thoughts have constantly been with this son of mine, but I had no way of seeing him. Now suddenly he has appeared of himself, which is exactly what I would have wished. Though I am old and decrepit, I still care what becomes of my belongings.

"Thereupon he dispatched a bystander to go after the son as quickly as possible and bring him back. At that time the messenger raced swiftly after the son and laid hold of him. The impoverished son, alarmed and fearful, cried out in an angry voice, 'I have done nothing wrong! Why am I being seized?' But the messenger held on to him more tightly than ever and forcibly dragged him back.

"At that time the son thought to himself, I have committed no crime and yet I am taken prisoner. Surely I am going to be put to death! He was more terrified than ever and sank to the ground, fainting with despair.

"The father, observing this from a distance, spoke to the messenger, saying, 'I have no need of this man. Don't force him to come here, but sprinkle cold water on his face so he will regain his senses. Then say nothing more to him!'

"Why did he do that? Because the father knew that his son was of humble outlook and ambition, and that his own rich and eminent position would be difficult for the son to accept. He knew very well that this was his son, but as a form of expedient means he refrained from saying to anyone, 'This is my son.'

"The messenger said to the son, 'I am releasing you now. You may go anywhere you wish.' The impoverished son was delighted, having gained what he had not had before, and picked himself up from the ground and went off to the poor village in order to look for food and clothing.

"At that time the rich man, hoping to entice his son back again, decided to employ an expedient means and sent two men as secret messengers, men who were lean and haggard and had no imposing appearance. 'Go seek out that poor man and approach him casually. Tell him you know a place where he can earn twice the regular wage. If he agrees to the arrangement, then bring him here and put him to work. If he asks what sort of work he will be put to, say that he will be employed to clear away excrement, and that the two of you will be working with him.'

"The two messengers then set out at once to find the poor man, and when they had done so, spoke to him as they had been instructed. At that time the impoverished son asked for an advance on his wages and then went with the men to help clear away excrement.

"When the father saw his son, he pitied and wondered at him. Another day, when he was gazing out the window, he saw his son in the distance, his body thin and haggard, filthy with excrement, dirt, sweat, and defilement. The father immediately took off his necklaces, his soft fine garments and his other adornments and put on clothes that were ragged and soiled. He smeared dirt on his body, took in his right hand a utensil for removing excrement, and assuming a gruff manner, spoke to the laborers, saying, 'Keep at your work! You mustn't be lazy!' By employing this expedient means, he was able to approach his son.

"Later he spoke to his son again, saying, 'Now then, young man! You must keep on at this work and not leave me anymore. I will increase your wages, and whatever you need in the way of utensils, rice, flour, salt, vinegar, and the like you should be in no worry about. I have an old servant I can lend you when you need him. You may set your mind at ease. I will be like a father to you, so have no more worries. Why do I say this? Because I am well along in years, but you are still young and sturdy. When you are at work, you are never deceitful or lazy or speak angry or resentful words. You don't seem to have any faults of that kind the way my other workers do. From now on, you will be like my own son.' And the rich man proceeded to select a name and assign it to the man as though he were his child.

"At this time the impoverished son, though he was delighted at such treatment, still thought of himself as a person of humble station who was in the employ of another. Therefore the rich man kept him clearing away excrement for the next twenty years. By the end of this time, the son felt that he was understood and trusted, and he could come and go at ease, but he continued to live in the same place as before.

"World-Honored One, at that time the rich man fell ill and knew that he would die before long. He spoke to his impoverished son, saying, 'I now have great quantities of gold, silver, and rare treasures that fill and overflow from my storehouses. You are to take complete charge of the amounts I have and of what is to be handed out and gathered in. This is what I have in mind, and I want you to carry out my wishes. Why is this? Because from now on, you and I will not behave as two different persons. So you must keep your wits about you and see that there are no mistakes or losses.' At that time the impoverished son, having received these instructions, took over the surveillance of all the goods, the gold, silver, and rare treasures, and the various storehouses, but never thought of appropriating for himself so much as the cost of a single meal. He continued to live where he had before, unable to cease thinking of himself as mean and lowly.

"After some time had passed, the father perceived that his son was bit by bit becoming more self-assured and magnanimous in outlook, that he was determined to accomplish great things and despised his former low opinion of himself. Realizing that his own end was approaching, he ordered his son to arrange a meeting with his relatives and the king of the country, the high ministers, and the noblemen and householders. When they were all gathered together, he proceeded to make this announcement: 'Gentlemen, you should know that this is my son, who was born to me. In such-and-such a city he abandoned me and ran away, and for over fifty years he wandered about suffering hardship. His original name is such-and-such, and my name is such-and-such. In the past, when I was still living in my native city, I worried about him and so I set out in search of him. Sometime after, I suddenly chanced to meet up with him. This is in truth my son, and I in truth am his father. Now everything that belongs to me, all my wealth and possessions, shall belong entirely to this son of mine. Matters of outlay and income that have occurred in the past this son of mine is familiar with.'

"World-Honored One, when the impoverished son heard these words of his father, he was filled with great joy, having gained what he never had before, and he thought to himself, I originally had no mind to covet or seek such things. Yet now these stores of treasures have come of their own accord!

"World-Honored One, this old man with his great riches is none other than the Thus Come One, and we are all like the Buddha's sons. The Thus Come One constantly tells us that we are his sons. But because of the three sufferings, World-Honored One, in the midst of birth and death we undergo burning anxieties, delusions, and ignorance, delighting in and clinging to lesser doctrines. But today the World-Honored One causes us to ponder carefully, to cast aside such doctrines, the filth of frivolous debate.

"We were diligent and exerted ourselves in this matter until we had attained nirvana, which is like one day's wages. And once we had attained it, our hearts were filled with great joy and we considered that this was enough. At once we said to ourselves, 'Because we have been diligent and exerted ourselves with regard to the Buddhist Law, we have gained this breadth and wealth of understanding.'

"But the World-Honored One, knowing from past times how our minds cling to unworthy desires and delight in lesser doctrines, pardoned us and let us be, not trying to explain to us by saying, 'You will come to possess the insight of the Thus Come One, your portion of the store of treasures!' Instead the World-Honored One employed the power of expedient means, preaching to us the wisdom of the Thus Come One in such a way that we might heed the Buddha and attain nirvana, which is one day's wages. And because we considered this to be a great gain, we had no wish to pursue the Great Vehicle [the Mahayana form of Buddhism].

"In addition, though we expounded and set forth the Buddha wisdom for the sake of the bodhisattvas, we ourselves did not aspire to attain it. Why do I say this? Because the Buddha, knowing that our minds delight in lesser doctrines, employed the power of expedient means to preach in a way that was appropriate for us, So we did not know that we were in truth the sons of the Buddha. But now at last we know it.

"With regard to the Buddha wisdom, the World-Honored One is never begrudging. Why do I say this? From times past we have in truth been the sons of the Buddha, but we delighted in nothing but lesser doctrines. If we had had the kind of mind that delighted in great ones, then the Buddha would have preached the Law of the Great Vehicle for us.

"Now in this sutra the Buddha expounds only the one vehicle. And in the past, when in the presence of the bodhisattvas he disparaged the voice-hearers [traditional Buddhists] as those who delight in a lesser doctrine [the Hinayana], the Buddha was in fact employing the Great Vehicle to teach and convert us. Therefore we say that, though originally we had no mind to covet or seek such a thing, now the great treasure of the Dharma King has come to us of its own accord. It is something that the sons of the Buddha have a right to acquire, and now they have acquired all of it."

Source: Kumarajiva's Chinese version of the *The Lotus Sutra*, translated by Burton Watson (New York: Columbia University Press, 1993), 81–86.

East Asian Sources

Monkly Sons Who Save Their Mothers, and Ancestors

In developing the motif of the perfect Buddhist son who saves his mother, the following sutra, written in China in the sixth century, explains how Mulian's Buddhist career culminates in his efforts to save his mother. In this version of the story—when it was still relatively simple and free of the graphic descriptions of Mulian's mother's torture in hell—the author is arguing that sons should realize that their lives are not just gifts from their mothers, but gifts that entail repayment. Thus Mulian, and by extension, all sons, ought to recognize the gravity of "milk-debts," and furthermore, realize that refusing to pay these "milk-debts" likely would condemn their mothers to endless eons of suffering in hell. In short, this text makes it clear that to be a good son is to be a good Buddhist in the specific sense of making donations to the Buddhist monasteries during the annual Ghost Festival. Moreover, as several passages make clear, this text works to join Buddhist ethics, and Buddhist identities, with at-home ethics and identities. Thus it is that

Mulian is both a filial son and an elite monk. And, since readers from all levels of society are called on to mimic Mulian, it seems fair to assume that the identity that the text creates for the believing reader is one in which Buddhist models of monkly discipline are conjoined with filial expectations in which care for parents, and ancestors, is paramount.

One last thing is important to note: a careful reading of this text, especially against its earlier and later versions, suggests that at this point in sixth-century China, Buddhist cosmology basically put the Buddha, and Buddhist institutions, in charge of hell and purgatory. Thus, the date of the fifteenth day of the seventh lunar month, which the text promises as a particularly efficacious day for making offerings to the monastery, appears as a jubilee date when a kind of Buddhist indulgence (often referred to as an "expedient means") is for sale to those who find this account of family realities convincing and respond accordingly. Thinking about the Buddhist effort to present itself as the guardian of the family—in this world and the next—seems all the more warranted when in the following centuries, in China and Japan, a range of textual statements appear in which Buddhist authors describe scenes from the underworld in which Buddhist figures—Dizang (Japanese: Jizo), in particular—are clearly in charge of the dead. Thus, it seems that a variety of Buddhist deities became central figures in Buddhist-styled ancestor cults that were designed to funnel devotion to both the previous generations and the Buddhist hell-figures who controlled their fates in the netherworld.

In the following sutra, the author has gone out of his way to denounce non-Buddhist forms of ancestor worship—marked by the Confucian-styled effort to directly feed the dead—as not only worthless but the cause of additional suffering for one's loved ones.

Document 5–10

The Ghost Festival Sutra (*Yulanpen Jing*)

Thus have I heard. Once the Buddha resided in the kingdom of Sravasti, among the Jetavana trees in the garden of Anathapindika. The Great Mu Qian Lian [Mulian] first obtained the six penetrations and then, desiring to save his parents to repay the kindness of breast-feeding, he used his divine eye to search the worlds. He saw that his departed mother had been reborn among the hungry ghosts where she never saw food or drink—[it was so bad] that her skin hung off her bones. Mulian took pity, filled his bowl with rice, and sent it to his mother. When his mother received the bowl of rice, she used her left hand to guard the bowl and her right hand to gather up the rice, but before the food entered her mouth it changed into flaming coals, so in the end she could not eat. Mulian cried out in grief and wept tears. He rushed back to tell the Buddha and explained everything as it had happened.

The Buddha said, "The roots of your mother's sins are deep and tenacious. It is not within your power as a single individual to do anything about it. Even though the fame of your filial devotion moves heaven and earth, still [all] the spirits of heaven and the spirits of earth, harmful demons and masters of the heterodox paths—the Daoist priests—and the four spirit kings of heaven, cannot do anything about it. You must rely on the mighty spiritual power of the assembled monks of the ten directions in order to obtain her deliverance. I shall now preach for you the method of salvation, so that all beings in dire straights may leave sadness and suffering, and have their sinful impediments swept way."

The Buddha told Mulian, "On the fifteenth day of the seventh month, when the assembled monks of the ten directions release themselves, you should, for the sake of seven generations of ancestors, up to and including your current parents—those in dire straights—gather food of the one hundred flavors and five kinds of fruit, basins for washing and rinsing, incense, oil lamps and candles, and mattresses and bedding. Then place these, the sweetest, prettiest things in the world, in a bowl and offer it to the assembled monks, those of great virtue of the ten directions. On this day, . . . all of those who are part of the great assembly shall with one mind receive the bowls of rice. The assembly of saints possesses fully the purity of the precepts and the Way—their virtue is vast indeed. When you make offerings to these kinds of monks as they release themselves, then your current parents, your seven generations of ancestors, and your six kinds of relatives will obtain release from the suffering of the three evil paths of rebirth and will be liberated and clothed and fed naturally. If one's parents are still living, then they will have one hundred years of joy and happiness [from this offering]. If they are already deceased, then [they and] the seven generations of ancestors will be reborn in the heavens; born freely through magical transformation, they will enter into the light of heavenly flowers and receive unlimited joy."

Then the Buddha decreed that the assembled monks of the ten directions should first chant prayers on behalf of the family of the donor [and for] for the seven generations of ancestors, and practice meditation and concentrate their thoughts before receiving the food. In receiving the bowls, they should first place them in front of the Buddha's stupa, and when the assembled monks have finished chanting prayers, they may then individually partake of the food.

At this time the monk Mulian and the assembly of great bodhisattvas rejoiced. Mulian's sorrowful tears ended and the sound of his crying died out. Then, on that very day, Mulian's mother gained release from an eon of suffering as a hungry ghost.

Then Mulian told the Buddha, "The parents who gave birth to me, your disciple, are able to receive the power of the merit of the Three Jewels because of the mighty spiritual power of the assembly of monks. But all of the future disciples of the Buddha, those who practice filial devotion, may they or may they not also present *yulan* bowls as required to save their parents and their seven generations of ancestors?"

The Buddha said, "Excellent! This question pleases me very much. It is just what I would like to preach, so listen well! My good sons, if there are monks, or nuns, kings of states, princes, sons of kings, great ministers, counselors, dignitaries of the three ranks, any government officials, or the tens of thousands of common people who practice filial compassion, then on behalf of their current parents and the past seven generations of ancestors, on the fifteenth day of the seventh month, the day on which the Buddha is happy, the day on which the monks release themselves, they must all place food and drink of the one hundred flavors inside the *yulan* bowl and donate it to monks of the ten directions who are releasing themselves. When the prayers are finished, one's present parents will attain long life, passing one hundred years without sickness and without any of the torments of sufferings of hungry ghosthood, attaining rebirth among gods and humans, and blessings without limit."

The Buddha told all of the good sons and good daughters, "Those disciples of the Buddha who practice filial devotion must in every moment of consciousness think of, and care for, their parents and their seven generations of ancestors. Each year on the fifteen day of the seventh month, out of filial devotion and compassionate consideration for the parents who gave birth to them, and for the seven generations of ancestors, they should always prepare a *yulan* bowl and donate it to the Buddha and Sangha to repay the kindness bestowed by parents in nurturing and caring for them. All disciples of the Buddha must carry out this law."

Upon hearing what the Buddha preached, the monk Mulian and the four classes of disciples rejoiced and put it into practice.

Source: Alan Cole, translation from the *Taisho shinshu daizokyo*, T. 16.779, based, in part, on Stephen F. Teiser's translation in his *The Ghost Festival in Medieval China* (Princeton: Princeton University Press, 1988), 49–54; for more discussion of this text, see my *Mothers and Sons in Chinese Buddhism* (Stanford: Stanford University Press, 1998), chapter 5.

The Story of Dizang Bodhisattva

The narrative below appears to have been crafted in the tenth or eleventh century and is designed to give the reader a better sense of Dizang's lifestory. Dizang, as the (male) warden of hell, is explained to have been an unusually filial daughter (Bright Eyes), who nonetheless had the misfortune of having a very unBuddhist mother. After her mother's death, Bright Eyes comes to terms with her mother's pitiful fate and sets out to right not just her mother's postmortem woes but also to turn herself into a place of refuge for all those who wish to free their loved ones from hell.

In this account, Dizang's past childhood, and filial resolve, are presented as the cause of his final Buddhist identity—just as in the case of Mulian. Thus, it was precisely due to his previous life as an exceptionally filial and concerned daughter that he achieved the exalted role of Bodhisattva Dizang in charge of the fates of all deceased humans. Of course, looked at from a wider point of view, this narrative again puts Buddhist deities in charge of hell in a way that suggests that the dead are essentially captives of the Buddhist power figures who, when correctly propitiated, will deliver the dead from their sufferings, provided that their descendents manifest a suitable level of Buddhist devotion and generosity. It would seem that in offering this ideological package, Buddhist authors had found a way to ensure both their own institutional viability and that of the patriarchal family, while also trumping Confucian charges that the Buddhists were unfilial, since, in fact, this entire Buddhist apparatus was motivated by the hallmark Confucian ethic of filial piety. In short, again as in the case of Mulian, being a good son or daughter in the at-home family was wrapped in a package with being a good and supportive Buddhist. Of course, that Dizang was a daughter in his final human life suggests that the form of Buddhist filial piety that had been centered on Mulian—and by implication, sons—had morphed and extended to cover daughters as well.

Document 5–11

The Sutra on the Original Vow of Bodhisattva Dizang

"Moreover, limitless eons ago a Buddha named Pure-Lotus-Eyes Thus Come One appeared in the world. His lifespan was forty eons. During his period of the semblance of Dharma, an Arhat who had great merit and who saved living beings, teaching them as he encountered them, met a woman named Bright Eyes who made an offering of food to him.

" 'What is your wish?' asked the Arhat.

"Bright Eyes replied, 'On the day of my mother's death I performed meritorious deeds for her rescue, but I do not yet know in what path she has been born.'

"Out of pity for her, the Arhat entered into samadhi to contemplate and saw that Bright Eyes' mother had fallen into an evil path where she was undergoing extremely great suffering. The Arhat asked, 'When your mother was alive, what deeds did she do that she should now be undergoing such great punishment in an evil path?'

"Bright Eyes replied, 'My mother enjoyed eating fish, turtles, and the like. She particularly relished their fried or boiled roe, and because she was fond of eating, she took thousands of lives. Oh, Venerable Compassionate One, how can she be saved?'

"The Arhat pitied her and established an expedient means and said, 'With a sincere motivation be mindful of Pure-Lotus-Eyes Thus Come One, and also make carved and painted images for the benefit of the living and the dead.'

"On hearing this, Bright Eyes renounced everything she loved, drew an image of that Buddha, and made offerings before it. Moreover, she wept sorrowfully as she respectfully gazed at and worshiped that Buddha. Suddenly, in the small hours of the night, as if in a dream, she saw that Buddha's body, dazzling gold in color and as large as Mount Sumeru, emitting great light.

"This Buddha said to Bright Eyes, 'Before long your mother will be born in your own household and as soon as she can know hunger and cold she will speak.'

"Shortly thereafter, a maidservant in the house bore a son who spoke within three days of his birth. Lowering his head and weeping mournfully, he said, 'In life and death one must undergo retributions for his own deeds, I am your mother and have been in darkness for a long time. Since leaving you I have constantly been reborn in the great hells. As a result of receiving the power of your meritorious deeds, I have been able to be reborn, but only as a poor son of low class. My lifespan, moreover, will be short, and after thirteen years I will fall into an evil path again. Do you not have some way to effect my liberation?'. . . .

"Bright Eyes heard this and wept bitterly and said into empty space, 'May my mother be eternally separated from the hells, and after these thirteen years may she be free of her heavy offenses and leave the Evil Paths [of rebirth]. O Buddhas of the ten directions, have compassion and pity on me. Hear the far-reaching vows which I am making for the sake of my mother. If she can leave the Three Paths [of existence] forever, leave the lower classes, leave the body of a woman, and never again have to endure them, then, before the image of the Thus Come One Pure-Lotus-Eyes, I vow that from this day forth, throughout hundreds of thousands of tens of thousands of millions of eons, I will rescue living beings who are suffering in the hells for their offenses, and others of the Three Evil Paths. . . .' "

The story closes out with the Buddha confirming that this vow will take effect, and that Bright Eyes' mother will be saved from hell and that Bright Eyes will become Dizang Bodhisattva, in charge of saving all others from hell.

Source: Heng Ching, trans., *Sutra of the Past Vows of the Earth Store Bodhisattva: The Collected Lectures of Tripitaka Master Hsuan Hua* (New York: Buddhist Text Translation Society, 1974), 124–126, with minor stylistic changes.

Jizo (Dizang), The Bodhisattva Who Saves Children

The popular medieval song presented below, probably dating from fourteenth-century Japan, shows Jizo (the Japanese pronounciation of Dizang) performing the Mulian-like role of meditating the triangle of the dead, the Buddhist monasteries, and the family. The difference, though, is that Jizo is clearly imagined to be especially involved with the postmortem fate of deceased children, or at least all those so unfortunate as to have died before the age of ten. Thus, instead of the tortured mother in hell, as in the Mulian stories, it is the tortured children that are brought on stage to coerce still-alive parents into fulfilling their ritual obligations.

Arguably, whether the Buddhists are arranging for the postmortem care of mothers or children, their fundamental three-part agenda is the same: working up a sustainable fear of postmortem lands, showing that the Buddhists and their representatives can tame these dangerous zones, and demonstrating these realities with sufficient emotion to hold their audiences' attention and to draw them to pro-Buddhist activities. The song is particularly heavy on pathos as the children by the River Sai are shown trying to be good Buddhists even as they are regularly thwarted, and tortured, by a demon, though all this calamity is explained as a failure on the part of parents to correctly memorialize them. In fact, the song works up an interesting mirror with the children memorializing their parents by building Buddhist reliquaries for their parents and siblings in their hell-zone, even as their parents fail to uphold their mimetic ritual duties on earth. Jizo appears, for his part, as the perfect blend of father and mother, and saves the children, at least for a set time each day, with love and tenderness.

Document 5–12

A Song about the Riverbank of Sai

This is a tale that comes not from this world,
But is the story of the Riverbank of Sai
By the road on the edge of Death Mountain.
Hear it and you will know its sorrow.
Little children of two, three, four,
Five—all under ten years of age—
Are gathered at the Riverbank of Sai
Longing for their fathers and mothers;
Their "I want you" cries are uttered

From voices in another world.
Their sorrow bites, penetrates
And the activity of these infants
Consists of gathering river stones
And of making merit stupas out of them;
The first storey is for their fathers
And the second for their mothers,
And the third makes merits for siblings
Who are at home in the land of the living;
This stupa-building is their game
During the day, but when the sun sets
A demon from hell appears, saying
"Hey! your parents back in the world
Aren't busy doing memorial rites for you.
Their day-in, day-out grieving has in it
Much that's cruel, sad, and wretched.
The source of your suffering down here is
That sorrow of your parents up there.
So don't hold any grudge against me!"
With that the demon wields his black
Iron pole and smashes the children's
Little stupas to smithereens.
Just then the much-revered Jizo
Makes an awe-inspiring entrance, telling
The children, "Your lives were short;
Now you've come into the realm of darkness
Very far away from the world you left.
Take me, trust me always—as your father
And as your mother in this realm."
With that he wraps the little ones
Inside the folds of his priest robes,
Showing a wondrous compassion.
Those who can't yet walk are helped
By him to grasp his stick with bells on top.
He draws them close to his own comforting,
Merciful skin, hugging and stroking them,
Showing a wondrous compassion.
Praise be to Life-sustaining
Bodhisattva Jizo!

Source: William R. LaFleur, trans., *Liquid Life: Abortion and Buddhism in Japan* (Princeton: Princeton University Press, 1992), 63–64.

Buddhist Rites to Save Aborted Fetuses

A 1980s pamphlet from the Japanese monastery Purple Cloud Villa–clearly designed for general family consumption–makes clear that East Asian forms of Buddhism continue to promote a style of family ethics in which filial piety is fused with calls to support the monasteries. However, as even a cursory reading of this document makes clear, the obligation to repay the dead, via Buddhist offerings, has now shifted so that parents–mothers, in particular–are invited to fantasize about their aborted fetuses, referred to as *mizuko,* who are depicted as alive in the netherworld and in urgent need of assistance. More explicitly threatening than earlier versions of this scenario–as seen in the song above–these quasi children in limbo are described as threatening and intent on ruining the family to which they never had a chance to belong.

The text opens by explaining to parents why the mizuko is angry and in need of placation. The text is particularly "advanced" within this style of Buddhist writing in the way that it explains normal troubles in the family–such as children's nightmares–as the result of attacks from the vengeful mizukos. In this formulation, closely in line with the two entries above, Jizo is imagined to perform the necessary mediation between the family, their deceased "members," and the Buddhist institution. Here, though, Jizo statues are required both at home on the alter, and on monastery's grounds, where they serve as focal point for the family's devotions–devotions that will, as usual, link the life and well-being of the family to the monastery's economy, but now with that link ensured by fears over aborted fetuses.

Document 5–13

The Way To Memorialize One's Mizuko

1. The mizuko resulting from a terminated pregnancy is a child existing in the realm of darkness. The principal things that have to be done for its sake are the making of a full apology and the making of amends to such a child.

In contrast to the child in darkness because of an ordinary miscarriage or by natural death after being born, the child here discussed is in its present location because its parents took active steps to prevent it from being born alive in our world. If the parents merely carry out ordinary memorial rites but fail to make a full apology to their child, their mizuko will never be able to accept their act.

Think for a moment how even birds and beasts, when about to be killed, show a good deal of anger and distress. Then how much more must be the shock and hurt felt by a fetus when its parent or parents have decided to abort it? And on top of that it does not even yet have a voice with which to make complaint about what is happening.

It often happens that the living children of persons who have repeatedly had abortions will in the middle of the night cry out "Father, help!" or "Help me, Mommy!" because of nightmares. Uncontrollable weeping or cries of "I'm scared! I'm scared!" on the part of children are really caused by dreams through which their aborted siblings deep in the realm of darkness give expression to their own distress and anger. Persons who are not satisfied with this explanation would do well to have a look at two publications of the Purple Cloud Villa; these are entitled *Mizuko Jizo-ji's Collection of the Experiences of Departed Souls* and *The Medical Dictionary of Life*.

2. The next thing to do in remembering the mizuko is to set up an image of Jizo on the Buddhist altar in one's own home. That will serve as a substitute for a memorial tablet for the mizuko. Such a Jizo can do double service. On one hand it can represent the soul of the mizuko for parents doing rites of apology to it. Simultaneously, however, the Jizo is the one to whom can be made an appeal in prayer to guide the fetus through the realm of departed souls. Such Jizo images for home use can be obtained from the Purple Cloud Villa but can also be purchased at any shop specializing in Buddhist art and implements. As long as one performs this worship with a pure heart, it is bound to have a positive effect.

Some prices follow. Jizo images made of metal are either 3,000 yen for silver ones or 4,000 yen for gold. Add 1,100 yen to the price of either of these if home delivery is desired. These are prices as of September 1984.

3. Inasmuch as the Jizo image on the Buddhist altar also does double duty as a memorial tablet for a terminated fetus, it is allowable—after asking permission of the Jizo—to give it a place on the altar lower than the memorial tablets for one's parents and ancestors. Also it does not matter greatly whether it is to the right or the left on the altar.

4. The next thing of importance is to set up a stone Jizo image either in the cemetery of the Mizuko Jizo Temple or at one's own family temple. Such will serve as substitute for a gravestone for the aborted child and will constitute an eternal, ongoing ritual of apology and remembrance. Such action will undoubtedly have a good effect—a fact shown in things published in our monthly periodical *The Purple Cloud*. The expenses involved in setting up a stone Jizo Buddha at our place are fully detailed in our publication *Concerning the 10,000 Jizos*. If requested, we will be pleased to send it.

5. The following pertains to the number of images needed if a person is the parent of more than one mizuko. One of each on the home altar and in the cemetery will suffice if all the mizukos were produced by a single couple—whether married or not. If, however, the father of a later mizuko was different from that of

an earlier one—and, of course, also had a different family registry—separate Jizo images will be required. An exception to this could be made if a woman were to discuss this candidly with her second husband and get his permission. Then it would be just as in the case of a woman bringing along into her second marriage the children begotten in an earlier one. In such a case, if she requests that the deceased ancestors understand the situation, it is allowable for all her mizukos to be collectively remembered with a single image.

6. When at your home altar you are giving a daily portion of rice and water offering to your deceased ancestors, be sure to include the mizuko too—and let them know of their inclusion. Also pray for the well-being of your mizuko in the other world. Do this by standing before the buddhas there and reciting either the *Heart Sutra* or the *Psalm to Jizo* used at the Jizo cemetery in Chichibu. In addition to that, if as an ongoing remembrance of your mizuko you write out in longhand a copy of the *Heart Sutra* once a day, you will at some point along the way receive the assurance that your child has most certainly reached buddhahood. Until you receive such an assurance, you should continue to perform these rites of apology and remembrance.

7. To make amends for the fact that you never had to pay anything for the upbringing and education of a mizuko, you should give to the buddha everyday an offering of 100 yen for each of your mizuko. However, if you have had as many as ten terminated pregnancies, there may be hardship in laying out 1,000 yen every day; in such cases it is permissible to give only 300 or 500 yen—or even to give more or less depending on one's income. This is an expression of apology to the child for not having given it a love-filled upbringing. Therefore, you should put your love into these acts of remembrance, not being stingy with your time and resources. Once you get into the habit of thinking how much easier it would be simply to make a 10,000-yen contribution once a month, you are missing the whole point. It is far better to put a daily offering on the altar every day and then on a special, designated day pay a visit to the Jizo Temple at Chichibu and make a contribution to the temple. Alternatively, you could do it while making the eighty-eight-temple pilgrimage on the island of Shikoku or the pilgrimage to the one hundred Kannon sites in western Japan.

8. When a person has awakened to the value and importance of remembering mizuko, one gains a much deeper faith and makes efforts to live as a bodhisattva, setting one's mind to performing at least one act of goodness each day. Also vowing to go on pilgrimage to Shikoku or the Kannon sites is an excellent way to be total and thorough-going in one's act of apologizing to and remembering the mizuko. It is important to be of a mind to do more than enough; to be of the opinion that one has already done plenty is just the kind of attitude that evokes a bad effect.

9. Children who are miscarried, born dead, or die shortly after being born differ, of course, from those whose lives are cut short by being terminated by their parents. Nevertheless, they too are mizuko and, when one gives consid-

eration to his or her responsibility for the fact that these too did not enter life successfully, it would seem good to provide them too with mizuko rites, just as one would in the case of aborted fetuses.

10. Households whose members think about the seriousness of karmic laws related to abortion are also households that can take advantage of such occasions in order to deepen the faith of those within them. By continuing to perform adequate rites of apology and memorial, such persons later are blessed with the birth of fine, healthy children. Or, as an extension of good fortune, there are many instances of people really thriving. Some persons find that their own severe heart diseases are cured or that the rebelliousness of children or neuroses go away. When on top of all that there is increased prosperity in the family business, there is good cause for lots of happiness.

Why not find out more about this by simply paying a visit to the Jizo Temple in Chichibu?

Source: William R. LaFleur, trans., *Liquid Life: Abortion and Buddhism in Japan* (Princeton: Princeton University Press, 1992), 221–222.

Chan (Zen) Discipleship as Sonship

The narrative below is a snippet taken from an eighth-century work—often referred to as the "Huineng biezhuan"—dedicated to explaining the life and teachings of Chan master Huineng. In this scene Huineng, referred to throughout as "the Master," debates with Shenhui, referred to as "the novice." The central point of the debate, once they are in private, is the nature of the public beating that Huineng has given Shenhui. As the debate develops it seems clear that the vignette is intent not just on forging a close connection between the two—something that would have been politically useful to later partisans of Shenhui and which the final comment about Huineng conferring transmission on Shenhui highlights—but also to link corporal punishment and the deepest kind of reflection on Buddhist realities. In short, this narrative works hard at somaticizing Buddhist truths and does so by suggesting that a beating is not just a beating, but rather is a place to uncover the riches of Buddhist practice, devotion, and understanding. Of course, that Shenhui is but thirteen in this episode casts the entire exchange as a kind of father-son matter in which the Master uses words and blows to instruct and discipline his Buddhist progeny.

Document 5-14

Chan Master Huineng Gives Young Shenhui a Beating

On the eighth day of the fourth month of this year, the Master for the first time taught the Dharma-gate for the full assembly, saying, "I have a Dharma that is nameless and unlettered, eyeless and earless, bodiless and mindless, wordless and signless, headless and tailless, without exterior or interior, nor with in-between, not going or coming, not green, yellow, red, white or black, neither existent nor non-existent, neither cause nor result."

The Master asked, "What is this?"

The full assembly looked at each other in pairs, and did not dare reply. At the time there was a small novice, Shenhui of Hotse Monastery, just in his thirteenth year, who answered, "This is the original source of the Buddha."

The Master asked, "What is the original source?"

The novice replied, "The original source is the original nature of the buddhas."

The Master said, "I preached the nameless and unlettered. How can you say the Buddhanature has name and letters?"

The novice said, "The Buddhanature is nameless. It was your question that gave it a name. When the name is correct, that is nameless."

The Master hit the novice several times. The full assembly respectfully apologized, "The novice is a minor, and has irritated the Teacher."

The Master said, "The full assembly disperse now. Leave behind that loquacious novice."

When night came, the Master asked the novice, "When I hit you, did the Buddhanature feel it or not?"

"The Buddhanature lacks feeling."

The Master asked, "Do you know pain?"

The novice replied, "I know pain."

The Master asked, "Since you know pain, how can you say that the Buddhanature lacks feeling?"

The novice replied, "How can it be the same as trees and stones? Even though it hurts, the mind-nature does not feel it."

The Master said to the novice, "When you are dissected piece by piece, and you do not give birth to anger and resentment, that is called lacking feeling. I have forgotten my body for the Way. I trod the pestle right up until I overcame [the bodily pain], and I did not think it painful. That is what is called lacking feeling. [Even though] you now were beaten, the mind-nature did not feel it. If you feel the various sensations as if with the insightful realization, you have attained the true correct-feeling samadhi."

The novice secretly received transmission [from Huineng].

Source: John Jorgensen, trans., *Inventing Hui-neng, the Sixth Patriarch: Hagiography and Biography in Early Ch'an* (Leiden: E. J. Brill, 2005), 689–691, with minor stylistic changes.

NOTES

1. See John S. Strong, trans., "The Divyavadana" in his *The Experience of Buddhism: Sources and Interpretations* (Belmont, CA: Wadsworth, 1995), 7.

2. For discussion of this story, see my *Mothers and Sons in Chinese Buddhism* (Stanford: Stanford University Press, 1998), 64–68.

3. For a translation of this story, see John S. Strong, *The Experience of Buddhism* (Belmont, Cal.: Wadsworth Thomas, 2002), 52–56.

4. For an useful discussion of this story, see Reiko Ohnuma's "Mother-Love and Mother-Grief: South Asian Buddhist Variations on a Theme," forthcoming in the *Journal of Feminist Studies in Religion*.

5. For Richard Cohen's discussion, see his "Naga, Yaksini, Buddha: Local Deities and Local Buddhism at Ajanta," *History of Religions* 37.4 (1998): 360–400.

6. For her discussion, see "Debt to the Mother: A Neglected Aspect of the Founding of the Buddhist Nuns' Order," *Journal of the American Academy of Religion* 74.2 (2006): 861–901.

7. For more discussion of this trope, see my *Text as Father: Paternal Seductions in Early Mahayana Buddhist Literature* (Berkeley: University of California Press, 2005).

8. For a translation of this sequence, see Burton Watson, *The Lotus Sutra* (New York: Columbia University Press, 1993), 48.

9. For more discussion of the complexities involved in these narratives, see my *Text as Father*, chapter 5.

10. See his "Kinsmen of the Son: Sakyabhiksus and the Institutionalization of the Bodhisattva Ideal," *History of Religions* 40.1 (August 2000): 1–31.

11. For discussion of Guanyin, see Chun-fang Yu's *Kuan-yin: The Chinese Transformation of Avalokitesvara* (New York: Columbia University Press, 2001); see also Barbara E. Reed, "The Gender Symbolism of Kuan-yin [Guanyin] Bodhisattva," in *Buddhism, Sexuality, and Gender*, edited by Jose Ignacio Cabezon (Albany: State University of New York Press, 1992), 159–180.

12. For discussion of the cult of Dizang in medieval China, see F. Wang-Toutain, *Le Bodhisattva Ksitigarbha en Chine Vè au XIIIè siècle* (Paris: Presses de l'Ecole Française d'Extrême-Orient, 1998); see also, Zhiru Ng, *The Making of a Savior Bodhisattva: Dizang in Medieval China* (Honolulu: Kuroda Institute Studies in East Asian Buddhism, forthcoming).

13. Not surprisingly, given the volatile nature of abortion debates in the United States, this set of practices has been judged quite differently by American scholars. Thus, William LaFleur argues in his *Liquid Life: Abortion and Buddhism in Japan* (Princeton: Princeton University Press, 1992) that this set of beliefs and practices fits well within long-standing patterns in Japanese Buddhist thought and ought to be recognized as a modern adaptation intent on easing the suffering of women. Conversely, Helen Hardacre argues in her *Marketing the Menacing Fetus in Japan* (Berkeley: University of California Press, 1997) that these Buddhist rites are highly opportunistic and are designed to generate maximum guilt in women and then "harvest" that guilt via expensive temple rituals recently created to capitalize on Japan's rather underdeveloped system of family planning.

14. For discussion of father-son motifs in Chan funerals, see my "Upside Down/Right Side Up: A Revisionist History of Buddhist Funerals in China," *History of Religions* 35.4 (1996): 307–338.

15. For discussion of the story of Huike's offering and how it was pieced together from disparate narratives, see my *Fathering Your Father: The Zen of Fabrication in Tang Buddhism* (Berkeley: University of California Press, 2009).

16. The introduction to this text is taken from my chapter on Buddhism in *Sex, Marriage, & Family in World Religions*, edited by Don S. Browning, M. Christian Green, and John Witte Jr. (New York: Columbia University Press: 2005), 338–339.

17. The introduction to this text is reprinted (slightly edited) from my chapter on Buddhism in *Sex, Marriage, & Family in World Religions*, 343.

6

Confucianism

YIQUN ZHOU

For most of its long history in China, Confucianism was a moral system that rested on the religious underpinnings of ancestor worship and operated with the strong support of the state's political and legal apparatus. A good way to approach our topic, as a chapter in *Children and Childhood in World Religions*, is to begin with ancestor worship, what it is, and how it provides a key to understanding the perception and treatment of children in Confucianism.

Known as the "essential form of Chinese religion," ancestor worship had been practiced in China long before the time of Confucius (551–479 BCE). Taking place in the household and consisting of regular offerings and rituals that commemorated patrilineal ancestors and celebrated the continuity and prosperity of the patriline, ancestor worship was a quintessential domestic religion with an explicitly male-centered and patriarchal character. The contribution Confucianism made to the hoary practice of ancestor worship was of great and far-reaching significance. Confucian thinkers, whose central concern was the regulation of human relationships and the establishment of a hierarchy-based, harmonious familial and social order, theorized the values embodied in ancestor worship so that filial piety—obedience and devotion to one's parents and commitment to the well-being of the patriline—became the ethical corollary of the religious duty of ancestral piety. The homology between the ethical and the religious was such in Confucianism that it is difficult to separate the two in discussing the enduring domination enjoyed by Confucianism in premodern China.

Such inseparability resulted in the following points about the position of the child in Confucianism.

First, because ancestor worship was about the continuity and prosperity of the patrilineal family through the joint efforts of an endless chain of ancestors and descendants, the parents-children (in particular, father-son) relationship was at the very heart of Confucian ethics. To begin with, it was essential to acquire male heirs. This task was as much for the safeguard of one's own old age and the satisfaction of one's own emotional needs as for the fulfillment of a religious responsibility to the long line of ancestors and offspring before and after oneself. The corporate concept of the family as composed of mutually dependent ancestors and descendants meant that both parties shouldered weighty and irresolvable responsibilities not only to each other but ultimately to the collective to which they both belonged. It should be noted that this "collective" did not just exist at a conceptual level; various forms and sizes of patrilineal kinship networks in Chinese society, from the extended family to the lineage and the clan, helped to endow that concept with a concrete entity. This means that besides the parents there were many other adults who had serious interests and stakes in the life of a child and that Chinese children learned their roles and responsibilities by moving within an adult world that was typically larger and more complex than that of their Western counterparts. The notion of one's membership in and obligations to the patriline was instilled in young children by, among other things, having them participate in the numerous ancestral rites that included varying ranges of members of a descent group. The tie that was most emphasized and most assiduously cultivated in both quotidian and ritual situations, however, was of course that between parents and children, which formed the axis of the entire family hierarchy.

Second, the mutual responsibility between parents and children was nevertheless perceived as asymmetrical, with the parents being seen as making sacrifices for their children that could never be repaid. Chinese parents were (and still are) noted for their dedication, in time, material means, and emotional energies, to the upbringing and education of their children. It is also perhaps hard to find in other traditions a match for the seriousness and enthusiasm with which the Confucian educated elite composed and published children's primers and didactic handbooks. The goal of such devotion and passion on the part of householders and moralists was that children might acquire the skills, ritualized manners, and virtues that would bring fame, status, material benefits, or at least respect for the family when they grew up. Besides these social successes, children owed to their parents love, obedience, and care, all of which were lifelong filial duties that had to be learned and practiced from early childhood. The vast body of inspirational stories about filial paragons frequently had young children as their protagonists.

Third, if it is the case that children were generally in a subordinated and oppressed position vis-à-vis adults in premodern societies, this might have been especially true of a land where ancestors were revered as deities (and parents as quasi deities) and age provided the basis for one of the most important social hierarchies. A telling indicator of the marginal status of children as incomplete human beings in the Confucian scheme of things is that children who died before reaching maturity were to be mourned for reduced lengths of time and with curtailed expressions of sorrow, to the extent that no formal mourning was prescribed for those younger than eight (see Docs. 6-4, 6-15).[1] Children were regarded as not only incomplete but also ignorant beings who had to be subjected to strenuous processes of training and discipline. Aside from literacy, the core of children's education in the Confucian curriculum was to inculcate such virtues as filial piety, respect for seniors, self-restraint, and compliance, both through the teaching of principles and examples and through the learning of restrictive ritualized conduct. Precocious children who behaved like adults brought comfort and pride to their parents and relatives and were held up as exemplars for their peers.

To be ritually marginalized and to be regarded as immature and ignorant beings that called for molding and restraining do not mean that childhood was not recognized as a distinctive stage deserving of special treatment or that young children did not have much claim to their parents' emotions and affections. In fact, canonical Confucian texts, major Confucian ritual treatises of later times, and the Confucianized law of imperial times all recognized children as a special group that should be granted various degrees of indulgence and mercy (Docs. 6-5, 6-15, 6-25).

In the sources just mentioned, childhood seems to have been divided into two major stages: from one to seven, which was the stage of freedom and indulgence (while being ritually insignificant in the mourning system); and from eight to fifteen, which began to take on ritual significance and might have been accompanied by drastic changes in adult attitudes and expectations.[2] Now study and other types of training became serious and demanding, and harsh discipline could be administered by parents, teachers, and other relevant adults—all presumably because children of this age group were seen to have survived the great uncertainties of early childhood and to have entered a stage where they should be prepared to assume their future places in family and society. Family interests and ancestral and parental expectations were the most frequently and effectively invoked incentives and excuses to motivate children who labored in their studies and training, and to justify what could often be tough and unreasonable demands and punishments from adults. The rupture around age eight, ushering in what seems to have been a parent-child relationship characterized by distance, demand, and duty, might have brought great pain for both parents and children and have been particularly shocking for the children. However, if we view the change in light of both parties' common membership in the corporate family and the start of their cooperation to contribute to the (ideally) endlessly extending patriline, the question about how much the stereotypically dominating and demanding Chinese parents loved their children becomes less relevant. In the famous phrase of Francis Hsu, everybody, parent or offspring, adult or child, lived "under the ancestors' shadow," and their relationship was defined in the broad context of a descent line that transcended any bond between specific individuals.

The fourth point is that the concern with the patrilineal family in ancestor worship had obvious implications for the different positions of boys and girls. Whereas boys were to carry the family line, girls had no formal role in ancestor worship or the patriline until after they had married and, by giving birth to male heirs, assumed their proper place in their husbands' line. This difference in expectations resulted in great, gender-specific differences in such matters as parental attitudes and training of character and skills. Generally speaking, boys received more attention and resources as they grew up, and their education and training were geared toward their future responsibility to raise the family, whereas most girls were mainly instructed in household management. Filial piety was the supreme virtue to be learned by both boys and girls, but for boys that virtue entailed active responsibilities and achievements in society besides love and obedience to their parents, whereas for girls it was mostly about obedience to their parents, which would prepare them for their later service to their parents-in-law.

The gender difference also had its physical manifestation. The principle of sexual separation that governed the adult society began to be enforced when boys and girls reached a certain age (seven being the canonical stipulation) and stopped occupying the same space in their activities (e.g., eating, playing, and sitting). The danger of sexual attraction between boys and girls, though clearly in the awareness of the householders and moralists, was rarely explicitly alluded to in the sources.

Presumably, enforcing sexual separation among children gave boys and girls the benefit of learning their distinct roles and tasks from early on and without interference, so that in the future they would be able to coexist and contribute to the well-being of the family in an orderly and harmonious manner.

An important point about gender and children in ancestor worship and Confucianism concerns the role of the mother. On the one hand, the patrilineal and patriarchal nature of ancestor worship meant that the mother essentially depended on her ties to her sons for her place in the family. On the other hand, however, ancestresses (that is, those with male heirs, including adopted ones) were worshiped alongside ancestors, and the ethical corollary of filial piety dictated that sons serve and obey their mothers. The mother's keen interest in cultivating a bond with her son and incurring his feelings of indebtedness, his absolute duty to love her and sacrifice himself for her, and the fact that fathers typically spent most of their time taking care of extra-domestic affairs—all these factors combined to make the mother a key figure in the upbringing and education of young children despite the theoretically male-centered and male-dominant nature of the Chinese family. Numerous sources testify to the mother's great personal responsibility for the education of her sons, which started with pregnancy (see Docs. 6–10, 6–12, 6–15 on so-called prenatal education) and could continue at least until the child began to attend school. It is perhaps for this reason that many other sources reveal the Confucian moralists' concern and fear that mothers might spoil their children or lead them astray by their indulgence, selfish desires, or sheer ignorance.

So far we have made some general observations on the position of the child in Confucianism, in both the religious and the moral or ethical contexts. It is of course important to keep in mind that those generalities have to be modified by changes and variations in time, place, individual temperaments, school affiliations, and other factors. The first thing to note is that Confucianism enjoyed long domination, but not monopoly, in premodern China. There were times, most notably the Period of Disunity (third to sixth centuries) and the Tang dynasty (618–907), when Buddhism and Daoism commanded great influence, and the late imperial period (ca. 1300–1911) was marked by a so-called syncretism of Confucianism, Buddhism, and Daoism. People, not just "ignorant" women and peasants but also self-styled Confucians, often readily adopted non-Confucian beliefs and practices under various circumstances and for a variety of purposes. It probably took the most orthodox and purist family to give their children an ideal Confucian upbringing.

With this caveat in place, however, we should stress that the core values of Confucian ethics—such as filial piety, importance of the family, and hierarchical social organization—remained intact and exerted the greatest influence in premodern China despite all the flexibility and syncretism among the general population. Ancestor worship continued to prevail at least until the early twentieth century, and acceptance of its rationale and ethical corollaries was the basis on which other religious and ritual practices were able to coexist and develop in Chinese society.

In fact, it seems that the core of Confucian views and practices regarding children not only remained intact but also overall underwent a process of hardening and reinforcement in the course of China's imperial history (221 BCE–1911 CE). For example, in the early texts the father-son relationship seems to have been characterized by greater affection and reciprocity than in later times, when paternal reserve and authoritarianism increasingly came to be represented as the norm. The growing entrenchment of the old-young hierarchy and the absolute dictates of filial piety had much to do with the steady ascendancy of Confucianism as the state ideology and as the key to public success in imperial China. Children seem to have been subjected to increasingly systematic and rigid regimens in their upbringing and education as the Confucian householders and scholar-officials raised the stake in that enterprise. More children appeared as the protagonists of filial piety stories, their ages getting younger, and their filial acts becoming more drastic and sensational. Moreover, the full-fledged institutionalization of the civil service examination (testing mastery of the Confucian classics and providing the most prestigious channel of upward mobility) from the seventh century onward and the intensification of the competition in late imperial times seem to have considerably affected children (boys) for the worse. Whereas traditionally the critical transition in a child's education had occurred around seven years of age, now it was not infrequent to hear of four- or five-year-olds embarking on the quest for examination success under the supervision of their eager and self-sacrificing parents who put all their hopes in the little boy.

We also have to note some important differences within the broadly similar Confucian views of the child. In the preimperial period, the two great masters Mencius (ca. 372–289 BCE) and Xunzi (ca. 310–230 BCE) adopted quite different views of human nature, with significant implications for attitudes toward children. Considering the innate goodness of human beings as something to be brought out and nourished by environment and education, Mencius saw in the newborn infant a symbol of moral perfection. By contrast, Xunzi regarded human nature as being inherently evil and needing constant and rigorous molding and correction, which was precisely what teachers did for their pupils, and which implied a much less sanguine opinion of children. The divergence between Mencius and Xunzi was considerable but should not be exaggerated, however. Both thinkers accepted the fundamental necessity for Confucian education in ethics and ritual, and their major difference lay in their approaches as to how to carry out such education and how to make it most effective. The same may be said of a much-discussed contrast in later times, that between Zhu Xi (1130–1200) and Wang Yangming (1472–1529). Zhu, representing the late imperial orthodox, advocated serious and diligent study and investigation as the only path to sagehood, and adopted an educational approach that was characterized by its stringency and formalism. By contrast, Wang, who championed the Mencian view of innate human goodness and exalted intuitive understanding, held a theory of education that recognized and accommodated children's natural tendencies for play and fun. Again, true and important as the Zhu-Wang divergence is, it may be far from fundamental, because Wang unquestionably endorsed the value of Confucian moral teachings and ritual practices, and his dispute with Zhu Xi concerned how to make children learn those teachings and practices with ease and pleasure and without distorting their nature (Docs. 6–22, 6–23).

That being said, it is nevertheless true that Zhu and Wang have met with different fates in the modern age, when the status of the child has undergone a radical elevation first in the West and then in the other parts of the world. The end of China's two-millennium-long imperial period under the impact of Western military, economic, and cultural superiority at the beginning of the twentieth century precipitated a barrage of fundamental criticisms of Confucianism, most notably its maintenance of strict hierarchies and its suppression of women and young people. Accordingly, the Zhu school has been condemned as the major villain in perpetrating such injustice, while Wang Yangming and his followers are lauded for their apparently liberal and "modern" view of children and education. For social reformers and a new generation of Neo-Confucians who believe that Confucianism could undergo yet another revival and continue to provide moral and spiritual guidance for Chinese societies, Wang Yangming represents a precious fount of wisdom. From the Republican period (1912–1949) to post-Mao mainland China, and from Taiwan to Singapore, it is often in the spirit of Wang's theory and activism that children are targeted in the recurring waves of educational movements, moral campaigns, and social projects to rejuvenate and modernize Confucianism.

Great uncertainty revolves around the prospect of this revival. On the one hand, it is true that in such things as the mutual dependency between parents and children, parents' dedication to their children's education, and the imperative force of filial piety, Chinese family life and social practices retain many features that are recognizably and distinctively Confucian. On the other hand, there is good reason to be doubtful about the tenability of the contemporary vestige of Confucian family and educational practices. With the rapidly growing influence of Western individual- and youth-oriented culture, and with the abandonment of the entire apparatus of religion, ritual, education, and law that contributed to the formation of a unique Confucian culture in premodern China, will the "Confucian child" not be an impossible creature in the contemporary world? Confucianism, with ancestor worship and all, was about the opposite of a child-centered world. Mencius and Wang Yangming may have been hailed as heroes and prophets in modern times for their valuation of children, but they were by no means revolutionaries. The child in their ideal world is one who is successfully brought up to take delight in the Confucian rituals and moral teachings and to exercise his freedom in living under the ancestors' shadow. Modern neo-Confucian thinkers and activists have yet to show us what kind of reorientation will be necessary so that there will be a rich and compelling view of the child that is deeply rooted in the Confucian tradition and not only seeks compatibility with the increasingly individual- and child-centered character of our world but also promises challenges and alternatives to what seems to be the irreversible trend.

Selection of Texts

Texts are selected to illustrate both the common ideas and practices concerning children in Confucianism and the changes and variations in historical times, school affiliations, and individual approaches. Understandably, in keeping with the unusual degree of continuity and domination of the Confucian tradition in Chinese history, the selections aim at conveying a sense of fundamental and lasting homogeneity over and above constant and significant modifications, shifts, and transformations.

The chronological organization of the materials is intended to help the reader grasp the overall shape of the tradition while paying proper attention to the internal changes and variations. The first seven selections are from the Classics (the latest of which could be dated to the second century BCE). The reader will be struck by how later Confucian thinkers, writers, and officials consciously and piously looked back to these texts and used adaptation, reinterpretation, or straightforward appropriation in formulating their own beliefs and practices regarding children. The fundamental criticism and rejection of the tradition only occurred in the twentieth century, and three selections have been made to give an idea of the Western-inspired modern reaction.

I have tried to represent different genres in the selections, though they are predominantly of a prescriptive rather than descriptive nature. This is due to the fact that the sources from traditional China, as from elsewhere in the premodern world, typically reveal much more about adult expectations and fears concerning children than about the actual treatment of children. Aside from the Classics, the selections mainly consist of ritual texts, family rules, didactic handbooks for women, children's primers, school regulations, official instructions, and legal stipulations. A glimpse of how children actually coped with adult expectations and demands is offered by two personal reminiscences (Docs. 6-12 and 6-26), though the fact that they were written by adults immediately raises the problem of consciously or unconsciously filtered and twisted memories. I have also included an emotional and deeply personal requiem that a leading Tang Confucian wrote for his daughter (Doc. 6-13), in order to remind the reader that the Confucian moralists' preoccupation with molding and prescribing for children does not mean that society only operated on those rules. I have refrained from incorporating more texts that corroborate this important insight, because the aim of this chapter is to present the most influential and representative texts in the Confucian tradition. Undercurrents of human feelings and desires that ran in a different direction from the Confucian principles there no doubt always were, and they should always be kept in mind when we approach the world presented in this chapter. However, those undercurrents only modify the contours but do not change the direction of the Confucian "mainstream" that flowed down the long and deep course of Chinese history.

Note on Translation and Romanization

With the exception of three cases (Docs. 6-20, 6-26, 6-29, newly translated for this anthology), all the translations are taken from published sources. For the sake of consistency I have modified some of the translations so that the *pinyin* Romanization system is used throughout the chapter.

The Book of Poetry

An anthology of 305 poems that range from love songs to sacrificial hymns, most dating from the tenth to the sixth century BCE, the *Book of Poetry* (*Shijing*) was, according to the Confucian tradition, compiled by Confucius himself from a large corpus of poems that had long played an important role in elite ritual, sociable, and educational contexts. Confucius highly valued the didactic function of those poems, believing that they served to arouse the correct sentiments in young people, acquaint them with social customs and values, and give them an idiom that befitted a well-educated gentleman. The following selection shows the different treatments and expectations for boys and girls.

Document 6–1

Poem 189

> So he bears a son,
> And puts him to sleep upon a bed,
> Clothes him in robes,
> Gives him a jade scepter to play with.
> The child's howling is very lusty;
> In red greaves shall he flare,
> Be lord and king of house and home.
> Then he bears a daughter,
> And puts her upon the ground,
> Clothes her in swaddling-clothes,
> Gives her a loom-whorl to play with.
> For her no decorations, no emblems;
> Her only care, the wine and food,
> And how to give no trouble to father and mother.

Source: *The Book of Songs: The Ancient Chinese Classic of Poetry*, translated by Arthur Waley, edited with additional translations by Joseph R. Allen (New York: Grove, 1996), 162–163.

The Book of Changes

Originally a handbook of divination consisting of hexagrams and interpretations of the hexagrams, the *Book of Changes* (*Yijing*) came to be used as a wisdom text by Han times (206 BCE–220 CE) and as such was treated as the first among the Confucian classics. The selection is about the fourth hexagram, "Meng," which literally means "youthful ignorance." Commentators have taken the text to be about the correct relationship between teachers and pupils: the youth must be aware of his ignorance and must seek out the teacher, and in learning he should avoid annoying the teacher by persistent and unintelligent questioning.

Document 6–2

Meng

Youthful folly has success.
It is not I who seek the young fool;
The young fool seeks me.
At the first oracle I inform him.
If he asks two or three times, it is importunity.
If he importunes, I give him no information.
Perseverance furthers.

Source: *The I Ching, or Book of Changes*, the Richard Wilhelm translation rendered into English by Cary F. Baynes (Princeton: Princeton University Press, 1967), 20–21.

The Analects

The *Analects* (*Lunyu*) consists of records of Confucius's (551–479 BCE) sayings and deeds. According to Sima Qian's (ca. 145–86 BCE) biography of Confucius, while still a child Confucius enjoyed imitating the adults' performance of rites, behavior that foreshadowed the greatest Chinese philosopher and teacher that he was to become. Confucius (referred to as "Master") as seen in the *Analects*, however, does not appear eager to demand serious study or speedy moral growth of children. Nor does he regard children as ignorant beings. Instead, he seems to acknowledge developmental stages and to treat children and youths with respect and affection. Meanwhile, the selections show Confucius approving of the importance of filial piety and observing the principle that fathers maintain a distance from their children while taking an interest in their education.

Document 6–3

2.4 The Master said, "At fifteen, I had my mind bent on learning."

9.22 The Master said, "A youth is to be regarded with respect. How do we know that his future will not be equal to our present? If he reaches the age of forty or fifty, and has not made himself heard of, then indeed he will not be worth being regarded with respect."

11.25 [Confucius asks four of his disciples to describe the most ideal use of their talents. Zeng Dian, the last to speak, says,] "In the last month of spring, with the dress of the season all complete, along with five or six young men who have assumed the cap,[3] and six or seven boys, I would wash in the Yi, enjoy the breeze among the rain altars, and return home singing." The master heaved a sigh and said, "I give my approval to Dian."

14.47 A youth of the village was employed by Confucius to carry the message between him and his visitors. Some one asked about him, saying, "I suppose he has made progress." The master said, "I observe that he is fond of occupying the seat of a full-grown man; I observe that he walks shoulder to shoulder with his elders. He is not one who is seeking to make progress in learning. He wishes quickly to become a man."

16.13 Chen Kang asked Boyu, saying, "Have you heard any lessons from your father different from what we have all heard?"

Boyu replied, "No. He was standing alone once, when I passed below the hall with hasty steps, and said to me, 'Have you learned the Odes [Book of Poetry]?' On my replying 'Not yet,' he added, 'If you do not learn the Odes, you will not be fit to converse with.' I retired and studied the Odes. Another day, he was in the same way standing alone, when I passed by below the hall with hasty steps, and said to me, 'Have you learned the rules of Rites?' On my replying 'Not yet,' he added, 'If you do not learn the rules of Propriety, your character cannot be established.' I then retired, and learned the rules of Propriety. I have heard only these two things from him."

Chen Kang retired, and, quite delighted, said, "I asked one thing, and have got three things. I have heard about the Odes. I have heard about the rules of Propriety. I have also heard that the superior man maintains a distant reserve towards his son."

17.21 Zai Wo asked about the three years' mourning for parents, saying that one year was long enough. . . . Zai Wo then went out, and the Master said, "This shows [Zai Wo's] want of virtue. It is not till a child is three years old that it is allowed to leave the arms of its parents. And the three years' mourning is universally observed throughout the empire. Did [Zai Wo] enjoy the three years' love of his parents?"

Source: *Analects*, in *The Chinese Classics*, vol. 1, translated by James Legge (Hong Kong: Hong Kong University Press, 1960), 146, 223, 248, 293, 315–316, 327–328.

The Book of Etiquette and Ceremonial

The *Book of Etiquette and Ceremonial (Yili)* might have existed in various forms in the two centuries prior to the Qin unification of China in 221 BCE, and its contents may have had something to do with the "rules of Rites" and "rules of Propriety" referred to in *Analects* 16.13. The extant seventeen chapters contain detailed rules for such ritual occasions as capping, wedding, mourning, sacrifices, and diplomatic meetings. The selections on the capping ceremony show capping as a domestic ritual initiating the "childish" male youth (aged twenty) into the responsibilities and virtues of adulthood, marked by the assumption of different garments and a Style name.[4] The selection from the chapter on the different mourning garments to be worn for different people depending on their age, gender, and kinship relationship to oneself indicates that children were treated as "incomplete" human beings and granted less elaborate and shorter periods of mourning.

Document 6–4
The Blessings at the Cappings

At the first capping the blessing runs: "In this auspicious month, and on this lucky day, we endue you with the headgear for the first time. Put from you your childish thoughts, and see that you keep guard upon the virtues of your manhood. Then shall your years all be fair, and your good fortune grow from more to more."

At the second capping it runs: "In this lucky month, at this auspicious hour, we add to your garments. Guard reverently your demeanor, preserve the integrity of your virtue. Then will your years be without end, and good luck attend you for ever and ever."

At the third capping it runs: "In this best of years, and most auspicious of months, we complete the tale of your robes. Your kinsmen are all here to perfect this virtuous act. May your years be age long, and Heaven's blessing attend you."

The Blessing at the Giving of the "Style"

At the giving of the Style the blessing runs thus: "Now that the ceremony is complete, I announce your Style in this auspicious month, and on this lucky day. May that Style become greatly honored, and may you attain to eminence, holding fast to what is right, for right leads to happiness. May you receive and ever hold this gift." Then he addresses him as eldest son of such and such a Style. If second, third, or youngest son, the appropriate character is used according to his status.

The Dagong Mourning Garments Worn for Early Death, for Nine or Seven Month's Mourning

a. The *dagong* mourning consists of a grass-cloth coat and skirt, and male hemp nettle fillet. There is no other mourning to follow this.

b. It is worn for a child, boy or girl, who has died in mature or middle youth.

c. The commentary asks, Why? Because he has not yet reached maturity. Why does no other mourning follow this? Because in mourning for an adult the details of changing and putting off mourning are taken account of, but not in the case of one who has not yet reached adult age. Therefore there are no streamers in the fillet worn for one who has died in youth. The time from nineteen to sixteen is "mature youth"; from fifteen to twelve "middle youth"; and from eleven to eight "early youth." Children who have not reached the age of eight full years are spoken of as dying "a mourningless death." In such a case, one day of wailing is undertaken for every month of the child's age. So when a child is three months old, the father gives it a name, and when it dies it is wailed for. But if it has not yet received a name it is not wailed for.

d. This mourning is worn for the following, who have died in middle or mature youth: a younger uncle, older and younger paternal aunts, brothers older and younger, and a husband's nephews and nieces.

e. It is worn for a grandson in the succession; the sons of great officers by concubines wear it for their brothers born of the wife; a Duke or great officer wears it for his son in the succession; when in any of these cases death occurs in mature or middle youth.

f. The mourning for those who die in mature youth is for nine months, and the fillet has tie-strings to it. For those dying in middle youth it is worn for seven months, and the fillet has no strings.

Source: *The I-Li, Book of Etiquette and Ceremonial*, 2 vols., translated by John Steele (London: Probsthain, 1917), 1:14–15; 2:27–28.

The Record of Ritual

The *Record of Ritual* (*Liji*) was compiled sometime during the second century BCE but might have included much earlier materials. It contains extensive prescriptions on domestic life, many of which bear on the status of children in family and society, expectations for children, and children's education. The selections show that whereas there were numerous rules for children to obey, very young children received special treatment in law and by adult family members. The different treatments of boys and girls can also be seen in a variety of areas. Many of the ideas in the selections were continually implemented and reinvented in later Chinese history, as Confucian scholar-officials of various dynasties kept returning to this classic in writing family instructions, proposing educational policies, and envisioning moral reforms. The numbering of parts and paragraphs in James Legge's translation has been retained for the convenience of the reader.

Document 6–5

Summary of the Rules of Propriety

1.7.27. When one is ten years old, we call him a boy; he goes [out] to school. When he is twenty, we call him a youth; he is capped. When he is thirty, we say, "He is at his maturity"; he has a wife. . . . At eighty or ninety, we say of him, "He is very old." When he is seven, we say that he is an object of pitying love. Such a child and one who is very old, though they may be chargeable with crime, are not subjected to punishment.

II.5.17. A boy should never be allowed to see an instance of deceit. A lad should not wear a jacket of fur nor the skirt [translator's note: To make him handy, and leave him free to execute any service required of him]. He must stand straight and square, and not incline his head in hearing. When an elder is holding him with the hand, he should hold the elder's hand with both his hands. When the elder has shifted his sword to his back and is speaking to him with the side of his face bent down, he should cover his mouth with his hand in answering. When he is following his teacher, he should not quit the road to speak with another person. When he meets his teacher on the road, he should hasten forward to him, and stand with his hands joined across his breast. If the teacher speak to him, he will answer; if he do not, he will retire with hasty steps. When, following an elder, they ascend a level height, he must keep his face towards the quarter to which the elder is looking.

The Pattern of the Family

1.5. Youths who have not yet been capped, and maidens who have not yet assumed the hair-pin, at the first crowing of the cock, should wash their hands, rinse their mouths, comb their hair, draw over it the covering of silk, brush the dust from that which is left free, bind it up in the shape of a horn, and put on their necklaces. They should all hang at their girdles the ornamental [bags of] perfume; and as soon as it is daybreak, they should [go to] pay their respects [to their parents] and ask what they will eat and drink. If they have eaten already, they should retire; if they have not eaten, they will [remain to] assist their elder [brothers and sisters] and see what has been prepared.

1.6. The children go earlier to bed, and get up later, according to their pleasure. There is no fixed time for their meals.

II.16. When a wife was about to have a child, and the month of her confinement had arrived, she occupied one of the side apartments, where her husband sent twice a day to ask for her. If he were moved and came himself to ask about her, she did not presume to see him, but made her governess dress herself and reply to him.

When the child was born, the husband again sent twice a day to inquire for her. He fasted now, and did not enter the door of the side apartment. If the child were a boy, a bow was placed on the left of the door; and if a girl, a handkerchief on the right of it. After three days the child began to be carried, and some archery was practiced for a boy, but not for a girl.

II.17.   When a son and heir to the ruler of a state was born, and information of the fact was carried to him, he made arrangements to receive him at a feast where the three animals should all be provided; and the cook took in hand the [necessary] preparations. On the third day the tortoise-shell was consulted for a good man to carry the child; and he who was the lucky choice, kept a vigil over night, and then in his court robes, received him in his arms outside the chamber. The master of the archers then took a bow of mulberry wood, and six arrows of the wild rubus, and shot towards heaven, earth, and the four cardinal points. After this the nurse received the child and carried it in her arms. The cook [at the same time] gave [a cup of] sweet wine to the man who had carried the child, and presented him with a bundle of silks, and the tortoise-shell was again employed to determine the wife of an officer, or the concubine of a Great officer, who should be nurse.

II.18.   In all cases of receiving a son, a day was chosen; and if it were the eldest son of the king, the three animals were killed [for the occasion]. For the son of a common man, a sucking-pig was killed; for the son of an officer, a single pig; for the son of a Great officer, the two smaller animals; and for the son of the ruler of a state, all the three. If it were not the eldest son, the provision was diminished in every case one degree.

II.19.   A special apartment was prepared in the palace for the child, and from all the concubines and other likely individuals there was sought one distinguished for her generosity of mind, her gentle kindness, her mild integrity, her respectful bearing, her carefulness and freedom from talkativeness, who should be appointed the boy's teacher; one was next chosen who should be his indulgent mother, and a third who should be his guardian mother. These all lived in his apartment, which others did not enter unless on some [special] business.

II.28.   Among the common people who had no side chambers, when the month of confinement was come, the husband left his bed-chamber, and occupied a common apartment. In his inquiries for his wife, however, and on his son's being presented to him, there was no difference [from the observances that have been detailed].

II.30. The nurse of the ruler's boy quitted the palace after three years, and, when she appeared before the ruler, was rewarded for her toilsome work. The son of a Great officer had a nurse. The wife of an ordinary officer nourished her child herself.

II.32. When the child was able to take its own food, it was taught to use the right hand. When it was able to speak, a boy [was taught to] respond boldly and clearly; a girl, submissively and low. The former was fitted with a girdle of leather; the latter, with one of silk.

II.33. At six years, they were taught the numbers and the names of the cardinal points; at the age of seven, boys and girls did not occupy the same mat nor eat together; at eight, when going out or coming in at a gate or door, and going to their mats to eat and drink, they were required to follow their elders:—the teaching of yielding to others was now begun; at nine, they were taught how to number the days.

At ten, [the boy] went to a master outside, and stayed with him [even] over the night. He learned the [different classes of] characters and calculation; he did not wear his jacket or trousers of silk; in his manners he followed his early lessons; morning and evening he learned the behavior of a youth; he would ask to be exercised in [reading] the tablets, and in the forms of polite conversation.

II.34. At thirteen, he learned music, and to repeat the odes, and to dance the Zhuo [of the duke of Zhou]. When a full-grown lad, he danced the Xiang [of King Wu]. He learned archery and chariot-driving. At twenty, he was capped, and first learned the [different classes of] ceremonies, and might wear furs and silk. He danced the Daxia [of Yu], and attended sedulously to filial and fraternal duties. He might become very learned, but did not teach others;—[his object being still] to receive and not to give out.

II.36. A girl at the age of ten ceased to go out [from the women's apartments]. Her governess taught her [the arts of] pleasing speech and manners, to be docile and obedient, to handle the hempen fibers, to deal with the cocoons, to weave silks and form fillets, to learn [all] woman's work, how to furnish garments, to watch the sacrifices, to supply the liquors and sauces, to fill the various stands and dishes with pickles and brine, and to assist in setting forth the appurtenances for the ceremonies.

II.37. At fifteen, she assumed the hair-pin; at twenty, she was married, or, if there were occasion [for the delay], at twenty-three.

Source: *Li Chi, Book of Rites: An Encyclopedia of Ancient Ceremonial Usages, Religious Creeds, and Social Institutions*, 2 vols., translated by James Legge (New York: University Books, 1967), I: 65–66, 69–70, 451–452, 471–472, 477–479.

Mencius

Revered as the Second Sage in later Chinese history, Mencius (ca. 372–289 BCE) was a major thinker in early Confucianism. His activities and thought, as recorded in *Mencius*, were predominantly concerned with ending the perennial chaos of the age (the Warring States Period) and restoring the harmonious sociopolitical and moral order of the legendary sage kings. Mencius is best known for his theory on the innate goodness of human nature, which education and correct environment will serve to nourish. Moral perfection can therefore be understood in terms of retaining the innocence of the newborn infant. Later the education of the young Mencius became the subject of some famous stories (Docs. 6–9, 6–10). Mencius was also often quoted for his pronouncement on the importance of bearing male children in order to fulfill one's duty to the family line.

Document 6–6

1A7. [Mencius expounds the Way of the true King for King Xuan of Qi.] "Treat the aged of your own family in a manner befitting their venerable age and extend this treatment to the aged of other families; treat your own young in a manner befitting their tender age and extend this to the young of other families, and you can roll the Empire on your palm."

1B5. [Mencius explains Kingly government for King Xuan of Qi, using the example of King Wen, one of the sage kings.] "Old men without wives, old women without husbands, old people without children, young children without fathers—these four types of people are the most destitute and have no one to turn to for help. Whenever King Wen put benevolent measures into effect, he always gave them first consideration. The *Book of Odes* says,

> Happy are the rich;
> But have pity on the helpless."

2A6. Mencius said, "No man is devoid of a heart sensitive to the suffering of others. . . . Suppose a man were, all of a sudden, to see a young child on the verge of falling into a well. He would certainly be moved to compassion, not because he wanted to get in the good graces of the parents, nor because he wished to win the praise of his fellow villagers or friends, nor yet because he disliked the cry of the child. From it can be seen that whoever is devoid of the heart of compassion is not human, that whoever is devoid of the heart of shame is not human, whoever is devoid of the heart of courtesy and modesty is not human, and whoever is devoid of the heart of right and wrong is not human. The heart of compassion is the germ of benevolence; the heart of shame, of dutifulness; the heart of courtesy and modesty, of observance of the rites; the heart of right and wrong, of wisdom. Man has these four germs just as he has four limbs. For a man possessing these four germs to deny his own potentialities is for him to cripple himself; for him to deny the potentialities of his prince is for him to cripple his prince. If a man is able to develop all these four germs that he possesses, it will be like a fire starting up or a spring coming through. When these are fully developed, he can take under his protection the whole realm within the Four Seas, but if he fails to develop them, he will not be able even to serve his parents."

3A4.   [Mencius on a true king's duty to educate his people.] "Hou Ji [a legendary culture hero and sage king] . . . appointed Xie as the Minister of Education whose duty was to teach the people human relationships: love between father and son, duty between ruler and subject, distinction between husband and wife, precedence of the old over the young, and faith between friends."

4A18.   Gongsun Chou said, "Why does a gentleman not take on the teaching of his own sons?"

"Because in the nature of things," said Mencius, "it will not work. A teacher necessarily resorts to correction, and if correction produces no effect, he will end by losing his temper. When this happens, father and son will hurt each other instead. 'You teach me by correcting me, but you yourself are not correct.' So father and son hurt each other, and it is bad that such a thing should happen. In antiquity people taught one another's sons. Father and son should not demand goodness from each other. To do so will estrange them, and there is nothing more inauspicious than estrangement between father and son."

4A26.   "There are three ways of being a bad son. The most serious is to have no heir."

4B12.   "A great man is one who retains the heart of a new-born babe."

Source: *Mencius*, translated by D. C. Lau (Harmondsworth: Penguin, 1970), 56, 65–66, 82–83, 102, 125, 127, 130.

The Book of Filial Piety

The *Book of Filial Piety* (*Xiaojing*) may have been compiled around the beginning of China's imperial period. It posits filial piety as the "foundation of virtue and the root of civilization" and the violation of filial piety as the most heinous of all crimes. Moreover, it establishes a homology between filial piety and loyalty to rulers, thereby creating a unity of familial and political virtue. Though the text seldom directly addresses small children, it was used as a basic text in elementary education from Han times onward, apparently because it conveys in succinct language the central virtue of Confucianism that children should learn from the very beginning.

Document 6-7

Now the feeling of affection for parents grows up in early childhood. When the duty of nourishing those parents is exercised, the affection daily develops into a sense of awe. The sages proceed from the feeling of awe to teach the duties of respect, and from that affection to teach those of love. . . . What they proceeded from [i.e., affection for parents] was the root. The relation and duties between father and son thus belong to the Heaven-conferred nature; they contain in them the principle of righteousness between ruler and subject.

Source: *The Sacred Books of China: The Texts of Confucianism.* Vol. 3 of *The Sacred Books of the East*, edited by F. Max Müller (Oxford: Clarendon Press, 1899), 478–479.

Xunzi

Xunzi (ca. 310–230 BCE), the other great early Confucian philosopher after Confucius and Mencius, formed a contrast with Mencius in his emphasis on the need to control and rectify human beings' innate evil tendencies. Whereas Mencius understood education in terms of the retaining, nourishing, and perfecting of the inherent goodness of the child, Xunzi compared the necessary imposition of ritual training, moral discipline, and correct environment to the shaping, straightening, and correcting of warped materials. Thanks to his great success as a teacher, Xunzi played a very important role in the transmission and interpretation of the Confucian canon at the beginning of China's imperial period.

Document 6-8

Encouraging Learning

The gentleman says: Learning should never cease. Blue comes from the indigo plant but is bluer than the plant itself. Ice is made of water but is colder than water ever is. A piece of wood as straight as a plumb line may be bent into a circle as true as any drawn with a compass and, even after the wood has dried, it will not straighten out again. The bending process has made it that way. Thus, if wood is pressed against a straightening board, it can be made straight; if metal is put to the grindstone, it can be sharpened and if the gentleman studies widely and each day examines himself, his wisdom will become clear and his conduct be without fault. . . . Children born among the Han or Yüeh people of the south and among the Mo barbarians of the north cry with the same voice at birth, but as they grow older they follow different customs. Education causes them to differ.

Man's Nature is Evil

Those who maintain that the nature is good praise and approve whatever has not departed from the original simplicity and naïveté of the child. . . . Now it is the nature of man that when he is hungry he will desire satisfaction, when he is cold he will desire warmth, and when he is weary he will desire rest. This is his emotional nature. And yet a man, although he is hungry, will not dare to be the first to eat if he is in the presence of his elders, because he knows that he should yield to them, and although he is weary, he will not dare to demand rest because he knows that he should relieve others of the burden of labor. For a son to yield to his father or a younger brother to yield to his elder brother, for a son to relieve his father of work or a younger brother to relieve his elder brother—acts such as these are all contrary to man's nature and run counter to his emotions. And yet they represent the way of filial piety and the proper forms enjoined by ritual principles. Hence, if men follow their emotional nature, there will be no courtesy or humility; courtesy and humility in fact run counter to man's emotional nature. From this it is obvious, then, that man's nature is evil, and that his goodness is the result of conscious activity.

Source: *Hsun Tzu: Basic Writings*, translated by Burton Watson (New York: Columbia University Press, 1963), 15, 159–160.

Exoteric Commentary on the Han School Text of the Book of Poetry

The *Exoteric Commentary on the Han School Text of the Book of Poetry* (*Hanshi waizhuan*), a collection of moralizing anecdotes illustrated by quotations from the *Book of Poetry,* was attributed to the Han dynasty scholar Han Ying (fl. 150 BCE). The first selection is reminiscent of *Mencius* 4A18 (Doc. 6–6) in its advocacy of love and toleration in the art of being a father, and it is also noteworthy for suggesting that children should be treated differently before and after the capping ceremony. The two anecdotes about young Mencius demonstrate the important role mothers played in their children's upbringing.

Document 6-9

7.27. To practice the art of being a father, one must embrace a tender and benevolent (*ren*) love with which to rear a son. One quiets him with food and drink, so that his body may be perfect. When he begins to have understanding, [the father] must maintain a stern demeanor and speak correctly to lead him forward. When it is time to tie up his hair [translator's footnote: at puberty], [the father] provides him with an intelligent teacher to perfect his abilities. At nineteen he shows his ambitions, and [his father] invites a guest to cap him. This serves to complete his virtue. His blood is pure and his pulse steady, and so [his father] betroths him so as to keep it that way. The relations [between father and son] are characterized by honesty and friendliness, with no trace of suspicion. After the son is capped, [his father] does not curse him, nor does he beat him after his hair is bound up. He listens to [his son's] subtle reproach and does not let him worry. Such is the art of being a father.

The Ode says,

> Oh my father, who begat me!
> Oh my mother, who nourished me!
> Ye indulged me, ye fed me,
> Ye held me up, ye supported me.
> Ye looked after me, ye never left me,
> Out and in ye bore me in your arms

9.1 Mencius as a child was once reciting his lessons when his mother happened to be spinning. Breaking off suddenly, he stopped in the middle, then started up again. His mother knew his mind was wandering, and called out to ask, "Why do you stop in the middle?"

He replied, "I had forgotten part of it, and then I remembered it again." His mother took a knife and cut her thread. She did this as a warning to him. After that Mencius did not let his mind wander again.

When Mencius was a child, their neighbor on the east killed a pig. Mencius asked his mother, "What did our neighbor on the east kill the pig for?

His mother said, "To feed you." His mother then regretted [her words] and said, "When I was pregnant with this child I would not sit on a mat that was not straight, nor would I eat meat that was not cut properly—this was teaching him in the womb. To deceive him now when he has grown to have understanding is to teach him to be distrustful." Whereupon she purchased some of the pork from the neighbor on the east and fed it to him to show that she had not been deceiving him. The Ode says,

Right it is that your descendants
Should be as in unbroken strings.

It speaks of a worthy mother making her son worthy.

Source: *Han Shih Wai Chuan: Han Ying's Illustrations of the Didactic Application of the Classic of Songs*, translated by James Robert Hightower (Cambridge: Harvard University Press, 1952), 250–251, 290.

The Biographies of Women

Attributed to Liu Xiang (ca. 79–8 BCE), the Han scholar and bibliographer, the *Biographies of Women (Lienü zhuan)* was an anthology of life stories of historical or quasi-historical women intended to offer a moral guide for female conduct. The tremendous influence of this work can be seen from the fact that it inspired countless imitations and expanded editions, and served as a basic text for girls' and women's education in the next two thousand years. The selected stories, which are about mothers' crucial responsibilities for the upbringing of their children, show that such responsibilities start with the so-called "prenatal instruction" and continue through a long process that requires determined efforts, wise judgments, and skillful persuasion.

Document 6–10
Tairen, Mother of King Wen

Tairen's disposition was upright, sincere, decorous, and engaged solely in virtuous conduct. When she was with child, her eyes would not gaze on evil things; her ears would not listen to lewd sounds; and her mouth would not emit insolent words. She was capable in prenatal instruction. She gave birth to King Wen as she was about to urinate in the pigsty. King Wen grew up and became an illustrious sage. Tairen taught him one thing and [from that] he comprehended a hundred others.

The Man of Noble Sentiments says: Tairen was capable in prenatal instruction. In ancient times, a woman with child did not lie on her side as she slept; neither would she sit sidewise nor stand on one foot. She would not eat dishes having harmful flavors; if the food was cut awry, she would not eat it; if the mat was not placed straight, she would not sit on it. She did not let her eyes gaze on lewd sights nor let her ears listen to depraved sounds. At night she ordered the blind musicians to chant poetry. She used right reason to adjust affairs, and thus gave birth to children of correct physical form who excelled others in talent and virtue. For this reason a woman with child should be careful about things that affect her. If she is affected by good things, the child will be good; if she is affected by evil things, the child will be evil. Men resemble the natural order because their mothers were influenced by that order. For that reason their features and sounds correspond to it. King Wen's mother may be said to have known how to make her child conform to it.

The Mother of Mencius

She was living near a graveyard when Mencius was small and he enjoyed going out to play as if he were working among the graves. He enthusiastically built up the graves and performed burials. His mother said, "This is not the place for me to keep my son." Then she departed and dwelt beside a market place. Since he enjoyed playing as if his business were that of the merchant and bargainer, his mother again said, "This is not the place for me to live with my son." She once more moved her abode and dwelt beside a schoolhouse. He [Mencius] amused himself by setting up the instruments of worship and by bowing politely to those coming and going. Mencius' mother said, "Truly my son can dwell here." Thereafter they dwelt there and as Mencius grew up he learned the six liberal arts. In the end he attained fame as a great scholar. The Man of Noble Sentiments says: Mencius' mother was able to improve others gradually. . . .

While Mencius was young yet, he was studying at school. When he returned home, Mencius' mother, who was weaving, asked him, saying, "How much have you learned?" Mencius said, "About as usual." Mencius' mother took up a knife and cut the web of her loom. Mencius was frightened and asked the reason for her doing that. Mencius' mother said, "Your being remiss in your studies is like my cutting the web of my loom. Now, the Superior Man learns that he may establish a reputation; he investigates that he may broaden his knowledge. Therefore if you remain inactive, you will be peaceful; if you arouse yourself, you will keep harm away. If you now abandon your studies, you will not avoid becoming a privy servant and will be without means of freeing yourself from your misfortune. What difference is there [in your studying] and my weaving? I spin thread that we may have food. If the woman abandons her weaving when she half way through, how shall she clothe her husband and how shall he grow without grain to eat? Just as the woman who abandons what she has to eat, so the man who fails in his cultivation of virtue, if he does not become a thief or robber, will become a captive or slave." Mencius, having become frightened, studied diligently morning and evening without respite. He served his teacher, Zisi [translator's footnote: grandson of Confucius], and consequently became the most famous scholar of the whole nation.

Source: *The Position of Woman in Early China: According to the Lieh Nü Chuan, "The Biographies of Eminent Chinese Women,"* translated by Albert Richard O'Hara (Taipei: Mei Ya Publications, 1978), 23–24, 39–40.

The Precepts for Women

The author of the *Precepts for Women* (*Nüjie*) was Ban Zhao (d. 116 CE), the most celebrated woman scholar in premodern China. Widowed at a young age, Ban Zhao brought up her son and apparently had a busy and productive life. She took over the writing of the *History of the Western Han* when her historian brother died in 92 CE. At the emperor's request she taught the classics, history, and other subjects to the women in the imperial palace, and she also offered instruction for the young women of her own extended family (who were the original recipients of the *Precepts*). In the first selection Ban Zhao interprets Ode 189 of the *Book of Poetry* (Doc. 6-1) to illustrate the different expectations for boys and girls. In the second she argues, against current practice, that girls should be educated so that they might make better wives.

Document 6–11

Humility

On the third day after the birth of a girl the ancients observed three customs: [first] to place the baby below the bed; [second] to give her a potsherd with which to play; and [third] to announce her birth to her ancestors by an offering. Now to lay the baby below the bed plainly indicated that she is lowly and weak, and should regard it as her primary duty to humble herself before others. To give her potsherds with which to play indubitably signified that she should practice labor and consider it her primary duty to be industrious. To announce her birth before her ancestors clearly meant that she ought to esteem as her primary duty the continuation of the observance of worship in the home.

Husband and Wife

[The gentlemen of the present age] only know that wives must be controlled, and that the husband's rules of conduct manifesting his authority must be established. They therefore teach their boys to read books and [study] histories. But they do not in the least understand that husbands and masters must [also] be served, and that the proper relationship and the rites should be maintained.

Yet only to teach men and not to teach women,—is that not ignoring the essential relationship between them? According to the "Record of Ritual," it is the rules to begin to teach children to read at the age of eight years, and by the age of fifteen years they ought then to be ready for cultural training. Only why should it not be [that girls' education as well as boys' be] according to this principle?

Source: *Pan Chao: Foremost Woman Scholar of China*, translated by Nancy Lee Swann (New York: Russell & Russell, 1932), 83, 84–85.

Yan's Family Instructions

Yan's Family Instructions (*Yanshi jiaxun*) by Yan Zhitui (531–591), was the first famous work in the genre of "family instructions," usually written by patriarchs to set rules and injunctions and to offer moral and practical advice for their family members. Living at a time marked by severe sociopolitical breakdown and flourishing of Buddhism, Yan freely allowed Buddhism a place in his teachings, although his central attention to managing the household and regulating family relationships demonstrated unmistakably Confucian concerns. The first selection, from Yan's preface to the work, is especially valuable as a recollection of his own childhood experience.

Document 6–12

Preface

The habits and teaching of our family have always been regular and strict. In my childhood I had the advantage of good instruction from my parents. With my two elder brothers I went to greet our parents each morning and evening to ask in winter whether they were warm and in summer whether they were cool; we walked steadily with regular steps, talked slowly with good manners and moved about as dignified and reverent as though we were visiting the awe-inspiring rulers at court. They gave us good advice, asked about our particular interests, criticized our defects and encouraged our good points—always zealous and sincere. When I was just nine years old, my father died. The family members were divided and scattered, every one of us living in poverty. I was brought up by my loving brothers, who went through hardships and difficulties. They were kind but not exacting; their guidance and advice to me were not strict. Though I read the *Book of Decorum* and its commentaries and was somewhat fond of composition, I was greatly influenced by vulgar practices, uncontrolled in feelings, careless in speech and slovenly in dress. When about eighteen or nineteen years old I learned to refine my conduct a little. As these bad habits had become second nature, it was difficult to get rid of them entirely. After my thirtieth year gross faults were few but still I had to be careful always; for my words and my reason, my passions and my nature were like enemies to each other. Each evening I became conscious of the faults committed that morning and today I regretted the errors of yesterday. How pitiful that the lack of instruction brought me to this condition! Recalling past experience, not merely precepts once learned from old books but my own experience engraved upon the bone and muscle of physical nature, I leave these twenty chapters to warn and guard you boys.

Teaching Children

Those of the highest intelligence will succeed without teaching; those of great stupidity even if taught will amount to nothing; those of medium ability will be ignorant unless taught. The ancient sage-kings had rules for pre-natal training. Women when pregnant for three months moved from their living quarters to a detached palace where sly glances would not be seen nor disturbing sounds heard, and where the tone of music and the flavor of flood were controlled by the rules of decorum. These rules were written on jade tablets and kept in a golden box. After the child was born, imperial tutors conversant with filial piety, human-heartedness, decorum, and righteousness guided and trained him.

The common people cannot follow such ways. But as soon as a baby can recognize facial expressions and understand approval and disapproval, training should be begun in doing what he is told and stopping when so ordered. For several years punishment with the bamboo rod should be avoided. Parental strictness and dignity mingled with tenderness will usually lead boys and girls to a feeling of respect and carefulness and so arouse filial piety. I have noticed in this generation that where there is merely love without training this result is never achieved. Children eat, drink, speak and act as they please. Instead of needed prohibitions they receive praise; instead of urgent reprimands they receive smiles. Even when children are old enough to learn, such treatment is still regarded as the proper method. After the child has formed proud and arrogant habits, they begin to control him. But whipping the child even to death will not lead him to repentance, while the growing anger of the parents only increases his resentment. After he grows up such a child becomes at last nothing but a scoundrel. Confucius was right in saying, "What is acquired in babyhood is like original nature; what has been formed into habits is equal to instinct." A common proverb says, "Train a wife from her first arrival; teach a son in his babyhood." How true such sayings are!

Ordinary parents who cannot teach their sons and daughters do not intend to involve them in wickedness; they merely fear that heavy reprimands will cause loss of face, and that unbearable beating will injure their bodies. We should take illness as an illustration. If drugs, medicines, acupuncture and cautery are not used, can there be any cure? Should we think, then, that those who are strict in reproving and training are cruel to their own flesh and blood? No, indeed, they have no choice!

Relations between parents and children should be dignified without familiarity; in the love between blood-relations there should be no rudeness. If there is rudeness, affection and fidelity cannot unite; if there is familiarity, carelessness and disrespect will grow.

Source: *Family Instructions for the Yen Clan*, translated by Teng Ssu-yü (Leiden: E. J. Brill, 1968), 1–5.

Han Yu

Han Yu (768-824), scholar and essayist, was a major figure in the Tang (618-907) revival of Confucianism following several centuries of relative decline amid sociopolitical disunity and flourishing of Buddhism and Daoism. Aside from his accomplishments in prose writing, Han was known for his attempt to establish a lineage of the Confucian masters and for his special exaltation of Mencius. The following is the requiem Han wrote for his fourth daughter named Na, who died at twelve in 819. The essay, composed in 823, recounts the unhappy circumstances of the girl's death and burial and expresses the father's sorrow over his inability to save his child.

Document 6–13

Requiem for Na

On such a day, such a month, and such a year, your dad and mom send your wet nurse to your grave with pure wine, seasonal fruit, and a variety of delicious food to be offered to the spirit of Nazi, their fourth daughter.

Alas, you were gravely ill just when I was about to be exiled to the south. The parting came so suddenly that you were both startled and grieved. When I caught my last glimpse of you, I knew death would make our separation permanent. When you looked at me, you were too sad to cry. After I left for the south, the family was also driven out. You were helped into a sedan chair and traveled from early morning to night. Snow and ice injured your weakened flesh. Shaken and rocked, you did not have any rest. There was no time to eat and drink, so you suffered from frequent thirst and hunger. To die in the wild mountains was not the fate you deserved. It is usually the parents' guilt that brings calamities to their children. Was I not the cause of your coming to such a pass?

You were buried hastily by the roadside in a coffin which could hardly be called a coffin. After you were interred the group had to leave. There was no one to care for your grave or watch over it. Your soul was solitary and your bones were cold. Although everyone must die, you died unjustly. When I traveled back from the south I made a stop at your grave. As I wept over you I could see your eyes and face. How could I ever forget your words and expressions?

Now on an auspicious day I am having you moved to our ancestral cemetery. Do not be frightened or fearful: you will be safe along the way. There will be fragrant drink and sweet food for you, and you will arrive in your permanent resting place in a nice new coffin. Peace will be with you for ten thousand years!

Source: Pei-yi Wu, trans., "Childhood Remembered: Parents and Children in China, 800 to 1700," in Anne Behnke Kinney, ed., *Chinese Views of Childhood* (Honolulu: University of Hawai'i Press, 1995), 139.

The Analects for Women

The *Analects for Women* (*Nü Lunyu*) was by Song Ruozhao (ninth century), one of the five learned sisters of the Song family in the Tang dynasty. Emulating Ban Zhao's achievements, Song Ruozhao never married and won fame for her scholarship when she was summoned by the emperor to provide instruction for the palace women. The title of her most famous work indicates its aspiration to provide an authoritative guide for women's conduct, a goal that presumably would be facilitated by its adoption of the verse form and a colloquial idiom (not easily seen in the translation). The selection, from the chapter on "Instructing Girls and Boys," not only reiterates the different treatments for boys and girls and the importance of the mother in childrearing but also describes in vivid language the kinds of undesirable behavior to be forbidden in children.

Document 6–14

Instructing Girls and Boys

Most all families have sons and daughters. As they grow and develop, there should be a definite sequence and order in their education. But the authority/responsibility to instruct them rests solely with the mother. When the sons go out to school, they seek instruction from a teacher who teaches them proper [ritual] form and etiquette, how to chant poetry, how to write essays. . . .

Daughters remain behind in the women's quarters and should not be allowed to go out very often. . . . Teach them sewing, cooking, and etiquette. . . . Don't allow them to be indulged, lest they throw tantrums to get their own way; don't allow them to defy authority, lest they become rude and haughty; don't allow them to sing songs, lest they become dissolute; and don't allow them to go on outings, lest some scandal spoil their good names.

Worthy of derision are those who don't take charge of their responsibility [in this area]. The sons of such women remain illiterate, they poke fun at their elders, they get into fights and drink too much, and they become addicted to singing and dancing . . . the daughters of such women know nothing about ritual decorum, speak in an overbearing manner, can't distinguish between the honorable and the mean, and don't know how to serve or sew. They bring shame on their honorable relatives and disgrace on their father and mother. Mothers who fail to raise their children correctly are as if they had raised pigs and rats!

Source: In Wm. Theodore de Bary and Irene Bloom, eds., *Sources of Chinese Tradition*, vol.1, *From Earliest Times to 1600*, second edition (New York: Columbia University Press, 1999), 830.

Zhu Xi

Zhu Xi (1130–1200), the Song (960–1279) scholar-official, was arguably the most influential Chinese philosopher after the Han. Through his authoritative commentaries on the Confucian classics and his diligent work as editor and educator, Zhu provided a synthesis of Neo-Confucianism that was to become the orthodox ideology in the last few centuries of China's imperial period. Children's upbringing and education being an inherent part of Zhu's vision on Confucian moral cultivation, he treated it in a variety of works, most of which were compiled from the Confucian classics or the sayings of both past and contemporary Confucian thinkers. The selections are from *Family Rituals* (*Jiali*) and *Reflections on Things at Hand* (*Jinsi lu*, co-edited with Lü Zuqian, 1137–1181). Though they are largely concerned with the child as an object of moral training and discipline, there are also precious indications of the awareness that adults can benefit from teaching children and that interest is important for children's learning.

Document 6–15

Family Rituals

If a wet nurse is sought for a newborn son, a woman from a respectable family of a gentle and modest nature should be chosen. (Not only would a bad nurse violate family regulations, but she would also influence the temperament and behavior of the child in her care.) Children old enough to eat should be given food and taught to use their right hands in eating. Those old enough to talk should be taught their names and greetings such as "at your service," "bless you," and "sleep well." As they gain some understanding, they should be taught to respect their seniors. Anytime they fail to behave properly toward them, they must be scolded and warned not to act that way again.

In ancient times even prenatal instruction was practiced, not to mention postnatal education. From the time of a child's birth, even before he can understand, we familiarize him with the proprieties. How, then, can we ignore proper behavior when he is old enough to understand it? Confucius said that what is formed in childhood is like part of one's nature, what has been learned through practice becomes like instinct. *The Family Instructions of Mr. Yan* says, "Teach a bride when she first arrives; teach a child while it is still a baby." Therefore, from the time children begin to understand, they must be made to learn the distinctions of etiquette based on age and generation. In cases where they insult their parents or hit their elder brothers and sisters, if their parents laugh and praise them instead of scolding or punishing them, the children, not knowing right from wrong, will think such behavior is natural. By the time they are grown, their habits have been formed. Their parents now become angry and forbid them to do such things, but they find themselves unable to control them. As a result, the father will hate his son, and the son will resent his father. Cruelty and defiance of any sort can then occur, and all because the parents were short-sighted and failed to prevent the evil from the beginning; in other words, bad character is nourished by indulgence.

At the age of six, a child is taught the words for numbers (1, 10, 100, 1,000, 10,000) and directions (east, west, south, north). Boys should begin learning how to write, and girls should be taught simple women's work. At the age of seven, boys and girls no longer sit together or eat together. At this age boys recite the *Classic of Filial Piety* and the *Analects*. It is a good idea for girls to recite them too.

Before the seventh year, children are called youngsters; they can go to sleep early, get up late, and eat whenever they wish. Beginning with the eighth year, however, whenever they enter or exist through a doorway or whenever they sit down to eat, they must wait their turn, which will come after all those who are older. At this age they begin to learn modesty and yielding. Boys recite the *Book of Documents* and young girls no longer go past the door of the inner quarters.

At nine years boys recite the *Spring and Autumn Annals* and other histories. The texts are now explained to them, so that they can understand moral principle. At this age girls have explained to them the *Analects*, the *Classic of Filial Piety*, and such books as *Biographies of Admirable Women*[5] and *Warnings for Women*[6] so that they comprehend the main ideas.

In ancient times all virtuous women read illustrated histories to educate themselves; some, such as Cao Dagu (Ban Zhao), became quite conversant in the classics and could discuss issues intelligently. Nowadays, some people teach their daughters to write songs and poems and popular music; these are entirely inappropriate activities.

At the age of ten, boys ought to go out to study under a school master and should stay in the outer quarters or away from home. They should study the commentaries to the *Classic of Poetry* and the *Record of Ritual*, which will be explained to them by their teacher. They should also be taught the essence of benevolence, moral duty, etiquette, wisdom, and faithfulness. From this time on, they can study Mencius, Xunzi, Yangzi, and read widely in other works. The essential ones, however, should be recited. (These include the *Record of Ritual*'s "Record of Learning," "Great Learning," "Centrality and Commonality," and "Record of Music.") At the same time heretical books not written by sages ought to be prohibited so that the student will not become confused. Not until boys understand all of these books should they begin composition. For girls, at this age instruction in compliance and obedience and the principal household tasks should begin.

Household tasks such as breeding silkworms, weaving, sewing, and cooking are the proper duties of a woman. In addition, instruction in them lets a girl learn the hardships through which food and clothing are obtained so that she will not dare to be extravagant. Concerning delicate crafts, however, no instruction is needed.

Before they are capped or pinned, young boys and girls should rise at daybreak, comb their hair into top-knots, wash their faces, and then call on their elders. When assisting their elders at meals or ancestral rites, they should help by holding the food and wine. After the capping or pinning ceremonies, however, they will be expected to behave with the proper manners of adults and can no longer be regarded as children.

As a rule, mourning is reduced one degree for those who die young. Those aged from sixteen to nineteen are classed as upper early deaths, those from twelve to fifteen middle early deaths, and those from eight to eleven lower early deaths. In cases where they would otherwise have been mourned for a year, for upper early death, it is reduced to greater processed cloth for nine months; for middle early death, to seven months; for lower early death, to lesser processed cloth for five months. In cases where they would otherwise have been mourned at the level of "greater processed cloth" [nine months] or lower, it is reduced one degree. Anyone who dies before a full eight years does not have mourning garments worn for him or her. One wails for them for a limited period, converting months into days. Those who do not live three months are wept over. A man who has married or a daughter who is engaged is not classed as an early death.

Source: *Chu Hsi's Family Rituals: A Twelfth-Century Chinese Manual for the Performance of Cappings, Weddings, Funerals, and Ancestral Rites*, translated by Patricia Ebrey (Princeton: Princeton University Press, 1991), 31–33, 95–96.

Document 6–16
Reflections on Things at Hand

V. Correcting Mistakes

41. Since the training of children is neglected today, people from childhood on are proud, lazy, and spoiled. As they grow up, they become even more wicked. Because they have never performed the duties of younger people, they consider their parents as separated from them and refuse to submit to them. The root of this trouble is always present. It will grow according to circumstances and will remain unchanged until their death. As young people they will not be happy with sweeping the floor and answering questions. As friends they cannot be humble toward their associates. As government officials they cannot bow to other officials. And as prime ministers they cannot bow to men of virtue in the world. In extreme cases they will follow their selfish desires, and all moral prin-

ciples will be destroyed. All this because the root of the trouble is not removed and will grow according to the place one lives in and the people he associates with. One must get rid of this trouble in everything. Then moral principles will always win.

Methods of Handling Affairs

64. One can benefit from teaching young boys. They keep one busy so one will not be going in and out. This is the first benefit. In teaching others, one goes over the lesson again and again and thus understands the meaning himself. This is the second benefit. In front of boys, one must be correct in attire and serious in expressions. This is the third benefit. One dares not be lazy for fear that one might spoil the talents of others. This is the fourth benefit.

XI. The Way to Teach

2. Master Yichuan [Cheng Yi] said: In bringing up children, the ancients taught them as soon as they could eat or speak. In the method of great learning, the first thing is to prevent evil before it starts. When a person is young, he is not master of his own knowledge or thought. Proverbs and sound doctrines should be spread before him every day. Although he does not yet understand, let their fragrance and sound surround him so his ears and mind can be filled with them. In time he will get used to them as if he had originally had them. Even if someone tries to delude him with other ideas, they will not be able to penetrate him. But if there has been no prevention, when he grows older selfish ideas and unbalanced desires will grow within and arguments from many mouths will drill from the outside, and it will be impossible for him to be pure and perfect.

8. In teaching people, if no interest is aroused, the people will surely not enjoy their study. . . . I want to write some poems generally instructing boys to attend to the duties of sprinkling, sweeping, answering questions, and serving elders [translator's footnote: first items in a boy's education], and let them sing these morning and evening. This should be of some help.

9. Zihou [Zhang Zai] teaches his students ceremonies. This is excellent, for that will enable the students to have something to hold on to from the beginning.

20. In ancient times a child was already able to be serious about things. When an elder held him by his hand, he held the elder's hand with both of his, and when he was asked a question, he covered his mouth with his hand while he answered. As soon as one is not serious about things, he will not be loyal or faithful. Therefore, in teaching children, let them first be quiet, careful, respectful, and reverent.

Source: *Reflections on Things at Hand: The Neo-Confucian Anthology*, translated by Wing-tsit Chan (New York: Columbia University Press, 1967), 169–170, 258–261, 263, 267.

Yuan's Precepts for Social Life

Yuan's Precepts for Social Life (*Yuanshi shifan*) was written by Yuan Cai (fl. 1140–1195), a Song scholar-official, as a practical guide for householders. Parent-child relationship was a central concern in the author's discussion of parental responsibilities and parenting skills. The advice on the importance of treating all the children impartially, starting education early, and avoiding spoiling young children suggests that there were many ways in which parents' misguided love could ruin their children and affect the well-being of the family. The strongly pragmatic and down-to-earth character of Yuan's work shows that the Confucian elite's deep interest in family life concerns both principles and practical management.

Document 6–17

1.11. Filial Sentiments

Babies are closely attached to their parents, and parents are extremely generous with their love for their babies, doing everything possible to care for them. The reason would seem to be that not long has passed since they were one flesh and blood, and besides, a baby's sounds, smiles, and gestures are such that they bring out the love in people. Furthermore, the Creator has made such attachment a principle of nature, to ensure that the succession of births will continue uninterrupted. Even the most insignificant insect, bird, or animal behaves this way. When the young first emerges from the womb or shell, these creatures suckle it or feed it pre-chewed food, going to all lengths to care for it. If something threatens their young, they protect it, heedless of their own safety.

When human beings are full grown, distinctions in status become stricter and distance becomes established; parents then are expected to express fully their kindness and children to express fully their filial duty. By contrast, when insect, birds, and animals mature a little, they no longer recognize their mothers nor their mothers them. This difference separates human beings from other creatures.

It is impossible to recount fully how parents care for their children in their earliest years. Thus the children will never be able to repay them for the care they received, even if they are solicitous of their parents their whole lives, entirely fulfilling their filial duties. How much more true is this for those whose filial conduct has been imperfect!

I would ask those who are not able to fulfill their duties to observe how people care for infants, how much they love them. This ought to bring them to their senses. The life-giving and life-nurturing principles of Heaven and Earth reach their fullest manifestation in man. But how do men repay Heaven and Earth? Some burn incense and kneel in prayer before the "void" (*hsü-k'ung*).

Some summon Taoist priests to offer sacrifices to God (*Shang-ti*). In this way they think they are repaying Heaven and Earth. In fact, they are only repaying one part in ten thousand of what they owe! And this is even more true of those who resent and blame Heaven and Earth! Such errors come from not reflecting.

1.12. Parental Blindness

Very often parents, during their son's infancy and childhood, love him so much they forget his faults; they give in to his every demand and tolerate his every action. If he cries for no reason, they do not have the sense to make him stop, but blame his nanny. If he bullies his playmates, his parents do not have the sense to correct him, but instead blame the other children. If someone tries to tell them that their child was the one in the wrong, they reply that he is too young to be blamed. As the days and months go by, they nurture his depravity. All this is the fault of the parents' misguided love.

As the boy grows older, the parents' love gradually lessens. They get angry at the slightest misdeed, treating it as a major crime. When they meet relatives and old friends, they relate every incident of misbehavior with great embellishments, guaranteeing that the boy gets labeled very unfilial, a label he does not deserve. All this is the fault of the parents' irrational disapproval.

The mother is usually the source of such unreasonable likes and dislikes. When the father fails to recognize this and listens to what she says, the situation can become irretrievable. Fathers must examine this situation with care. They must be strict with their sons when they are young and must not let their love grow thin as the sons reach maturity.

1.14. Educating Young Family Members

When rich and high-ranking families teach their boys to read, they certainly hope that they will pass the civil service examinations and also absorb the essence of the words and actions of the sages. But you cannot demand that your children all succeed, since people differ in their destinies and their intellectual capacities. Above all, you should not make them give up their education because they are not succeeding in the goal of entering civil service.

When young people are well-read, they gain what is called the "usefulness of the useless." Histories record stories. Literary collections contain elegant poems and essays. Even books on Yin-Yang, divination, magic, and fiction contain delightful tales. But there are so many books that no one can exhaust them in a few years. If young people spend their mornings and evenings amid such books they will certainly profit from them, and they will not have time for other affairs. Moreover, they will make friends with professional scholars and carry on discussions with them when they visit one another. Then how could they spend whole days like those who get enough to eat but apply their minds to nothing and get into trouble with riffraff?

1.15. Starting Education Early

When people have several sons, the care they give them in food, drink, and clothing must be equal. At the same time they must teach them to be scrupulous in observing distinctions based on age and rank and must teach them to distinguish wisdom from folly and truth from falsehood. If sons are shown equality when young, when grown they will not get into disputes about property. If they are taught the niceties, when grown they will not cause trouble through willful and arrogant behavior. If they are taught to make value judgments, when grown they will not do wrong.

Nowadays, people treat their sons in the contrary fashion. They are generous to those they like and stingy with those they dislike. But if in the beginning sons are not treated equally, how can the parents prevent them from later getting into disputes? Parents also let their sons insult their seniors and bully their juniors. But if such behavior is not corrected by reproof and punishment at the start, how can the parents prevent them from later becoming defiant? Parents also sometimes hate their good sons and love their unworthy ones. But if treatment starts unfairly, how can the parents prevent them from one day becoming bad?

1.19. Spoiling the Youngest Child

Among boys of the same mother, the oldest is often despised by his parents while the youngest is doted on. I once gave this perplexing phenomenon careful thought and now think I know the explanation. In the first and second year of life, a baby's every action, smile, and word makes us love him. Even strangers love little babies, so need I speak of their parents! From his third and fourth to his fifth and sixth years, the child becomes willful, screams and yells, and is generally contrary. He breaks things and is foolhardy. Everything he says or does elicits disapproval. Moreover, he is often obstinate and intractable. Therefore even his parents detest him.

Just when the older boy is at the most insufferable stage, his younger brother will be at the most adorable. The parents then transfer their love from the older to the younger boy, whom they love all the more. From then on the parents' affections follow separate course. When the youngest son reaches the detestable stage, there is no one who is lovable, so the parents have no one to transfer their love to and continue to dote on him. This is how the development seems to proceed.

Sons should recognize where their parents' love lies. Older ones ought to yield a little and younger ones ought to practice self-restraint. In addition parents must wake up to what they are doing and try to compensate a little. They should not do whatever they like or they will make the older ones resentful and the younger ones spoiled, leading to the ruin of the patrimony.

1.20. Spoiling the First Grandson
Whereas parents often dislike their oldest son, the grandparents often dote on him excessively. This situation is also perplexing. Could it be that the grandparents transfer their love for their youngest son to him?

3.15. Adoring Children
Rich people who dote on their little children deck them out with gold, silver, pearls, and jewels. Covetous inferior people will waylay the children in some quiet out-of-the-way spot and kill them to get the jewels. Even if the culprit is reported to the government and sentenced by the law, what good is this for you?

3.16. Leaving Children Unattended
In the city, because of the danger of kidnappers, do not allow little children out in the streets and alleys unless an adult male is carrying them or holding their hands.

3.17. Child Safety
Wells in people's houses should have railings around them, as should ponds. Care is needed at spots with deep ravines and rapid streams, high points where one could fall, and near machines that can be set off by a touch. Do not let little children get right up to them. If by any chance someone is careless, it will be too late to place the blame elsewhere.

Source: *Precepts for Social Life*, translated by Patricia Ebrey (Princeton: Princeton University Press, 1984), 188–192, 194–195, 284.

Zhen Dexiu's Instructions for Children

Zhen Dexiu (1178–1235) studied with one of Zhu Xi's disciples and was the most famous Neo-Confucian scholar after Zhu's generation in the Song dynasty. His *Instructions for Children* (*Jiaozi zhaigui*) was widely adopted in schools and anthologized in basic educational texts. Consisting of a series of stern commands and injunctions, the *Instructions* can be regarded as the epitome of the view in which the aim of education is quickly and efficiently to turn unruly children into adults and to instill in them the virtues of self-restraint, obedience, and industriousness. Inasmuch as this kind of regimented school code achieved great influence in late imperial times, it has been subjected to fierce criticism after modern Western theories of education were introduced to China.

Document 6–18

1. Learning the rites: to be [truly] human, one must know the Way and its principles and the different ritual prescriptions. At home one must serve parents; at the academy one must serve his teacher. They are entitled to equal respect and compliance. Follow their instructions. Listen to what they say; do what they prescribe. Do not be lazy, careless, or presumptuous.

2. Learning to sit: Settle yourself and sit straight; control your hands and feet; do not sit cross-legged or lean on anything; do not lie back or lean down.

3. Learning to walk: hold your arms in and walk slowly; do not swing your arms or jump about.

4. Learning to stand: Fold your hands and straighten your body; do not lean to one side or slouch over.

5. Learning to speak: Be plain and honest in your speech; do not lie or boast; speak softly and circumspectly; do not yell or shout.

6. Learning to bow [in salute]: Lower the head and bend at the waist; speak without gesticulating; do not be flippant or rude.

7. Learning to recite: Look at the characters with undivided attention; read slowly, short passages at a time; clearly distinguish, character by character; do not look at anything else or let your hands fiddle with anything.

8. Learning to write: Grasp the brush with firm intent; the characters must be balanced, regular, and perfectly clear; there must be no carelessness or messiness.

Source: In Wm. Theodore de Bary and Irene Bloom, eds., *Sources of Chinese Tradition*, vol.I, *From Earliest Times to 1600*, second edition (New York: Columbia University Press, 1999), 812.

Three-Character Classic

Attributed to Wang Yinglin (1223-1296), the eminent Song scholar, the *Three-Character Classic (Sanzi jing)* was perhaps the most commonly used primer when children started their education in late imperial China. Written in rhymed short verses (with three characters in each line), this text contains 508 different characters and covers such diverse subjects as the seasons, plants, animals, dynastic history, kinship terms, titles and contents of Confucian classics, and Confucian ethical values. Simplicity, broad coverage, and combination of literacy skills and moral knowledge accounted for the enduring popularity of this primer. The excerpt, which offers a flavor of this unique text, is peppered with the examples of various historical paragons–children celebrated for their exceptional virtues as well as talents–that the young students were exhorted to emulate.

Document 6–19

Men, one and all, in infancy are virtuous at heart;
Their moral tendencies the same, their practice wide apart.
Without Instruction's friendly aid our instincts grow less pure;
But application only can proficiency ensure.
The sage's mother chose with care her humble dwelling-place;
And rent the web in ire before her idle offspring's face.
Old Dou Yanshan, of days gone by, in virtue's school was trained,
And taught five sons who afterwards great reputation gained.
To feed the body, not the mind—fathers, on you the blame!
Instruction without discipline, the idle teacher's shame.
Study alone directs the course of youthful minds aright:
How, with a youth of idleness, can age escape the blight?
Each shapeless mass of jade must by the artisan be wrought,
And man by constant study moral rectitude be taught.
Be wise in time, nor idly spend youth's fleeting days and nights:
Love tutor, friend, and practice oft Decorum's sacred rights.
The little Xiang at nine years old could warm his parents' bed:—
Ah, would that all of us were by like filial precepts led!
The baby Rong when only four resigned the envied pear:
Deference to elder brothers then should be our early care.
Affection stands the first of all, and study follows next;
The laws of numbers must be learnt and then the letter-text.
In numbers, hundred, units, tens, in like proportion meet;
Thus on to thousands, ten of which a myriad complete.
Nature's three mighty motive-powers are Heaven and Earth and Man:
The sun, the moon, and stars make up the great celestial plan.
So also, three in number are the closest ties in life:—
The bonds between minister and prince; son, father; man and wife.

. . .

On then, ye youths who learn, let nought your resolution tire.
The little Ying, at eight years old, could read the Odes aright;
And Mi, at seven, direct with skill the chessboard's mimic fight.
Talent like this is sure to meet its well-earned meed of praise:
Ye youths who learn, let each and all thus strive himself to raise.
Cai tuned her lute and sweetly thence responsive echoes came;
And Xie Daoyun, the poet-girl, has earned a deathless fame.
In art and likewise literature these gifted maidens shone:
Ye who are *youths*, reflect before the precious hours are gone.

. . .

To your parents let your own renown the place of fame supply:
Shed luster on your ancestors, enrich posterity.
Man's hearts rejoice to leave their children wealth and golden store:

I give my sons this little book and give them nothing more.

Waste not the flying moments in unprofitable play!

Strive, O ye youths, with might and main these precepts to obey!

Source: *The San Tzu Ching, or Three Character Classic, and the Ch'ien Tsu Wen, or Thousand Character Essay*, translated by Herbert A. Giles (Shanghai: A. H. de Carvalho, 1873), 1–3, 10–12

Rules of the Zheng Clan

The Zheng clan epitomized the "communal family" ideal that was widely admired but rarely accomplished in Chinese history. For a span of three centuries (thirteenth to sixteenth centuries) and ten generations, all the members of the Zheng clan lived together, shared corporate property, and participated in common ancestral rites. The Zheng clan rules, which were first written down in mid-Yuan times (1279–1368) and revised for a last time in 1379, governed the daily operation of this remarkable communal organization and received much adulation among contemporary and later Confucian thinkers. The selection is a translation based on one of the extant versions.

Document 6–20

Item. Every morning, when the bell has been struck twenty-four times, all members of the family rise. Another four times, all make their toilet. Another eight times, all enter the Hall of Orderliness. The head of the family sits in the middle, men and women sit on left and right, and the youths who have not been capped and pinned recite the precepts for sons and daughters.... After the recitation, the youths first bow to the head of the family and then to the adults on left and right, before retiring quietly. All males then dine together in the Hall of United Hearts, all females dine at the Hall of Peace and Chastity. Those who fail to appear will be reprimanded by the family head.

Item. Uncapped sons will not be permitted to eat meat, because they have not yet accomplished their studies. This rule, based on the family's old practice, not only helps train industriousness and forbearance but also allows the youths to know the taste of pickles and salt [poor food].

Item. The capping ceremony may be performed when sons reach sixteen. For that ceremony to take place, they must be able to memorize the text of one of the Four Books [*Analects, Mencius,* and two chapters culled from the *Record of Ritual*] and expound its gist. Otherwise, the ceremony will be delayed until they are twenty-one. If a younger brother fulfills the requirements earlier [than the elder brother], cap him first so as to shame the elder sibling.

Item. For the capping ceremony of sons, a virtuous guest must be invited to serve as the sponsor so that he might instruct the youth on the way of adulthood. All of the rituals should be conducted according to Master Zhu's *Family Rituals*.

Item. Every other ten days in a month, sons who have been capped and who are studying should be summoned to recite the texts that they have memorized, or the clan genealogy and family rules, or the like. The first time someone fails in this test he will have his cap removed for a day; the second time the punishment will be doubled; the third time his rations [food, clothing, etc.] will be reduced to those of one who has not been capped. Reinstatement will occur when he passes.

Item. When daughters have reached the age for pinning, their mothers should select a guest sponsor to perform the ceremony, offer blessings and injunctions, and confer a Style name.

Item. When sons and grandsons are scolded by their seniors, they must receive it quietly and not talk back, regardless of whether they are right or wrong.

Item. Sons and grandsons must not read books that are against the rituals. Books that contain undignified or licentious language will be burned immediately. The same with those about magic practices.

Item. Boys who have reached five can be made to learn the rituals when they attend the lectures on the first and fifteenth of each month as well as the sacrifices on the ancestors' anniversaries. Those who have entered primary school should participate in the ancestral sacrifices of the four seasons. . . .

Item. Sons enter primary school at eight, leave home to seek teachers at twelve, and begin advanced education at sixteen. Knowledgeable teachers should be engaged to offer instructions in filiality, fraternity, loyalty, and faithfulness, with the aim of achieving the [Confucian] Way. If someone fails to accomplish anything in his study by the age of twenty-one, he will be ordered to learn the skills of managing the household and finance. This restriction does not apply to those who desire to learn and have made progress.

Item. Sons and grandsons who are pursuing their studies must be first and foremost concerned about [the learning of] filial and righteous conduct. It is highly undesirable to focus on the words of the texts. This is indeed the most important thing about maintaining the family tradition, and one cannot afford not to be careful about it.

Item. People in the world often drown their infant daughters. [However,] although it is true that daughters are difficult to marry [because of the burden of having to pay large dowries], why is it bad if we only endow our daughters with plain trousseaux? Wives who violate this rule will be considered for punishment.

Item. When wives return to visit their parents, they must not take with them their daughters who are eight years of age or older. The same applies to visits to other relatives, no matter how close the relationship is. The mother is to be punished in cases of violation.

Source: Translated by Yiqun Zhou.

Twenty-four Paragons of Filial Piety

Stories of filial offspring had circulated widely and in both literary and artistic media for centuries in China before they crystallized into various groups of twenty-four examples, probably during Song and Yuan times. The selections follow one version of the list of the twenty-four paragons. Three of the four selected examples involve young children whose interests are subjected to those of their parents or grandparents, and in the other an old man plays the child in order to entertain his parents. In that they may have shown filial piety at its most radical and the Confucian oppression of children in its most undesirable light, these stories have provided ready ammunition for modern critics of Confucianism.

Document 6–21

In the Zhou dynasty there flourished Lao Laizi, who was very obedient and reverent toward his parents, manifesting his dutifulness by exerting himself to provide them with every delicacy. Although upwards of seventy years of age, he declared that he was not yet too old, and, dressed in gaudy-colored garments, would frisk and cut capers like a child in front of his parents. He would also take up buckets of water and try to carry them into the house; but, feigning to slip, would fall to the ground, wailing and crying like a child; and all these things he did in order to divert his parents.

In the days of the Han dynasty lived Guo Ju, who was very poor. He had one child three years old; and such was his poverty that his mother usually divided her portion of food with this little one. Guo says to his wife: "We are so poor that our mother cannot be supported, for the child divides with her the portion of food that belongs to her. Why not bury this child? Another child may be born to us, but a mother, once gone, will never return." His wife did not venture to object to the proposal, and Guo immediately digs a hole about three cubits deep, when suddenly he lights upon a pot of gold, and on the metal reads the following inscription: "Heaven bestows this treasure upon Guo Ju, the dutiful son; the magistrate may not seize it, nor shall the neighbors take it from him."

Lu Ji, a lad six years old, who lived in the time of Han and in the district of Jiujiang, once met the celebrated general Yuan Shu, who gave him a few oranges. Two of them the lad put in his bosom, and when turning to thank the giver, they fell out on the ground. When the general saw this, he said: "Why does my young friend, who is now a guest, put the fruit away in his bosom?" The youth, bowing, replied: "My mother is very fond of oranges, and I wished, when I returned home, to present them to her." At this answer Yuan was much astonished.

Wu Meng, a lad eight years of age, who lived in the Jin dynasty, was very dutiful to his parents. They were so poor that they could not afford to furnish their beds with mosquito-curtains; and every summer night myriads of mosquitoes attacked them without restraint, feasting upon their flesh and blood. Although there were so many, yet Wu would not drive them away from himself, lest they should go to his parents and annoy them. Such was his filial affection!

Source: *The Book of Filial Duty*, translated by Ivan Chen (London: John Murray, 1920), 40, 48, 52, 57.

The Wang School of Neo-Confucianism

The Wang school of Neo-Confucianism, founded by Wang Yangming (1472–1529) and best known for its advocacy of "innate knowledge," "unity of knowledge and action," and an intuitive approach to sagehood, was a reaction against the emphasis on serious intellectual inquiry and moral cultivation in the Cheng-Zhu school (Cheng Hao 1032–1085, Cheng Yi 1033–1107, and Zhu Xi 1130–1200). A corollary of the philosophical departure taken by the Wang school was its more positive understanding of children's nature and their status in the Confucian moral hierarchy. Modern scholars have credited the Wang school with an increased interest in children's life in sixteenth- and seventeenth-century texts. The selections come from three sources. The first two are the instructions and regulations Wang Yangming issued for the community schools he established in Southern Jiangxi in 1518. The third is from the essay "On the Mind of a Child" (*Tongxin shuo*) by Li Zhi (1527–1602), a radical follower of the Wang school who eventually lost his life for his iconoclastic ideas and behavior.

Document 6–22

Instructions for Practical Living

In education the ancients taught the fundamental principles of human relations. As the habits of memorization, recitation, and the writing of flowery compositions of later generations arose, the teachings of ancient kings disappeared. In educating young boys today, the sole task should be to teach filial piety, brotherly respect, loyalty, faithfulness, propriety, righteousness, integrity, and the sense of shame. The ways to raise and cultivate them are to lure them to singing so their will will be roused, to direct them to practice etiquette so their demeanor will be dignified, and to urge them to read so their intellectual horizon will be widened. Today singing songs and practicing etiquette are often regarded as unrelated to present needs. This is the view of small and vulgar people of this degenerate modern age. How can they know the purpose of the ancients in instituting education?

Generally speaking, it is the nature of young boys to love to play and to dislike restriction. Like plants beginning to sprout, if they are allowed to grow freely, they will develop smoothly. If twisted and interfered with, they will wither and decline. In teaching young boys today, we must make them lean toward rousing themselves so that they will be happy and cheerful at heart, and then nothing can check their development. As in the case of plants, if nourished by timely rain and spring wind, they will all sprout, shoot up, and flourish, and will naturally grow by sunlight and develop under the moon. If ice and frost strip them of leaves, their spirit of life will be dissipated and they will gradually dry up. Therefore, to teach young boys to sing is not merely to rouse their will. It is also to release through singing their [energy as expressed in] jumping around and shouting, and to free them through rhythm from depression and repression. To lead them to practice etiquette is not only to make their demeanor dignified. It is also to exhilarate their blood circulation through such activities as bowing and walking politely, and to strengthen their tendons and bones through kneeling, rising, and extending and contracting their limbs. To urge them to read is not only to widen their intellectual horizon. It is also to preserve their minds through absorption in repeating passages and to express their will through recitation, now loudly and now softly. All this is smoothly to direct their will, adjust and regulate their nature and feelings, quietly to get rid of their meanness and stinginess, and silently to transform their crudeness and mischievousness, so that they will gradually approach propriety and righteousness without feeling that it is difficult to do so and will steep themselves in equilibrium and harmony without knowing why. This is the subtle purpose of the ancient kings in instituting education.

However, in recent generations the teachers of youngsters merely supervise them every day as they recite phrases and sentences and imitate civil service examination papers. They stress restraint and discipline instead of directing their pupils in the practice of propriety. They emphasize intelligence instead of nourishing goodness. They beat the pupils with a whip and tie them with ropes, treating them like prisoners. The youngsters look upon their school as a prison and refuse to enter. They regard their teachers as enemies and do not want to see them. They avoid this and conceal that in order to satisfy their desire for play and fun. They pretend, deceive, and cheat in order to indulge in mischief and meanness. They become negligent and inferior, and daily degenerate. Such education drives them to do evil. How can they be expected to do good?

In truth the following is my idea of education. I fear that ordinary folk do not understand it and look upon it as being wide of the mark, and moreover, since I am about to leave, I therefore earnestly say to all you teachers: Please understand and follow my idea and forever take it as a counsel to you. Never alter or give up your standard just because ordinary folk may say something against it. Then your effort to cultivate correctness in youngsters will succeed. Please bear this in mind.

Source: *Instructions for Practical Living and Other Neo-Confucian Writings by Wang Yang-ming*, translated by Wing-tsit Chan (New York: Columbia University Press, 1963), 182–184.

Document 6–23

School Regulations

Every day, early in the morning, after the pupils have assembled and bowed, the teachers should ask all of them one by one whether at home they have been negligent and lacked sincerity and earnestness in their desire to love their parents and to respect their elders, whether they have overlooked or failed to carry out any details in caring for their parents in the summer or the winter, whether in walking along the streets their movements and etiquette have been disorderly or careless, and whether in all their words, acts, and thoughts they have been deceitful or depraved, and not loyal, faithful, sincere, and respectful. All boys must answer honestly. If they have made any mistake, they should correct it. If not, they should devote themselves to greater effort. In addition, the teachers should at all times, and in connection with anything that may occur, use special means to explain and teach them. After that, each pupil should withdraw to his seat and attend to his lessons.

In singing, let the pupils be tidy in appearance and calm in expression. Let their voices be clear and distinct. Let their rhythm be even and exact. Let them not be hasty or hurried. Let them not be reckless or disorderly. And let them not sound feeble or timid. In time their spirits will be free and their minds will be peaceful. Depending on the number of pupils, each school should be divided into four classes. In rotation each class sings on one day, while the others sit down to listen respectfully with a serious expression. Every five days all the four classes will sing one after another in their own school assembly. On the first and the fifteenth day of every month the several schools will assemble to sing together in the academy.

In the practice of etiquette, let the pupils be clear in their minds and serious in their thoughts. Let them be careful with details and correct in demeanor. Let them not be negligent or lazy. Let them not be low-spirited or disconcerted. And let them not be uncontrolled or rough. Let them be leisurely but not to the point of being dilatory and be serious but not to the point of being rigid. In time their appearance and behavior will be natural and their moral nature will be firmly established. The order for the pupils to follow should be the same as that in singing. Every other day it will be the turn of one class to practice etiquette, while others are seated to observe respectfully with a serious expression. On the day of etiquette practice, the pupils will be excused from composition. Every ten days all four classes will assemble in their own schools and practice in rotation. On the first and fifteenth day of every month, all schools will assemble and jointly practice in the academy.

In reading, the value does not lie in the amount but in learning the material well. Reckoning the pupils' natural endowments, if one can handle two hundred words, teach him only one hundred so that he always has surplus energy and strength and then he will not suffer or feel tired but will have the beauty of being at ease with himself. While reciting the pupils must be concentrated in mind and united in purpose. As they recite with their mouths, let them ponder with their minds. Every word and every phrase should be investigated and gone over again and again. The voice and rhythm should go up and down and their thoughts should be relaxed and empty. In time they will be in harmony with propriety and righteousness and their intelligence will gradually unfold.

In the daily work first examine the pupils' moral conduct. Next let them repeat their old lessons and recite new ones. Then comes the practice of etiquette or composition, then repeating and recitation again, and finally singing. The practice of etiquette, singing, and so forth is intended to preserve the boys' minds so that they enjoy their study without getting tired and have no time for bad conduct. If teachers know this principle, they will know what to do. However, these are the essentials. "To see the spirit [of changes and transformations] and manifest them depends on the proper men."

Source: *Instructions for Practical Living and Other Neo-Confucian Writing by Wang Yang-ming*, translated by Wing-tsit Chan (New York: Columbia University Press, 1963), 184–186.

Document 6–24

On the Mind of a Child

A child is the beginning of a person. The mind of a child is the beginning of a mind. How can one afford to lose the beginning of a mind? Now, how does one suddenly lose the mind of a child? It is because at the beginning stage, some information enters the mind through the ears and the eyes; when it is allowed to dominate inside, the mind of a child is lost. As one grows up, some reasoning enters the mind from the information, and when it is allowed to dominate inside, the mind of the child is lost. By and by, with the daily increase in reasoning and information, one knows and feels more each day. When one knows that a good reputation is something desirable, and when one tries one's best to attain that, the mind of a child is lost. When one knows that a bad reputation is something undesirable, and when one tries one's best to avoid it, the mind of a child is lost. Now, all reasoning and information comes from extensive reading and moral reasoning, and who among the ancient sages didn't read? But, even when they didn't read, they would still keep their mind of a child, and even when they did read a lot, they would protect and preserve their mind of a child, unlike scholars today, who have blocked up their child's mind with extensive reading and moral reasoning. Since our scholars have blocked up their child's mind with extensive reading and moral reasoning, then why did the sages expound their ideas in writing, thus keeping our scholars benighted? Once the mind of a child is blocked up, when they say something, what they say is insincere. When they do something in their administrative affairs, what they do becomes groundless. And when they write something, what they write makes no sense. It has no depth, no grace, no substance, and no illumination. Not a single word of virtue may be found therein. Why is it so? It is only because the mind of a child has been blocked up, and information and reasoning that come from outside have taken its place inside.

Now, when information and reasoning dominate the mind, then when one speaks, it is from that information and reasoning, not from the mind of a child itself. Even when the saying is artful, what's the good to me? Isn't it a false person saying false words, doing false things, and writing false compositions? When a person is false, then everything he does is false. Accordingly, if one says false words to false people, they will be pleased; if one talks about false things to false people, they will be pleased; if one discusses false compositions with false people, they will be pleased. If everything one does is false, then everyone one talks to is pleased. When the entire theater is false, how can a short person make any distinction? Hence, although the very best of writings do exist in the world, there must have been much that sank into oblivion among short people, never to be read by later generations! Why? It is because all the world's very best writings originate from the mind of a child. If the mind of a child is always preserved, then all that information and reasoning will never take its place, and there will be great literature in every age, from every person, and in every creative and original form and style. . . . Past or present, as long as it is a great sage talking about the "way of the sages," it is excellent writing, and one should not judge by priority in temporal order. From this, I have therefore come to the conclusion that all that comes from the mind of a child is excellent writing by itself. Why should one talk about the Six Classics, *The Analects*, and *Mencius* only?

Source: *Vignettes from the Late Ming: A Hsiao-p'in Anthology*, translated by Yang Ye (Seattle: University of Washington Press, 1999), 26–28.

The Qing Code

China's imperial legal codes, from the oldest surviving Tang Code (653 CE) to the last Qing Code (first adopted in 1646 and finalized in 1740), exemplified the Confucian principles of particularism and familism. The law recognized special groups, allowed for differential treatments in accordance with social status, and made intrafamily distinctions on the basis of the age, seniority, and degree of kinship of the parties involved. Children and the elderly belonged to a special group who deserved clemency because of their age. It is unclear to what extent minors actually benefited from their theoretical special legal status. In the selections below, the italicized passages indicate the interlinear commentary to the Code, which seems to have been regarded as essentially part of the Code.

Document 6–25

Article 22. *Redemption by Aged Persons, Youths, and Those Who Are Disabled.*
Whenever someone who is 70 or over, or 15 or under, or seriously disabled (*such as those who are blind in one eye or who have one limb disabled*) commits a crime punishable with exile or less, redemption will be received. (*If someone is convicted of an offence carrying the death penalty, or if he is sentenced to exiled by attaint in the case of plotting rebellion* [Art. 255], *treason* [Art. 254], *or high treason* [Art. 254], *or in a case where the members of the household of one who has made or kept gu poison* [Art. 289], *or mutilated a living person* [Art. 288] *or killed three persons in one household* [Art. 287]—*cases in which a household is still exiled despite an amnesty—this law is not used. But as for all other offences involving an injury to another, monetary redemption is permitted. As for those committing offences incurring a penalty of military exile, redemption will be received as in the case of exile.*) As for those 80 or over, or 10 or under, or critically disabled (*as one who is blind in both eyes or who has two limbs that are disabled*) who criminally kills another (*by plot* [Art. 282] *or intentionally or during an affray* [Art. 290]) so that he should be executed (*beheaded or strangled*), the said sentence will be proposed and memorialized to the Emperor. (*In the case of rebellion or high treason* [Art. 254], *this law is not used.*) The [final] decision [in the case] will be received from the Emperor. If it is a case of stealing, or injuring others (*where the offence is not capital*), then there may be redemption. (*This means that in the case of assaulting and injuring others, it is not permitted* [that the wrongdoer should] *totally avoid punishment, so it is also ordered that redemption will be received.*) As for other offences, they will not be punished. (*This means that apart from the previously mentioned cases of killing others, in which a rescript is requested from the Emperor, or stealing and injuring others where redemption is permitted, all the other offences* [committed by such persons] *are not punished.*) As for those 90 or above and 7 or under, even in the case of capital offence, there is no punishment. (*As for those 90 or above who commit rebellion or high treason, do not use this law.*) If there is another who induces [such] a person to commit the fact, then punish the one who induced him. If there is property illegally received that must be restored, then the one who has received the property must pay for it. (*This means that if a person is over 90 or under 7, he has very little intellect and strength; if there is one who induces him, then the punishment is inflicted on the one who induced him. If there is a theft of property, and another receives and makes use of it, the one who receives it must return it. If the old person or child himself uses it, then it is from him that restitution must be sought*).

Article 404. *Old Persons and Youths Are Not Put to the Question.*
In the case of all persons who are within the eight [categories of persons] whose cases are entitled to consideration [Art. 3] (*those for whom according to the principles of the Rites it is appropriate to grant indulgence*), or those of 70 or above (*those for whom old age makes it appropriate to be sympathetic*) or those of 15 or under

(those for whom youth makes it appropriate to be merciful), or those who are seriously disabled *(infirmity makes it appropriate to be compassionate, if an offence is committed, the officials)* should not *(use torture)* put them to the question. In all cases set the penalty in accordance with the evidence from others. Any violation will be punished in accordance with the law of intentionally or mistakenly increasing the penalty [erroneously] [Art. 409]. *(For intentionally increasing the penalty* [erroneously], *inflict the whole penalty. For mistakenly increasing the penalty* [erroneously], *reduce three degrees.)* As for those whom the law permits reciprocally to hide each other's offences *(because such concealment is an aspect of close relationship)* [Art. 32], as well as old people 80 or above, young people 10 or below, those who are critically disabled [Art. 22] *(because they can rely on escaping punishment)*, none may be ordered to give evidence. For any violation of this, sentence to 50 strokes of the light bamboo. *(In all cases take the clerk as the principal, and the penalty will be set [for others] by being diminished proportionately.)*

Source: *The Great Qing Code*, translated by William C. Jones (Oxford: Clarendon Press, 1994), 52–53, 376.

Jiang Shiquan's Childhood Memories

Jiang Shiquan (1725–1785) was an eminent poet of the Qing dynasty. The following excerpt is from the note he wrote upon the completion of a painting that he had commissioned for his mother. In the note Jiang remembers his difficult childhood, when his father was constantly away and his mother managed to raise him and supervise his education by defying poverty and poor health. (Jiang grew up to pass all three levels of the civil service examination, at the ages of 22, 23, and 33). Full of pathos and filial sentiments, this personal narrative offers precious insights into the expectations for boys, the relationship between parents and children, and the tremendous responsibilities mothers often had to shoulder for their children's upbringing in premodern Chinese families. (Jiang's mother hailed from a scholarly family and received a good education from her father before she married at eighteen.)

Document 6–26

Painting on Night Study by the Singing Loom

When I was four years old, every day my mother taught me several lines from the Four Books. Because I was too young to be able to hold the writing brush, she cut up bamboo branches into threads and used the threads to represent the strokes of the characters. She then held me in her lap and taught me to read the characters thus constructed. Once I had mastered a character, she took it apart. She would teach me ten characters the first day and on the next day order me to reconstruct the characters myself by using the bamboo threads, and would not stop until I made no mistakes. Only when I turned six did she make me write with the brush. The family of my maternal grandfather had never been wealthy and now they were even more hard pressed because of the famine in successive years. My mother made all the clothes, hats, and shoes for me and our young servant. My mother was such a good hand at embroidering and knitting that when our young servant took what she had made to the market people all vied to buy them. Thus the young servant and I never looked shabby.

My late maternal grandfather was tall and wore a white beard. He liked to drink wine. Whenever he got drunk, he recited the poems he had written in a loud voice and asked my mother to critique his composition. At every criticism my mother made, my grandfather would drain a full cup. After several rounds, he became exhilarated. Stroking his beard and bursting into laughter, he raised the wine cup and exclaimed, "How could an old man like me have such a daughter!" Then he stroked my head and asked, "Good son, how are you going to repay your mother in the future?" Being too young to answer, I only plunged into my mother's arms and started crying profusely. My mother also clasped me and wept sorrowfully. The melancholy wind over the eaves and the flickering candle on the table seemed to join us in our sadness.

In my memory, my mother taught me with her weaving and embroidering equipment placed beside her, a book opened in her lap, and me sitting beneath her lap. She imparted the lessons to me whilst keeping her hands at her own work, and the sounds of our recitation mingled with the humming of the loom. When I let up, she would administer a slight beating to me and soon afterwards hold me, weeping and saying, "Son, if you do not study, how could I face your father again?" When it became very cold at midnight, my mother would get into the bed, cover her two feet with the quilt, unbutton her jacket to warm my back with her chest, and recite lessons together with me. When I became tired from recitation and fell asleep against her chest, she would presently shake me and said, "You can wake up now." I opened my eyes to look at my mother and saw tears coursing down her face, so I also wept. But after a while she would order me to resume the recitation, and we wouldn't rest until the cocks crowed. My aunts once said to my mother, "Sister, you only have this son. Why do you treat him so harshly?" My mother replied, "It would be all right if I had many sons. He being my only child, on whom could I depend if he turned out to be an unworthy person?" . . .

When I was nine years old, my mother taught me the *Record of Ritual*, the *Book of Changes*, and the *Book of Poetry*, and I was able to memorize all of them.

When she had time, my mother also copied poems of the Tang and Song dynasties and taught me to recite them. Both my mother and I were weak and often ill. Whenever I fell ill, my mother would hold me in her arms and walk back and forth in the room, not getting any sleep. When I had recovered a little, she would point to the poems pasted on the walls and taught me to recite them in a soft voice for amusement. When my mother was ill, I would sit by her pillow and refuse to leave. My mother, looking at me, wept and could not say anything, and I, too, grieved and clung to her in silence. I once asked my mother, "Do you have worries?" She said, "Yes." "How can I make your worries go?" She answered, "If you, my son, could memorize the books that you have recited, my worries will be gone." Then I started to read aloud, and the resonating sound of my recitation competed with the sound of the boiling of my mother's medicine. Smiling faintly, she said, "I feel a little better already!" Ever since then, whenever my mother fell sick, I would take a book and recite at her bedside. It always helped her get well.

When I was ten years old my father returned. After another year, he took my mother and me with him when he traveled between Yan, Qin, Zhao, Wei, Qi, Liang, Wu, Chu [i.e., all over the country as he sought employment as a legal expert]. During those times, my father pushed me very hard in my study. Whenever I showed any sign of letting up, he would get angry and leave me, refusing to speak to me for days. [When that happened,] my mother would shed tears, cane me, and order me to kneel down to recite the lessons until I had memorized them by heart, never getting tired [in thus disciplining me]. This way I was prevented from squandering my time in play, and my mother became ever more rigorous in her discipline.

Source: Translated by Yiqun Zhou.

Lu Xun

Lu Xun (1881–1936) was one of the most gifted and most thoroughgoing critics of traditional Chinese culture during the May Fourth Movement (1919). While attacking filial piety for sacrificing children for the sake of their parents and blaming Confucian education for making children "more dead than alive," Lu also actively participated in the creation of a new type of literature for children. The excerpt, from an essay written in 1919, is deeply informed of social Darwinism (highly influential in China at that time) in its criticism of the "unnatural" and "backward" nature of the traditional hierarchy between children and adults, which Lu blamed for China's lack of vitality and the humiliation she had suffered at the hands of the youth-oriented West.

Document 6–27

What Is Required of Us as Fathers Today

Why must life be propagated? So that it can develop and evolve. Each individual is mortal, and no bounds at all are set to evolution; therefore life must continue, advancing along the path of evolution. For this, a certain inner urge is needed, like the urge of a unicellular creature which in time enables it to multiply, or the urge of invertebrate animals which in time enables the vertebrae to appear. This is why the later forms of life are always more significant and complete, hence more worthwhile and precious; and the earlier forms of life should be sacrificed to the later.

Unfortunately, the old way of thinking in China is just the reverse of this. The young should take first place, but instead it is taken by the old. The emphasis should be on the future, but instead it is on the past. The elder generation is sacrificed to the generation before it; yet, with no means to outlive itself, it expects the younger generation to sacrifice itself for the elder's sake, destroying all that could carry it forward. I do not mean—as those who attack me claim—that grandsons must spend their whole time beating their grandfathers, and daughters must for ever be cursing their mothers. I mean that henceforward those who have seen the light should purge themselves of the unsound ideas long handed down in the East, show a greater sense of responsibility towards their children and drastically cut down on all thought of privilege, to build up a new morality in which the young take place. And the young will not remain in a privileged position for ever; they will have to do their duty by their own children. All hand on the torch to those after them, only some come earlier in the race, some later.

Source: Yang Xianyi and Gladys Yang, trans., *Lu Xun, Selected Works* (Beijing: Foreign Languages Press, 1980), 2: 59–60.

Tao Xingzhi

A renowned educational theorist and reformer, Tao Xingzhi (1891–1946) was influenced by both the pragmatist educationist John Dewey (while studying at Columbia's Teachers' College from 1915–1917) and the neo-Confucian philosopher Wang Yangming. In fact, Tao took the name Zhixing (in the 1910s) and later Xingzhi (in the early 1930s) to indicate his identification with Wang's theory of "unity of knowledge (*zhi*) and action (*xing*)." Wang's view that education should accommodate and develop children's natural tendencies also guided much of Tao's educational practice. Besides advocating the universal establishment of kindergartens in China and promoting an elementary education that was more conducive to children's free development, Tao initiated in the 1930s the "little teacher" movement of having school children teach uneducated adults. Tao's essay on the movement, from which the excerpt is taken, exudes pride about the children whose pedagogical activities reversed the conventional hierarchy and proved them to be useful and creative members of society.

Document 6–28

The Little Teachers

The little teachers are the children who shared education with others. During the earlier stage of development the most prevailing type of little teachers is school children who volunteer to help their home folks and neighbors to acquire the elements of knowledge. As time goes on even children of the street pass on whatever they have learned to their friends. The first hint of the possibility of the little teacher was suggested by an incident some fourteen years ago when my mother, then fifty-seven years of age, got interested in learning. She wanted to read my letters sent home and wanted to know something of what was going on in the world. The only teacher available for her was my second boy who was then six years old and happened to have finished the first reader. The grandma and the grandson played and studied. In one month my mother finished the first book. This happy incident did not arouse much enthusiasm beyond my family circle at the time. But the fact that a six-year-old boy, without a diploma from a normal school or a certificate from a superintendent of education, succeeded in teaching a fifty-seven-year-old grandma to finish the first reader, had made upon my mind a very deep impression which was one of the determining factors in discovering "the little teacher."

When Manchuria was invaded and Shanghai attacked in 1931 and 1932, we began to be convinced that the nation could not be saved without national unity through a general awakening of the whole population. This calls for a free education for all at the lowest cost and within the shortest period of time. . . . With the rise of the little teachers we have been enabled not only to keep the guiding principle "all come all served," but in addition we have a new slogan, "they who cannot come will receive education on delivery without cash." Since then we have witnessed the little friends delivering education to housewives and cowboys who cannot possibly attend regular classes without breaking their rice bowls [i.e., losing their means of livelihood]. This feature of delivering education and home teaching has made the little teacher system unique and differentiated from the Lancastrian pupil-teacher. Another difference is found in the fact that sooner or later even the cowboys and housewives begin to share their education with others. . . .

The principle derived from the little teachers is very simple. Anyone who has learned a simple truth has the qualification to teach it and has the duty to share it with others. Speaking from our experience the little teacher movement has shown the following merits:

1. The children learn more by teaching others. He who keeps his knowledge in the cold storage of his head learns the least.
2. Knowledge is no longer a commodity for sale. Education becomes a free gift for all. It is like the water which everybody can drink, and like sunshine which everybody can enjoy.
3. The older generation and youths make progress together. The constant contact between adults and children in intellectual growth tends to make the old people younger.
4. It helps to solve the insurmountable difficulties of women's education and makes it possible for us to extend an essential education to half of our population which can be hardly reached by other means. [It is much easier for the little ones than for male adult teachers to enter the women's quarters and give lessons.]
5. A new change in the school itself coincided with the arrival of the little teachers. Formerly the village school was a lonely thing in the country. Now with the little teachers as live-wires connecting the village school with every home, the whole village becomes the school, and the light of education radiates everywhere while the school is in turn vitalized by the stream of problems calling for solution. The lonely teacher in a ruined temple, joined suddenly with tens of little comrades, cannot but see a new vision in his profession and feel elevated for the historic mission that he is to fulfill.

Source: www.txzmuseum.org.cn/xzyz/exzyz2.htm, official Web site of Tao Xingzhi Museum, Shanghai, translator unidentified.

Liang Shuming

A leading figure in modern neo-Confucianism, Liang Shuming (1893–1988) is best known for his writings on East-West cultural comparisons, his theoretical reflections on the modernization of Confucianism, his personal engagement in the rural reconstruction project in the 1930s, and his courage to challenge Communist ideology under Mao. The following selection, from a speech in 1937, bears the imprint of both the modern Western-inspired views of children and the clear influence of Wang Yangming, who was Liang's most important spiritual ancestor in the premodern Confucian tradition. In his practice, Liang devoted much time to the education of adults in the rural reconstruction project, believing that the critical situation of China at that time made it more expedient and effective to teach adults first. As seen in the excerpt, however, he was an admirer of the cause of Tao Xingzhi, including his "little teacher system."

Document 6–29

On the Psychology of Children

From my observation of children, I have discovered their strengths and weaknesses. The weaknesses lie in their lack of experience and habituation and inability to persevere and concentrate. The lack of experience and habituation is due to their young age, and they are unable to persevere and concentrate because their interests are too many and too strong. . . . With the exception of these two things, children lack nothing. As for their strengths, they are far superior to adults. Children do things with the whole heart and the true heart, that is, what the ancient Chinese called "sincerity." Whereas adults tend to cope with things in a perfunctory manner because of their complex and ulterior considerations, children apply themselves to the things they want to do with no reluctance or pretense. Their fundamental strength lies in their ability to focus their energies in carrying out their impulses. If we ask them to do something that captures their interest and is within their capability, they will devote their whole hearts to it and seldom fail. . . .

Children have another strong point. Adults who have had experience and formed habits and yet lack a superior education often end up having confused minds. By contrast, children have yet to have the opportunity to have their minds confused and therefore are less muddle-headed than adults. An example of the adults' confusion is that, when they write essays, they without fail will adopt the prescribed format and as a result say all sorts of irrelevant things. Children, on the other hand, because they do not know how to write essays, will only say things as they actually experience it, honestly and without ornamentation, and thus produce good essays. . . . Children do not have impure motives and all their actions are the pure expressions of true life. Even their tears and laughter have meaning and value and can be deeply moving. The worst things are affectation and mannerism, as is typical of the reports many people submit to their superiors. Long-winded and empty, those writings have to be dumped once they have been read, because they all are about falsehood and have nothing intimate and true. Children do not produce such voluminous falsities, because they do not know how to.

We should study how education can enlighten instead of confusing people. Ordinary education—at home or in society—often harms and destroys children by confusing them. Zhang Yaozu [a "little teacher" who met Liang and deeply impressed him the year before] is not that superior [in intelligence]; many other children are just like him. There are two reasons for his superiority. One is that Mr. Tao [Xingzhi] gave him adequate stimulation, making him a "little teacher" and asking him to write about his own experience. The other is that he has suffered little harm in his upbringing and education. These two reasons explain why he is able to bring his talents into full play, and there is otherwise not anything exceptional about his own abilities.

Source: Translated by Yiqun Zhou.

NOTES

1. According to the traditional Chinese way of calculating age, the infant is one year old at birth and adds a year at every Lunar New Year (i.e., the child turns two at the first New Year, three at the second New Year, and so on). Consequently, Chinese children said to be of a certain age in our sources were usually one and even two years younger than their Western counterparts.

2. Boys' passage into adulthood, in the ritual and social sense, could occur anywhere between fifteen and twenty (about fourteen and nineteen by Western reckoning) in traditional China, depending on historical period, the family's class and means, and other factors. For girls, fifteen usually marked the point of transition. In any case, though the period fifteen to nineteen could still be regarded as childhood in the Chinese context, it was the years before that received most of the attention from writers who concerned themselves with children.

3. According to the *Book of Etiquette and Ceremonial* and the *Record of Ritual*, a boy assumed the cap at twenty, when a capping ceremony was held to mark his passage into adulthood. See Docs. 6–4, 6–5.

4. A person acquired a Style name upon reaching adulthood. Henceforth, one's given name was usually reserved for use by one's elders and superiors, and the Style name would be used to show respect when peer adults referred to one another.

5. That is, *Biographies of Eminent Women*, Doc. 6–10.

6. That is, *Precepts for Women*, Doc. 6–11.

CONTRIBUTORS

ELISHEVA BAUMGARTEN teaches Jewish history at Bar Ilan University and specializes in medieval social history in the Jewish communities of Germany and northern France. She is author of *Mothers and Children: Jewish Family Life in Medieval Europe* (Princeton, 2004) and articles on family and gender in medieval Ashkenaz.

DON S. BROWNING is the Alexander Campbell Professor of Religious Ethics and the Social Sciences, Emeritus, Divinity School, University of Chicago. His books include *Generative Man* (1973, 1975; National Book Award Finalist, 1974), *Religious Thought and the Modern Psychologies* (1987, 2004), and the coedited *Sex, Marriage, and Family in the World Religions* (2006) and *American Religions and the Family* (2006).

MARCIA J. BUNGE is a professor of humanities and theology at Christ College, the Honors College of Valparaiso University, and director of the Child in Religion and Ethics Project. She edited *The Child in Christian Thought* (Eerdmans, 2001); coedited *The Child in the Bible* with Terence E. Fretheim and Beverly Roberts Gaventa (Eerdmans, 2008); and has written several articles on children and childhood.

ALAN COLE is a professor of religious studies at Lewis and Clark College. He recently published *Text as Father: Paternal Seductions in Early Mahayana Buddhist Literature* and currently has another book in press entitled *Fathering Your Father: The Zen of Fabrication in Tang China.*

AVNER GILADI is an associate professor in Islamic studies at the University of Haifa. His publications include *Children of Islam: Concepts of Childhood in Medieval Muslim Society* (Houndmills, 1992) and *Infants, Parents and Wet Nurses: Medieval Islamic Views on Breastfeeding and Their Social Implications,* (Leiden, 1999).

LAURIE L. PATTON, professor and chairperson of the religion department at Emory University, is the author or editor of seven books, most recently, *Bringing the Gods to Mind: Mantra and Ritual in Early Indian Sacrifice* (2004). She published a book of poems, *Fire's Goal: Poems from a Hindu Year, in* 2003. Her translation of the Bhagavad Gita is forthcoming from Penguin Press in 2008.

JOHN WALL is an associate professor of religion, with a joint appointment in childhood studies, at Rutgers University, Camden. He is the author of *Moral Creativity* (Oxford, 2005) and articles in social ethics, religious hermeneutics, and children. He is currently writing a book on how considering childhood transforms moral theory.

YIQUN ZHOU is an assistant professor in the Department of Asian Languages, Stanford University. Her research interests include Chinese and comparative family and women's history, Chinese religion, and China-Greece comparative studies.

INDEX

rabbinic literature, 26
rabbinic sources, 27, 36–43, 46, 50, 56, 58, 65–66, 68, 69, 74
Radha (Krishna's lover), 223
Raheja, Gloria, 228, 267–268
Rahner, Karl, 142
Rahula (Buddha's biological son), 286
Ramabai, Pandita, 225
Rashi (R. Isaac b. Solomon), 23
Ray, Satyajit, 226, 261, 264, 266
Record of Ritual (*Liji*), 350, 367
Reflections on Things at Hand (*Jinsi lu*, Zhu Xi and Lü Zuqian), 366
Reform Brahmo Samaj, 225, 226, 261, 264–265
Republic (Plato), 89
Rig (Verses), 218
Rig Veda (knowledge of the verses), 11, 218, 220, 230
rituals and ceremonies, 1–2, 6, 8, 9, 11; Buddhist, 277; Christian, 84, 87; Confucian, 349–350, 366–368, 377; Hindu, 11, 218–219, 220, 222, 228, 235; Islamic, 186–188; Jewish, 8–10, 21, 33, 35–36, 43–51, 48, 50, 59, 77n10, 80n55. *See also* baptism; bar mitzvah; circumcision; marriage; Moroccan Torah Initiation Ritual; mourning rituals
Roman Catholicism, 89, 92, 119, 142
Rousseau, Jean-Jacques, 91

Sabbath, 35–36, 40–42, 51, 63, 66–78, 82–84
sahih (sound tradition), 153
St. Paul's Cathedral, 119
St. Paul's School in London, 119
al-Sakhawi, Abd al-Rahman, 157
Sakyamuni (Buddha), 282, 286
Salah al-Din al-Ayyubi, 158
Sama (Chants), 218
samnyas (renunciation before death), 222
samsara, 10, 222, 233, 285, 305, 313
samskaras, 222, 235
Saptavadhri, 218, 229–230, 272
Sarda Act. *See* Marriage Bill
Sariputra (Buddha's son), 286, 313–316
Satyakama Jabvala, 219, 230–232
Schleiermacher, Friedrich, 91, 136
Schleitheim Confession, 124
The School of Infancy (Comenius), 128
The Search Institute, 4, 12n4, 13n9
Second Temple, 16
Sefer sources, 39, 43, 46–49, 58, 63, 66–67, 71, 73, 74, 77
Sen, Keshub Chandra, 225
Sen, Ramprasad, 224, 259–260
Sen, Satadru, 224, 273n16
Sephardic community, 44
"Sermons on the Christian Household" (Schleiermacher), 136
Sex, Marriage, and Family in the World Religions, 5
sexuality, 1, 6; and Buddhism, 281; and Christianity, 85, 91; and Confucianism, 340–341; and Hinduism, 271n1, 275n31;

and Islam, 160; and Judaism, 45–46. *See also* adultery; procreation
Shammai, 26
Shammai, school of, 28
shari'a (Islamic religious law). *See under* law
shastras. *See under* law
shastric literature, 219–222, 235
Shenhui ("the novice"), 289, 332–333
Shiva (god), 222
Sigalaka Sutta, 284, 310
Sima Qian, 347
Simons, Menno, 124
al-Siyasa al-shar'iyya fi islah al-ra'i wa-al-ra'iyya (Governance According to God's Law in Reforming both the Ruler and His Flock, Ibn Taymiyya,), 199, 207
Siyasat al-sibyan wa-tadbiruhum (The Book of Childrearing, Ibn al-Jazzar), 180
Smith, Christian, 4, 13n7
Soma (sacred drink), 229
Song Ruozhao, 365
Soul Searching (Smith and Denton), 4, 13n7
spiritual development and children, 2, 4, 6, 12n4; in Christianity, 87, 90, 91–92, 139; in Confucianism, 338–340
Spring and Autumn Annals, 367
Sulwan al-musab bi-furqat al-ahbab (Consoling Those Smitten by Calamity on the Separation from Their Beloved, Ibn Yusuf al-Maqdisi), 209
Summa Theologica (Aquinas), 114–117
Sur Das, 223
svadharma (one's own dharma), 222

tafsir (Qur'an exegesis), 153
Talmudic sources, 15, 29–35, 52, 60, 63–69, 74–90
tamyiz (good and evil), 150
Tandon, Trisha, 227, 274n24, 285n33
Tang dynasty, 278, 341, 365
Tao Xingzhi, 388, 390–392
tasawwuf (mystical theories), 153–154
Tasliyat ahl al-masa'ib (*fi mawt al-awlad wa-al-aqarib*) (Consolation for Those in Distress [over the Death of Children and Relatives], Ibn Muhammad al-Manbiji), 209
Theodosius I, 102
Thomas Aquinas, Saint, 89, 114
Three-Character Classic (*Sanzi jing*), 374
Thurman, Howard, 147–148
tkhines, 27, 78n25
Torah sources, 15, 29, 36, 73
Transmission (Kunzru), 228
The Treasure of the City of Ladies (de Pizan), 118–119
Tuhfat al-mawdud bi-ahkam al-mawlud (A Present for the Beloved on the Rules concerning the Treatment of Infants, Ibn Qayyim al-Jawziyya), 162–163, 166, 177, 180, 185, 188, 196
Tukaram, Saint, 224, 255–258

Uberoi, Patricia, 229, 272n1, 275n35
Uma (mother), 224

LaVergne, TN USA
03 May 2010
181407LV00002B/3/P